FROM HOMICIDE TO SLAVERY

FROM HOMICIDE
TO SLAVERY

Studies in American Culture

David Brion Davis

New York   Oxford
OXFORD UNIVERSITY PRESS
1986

Oxford University Press

Oxford   New York   Toronto
Delhi   Bombay   Calcutta   Madras   Karachi
Petaling Jaya   Singapore   Hong Kong   Tokyo
Nairobi   Dar es Salaam   Cape Town
Melbourne   Auckland

and associated companies in
Beirut   Berlin   Ibadan   Nicosia

Copyright © 1986 by Oxford University Press, Inc.

Published by Oxford University Press, Inc.,
200 Madison Avenue, New York, New York 10016

Oxford is a registered trademark of Oxford University Press

Library of Congress Cataloging-in-Publication Data
Davis, David Brion.
From homicide to slavery.
Includes index.
1. Slavery—United States.   2. Violence—United States—History.
3. Slavery—United States—Historiography.
4. United States—Race relations.   5. National characteristics, American.
6. West (U.S.)—Civilization.   I. Title.
E441.D249   1986   305.8'96073'073   86-8706
ISBN 0-19-504089-9

2 4 6 8 10 9 7 5 3 1

Printed in the United States of America
on acid-free paper

Again, To Toni, with Love and Admiration

Preface

Slavery first appeared in human history, according to the classical account, when warriors realized that it would be more advantageous to secure the services of captives than to kill them or eat them. The connection between homicide and slavery persisted, however, since the slave might at any moment resume the warfare that his capture had suspended and the master might choose to kill his slave even for disobedience. Homicide is thus a logical starting point for anyone interested in a long-term study of the "problem" of slavery.

But historians seldom work from logical plans, at least not over a period of thirty-odd years. When I wrote my first book, *Homicide in American Fiction,* I had no intention of moving on to slavery and had never heard of the theories of Dio Chrysostom and Thomas Hobbes regarding the enslavement of war captives. It was an interest in social reform, initially the movement to abolish capital punishment, that led me gradually into the origins of antislavery thought, a subject I pursued in *The Problem of Slavery in Western Culture.*

Though I had little idea where I was headed, my choice of topics was guided by certain preoccupations and underlying assumptions: an abhorrence of violence coupled with the conviction that self-understanding necessitates an understanding of the aggression, domination, and paranoid self-deception of which we are all capable. As a way of getting at the inner tensions and dynamics of our cultural past, I have chosen the extreme limits of dehumanization. The killer literally reduces a human being into a non-being, removed from the flow of time. The enslaver reduces a human being to a state of "social death," to use Orlando Patterson's phrase, in which the captive is defined as an object, a thing without history. It is significant that reformers accused both slaveholders and executioners of usurping the prerogatives of God, of violating hu-

man limits. Yet traditionalists found biblical justification for both slavery and capital punishment. This struggle over defining moral limits,
seriously initiated only in the eighteenth century, has represented a crucial test of modern culture. During the eighteenth and nineteenth centuries such controversies were intimately linked with the belief that man
was breaking free from historical constraints and acquiring the powers
of self-perfection.

These broad concerns have shaped my approach to cultural history
and are reflected in most of the nineteen essays reprinted here. The first
unit, "Violence and Virility in American Culture," begins with an obscure young New Hampshire tanner and farmhand who in 1843 was
convicted of murder and sentenced to death. The essays move on to the
issue of capital punishment, portrayals of violence in American literature, and attempts to channel or control man's apparently limitless desires to seek stress, danger, and victory over opponents.

The image of combat and struggle as the basic reality of life leads
into the second unit, "The Redeeming West." After examining the myth
of the cowboy in popular culture, the essays deal with the complex
relations between primitivism and progress and with changing interpretations of the Mormons, who sought in the West both redemption and
the kingdom of God. The Mormon exodus posed a fundamental challenge to American concepts of loyalty, toleration, and historical identity. These themes are explored in the third unit, "Problems of Loyalty
and Identity." Here I am also concerned with the model of American
society as a republican family, founded by the heroic sacrifices of the
Revolutionary fathers and endangered by materialistic self-indulgence
and the conspiracies of un-American subversives.

In the eyes of Lincoln and his fellow Republicans, the family or
"house" of the Revolutionary fathers had become fatally divided over
the institution of black slavery and the expansionist policies of the southern
Slave Power. In the fourth unit, "Studies in Slavery and Antislavery,"
I discuss some of the more influential modern interpretations of slavery;
the iconographic origins of racism; and the mid-eighteenth-century view
that slave emancipation was a necessary and practicable step toward the
ideal of human equality. Three essays on the Anglo-American antislavery movements suggest how efforts to achieve emancipation reflected
changing concepts of history and moral responsibility. The concluding
essay, "an experiment in disciplined fantasy," questions some common
assumptions about the meaning of the American Revolution and American independence.

Orange, Connecticut   D.B.D.
February 1986

Contents

IV. STUDIES IN SLAVERY AND ANTISLAVERY

I

VIOLENCE AND VIRILITY
IN AMERICAN CULTURE

1

Murder in New Hampshire

On September 6, 1843, the male readers of the Haverhill, New Hampshire, *Democratic Republican* indulged in a dream. Economic conditions were still uncertain and credit was tight. Lists of bankruptcies and foreclosures multiplied in the weekly papers. The population of many Connecticut valley towns had been declining for nearly ten years. With little better news from York State and Ohio, it was exciting to speculate about dazzling futures in a distant land called Oregon. On page one the *Democratic Republican* reprinted a long article from the *Edinburgh Review* which challenged the imaginations of sturdy New Englanders. After describing the magnificent scenery and healthful climate, the article predicted:

> The land which is to command the North Pacific, and give the law to its myriad islands, cannot long remain unoccupied. It calls loudly on those who have foresight—on those who can estimate the promise of the future—to forecast its destiny. The Americans never show themselves deficient in this branch of political wisdom.[1]

Apparently ignorant of the fact that wagon-trains had already arrived in the Willamette Valley, the author went on to assert that Western mountains and deserts would prevent overland colonization. Americans knew better. Even a man suffering from the depression could read about Oregon and wonder how he might raise some money.

Although William Freeman Comings was in Haverhill, New Hamp-

---

1. *Democratic Republican* (Haverhill, N. H.), XVI, Sept. 6, 1843.

From *The New England Quarterly,* Vol. XXVIII, No. 2, (June, 1955). Reprinted by permission of *The New England Quarterly.*

shire, on September 6, 1843, he did not read the paper and did not dream about Oregon. A young man of twenty-nine, an undistinguished tanner and farmer, he was one of the thousands of ordinary, little people never mentioned in history books. In 1843 he had the misfortune to be in the Haverhill jail. A small note in the same paper that described the attractions of Oregon mentions that the Court of Common Pleas had just commenced, Judge Tibbetts presiding: "It is understood that several important criminal trials will take place during the term . . . we do hope and trust, that all possible dispatch will be made of the business of the term, so that our people may be taxed as lightly as possible."[2] This was a casual comment, indeed, when one considers that a spectacular murder trial was about to begin, involving a case which electrified northern New England and aroused intense public interest for several years.

Perhaps William Comings was born ten years too soon. Since he was energetic and willing to take risks, had he reached maturity in the mid-forties, he might have considered emigrating West. But the late thirties were not auspicious years for a young New Hampshire man to marry and settle down with his own business.

The Comingses were an old, respected family dating back to seventeenth-century Massachusetts. Deacon Fenno Comings, William's father, soberly practiced the tanning and currying trade in Cornish, New Hampshire.[3] In 1816 and 1817 the family migrated to Plainfield and Berlin, Vermont. When Deacon Fenno died in 1830, sixteen-year-old William returned to an uncle in Cornish. Later he wrote that "in my childhood and youth, I felt more or less sensibly the force of divine truth as brought upon me by the continual droppings of the parental culture, the Sabbath school, public worship, &c, to which I was constantly subject."[4] At twelve he entertained the hope that he had made an effectual surrender to God, "but my goodness, like the early dew, soon vanished, and I became to a great extent as before."[5] After receiving a good common school education, Comings went to Hanover in 1831 to learn the tanner's trade. In the college town he found both love and religion. If respectability was not assured by his joining the Congregational Church in 1832, he did achieve a higher social status by his

2. *Democratic Republican*, XVI, Sept. 6, 1843, 2.

3. William H. Child, *History of the Town of Cornish, N. H.* (Concord, N. H., n.d.), II, 105–107.

4. *Report of the Trial of William F. Comings . . . Together with His Life, Written by Himself* (Boston, 1844), 130.

5. *Report*, 130.

marriage to Adeline Tenny, daughter of Captain John Tenny of Hanover.

The future was indeed full of bright prospects for the William Comingses in the spring of 1835. After the bridegroom had taken over his father's tannery yard in Berlin, Vermont, the young couple settled down to raise a family, to follow the traditional life of their ancestors in the rugged, beautifully peaceful hills of northern New England. They were probably little disturbed by Jackson's Specie Circular, by the frantic speculation in Western lands, canals, and banks. Certainly Adeline had faith in her husband's future, since he seemed to be persuasive and full of imaginative plans. But things had changed by June, 1837. It was disillusioning for a twenty-three-year-old tanner, just starting out, to lose his father's business, to migrate to Woodstock, and there to find conditions even worse. After William's second straight failure, Adeline suggested that he leave New England and explore opportunities in the fabulous West. "That she suffered much from blasted hopes and disappointed expectations," Comings wrote, "through my want of success in business, it is true, but in this we shared equally—her disappointment was not greater than mine, nor her suffering more afflictive, unless from a less yielding and submissive temperament of mind."[6] So William left his young wife with her parents in Hanover and struck out for Ohio in the summer of 1838. But Ohio, with its bank failures and constricting credit, had little promise for a beginner without capital.

The Tennys were fairly ambitious and not inclined to attribute failure to social or economic causes. Adeline, whose cousin had committed suicide when he found himself blocked in his pursuit of education, could not understand her husband's repeated failures. Her family did not encourage toleration of a man addicted to bankruptcy. When William returned in December with another story of bad luck, despite alleged struggles, it was simply too much. Had not other young men gone to the West and returned with fortunes? Adeline told her husband that he could not expect support from her parents, that she was tired of his bad luck, and that she was sorry he had returned.

Deeply hurt by his wife's remarks, William nevertheless decided to give it another try. He moved his family to Wells River, where he was engaged by a tannery firm. In 1841, however, a general curtailment of business forced Comings to abandon his trade and search for work as a laborer. At first, Adeline's fall in social rank brought family friction and bitterness. As time passed, she gradually accepted her humbled sta-

6. *Report,* 130.

tus and even asked William to forgive her previous unkindness. But he continued to brood over her lack of sympathy. When a promising partnership failed to materialize, he suspected that Adeline's brother had damaged his credit.

In Bath, New Hampshire, Comings became acquainted with the family of Moses Abbott, a farmer with several grown children. Abbott told William about an elderly, childless couple named Hoskins, who wanted a young couple to live with them and take care of the farm. Hoskins agreed to take the Comingses in November, 1841, but since it was then only April, Moses Abbott hired Comings as a farm hand for the summer and gave him room and board. It is a pity that the Comingses could not have gone directly to the home of Nemiah Hoskins.

Adeline's father came up to Bath that spring and took his daughter back to Hanover, which was an unwise thing to do. It left William alone on the Abbott farm, still smarting from successive failures and from a deep mistrust of the entire Tenny family. Moses Abbott, moreover, had two attractive daughters. For companionship William turned to the younger Moses Abbott, who was then twenty-three, and to Sarah Ann, who had just turned twenty.[7]

Young Moses was interested in wooing William Comings' sister, Ednah, but he had a bad reputation among the girls in Bath and Wells River because he had once eaten a grub worm on a dare for five dollars (he only got two-fifty), and was henceforth known as "Grub Abbott." With such a nickname and reputation, he thought it necessary to approach Ednah Comings through her brother, and proceeded to help William negotiate for a farm in Montpelier. Encouraged by prospects of obtaining his own farm, Comings wrote to his wife in Hanover. He was outraged when she replied that it was just another wild scheme and that she would not consider moving to an unknown place. Thus he was forced to abandon the idea of buying a farm, probably on risky credit, and was obliged to settle down to a dreary, lonely summer with the Abbotts.

But as May progressed and passed into June, as the days grew warmer and clearer, as the foliage thickened on the steep mountain slopes, the coming summer no longer seemed dreary or lonely. If "Grub Abbott" proved to be good company, there was also something about Sarah Ann that appealed to a frustrated young man of twenty-seven, whose wife lived forty miles away, whose sense of responsibility had been blunted by economic misfortune and marital tension. If Sarah Ann seemed a trifle flirtatious at times, she also had a sprightly sense of humor. Com-

7. Frederic P. Wells, *History of Newbury, Vt. with Genealogical Records of Many Families* (St. Johnsbury, Vt., 1900), 421.

ings wrote that "about June, 1841 . . . I discovered that Sarah Ann
was frequently gazing at me, and, as she caught my eyes, turned hers
off with a deep sigh."[8] Even a young ex-tanner in good standing at the
Congregational Church found it difficult not to gaze back. "At first she
avoided my detecting glances," since she was a subtle and cunning
young lady, "but soon she seemed to loose *(sic)* the control of her eyes,
when they were caught by my own, and she would still look at me, her
eyes speaking volumes and her bosom heaving sighs."[9] Thus did William Comings become convinced that through the sheer power of his
steely glances, Sarah Ann Abbott irresistibly surrendered the power over
her own eyes. Moreover, some fatal destiny seemed to drive them together when other members of the family were absent. One Sunday
evening, for instance, when William was talking to the Abbott daughters, Sarah Ann's sister mysteriously left the room. Sarah offered to
comb his hair, which was customary in those days, and afterwards commenced to read a book. William went to the bureau and took out one
of his books called *Pictorial Illustrations of the Bible,* whereupon Sarah
bounced up out of her chair and asked to see the pictures. Sitting closely
together, they slowly turned the pages, thinking anything but Biblical
thoughts:

> We turned from one plate to another, until we came to one where it
> represented a person as being very near or quite naked; and of this she
> spoke in high terms, and unwilling to leave it, and to all similar ones she
> appeared much attached, and to one in particular where the complete
> shape of a naked boy, 7 or 8 years old was standing in a posture facing
> the reader. I must confess I blushed at the idea of seeing it at the same
> time she did. . . .[10]

Apparently Sarah Ann did not blush, but leaned a little closer, and
William could not contain himself. In fact, he kissed her on the cheek,
"which she received without the least disposition to avoid. . . ."
If William Comings had reflected, he might have expected such behavior from a girl whose brother would eat a grub worm for five dollars.
But William was in no mood to reflect. The session with the *Pictorial
Illustrations* had marked his downfall. The relative who gave him the
book, probably as a child to "work some effectual surrender to God,"
little dreamed what surrender it would actually effect. For the first time
Comings had a confidante, a sympathizer, to whom he could recount
his tales of hardship and ill fortune. No doubt Sarah Ann was deeply

8. *Report* 134.
9. *Report,* 134.
10. *Report,* 134.

shocked by Adeline Comings' lack of understanding, by her cruel rejection and persecution of a deserving husband. Once, William wrote a note and proposed what he dared not say. He asked for Sarah's secret affections. She wrote a dramatic reply: ''and for me to resist your love, I *cannot*. . . . I cannot give you more than you have for many months past possessed.''[11] So commenced a series of stealthy and furtive meetings, a rendezvous in the cow-yard, stocking feet noiselessly ascending the farmhouse stairs. These meetings were still of a relatively innocent character, but when Comings spoke of a possible divorce, Sarah Ann calmly agreed that such action might be justified.

But just when the summer was reaching an exciting pitch, Captain Tenny arrived at the Abbott farm and returned Adeline to her husband. This time it was William's turn to be disappointed by the arrival of a spouse. If Adeline wondered why her husband appeared moody and unresponsive, Sarah Ann became distressed when she noticed her family's suspicion. She had probably never intended to carry the affair beyond a pleasant flirtation. With Adeline Comings as a member of the household, the Abbotts exerted pressure on their youngest daughter. At this point, the lovers agreed upon an incredible action, a uniquely New England action. They wrote and signed a confession and had it read before the entire family! They asked forgiveness for their illicit love, which was granted, and then pledged themselves to try to hate each other in the future.[12] It was not clear, when this confession was later described in court, whether the action had been spontaneous or forced. It is significant, however, that the guilty lovers chose the old New England form of a confession before an assembled group. But confessions and resolutions, even in New England, are apt to be fragile. A few days later Sarah Ann tiptoed into William's room and showered him with kisses.

The golden summer ended with the Comingses' move to Nemiah Hoskins' farm, but since the new farm lay scarcely a mile from the Abbotts, William continued to visit his friends. Adeline Comings, who had been pregnant all summer, did not venture out when the days turned cold and the snow finally blew down from the mountains. Although an epidemic of puerperal fever had killed nearly every pregnant woman in the Bath vicinity in 1842,[13] William did not worry about his wife's danger. He said if such a catastrophe occurred, he would have to get a housekeeper.

---

11. *Report*, 136.
12. *Report*, 139.
13. *Address Delivered to the Inhabitants of Bath, on the Evening of January 23, 1854 by Rev. David Sutherland, with an Historical Appendix* . . . (Boston, 1855), 101.

Sarah Ann volunteered. They also spoke vaguely of eloping to Canada. Meanwhile, Adeline prayed that the baby would win back her husband's affections.

In March, shortly after Adeline had survived the birth of a daughter, William met Sarah Ann in the Abbott hayloft. He had good reason to remember the day in later testimony, because it was the scheduled day of conquest, culminating nine months of romance. "While we were upon the hay," Comings wrote, "greater liberties were taken than had ever been before." [14] But deciding to proceed indirectly, he first suggested that he might bring his family the next day to sample some maple sugar. Sarah Ann thought such conversation inappropriate, not realizing that William was reticent and trying to think how best to phrase his proposal. After several lame starts, William finally said that if it could be done with safety and without injury, would it be any worse to do now what they already intended to do? Sarah feigned innocence and forced him to say quite bluntly, *"Sarah, what do you say to our playing with our 'passions?'"* [15] At this, she put her hand to his face and shook her head, whereupon, with classical male prerogative, he replied: "O, that's all, I only asked to see what you would say." [16]

Eighteen months later, when William Comings was being tried for first degree murder, Sarah Ann partially recalled this conversation as a witness for the prosecution. She remembered the words: *"if it could* be done without violence, would it be any worse than to do as others have done, or as some have done, or as we intend to do." Not wanting to reveal the true nature of the conversation, she allowed the State, perhaps with some maliciousness, to interpret this as a fiendish design to poison the sugar, as a murderous intention to kill Mrs. Comings. [17]

During the spring of 1842 it was not necessary to meet in sheds and haylofts, and apparently the sight of rolling green pastures had more effect on Sarah Ann than ambiguous questions. "About the first of May," Comings said, "I met her about 80 or 90 rods east from the house and back from the road . . . at about half past 10 o'clock, and then and there I knew her, (I suppose,) as Adam knew Eve. I had sexual intercourse with her, without any resistance on her part." [18] Since Sarah Ann encouraged the idea of a divorce or an elopement, only the lack of money seemed to hold Comings to his wife and job. As the affair con-

14. *Report*, 143.
15. *Report*, 143.
16. *Report*, 143.
17. *Report*, 38.
18. *Report*, 144.

tinued during the rest of the spring and summer, Adeline became increasingly depressed and tearful. Village gossip informed her that her prayers had gone unanswered.

On June 2, 1842, William Comings was so elated by his recent triumph that he missed the significance of Governor Henry Hubbard's address to the Legislature in Concord. He would probably have shown no interest in the fact that the Governor asked for the abolition of capital punishment. While Comings made love to his willing mistress, heading inevitably toward unforeseen disaster, the Governor said, "Certain it is, that such a degree of punishment defeats the very object of punishment. It takes away human life when its object is and should be human reform and amendment. Capital punishment is not in unison with that spirit of justice, humanity and christian feeling, which should ever characterize the acts of the legislator."[19] Eight days later the House of Representatives referred the question to a committee.

Nemiah Hoskins was accustomed to rise a little after four in the morning to start the chores, but his elderly wife had been confined to her bed for some time. The Comingses slept in a French bed in the kitchen, which was separated from the Hoskins' bedroom by the chimney and a narrow partition. In the early morning of September 9, 1842, Mrs. Hoskins heard a noise that sounded like the cat. After Nemiah had been at his chores for a half-hour or so, he heard the bed squeak in the kitchen, followed by a loud thump on the floor. Then William Comings dashed into the Hoskins' room, in great excitement. "Uncle," he said, "do come here."[20] Nemiah Hoskins went with him to the kitchen and Comings said, "my dear is dead."[21] Through the semi-darkness, Hoskins could make out the form of Adeline at the foot of the bed, partially suspended from the footboard. Her head was less than three feet from the floor, and yet she was hanging from a handkerchief, tied in a halter knot around her neck. A quick examination revealed that she was, indeed, dead.

For the rest of the day neighbor women and doctors arrived at the Hoskins house to examine the body, while William described the horrible events of the early morning. When he discovered that the bed was empty, he said that he had called Adeline's name, thinking she had gone to see the baby. Then he saw the ghastly shape of her head at the foot of the bed, her body slumped across the floor. William sprang out of bed, which caused the thump that the Hoskinses had heard. He was

19. *Journals of the Senate and House, June Session, 1842* (Concord, N. H., 1842). 29.
20. *Report*, 63.
21. *Report*, 12.

immediately stricken with remorse, sensing that Adeline had committed suicide as a result of his infidelity. He never denied that he was responsible for her death. From the beginning, he showed an eagerness to have every aspect of the case examined.

But even in the early morning of September 9, Comings was aware of his perilous position. Adeline had chosen to kill herself in a most peculiar way, she had many friends in the community, and, worst of all, New Hampshire farmers were not especially tolerant of adultery. A man guilty of a sexual crime might well be guilty of something worse. Even though he made love to Sarah a week after his wife's death, it was obvious to William that their meetings must cease. They talked of eventual marriage, but always there was the shadow of an angry mob in Comings' mind. The fury of the public was fermenting slowly, but the scent of retribution was very strong in the clear, autumnal air. Under the pressure of both neighbors and family, Sarah Ann wrote Comings that they must part forever.

A Court of Inquest had ruled that Adeline Comings "voluntarily and feloniously, as a felon of herself, did kill and murder herself, against the peace and dignity of the State."[22] William waited for a formal accusation of murder, but there was no move for an indictment. Life in Bath was increasingly uncomfortable, jobs were unavailable, and the fear of lynching haunted his mind. So William Comings did a natural but a very unwise thing. He left the state.

He made no attempt, however, to conceal his plans or route from the Hoskinses. Stopping in Berlin, he wrote to friends in Wells River and Hanover, then entered his name in the stage-book at Montpelier and in the steamboat books at Burlington. But his move to Rensselaerville, New York, only confirmed the suspicions of an already hostile public. The wheels of justice began to move; on February 21, 1843, he was arrested in Rensselaerville.

In May a Grand Jury at Plymouth, New Hampshire, indicted Comings on three counts. They accused him of strangling his wife, of hanging her with a handkerchief of the value of fifty cents, of beating, bruising, wounding, and striking her with his hands, fists, feet, and knees on her head, breast, heart, abdomen, and stomach.[23] Four months later, when young New Hampshire men were reading about the wonders of Oregon, William Comings faced his jury.

The ways of the law appeared unreasonable to angry farmers. The

22. *Report,* 118.
23. *Report,* 118.

Democratic Republican mourned that "We judge from the number of witnesses present that the trial will be a protracted one and consequently an expensive one." [24]

Little disagreement appeared among witnesses as to how Adeline Comings had been discovered. Amanda Abbott, Sarah's older sister and Adeline's friend, said that Mrs. Comings was cheerful at the meeting house the Sunday before her death, thus discounting the theory of suicide. Mrs. Abigail Thatcher sat in the same pew, however, and said that Adeline had been crying and whispering to her husband. Sarah Ann reported that William had even prepared a bill of divorce on one occasion, giving as an example of his wife's alienation the fact that she frequently compared him with a screech-owl.

The State implied that Comings had been thinking of poisoning his wife with an abortion remedy as well as with maple sugar, although evidence was extremely weak in both instances. On September 20 the *Democratic Republican* had to report that the court was still in session, burning up the taxpayers' money. Still, the case was of such import and murders were so rare in New Hampshire, that it was probably worth the cost to be certain that justice was done. The editor generously abstained from commenting on Comings' guilt in the interest of an impartial trial.

The case really hinged on the conflicting testimony of a battery of country doctors. But rural juries have a reputation for ignoring medical evidence. In addition to the red marks under the handkerchief, observers had noticed some abrasions on Adeline's neck and a protuberance of the abdomen. The prosecution maintained that Comings had strangled his wife, kicked her, and then hung her to the bedboard. They said it would be impossible for a woman to tie a halter knot and successfully hang herself to such a low object.

The defense countered this argument in several ways. Miss Harriet Hancock, a close friend of Adeline's, admitted that the victim could not only tie a halter knot but was proud of her knot-tying ability. Dr. Dixi Crosby of Hanover, who performed the autopsy, said there was nothing unusual about the abdomen, there had been no blow and there was no poison. Dr. John French, who examined the body on September 9, saw nothing to indicate the pressure of fingers and concluded that the abrasions were probably caused by a fingernail. He also said that it was perfectly possible for a person to kill himself by hanging with the head only a foot from the floor and the rest of the body reclining. If Comings had tried to strangle his wife in bed, it would have produced a consid-

24. *Democratic Republican*, XVI, Sept. 13, 1843, 2.

erable struggle, which would surely have wakened the Hoskinses. Dr. French thought that death would be easy and silent in a suicide with the body partially supported by the floor. In short, there was no conclusive evidence which could not be accounted for by the hypothesis of suicide.[25] But Comings was an admitted adulterer who had frequently spoken of abandoning his wife.

Although the Hon. Josiah Quincy[26] made a powerful plea for his client, there was no question about the verdict in the eyes of the multitude. After an absence of only three hours, the jury found William Comings guilty of murder in the first degree. Now free to express its long-secret opinion, the *Democratic Republican* upheld the jury's decision, but called for the legislature to abolish capital punishment in its next session.[27] Since justice had triumphed, the editor thought it unnecessary to take a fellow citizen's life.

For the next year Comings remained in jail while his case was unsuccessfully appealed. On September 20, 1844, he appeared before Judge Gilchrist at the Court of Common Pleas to receive his sentence. William maintained his innocence of the murder but admitted that he had sinned against Heaven and was guilty of "an unhallowed passion." "I know that my Redeemer lives . . . and, though justly meriting his eternal punishment, I cast myself upon his promises and mercy, and with an humble, broken, and penitent heart, cry in my trouble—*Lord remember me.*"[28]

Judge Gilchrist looked down upon the prisoner and began speaking in a solemn and impressive voice:

> Of this offense you have been found to be guilty . . . before your fellow-citizens whose laws you have violated, whose moral sense you have outraged, whose religious principles you have shocked. You stand among them, but hardly of them. By your own deliberate act, you have placed between yourself and them an impassable barrier.

The judge was especially concerned with Comings' pretensions of religion. The whole structure of New England society was threatened when a church member, a man with a sound religious and moral background, subverted the social order. "You have condemned yourself," the judge continued, "to be singled out from the mass of mankind, as one who has raised his fatal and merciless hand against her, whom every

---

25. *Report,* 84.
26. This was *not* the president of Harvard. New Hampshire's Josiah Quincy had been president of the State Senate in 1842, but was a practicing attorney in Grafton County in 1843.
27. *Democratic Republican,* XVI, Oct. 4, 1843, 2.
28. *Report,* 122.

principle of religion . . . every kind feeling of the human heart, called upon him . . . to cherish and protect. . . .'' And now Comings was to be faced with his real offense:

And what was the temptation which, step by step, led you to the brink of the abyss. . . . What was the secret spell, which gradually but surely caused you to lay aside the better feelings of a man . . . and by one cruel blow to deprive your innocent children of their natural protector?

Here, one can almost feel the stern judge pausing for breath and lowering his vocal pitch to a new register.

> It was an unhallowed and unlawful passion for another in violation of your marriage vows, the laws of man, and the commands of God. To indulge this without suspicion, you covered yourself with the mantle of religion. With the name of the Deity upon your lips, every impulse of your heart was far from him.

After describing how passion had sowed evil weeds in Comings' soul which had gradually corrupted his whole nature, the judge now swung into his softer, andante mood:

> . . . let your heart be softened, and your spirit bowed with remorse for the sin you have committed. . . . And as you look, for the last time, at the anxious and pitying crowd here assembled, let it be with an humble trust that the sharp punishment which awaits you here, will be accepted by the Almighty, as some atonement for your violation of his laws.[29]

Comings was sentenced to be hanged on October 30, 1844. The bill to abolish capital punishment had been stranded in committee doldrums for two years when, on June 6, 1844, Governor John H. Steele called for the removal of ''that barbarous penalty.''[30] On June 19 the Senate concurred with a House resolution to take ''the sense of the voters'' on the issue.[31] Comings received a reprieve until December 26, which allowed time for both the referendum and expected legislative action. Thus the life of William F. Comings was placed directly in the hands of the citizens of New Hampshire. It was a dramatic moment, some two years after Adeline Comings' death, one year after the trial, when the voters of New Hampshire ruled that a man should not live. In effect, Comings received 11,241 votes; 21,544 citizens said that he should die.[32] In his

29. *Report*, 123–124.
30. *Journal of the Senate, June Session, 1844* (Concord, N. H., 1844), 19.
31. *Journal of the Senate, June Session, 1844*, 80.
32. *Journal of the House, November Session, 1844*, 55.

own Grafton County, he lost, 1,390 to 3,800. November elections have seldom been so bleak and deadly.

Governor Steele was not happy when he wrote his address of November 20:

> The reasons which induced such decision, are known only to those who so voted. To me, it is a decision full of painful regret. A fellow mortal now lies confined in a dungeon, condemned to death—condemned, at most, on circumstantial evidence; and although that evidence was strong enough to induce an impartial jury to convict him, yet there is a *possibility* that he did not do the deed for which he is condemned to suffer. Guilty or not guilty, I cannot forbear urging the Legislature to commute his punishment from the penalty of death to that of imprisonment for life. Surely, if vengeance is not the object of the law, the security of the public can be effectually guarded by imprisonment.[33]

The next day a petition was introduced in the House to commute Comings' sentence. Both the Governor and groups of legislators seemed unafraid to oppose the public will. Although new agitation to abolish capital punishment and to relate the bill with Comings' commutation had arisen in the House, the appropriate committee reported on December 27 that it was not an expedient time for reform.[34] Meanwhile, the bill to save Comings' life moved slowly, as the date of execution approached. Several petitions were read on December 12, including one by Comings himself, but the bill was referred to the Committee on the Judiciary. On December 18, eight days before the scheduled execution, the House debated the bill in the morning, heard Comings' petition once again, and tabled the resolution. There was more debate in the afternoon, but New Hampshire legislators were kinder than their constituents. They voted 150 to 84 to give the Governor power to commute Comings' sentence to life imprisonment. Two days later, the Senate concurred.[35]

Demoralized by the depression of the 1830's, trapped in the backwater of a recklessly expanding nation, William Comings had been saved by the reform agitation of the 1840's. From Maine to Michigan the pressure to abolish the death penalty reached a peak in the mid-forties, only to subside in later decades. Because Comings had the fortune to be tried at a moment when capital punishment was a lively subject for debate, he had the distinction, in 1845, of being New Hampshire State Prison's single inmate convicted of first degree murder. In later years he might not have fared so well.

33. *Journal of the Senate, November Session, 1844,* 5.
34. *Journal of the House, November Session, 1844, 359.*
35. *Journal of the Senate, November Session, 1844, 74.*

While Sarah Ann Abbott had been unsuccessful in promoting an elopement to Canada, she partially realized her objective in marrying a man named Bishop in 1845 and dying in Quebec in 1882. In June, 1853, William Comings was finally pardoned by the executive authority. He belatedly caught up with Manifest Destiny and headed West, perhaps to Oregon.[36] Having unpleasant associations with the upper Connecticut valley, he now unfailingly sensed that his future lay with the setting sun.

36. William F. Whitcher, *History of the Town of Haverhill, N. H.* (n.p., 1919), 366.

2

The Movement To Abolish
Capital Punishment in America,
1787–1861

Interest in the history of American feminism, temperance, abolitionism, and utopianism, has obscured the fact that for a generation before the Civil War the movement to abolish the death penalty was an important reform enterprise which aroused violent debate over the ultimate source of justice, the degree of human responsibility, the fallibility of the courts, the progress or decline of society, the metaphysical origins of good and evil, and the authority of the Bible. Although seldom mentioned in the standard social and intellectual histories of the period,[1] the antigallows movement won the support of prominent ministers, reformers, and men of letters and for over thirty years was a subject of heated controversy in the legislatures of many Northern states. Moreover, the movement was moderately successful, since three of these legislatures became the first governments in modern times to abolish the death penalty permanently. The purpose of this essay is to examine the background and implications

---

1. The bibliography of secondary works on the history of the movement is surprisingly small. There is much sociological literature on the subject, but practically all of this concerns the contemporary problem. Louis Filler's "Movements to Abolish the Death Penalty in the United States," in *Annals of the American Academy of Political and Social Science*, Vol. 284, 124–36, sketches the major developments over a period of two centuries, but the only detailed studies are a number of articles by Albert Post on early state movements.

From *The American Historical Review*, Vol. LXIII, No. 1 (October 1957). Reprinted by permission.

of the capital punishment controversy in America and to trace the history of the movement before the Civil War.

Infliction of the death penalty for certain secular crimes, such as murder and robbery, was associated historically with the rise of the modern state, whose sovereign was both authorized and obligated to maintain peace within his particular domain.[2] In England the number of capital crimes multiplied in the sixteenth and seventeenth centuries, as the increasing power of the state blurred the ancient distinction between public and private offenses. Executions were frequently justified by the rational arguments that they prevented victims from committing further crimes and that they served as a deterrent to potential criminals. But though the death penalty was rationally defended as a means for protecting the king's peace, it was never entirely dissociated from the primitive doctrine of retaliation for private wrongs. In primitive and modern societies alike, capital punishment seems to afford an emotional release from the profound anxiety and resentment often excited by crime,[3] although such release through projected aggression is usually given the sanction of religion or natural law. Thus by the eighteenth century the acceptance of capital punishment in Western nations involved both a rational theory of society's self-defense and an emotional belief in retributive justice.

The persistence of belief in revenge as the basis for punishment may be seen in John Locke, who was considered a fundamental authority on jurisprudence in America as late as the 1820's.[4] Ironically, Locke not only failed to apply the principles of empirical psychology to crime and punishment, but he sought to combine the ancient, irrational doctrine of retribution with the rational concept of a social compact, wherein the state chooses the most expedient means to protect life and property. He assumed that retribution was an inherent right of man when dictated by calm reason and conscience, which meant when in accordance with natural law. Locke did not inquire how a human being, whose mind began life as *tabula rasa,* became a "noxious Creature" deserving death. Yet he ruled that under the social compact, as in the state of nature, natural law demanded that an act of murder, for which no reparation could compensate, be invariably punished with death. Although the state might withhold punishment designed for the restraint of criminals, since this was essentially a function of government, no magistrate had the right to

2. George W. Kirchwey, "Capital Punishment," in *Encyclopedia of the Social Sciences,* ed. Edwin R. A. Seligman (New York, 1930), III, 192.

3. J. C. Flugel, *Man, Morals and Society* (New York, 1945), pp. 143–74.

4. Nathan Dane, *A General Abridgment and Digest of American Law, with Occasional Notes and Comments* (Boston, 1824), VI, 626–27.

omit retributive punishment, thereby depriving injured citizens of reparation.[5]

Locke might try to preserve the ancient doctrine of "blood for blood" within his theory of social compact, but his sensational psychology was soon to undermine belief in retribution. For eighteenth-century liberals, who found the origins of evil in the human environment and not in agents of the devil or in man's innate depravity, retributive punishment violated both natural law and Christian sensibility. When the human mind was conceived as a plastic substance molded by accidental forces of experience, the criminal no longer seemed an alien from God's law, but rather an unfortunate victim of circumstances, perhaps still capable of penitence and salvation.

In the utilitarianism which emerged from Locke's sensational psychology, swift and harsh punishments were sanctioned in the name of deterrence and expediency. Jeremy Bentham and William Paley advocated penalties of such a degree as to outweigh the imagined profit or enjoyment derived from each offense, but their rejection of retributive punishment represented a significant departure from Lockian theory.[6] As reformers of the Enlightenment increasingly attacked cruel and barbarous punishments, conservatives found comfort in Paley's philosophy of social expediency, which justified capital punishment for any crime difficult to detect or prevent.[7] Without Locke's belief in an inherent right of retribution, however, the sensational psychology could also be used to demonstrate the essential guiltlessness of criminals and, combined with a compassionate sympathy for human suffering, could justify a humanitarian protest against the penalty of death.

In 1764, Cesare Beccaria, who was strongly influenced by Montesquieu and Voltaire, published his monumental *Essay on Crimes and Punishments*. The first systematic application of the principles of the Enlightenment to criminal law, Beccaria's treatise aroused the enthusiasm of reformers in Europe and America and strongly influenced Catherine II of Russia and Grand Duke Leopold of Tuscany, both of whom abolished capital punishment. Because Beccaria's *Essay* was reprinted in America as early as 1773 and thereafter provided arguments for re-

---

5. *The Works of John Locke . . .* (2d ed.; London, 1722), II, 161.

6. Bentham, *An Introduction to the Principles of Morals and Legislation* (London, 1879), pp. 170, 179, 193; Paley, *The Principles of Moral and Political Philosophy* (7th ed.; Philadelphia 1788), pp. 400–405.

7. Paley, p. 403. He argued, of course, that God punished in exact proportion to guilt, which left human law to deal with external circumstances. He thus approved the English penal code, which held the threat of death for nearly any crime but was executed without justice or consistency, because its very uncertainty restrained potential criminals. If an innocent man occasionally suffered, he would at least know that he had died gloriously for his country's security (p. 421).

formers, it is necessary to outline his position on capital punishment with some care.

Beccaria assumed that individuals were compelled by a uniform and incessant desire to act in their own self-interest, unless this selfish force were met with some opposing obstacle. Unlike Locke, he held that men had not voluntarily submitted to the social compact but were prevented only by force from regressing to barbarism and anarchy.[8] Punishments should, therefore, be "political obstacles," designed by the legislator to promote the greatest happiness for the greater number of citizens.[9] By dispensing with the voluntary social compact, Beccaria could avoid Locke's deduction that the natural rights of self-defense and retribution had been ceded to society by each individual.

But if the state was bound to enforce social harmony by associating "lasting impressions" of pain with improper acts, it would seem that Beccaria might join Paley in advocating harsh and terrifying penalties. Despite his emphasis on reason, however, Beccaria's primary appeal was to feeling and sentiment. After formulating an abstract social theory which was typical of the Enlightenment, he went on to anticipate the romantic protest against all unnecessary pain and suffering. The foundation of a sovereign's right to punish, he said, lay in "the indelible sentiments of the heart of man," and whatever deviated from this innate moral sense was unnatural and tyrannical.[10]

We find, then, that the first important treatise on criminology combined the sensational psychology with an emotional belief in an inherent and inalienable moral sense. In addition to his rational argument that capital punishment gave only a momentary example which could never improve mankind, whereas a criminal in prison made a "lasting impression" on his fellow countrymen, Beccaria concluded that since society lacked any right to kill a human being, such punishment was "a war of a whole nation against a citizen," which stimulated barbarity by teaching murder and violence to the people.[11]

When we turn to America we find that the new states, faced by the necessity of formulating their own laws, were reluctant to abandon so traditional a practice as capital punishment. Yet there was considerable interest in constructing a rational and humane system of penal law. Benjamin Rush, whose studies in pathology had convinced him that crime resulted from a disease of the moral sense, gave an address in 1787 advocating the total abolition of the death penalty. Borrowing from Bec-

---

8. Beccaria, *An Essay on Crimes and Punishments* (London, 1767), pp. 9–11.
9. *Ibid.*, p. 22.
10. *Ibid.*, p. 8.
11. *Ibid.*, p. 102.

caria's *Essay,* Rush answered critics in 1792 with his *Considerations on the Injustice and Impolity of Punishing Murder by Death.* Joined by William Bradford,[12] the attorney general of Pennsylvania, Rush was instrumental in achieving a compromise between total abolition and regulation of executions.

The Pennsylvania legislature adopted a law on April 22, 1794, which divided murder into two degrees, providing a unique system for diminishing the number of cases to which the death penalty might be applied and setting an example to be followed by other states during the next half century.[13] When malice or intent, giving evidence of "a depraved mind, regardless of human life," could not be inferred from the circumstances of a common law murder, it was generally defined as murder in the second degree.[14] Adoption of the degree system was associated with a reduction in number of other capital crimes, and both reforms made considerable progress during the early nineteenth century.[15]

When states went still further and defined four degrees of manslaughter, which, along with excusable and justifiable homicide, allowed eight different interpretations of killing, juries were, in effect, given the power to commute the penalty for almost any specific act of homicide.[16] Al-

12. Bradford felt that Pennsylvania's act of 1786 reducing the number of capital crimes proved that hanging was unnecessary as a deterrent; yet he also believed that the punishment for murder should be radically different from that for all other crimes. He favored varied penalties, graded precisely according to guilt (Bradford, *An Enquiry How Far the Punishment of Death Is Necessary in Pennsylvania* . . . [Philadelphia, 1793], pp. 20–36).

13. *The Statutes at Large of Pennsylvania from 1682 to 1801,* comp. James T. Mitchell and Henry Flanders (Harrisburg, 1911), XV, 174–81. In 1682 Penn's famous law had abolished capital punishment for all crimes except murder, but in 1718 Pennsylvania had been forced to accept the English code. After 1794, as new states were formed, they tended to adopt the division of degrees of murder modeled on the example of Pennsylvania's law. Ohio had the degree system in 1824; New York did not define degrees of murder and manslaughter until 1827; Missouri adopted the system in 1835, Michigan in 1846, and Texas in 1848.

14. Francis Wharton, *A Treatise on the Law of Homicide in the United States: to Which is Appended a Series of Leading Cases* (2d ed.; Philadelphia, 1875), pp. 135, 153–62; *The Revised Statutes of the State of New York* . . . (Albany, 1829), II, 656–57.

15. In 1815 Ohio reduced the number of capital crimes from four to two and in 1824 limited the death penalty to willful murder (Albert Post, "The Anti-gallows Movement in Ohio," *Ohio State Archaeological and Historical Quar.,* LIV [Apr.–June, 1945], 105). Capital punishment was restricted to murder in Kentucky in 1800 and in New Hampshire in 1842. In 1841 New York lowered the number to three, treason, murder, and arson in the first degree. On the other hand, North Carolina's revised statutes of 1837 listed twenty-two capital crimes. In Virginia there were at least seventy-one crimes for which slaves could be executed, but from which whites were exempt (Charles Spear, *Essays on the Punishment of Death* [8th ed.; Boston, 1844], pp. 221–27, app.).

16. Degrees of manslaughter were usually defined in the following ways: first degree—when the victim was engaged in a misdemeanor at the time of his death, when assistance was given to a suicide, when death resulted from abortion (this was second degree murder in some states, but second degree manslaughter in Missouri); second degree—when the defendant killed in a cruel and unusual manner, but had no design to effect death; third degree—when the defendant used a dangerous weapon but did not intend to kill, or when a drunken doctor killed a patient through negligence (Missouri), or when a steamboat captain's negligence caused a fatal accident; fourth degree—everything not included in the other categories, when neither excusable nor justifiable. See

though American legislators had preserved the common law distinction between murder and manslaughter, they also, by a redefinition of relative guilt, had limited the use of capital punishment to those murderers who supposedly evidenced a total moral alienation. If a man's intellect had been only temporarily ignored or subverted, or if he had acted from great provocation, there was hope that he might be saved. But when a murderer's entire personality had consented to the crime, it was evident to American jurists that his moral sense had been completely depraved, making him too dangerous to live.

These changes in American criminal law had several important implications for the antigallows movement. For one thing, states like Kentucky and Pennsylvania had abolished capital punishment for every crime except murder at a time when Sir Samuel Romilly was desparately trying to persuade Lord Ellenborough that the British character would not be hopelessly corrupted if Parliament repealed the death penalty for thefts from bleaching grounds or for stealing five shillings from a shop.[17] This meant that the advocates of reform in America were free to strike at the vestiges of "barbarism" without first clearing away the thick deposits of legal cruelty and violence. On the other hand, the fact that many American states had reduced the number of capital crimes and had further softened their penal codes by defining degrees of murder and manslaughter, produced a mood of self-satisfaction, which is always a bulwark against reform. Jurists might applaud the efforts of Bentham and Romilly in England, but the Whig reformers were seen struggling toward a goal already achieved in the United States.

Outside of Pennsylvania, where in 1809 and 1811 the governor urged the legislature to abolish the death penalty,[18] the early protest against hanging was confined to Quaker periodicals or to occasional pamphlets combining New Testament charity with a Jeffersonian view of ethics and society.[19] In one of these booklets, published in 1821 after a prominent doctor's young son had been executed for murder, we find the

---

Revised Statutes (New York), II, 660–61; *The Revised Statutes of the State of Missouri . . .* (St. Louis, 1835), pp. 168–70. It is fairly obvious that if malicious intent could not be inferred from killing in a cruel or unusual manner, or from the use of a deadly weapon, it would be very difficult to prove in any case of homicide involving a sudden "heat of passion."

17. *The Debates in the House of Commons, During the Year 1811, Upon Certain Bills for Abolishing the Punishment of Death,* comp. Basil Montagu (London, 1812), *passim.* Romilly cited William Bradford and pointed to the favorable results of Pennsylvania's legislation (p. 105).

18. Albert Post, "Early Efforts to Abolish Capital Punishment in Pennsylvania," *Pennsylvania Magazine of History and Biography,* LXVIII (1944), 42–43.

19. Elisha Bates, a Quaker, was the first to fight capital punishment in Ohio. Many of the early petitions to the New York legislature were from Quaker groups, but since the yearly meetings were generally silent on the issue, it is difficult to measure the Quaker influence on the reform. The Progressive Friends, who broke away from the Hicksites in 1848, strongly supported abolition of the death penalty, along with other reforms (*ibid.,* p. 50).

theory that crime is prevented not by law, but only by "a healthful state of public morals." Severe punishments corrupted this state of public morals, as could be seen by the increase in crime under the sanguinary laws of England; yet perpetual and solitary confinement in prison would, as Beccaria and Rush had maintained, be a "lasting monument of the ignominious effects of crime." The most significant arguments, however, did not concern theories of deterrence or natural rights. If the pamphlet echoed the rationalism of the Enlightment, it also gave expression to the evangelical faith in universal brotherhood which was gradually undermining the cultural and psychological dominance of the Old Testament. Americans had traditionally justified capital punishment by citing God's injunction to Noah: "Whoso sheddeth man's blood, by man shall his blood be shed: for in the image of God made he man." The author of the 1821 pamphlet argued that this was a prophecy, addressed to Noah before the formation of government or society, simply reminding man of the natural tendency for one act of violence to produce another. To justify the death penalty by appealing to the Old Testament was to violate the spirit and teachings of Christ. Moreover, the preservation of a "bloody fragment of Jewish institutions" identified religion with injustice and thus strengthened the hand of deists and atheists. Executions outraged the moral sentiments of Christians, for whatever the guilt of the victim, "his sufferings alone are enough to call for the compassion of the sensible heart."[20]

Such emphasis on the personal suffering of a condemned criminal, as opposed to more theoretical discussions of deterrence and responsibility, signified the growing importance of romanticism for the antigallows movement. Because the death penalty was associated with both Old Testament brutality and the cold utilitarianism of conservative rationalists, it was attacked by those who yearned for an emotional and pietistic brotherhood, for an all-inclusive love which would embrace the wayward murderer as well as the suffering slave and degraded drunkard. Although leaders of the antigallows movement relied heavily on the rational arguments of Montesquieu, Voltaire, and Beccaria, they also profited from the rise of evangelical religion and from the romantic sympathy for criminals and outcasts expressed in the fiction and poetry of Bulwer-Lytton, Dickens, Victor Hugo, William Gilmore Simms, Sylvester Judd, and John Greenleaf Whittier.

This romantic literature conveyed two ideas which are important for the history of the capital punishment controversy. First, the sensitive

---

20. [Anon.], *Remarks on Capital Punishment* (Utica, 1821). The argument was not original with the author of this pamphlet.

reader was frequently aroused by a vivid and emotional identification with a condemned criminal and his family. In *The Last Days of a Condemned* (1829) Hugo pictured the "intellectual dissection" and drawn-out agony of a criminal about to be executed, dwelling particularly upon the prisoner's memories of happiness and his horror at the thought of his grief-stricken family: "If the Jury had seen thee, my pretty little Mary, they would have understood it was wrong to kill the Father of a child three years old."[21] Although *The Last Days* was not translated until 1840, Hugo's thesis was popularized by English reviewers and lent emotional force to the antigallows movements in both England and America.[22]

Whittier repeated Hugo's theme in "The Gallows" (1842) and "The Human Sacrifice" (1843), wherein he contrasted the joy and vital spontaneity of life ("Again with merry heart he threw / His light line in the rippling brook. / Back crowded all his schoolday joys; / He urged the ball and quoit again, / And heard the shout of laughing boys.") with the prisoner's agony before the "black, giant-like" gallows. When readers became convinced that even the condemned murderer was a human being with cherished memories, a loving family, and tender feelings, they might reflect bitterly at Whittier's lines: "Not by the Koran and the Sword, / But by the Bible and the Cord!"[23]

The second romantic idea, expressed in many tales and novels, was that true repentance atoned for even the worst of crimes and that such repentance came not from fear, but from harmony with nature. By depriving the criminal of contemplation and gradual regeneration, capital punishment interfered with the natural balance of guilt and remorse. At the conclusion of Simms's *Confession* (1841) a murderer is spared from arrest and prosecution because, we are told, life is a sacred trust and only by living may a criminal make atonement to a higher law: "It was with this merciful purpose that God not only permitted Cain to live, but commanded that none should slay him."[24] In one of his short tales Walt

21. (London, 1840), p. 99.
22. Long before it was translated, Hugo's book was well known and discussed in England. American readers of *Blackwood's Magazine* and other English journals would have become acquainted with Hugo's theme. Sir P. Hasketh Fleetwood, who edited one of the English editions, used Hugo's arguments to arouse support for the antigallows movement (Kenneth Ward Hooker, *The Fortunes of Victor Hugo in England* [New York, 1938], pp. 22, 25). In 1855 *The North American Review* spoke of the work as a great success and recommended it as one of the most powerful indictments of capital punishment ever written ("Genius and Writings of Victor Hugo," *NAR*, LXXXI [Oct., 1855], 334). However, Hugo's works were not generally popular in America before the Civil War. Bulwer-Lytton, Eugène Sue, Dickens, and G. W. M. Reynolds were more important in shaping the image of the criminal in popular literature.
23. *The Complete Poetical Works of John Greenleaf Whittier* (Cambridge ed.; Boston, 1894), pp. 355–56.
24. *Confession; or, the Blind Heart* (Chicago, 1890), pp. 397–98.

Whitman also asked whether an unpunished murderer might not receive more justice at the hands of God than from human tribunals: "Involuntarily, he bent over a branch of red roses, and took them softly between his hands—those murderous, bloody hands! But the red roses neither wither'd nor smell'd less fragrant. And as the young man kiss'd them . . . it seem'd to him that he had found pity and sympathy from Heaven itself."[25] Romantic writers sometimes pictured the murderer not as an evil villain, but as a man of unusual sensitivity whose remorse was proportionate to the enormity of his crime. Capable of both sudden anger and profound compassion, he occasionally seemed to have been prepared by his offense for a nobler life than that of average men. To convict him of an infinite and irremediable guilt was to usurp the functions of God and nature and to ignore the divine potentialities within every human being.

Perhaps worst of all for the romantic writer was the unnatural regulation of human death. It was a usurpation of divine prerogative to assign a given day, a given moment in time, for the death of a human being; even a soldier in war or a victim of incurable disease was spared from anticipating the exact moment of his dying. Hugo, Dickens, and Whittier emphasized the horror of approaching a scheduled execution.

Such a mixture of romantic sentiment and evangelical doctrine formed an important part of the argument against capital punishment and doubtless helped to win the support of such figures as Longfellow, Theodore Parker, Horace Greeley, and Henry Ward Beecher. But the major source of inspiration to the antigallows movement was neither a romantic poem nor an evangelical sermon, but rather a pragmatic system of penal law.

Edward Livingston, who corresponded with Bentham and with Continental legal theorists, and was said by Sir Henry Maine to have been the first legal genius of modern times,[26] formulated in the 1820's a systematic set of arguments against capital punishment that were later expanded and adapted by Thomas Upham, Robert Rantoul, Jr., and John L. O'Sullivan, in their various efforts to reform the penal codes of American states. In drawing up his famous criminal code for Louisiana,[27] Livingston agreed with Rush that prison, by depriving a criminal of pleasure, would mortify the original passions and lead to repentance. Yet England's example proved that the threat of death was no deterrent even to minor theft. This was to assume that ideas, such as the abstract idea of death, had little influence on human behavior.

---

25. *The Complete Poetry and Prose of Walt Whitman* (New York, 1948), II, 361.
26. John F. Dillon, *The Laws and Jurisprudence of England and America* (Boston, 1894), pp. 337–38.
27. *A System of Penal Law, for the State of Louisiana . . .* (Philadelphia, 1833).

If Livingston's naturalistic view of the mind implied that the idea of death was no restraint to criminals, his belief in an inherent moral sense led him to fear the social consequences of public executions. Like Rush and Beccaria, he felt that man's natural sensitivity might easily be blunted or perverted by the environment. Public hangings were barbarous spectacles which might well deprave the public taste, stimulate violence, and corrupt juries.[28] To prove his argument, Livingston cited examples of murders and other crimes committed immediately after executions.

In as appeal which assumed a Jeffersonian philosophy of human nature and society, Livingston also warned that all nations were subject to political disorder, party warfare, and dictatorship. When civil discord exploded into violence, as Paine had previously remarked, "new punishments are not invented, but those already known are rigorously enforced against the innocent."[29] The dangerous process of condemning and executing men as aliens from God and Society might not, in other words, be limited to a few isolated criminals: "Beware then, how you sharpen the axe, and prepare the other instruments of death, for the hand of party violence."[30]

Livingston stressed the uncertainty of a punishment the severity of which caused juries to hesitate and governors to exercise their power of mercy, but the codifier's most dramatic plea was patriotic. The eyes of the world, he said, were focused upon the United States. Experiments in Russia and Tuscany had been successful, but despite the rapid spread of world sentiment against hanging, reaction had prevented reform from sweeping Europe. Should Louisiana be the first state to make the enlightened experiment, she would reflect glory upon the whole nation, giving the United States a reputation for moral progress and benevolence among civilized peoples for centuries to come.[31]

Livingston's appeal was ignored by the Louisiana legislature, but his lucid arguments were reprinted and distributed in the Northeast, where they proved an impetus to legislative action. The New York Assembly appointed a committee in 1832 to inquire into the expediency of abolishing capital punishment; its report echoed Livingston's legal philosophy as well as his specific arguments.[32] In response to this report, bills

28. *Ibid.*, p. 27.
29. *Ibid.*, p. 124.
30. *Ibid.*, p. 125.
31. *Ibid.*, p. 116.
32. *Journal of the Assembly of the State of New York, 1832* (Albany, 1832), p. 44; *State of New York, Assembly Doc. No. 187* (Mar. 7, 1832), pp. 22–23. Since this report appeared before the major counterattack by defenders of capital punishment, little space was devoted to theological debate. In the Massachusetts General Court agitation began in 1828 and the first bills were introduced in 1832 (*The Prisoners' Friend, A Monthly Magazine*, VI [Boston, Sept., 1853], 197–98).

opposing the death penalty were introduced in the Assembly in 1832 and 1834, and though they failed to progress to a final reading, they provoked agitation and debate.[33] Livingston's influence was also felt in Pennsylvania, where the issue excited more interest than before, and in Maine, where a compromise measure was finally enacted.

On December 30, 1835, Livingston wrote a letter to Tobias Purrington, a member of the Maine legislature, deploring the fact that Louisiana had failed to act and urging Maine to set an example for the other states.[34] Copies of Livingston's code were distributed to the governor and to each state senator, and Purrington wrote a report to the legislature incorporating the arguments of Livingston, together with phrenological evidence proving that faulty cerebral organization, not conscious choice, was the cause of criminality.[35] The movement in Maine was led by several able men, including Thomas C. Upham, professor of mental and moral philosophy at Bowdoin, who was also a supporter of temperance, universal peace, and colonization of American Negroes. In 1837 Upham and Purrington succeeded in obtaining a law which virtually abolished the death penalty. Under the so-called "Maine law" (not to be confused with the later prohibition law), every criminal sentenced to death was to be confined in the state prison for one year after the date of sentence and could be executed only upon a written warrant issued at the discretion of the governor.[36]

The Maine law was something more than a compromise between opponents and defenders of the death penalty. Despite their occasional statements that crime was a disease and that criminals did not deserve punishment, critics of capital punishment were not primarily concerned with the welfare of felons. Just as abolitionists had seldom associated with slaves, so those opposing the death penalty had seldom mixed with rapists and murderers. Their proposals for reforming criminals were singularly naïve, being based on the assumption that isolation and restraint of passions would revive the debilitated moral sense. While reformers were shocked by the thought of executions, they did not question the cruelty of solitary confinement for life. As we have seen, arguments against capital punishment centered on the corrupting example of public hangings and on the social guilt of depriving an individual of his ina-

33. *Journal of the Assembly, 1832*, p. 354; *Journal of the Assembly, 1834*, p. 410.

34. Purrington, *Report on Capital Punishment, Made to the Maine Legislature in 1836 . . .* (3d ed.; Washington, 1852), pp. 30–31.

35. *Ibid.*, pp. 8–10.

36. *Ibid.*, pp. 41–42. Governor Dana said in 1849 that he interpreted the law as inferring that the legislature did not desire enforcement. However, as similar statutes were adopted by other states, they did not always result in fewer executions. Maine totally abolished capital punishment in 1876, reinstated it in 1883, and abolished it again in 1887.

lienable right to live. It was this profound sense of guilt, resulting from "legal murders," which drove reformers to action. If the guilt could be transferred to the shoulders of a state governor, however, then society might rest with an easy conscience. It was generally assumed that the governor would never use his power to kill a condemned man, but if he did, the burden would rest on him alone.

A similar compromise, adopted first by Pennsylvania in 1834 and by New York the following year, was the abolition of public executions. By eliminating the fearful spectacle of a tense and ribald crowd, hooting and cheering a criminal at the gallows, these states removed one of the more powerful arguments advanced by Rush and Livingston.[37] The guilt felt by sensitive men at a public execution and the horror aroused by a bloodthirsty mob were considerably lessened when hangings occurred in the remote sanctity of a county jail.

Yet many reformers were not content with compromises which merely obscured communal guilt. We have seen that when Beccaria attacked the social compact theory, he went so far as to deny society's right to take human life. In the 1830's Beccaria's secular argument was reinvigorated by an upsurge of religious sentiment against violence of all kinds. By 1838 a minority of extreme radicals in the American peace movement had concluded that total nonresistance was the only Christian answer to evil.[38] For such advocates of nonresistance as William Lloyd Garrison and the Reverend Henry Clarke Wright, war could be abolished only by first eliminating the "man-killing principle" from human society and by substituting in its place the Christian principle of sympathetic love.[39] So long as men used self-defense as a justification for aggression, revenge and retaliation would continue to destroy social harmony. Wright, Garrison, and other radical pacifists, who opposed not only war and capital punishment but also legal suits for the redress of injuries, formed in 1838 the New England Non-Resistance Society, most of whose objectives were supported by Samuel May, Gerrit Smith, and Theodore Parker.[40] Although the society was repudiated by many members of the American Peace Society and was violently attacked by the orthodox clergy, it gave added significance to the antigallows movement. Regardless of one's views on the causes of criminality or the

37. In 1832 Massachusetts recommended private hangings and by 1849 fifteen states had adopted the reform (*The Prisoners' Friend*, I [Mar., 1849], 317). However, some states held public executions as late as the 1930's.

38. Merle E. Curti, "Non-Resistance in New England," *New England Quar.*, II (Jan., 1929), 40–45.

39. *Ibid.*, pp. 40–57; Curti, *The American Peace Crusade, 1815–1860* (Durham, N. C., 1929), pp. 71–72, 81–83.

40. "Non-Resistance in New England," p. 53; *American Peace Crusade*, p. 84.

expediency of punishments, it was troubling to think that the death penalty might violate fundamental principles of Christianity. If few Americans were willing to accept the extreme position that society should renounce all resistance to evil, the sermons, speeches, and editorials of radical pacifists aroused thought and debate and thus helped to spread the belief that capital punishment could not be justified by the state's alleged right of self-defense.

In his annual address of 1836, Governor Edward Everett of Massachusetts noted that "an increasing tenderness for human life is one of the most decided characteristics of the civilization of the day . . ." and suggested that as an experiment the punishment of death be dispensed with for all crimes except murder.[41] The legislature appointed a select committee, headed by Robert Rantoul, Jr., whose subsequent report became something of a classic for the leaders of the movement in the next decade. Whereas Governor Everett had touched only on the possible inexpediency of capital punishment, Rantoul was directly concerned with the inalienable rights of citizens and the limitations of governmental power. He agreed with Non-Resistants that the state had no sanction to take the life of a criminal, but he based his argument on the political theory of Paine and Jefferson. From them he drew his belief that legitimate government was limited in its powers to protection of property and opportunity and to provision for the common defense. Prisons, said Rantoul, were adequate to protect society, but governments, always tending to exceed their proper limits, attempted to judge the hearts and consciences of men as if degrees of moral guilt could be infallibly determined. Since no power was more flattering to ambition than that of disposing at will of human life, capital punishment represented a dangerous intrusion into the sphere of individual rights. The political and ecclesiastical butchery of past ages, which has been allowed under pretense of legal forms, showed that such an unnecessary power might easily be used to subvert republican society.[42]

In contrast to pacifists like Wright or to romantic poets like Whittier, Rantoul represented the spirit of the Enlightenment. He attacked capital punishment for the secular reason that it violated natural law as interpreted by reason. Yet even Rantoul was aware that in America rational theory had to be supplemented with appeals to Scripture. After observing that Old Testament laws were addressed to a people whose hearts were not softened even by stupendous miracles, a people "but a few

41. *Resolves of the General Court of the Commonwealth of Massachusetts* . . . (Boston, 1836), pp. 280–81.

42. *Commonwealth of Massachusetts, House Doc. No. 32* (Feb. 22, 1836), pp. 10–14, 24.

removes from the condition of savages, and almost universally addicted to the most heinous acts of wickedness,'' Rantoul went on to argue that God's covenant with Noah concerned the relation between men and animals and should therefore be read: ''Whatsoever sheddeth man's blood, by man shall its blood be shed.'' By interpreting Scripture within a broader contextual meaning, Rantoul arrived at the conclusion that God's communication with Noah was intended to ''inculcate the sanctity of human life.''[43]

Rantoul's report of 1836 was valuable because it attempted to answer every possible objection to the abolitionist position. It is significant that while the main argument was couched in terms of Jeffersonian political theory and drew liberally from Beccaria and Livingston, Rantoul felt compelled to resort to ingenious interpretations of Scripture. This indicated the source and strength of his major opposition. Despite the power of his several reports, agitation in the Massachusetts House was unsuccessful, and in 1836 and 1837 Senate committees vindicated the death penalty. The one tangible result of years of debate was the final abolition in 1839 of capital punishment for burglary and highway robbery.[44]

Meanwhile, similar reform efforts had failed in Michigan. After Ohio's Governor Joseph Vance had urged repeal in 1837 and 1838, legislative committees in that state defended the death penalty and refused to act.[45]

In New York the enthusiasm originally inspired by Livingston's code had waned, and the issue aroused little interest in the years immediately following the depression of 1837.[46] In reply to petitions claiming that the state had no right to kill, the New York Assembly judiciary committee made a report in 1839 defending existing laws as necessary for social order. Ironically, the authors of this report accepted the assumption of Beccaria, Rush, and Livingston that ''lasting impressions,'' not abstract ideas, were the only force which restrained criminals. But they argued that the destitute criminal would look upon prison as a blessing, since there he would enjoy food, clothing, and physical security, while the fear of death, which was as universal as the desire for life, would strike terror in even the most depraved and hardened soul: ''. . . the

43. *Ibid.*, pp. 79–80. Adapting his arguments from the German scholar, Michaelis, Rantoul said that the Hebrew participle translated ''whoso sheddeth'' was closer to the English ''shedding'' and might be logically rendered ''whatsoever sheddeth.'' Orthodox ministers and scholars treated this argument with icy contempt. See George Barrell Cheever, *A Defense of Capital Punishment* (New York, 1846), pp. 127–36.

44. *Commonwealth of Massachusetts, House Doc. No. 149* (Apr. 24, 1851), p. 4.

45. Post, ''The Anti-gallows Movement in Ohio,'' pp. 106–107.

46. No petitions or proposed bills were reported in 1837. In 1838 the only debates were over a committee resolution favoring capital punishment, and in 1839 petitions against the death penalty were tabled after the Assembly judiciary committee reported against the reform. See Assembly journals for 1837, 1838, 1839.

great body of people are affected only by what is palpable. . . . It is only what is plain and evident that is tangible to their gross conceptions."[47]

It was not enough, however, to defend capital punishment in terms of utilitarianism and Lockian psychology. The committee was obviously perplexed by the fact that its opponents had used religious and philosophical arguments to challenge the state's right to take human life. Although they observed that harsher punishments were necessary in a free society than in an authoritarian country where perpetual police control and regulation reduced crime by infringing on the rights of every citizen[48]—a utilitarian argument that had been used against Sir Samuel Romilly's reforms[49]—they fell back for ultimate justification upon the Noachic covenant and the instinctual "sentiment" of blood for blood.

It is important to note, however, that the committee report of 1839 was tentative, uncertain, and poorly organized. The case for capital punishment had not yet been stated clearly, and the members of the New York judiciary committee were groping for arguments. So weak a document was little protection against the mounting number of petitions which began to flood the legislature in 1840.[50]

Partly in response to these petitions, Governor Seward's message of January 5, 1841, suggested that capital punishment was being inflicted so frequently as to become "an encouragement, rather than a preventive of crime."[51] This portion of Seward's message was referred to an Assembly committee headed by John L. O'Sullivan, dynamic editor of the *United States Magazine and Democratic Review,* a fiery reformer, literary critic, and ultimate supporter of the Confederacy, who, according to his friend, Nathaniel Hawthorne, had a genius for embracing lost causes. The cause of abolishing capital punishment was not yet lost, however, for O'Sullivan collected facts and statistics, borrowed heavily from Rantoul and Livingston, and produced what was perhaps the most distinguished document of the entire controversy. He infuriated his opponents by flatly denying the authority of the Old Testament as a guide for contemporary legislation. Ignoring subtle distinctions between the Noachic covenant and Mosaic code, he reasoned that if the Old Testa-

---

47. *State of New York, Assembly Doc. No. 378* (Apr. 16, 1839), p. 7.

48. *Ibid.,* pp. 11–12. The committee reported that in Tuscany, where capital punishment had been temporarily abolished, the "common people were prohibited from wearing arms, or even carrying a knife." But in a democracy it was necessary to place trust in punishments and not restrictions.

49. *Debates in the House of Commons, 1811,* p. 35. In a similar vein, Frankland argued that England might have milder punishments if the people were "so swathed, and swaddled, as not to be able to commit crimes."

50. *State of New York, Assembly Doc. No. 363* (May 14, 1840), pp. 1–2.

51. *Journal of the Assembly of the State of New York, 1841,* p. 16.

ment was to be taken as a model for legislation, the death penalty might be applied to unconfessed impurity before marriage, witchcraft, blasphemy, or the gathering of sticks on the Sabbath.[52] In addition to the usual arguments, he also drew on the recent writings of the English alienist, James C. Prichard, whose theory of moral insanity, or psychopathic personality, suggested that many criminals suffered from a diseased or atrophied sensibility.[53] Since the subject of insanity was charged with uncertainty, O'Sullivan warned that legal tests might be faulty, that the state might be executing irresponsible men. Had his opponents limited their case to expediency, O'Sullivan's argument would have been superfluous, but since the defenders of capital punishment presumed that guilt could be determined, the question of moral insanity became increasingly important.

When O'Sullivan's bill for total abolition of the death penalty was rejected by a close vote of 46 to 52,[54] defenders of tradition rose to meet the challenge. In 1842 the legislature was besieged by an array of petitions, memorials, and remonstrances both for and against abolition,[55] the most remarkable being a lengthy document from J. S. Van Rensselaer and other leading citizens of Albany. Van Rensselaer's memorial was a caustic refutation of O'Sullivan's report, but more than that, it was a clear and forceful defense of legal executions. Previously, such justifications had been strongly influenced by Lockian psychology and by Paley's doctrine of social expediency, but Van Rensselaer gave notice of his new approach by launching a bitter attack against the shallow and mechanistic philosophy of Bentham.[56]

Since the time of Beccaria, reformers had charged that executions violated man's inherent sense of justice. Now, however, their opponents appropriated the moral sense philosophy and transformed it into a weapon

---

52. O'Sullivan, *Report in Favor of the Abolition of the Punishment of Death by Law* . . . (2d ed.; New York, 1841), p. 11.

53. *Ibid.*, pp. 111–13. Prichard's *Treatise on Insanity* had been published in Philadelphia in 1837. His concept of a diseased moral sense was a more systematic development of earlier theories of Rush, Phillipe Pinel, and Jean Esquirol.

54. *Journal of the Assembly, 1841*, pp. 1179–80, 1362. O'Sullivan later gave the vote as 47 to 52. The first vote had been in favor of the bill by 57 to 52, and O'Sullivan claimed that because the final vote had come at an evening session, attendance was light and some of his friends were absent (O'Sullivan, *Report,* pref.). On May 26 *The Albany Daily Argus* reported that O'Sullivan's actions in behalf of a general election law had incensed the Whigs and caused them to defeat his capital punishment bill: "Some of them, as we are informed, even expressly declared to the mover that they would *now* vote against his bill for the Abolition of Capital Punishment, though before in favor of it!" This was probably just anti-Whig propaganda, since the *Argus* had been actively pushing the election reforms and had portrayed the Whig opposition as allied with thugs, criminals, and crooks.

55. *Journal of the Assembly of the State of New York, 1842*. Petitions in favor of abolition far outnumbered those opposed, and also outnumbered petitions concerning slavery and temperance.

56. *State of New York, Senate Doc. No. 97* (Apr. 9, 1842), p. 1.

for the defense of tradition. According to Van Rensselaer, the moral sense for men like O'Sullivan was a sentimental emotion, which, if consistently applied to social problems, would logically result in the abolition of prisons.[57] Yet the true moral sense was not an effeminate emotion but an inherent, necessary, and absolute sense of duty. "That the criminal should be punished for his crime, is not a truth, summed up from the tardy teachings of experience; it is an immediate, and peremptory decision of the moral sense." Thus the Albany memorial abandoned both the compact theory and the sensational psychology of Locke, Paley, and Beccaria, justifying punishment by a moral sense whose rational and absolute content suggested the transcendental reason of Hegel. Society had no right to punish criminals as an example, for "The attempt to found justice upon utility is only another effort of a low material philosophy, seeking to solve a problem that lies as high above its reach as the heavens above the earth." Hence the English system of law, by ignoring "the intrinsic ill-desert of the offender," was based on an untenable philosophy of social expediency, which opened the way for reckless reformers:

> Nothing but guilt can break down the defences which stand around every moral being, and permit us to subject him to suffering for the advantage of others. It is from this prior consideration of justice that the penalties of law derive their utility. . . . Punishment is not just because it is useful; but it is useful because it is just.[58]

Henceforth, the debate over capital punishment would not be a dispute between Locke and Beccaria but would rest on a philosophic division between naturalistic and idealistic interpretations of the innate moral sense, the former emphasizing environmental causes of crime and the latter stressing intrinsic guilt and justice.

The Albany memorial was the most powerful attack on reform yet to appear. Condemning both the mawkish sentimentality of the romantics and the implied materialism of reformers who based their arguments on the theories of Locke, Montesquieu, and Beccaria, it furnished a new philosophy for defenders of tradition. The final insult was to identify O'Sullivan and Rantoul, who had frequently appealed to the enlightened example of Catherine of Russia, with the corruptions of godless Europe:

---

57. *Ibid.*, pp. 18–19. O'Sullivan and Rantoul were accused of gross inconsistency, since they sometimes argued that prison was more terrifying than death and thus made a more "lasting impression" on society, and at other times claimed that criminals should be cured and not punished. This dilemma, as we have seen, resulted from the abolitionists' principal concern with escaping communal guilt. Their opponents charged them with using capital punishment as a means for political advancement, without really caring about the welfare of criminals.

58. *Ibid.*, pp. 22–23.

"And if we are to be influenced by imitation, if 'patterns of noble clemency' are to be sought, we shall go somewhere else than to an Empress who was twice, at least, a murderer of the foulest degree, and always a loathsome adulteress."[59]

During the 1840's the issue of capital punishment kindled the passions of the orthodox clergy, who brought forth a mass of articles, pamphlets, and books echoing the philosophy of the Albany memorial. Although a few conservatives like William T. Dwight continued to struggle for the theory of deterrence, opposing the enemy's statistics with charts and percentages of their own,[60] the argument of "intrinsic justice" and "moral necessity" increasingly dominated the debate.

The doctrine of divine retaliation was most closely associated with the Reverend George Barrell Cheever, later prominent in the antislavery movement, who in 1843 confronted O'Sullivan in public debate at the Broadway Tabernacle and in 1846 published *A Defense of Capital Punishment*, which established him as the acknowledged leader of the opposition. Drawing from Schlegel the concept of innate reason serving as divine regulator, Cheever spoke of the "intrinsic enormity" of murder and rejected the utilitarian defense of punishment.[61]

There was a direct line of development between Cheever's theology and the philosophy of Francis Wharton, whose monumental *Treatise on the Criminal Law of the United States* was published in 1846, at the height of the capital punishment controversy. When Wharton later defended the death penalty, he pointedly dismissed theories that punishment was intended primarily to prevent crime, to reform offenders, or to incite terror. The justification for punishment was simple and absolute: government was the vindicator of right, crime was a violation of eternal moral law, and "crime as crime must be punished."[62] In the philosophy of Kant and Hegel, Wharton found justification for a theory of punishment as categorical imperative, demanded by the laws of reason. Penalties, as Hegel had said, were agencies with which to annihilate wrong in its continual effort to annihilate right.[63] Hence man was to be given a power which heretofore had been at least theoretically reserved for God—the measurement and negation of total guilt.

In the erratic course of ideas, the moral sense theory, which had at

59. *Ibid.*, p. 34.
60. Dwight, *A Discourse on the Rightfulness and Expediency of Capital Punishments* (Portland, Me., 1843), pp. 25–27.
61. Cheever, *Defence*, pp. 14–16.
62. Wharton, *Philosophy of Criminal Law* (Philadelphia, 1880), pp. 2–12. Since Wharton's views were largely a comment on the debate of an earlier period, his summary of legal philosophy is relevant to this discussion.
63. *Ibid.*, p. 14. Wharton also interpreted law as the united will of the people.

first reinforced the efforts of reformers to reclaim their deluded and erring brethren, had now been expanded into an inherent and absolute knowledge of right and wrong, vindicating the infliction of punishment graded in exact proportion to guilt. With the repudiation of sensational psychology in favor of intuitive knowledge and complete moral freedom, men achieved the power to punish those who were alienated, not from the social compact, but from the universal rules of transcendental mind. Thus was idealistic philosophy gradually converted into the strongest intellectual bulwark against reform. Only the sanction of a higher and absolute law could repress the guilt which drove reformers into action.

In 1846, the year of Cheever's *Defence,* an English phrenologist named M. B. Sampson published *The Rationale of Crime,* in which frank materialism offset the scriptural and philosophical arguments of the opposition. Applying "modern science" to the theories of Rush and Prichard, Sampson gave a physiological basis to moral insanity and stated flatly that all crime was the result of disease.[64] Moreover, since murder evidenced a perversion of the criminal's organs of destruction, which included a propensity toward self-destruction as well as outward aggression, capital punishment only gratified his morbid passions. Phrenology solved the ancient problem of gauging responsibility by simply eliminating it. When crime was conceived as merely the outward manifestation of a diseased brain, punishment became a frightful barbarism. Indeed, executions stimulated the destructive organs of ordinarily normal people, arousing them to acts of cruelty and depravity and inducing waves of suicide and violent crime.[65] Sampson's book was soon quoted extensively in legislative documents, making phrenology an integral part of the debate.

The significance of Sampson's book was that it pushed the naturalism of Rush and Livingston to a logical extreme, directly opposed to the position of Cheever and Wharton. By the 1840's reformers like Theodore Parker could assert that since individuals possessed different capacities for responsible action, and since crime was essentially a disease, it was no more rational for society to kill offenders than it would be for doctors to execute as an example a "patient sick of a disease which he had foolishly or wickedly brought upon himself. . . ."[66] But if reformers stressed the physical and psychological differences between men, their opponents held that by sharing a divine faculty, all men were equally

---

64. Sampson, *The Rationale of Crime, and its Appropriate Treatment; Being a Treatise on Criminal Jurisprudence Considered in Relation to Cerebral Organization* (New York, 1846), pp. 11–17.
65. *Ibid.,* pp. 80–83, 104–18.
66. Parker, *A Sermon of the Dangerous Classes of Society* (Boston, 1847), p. 45.

responsible. Ironically, those who emphasized human differences sought to redeem their depraved brethren, while those who believed in an equal and common divinity would have destroyed the total outcasts, the hopeless aliens.

Meanwhile, the antigallows movement stimulated controversy and aroused increasing resistance. After two governors of New Hampshire had urged that the death penalty be abolished, the legislature in 1844 agreed to a referendum, in which the citizens voted nearly two to one in support of capital punishment.[67] Five years later the Reverend Samuel Lee warned the legislature that to reject the Noachic covenant was to say that God was a liar.[68] The Pennsylvania House, after being swamped with petitions in 1843 and 1844, finally voted to maintain the death penalty for murder.[69]

In 1844 a Boston Universalist minister named Charles Spear published *Essays on the Punishment of Death,* which was dedicated to Thomas Upham and gave thanks to Rantoul and O'Sullivan. In addition to publicizing the arguments of Rantoul and Livingston, Spear edited a monthly magazine, *The Prisoners' Friend,* which dramatized the plight of condemned criminals and printed articles by prominent reformers, along with highly sentimental poems and illustrations attacking brutal punishments. The only magazine of its kind in the country, *The Prisoners' Friend* helped to coordinate the movements in various states; it furnished statistics on crime and reports of legislative debates and organized public protest against executions of specific criminals.[70]

The movement reached its zenith in the mid-1840's. Charles Spear, together with Rantoul, Wendell Phillips, and Whittier succeeded in 1844 in founding a Massachusetts society for the abolition of capital punishment.[71] The same year a similar organization appeared in New York, led by Samuel May, Greeley, William Balch, and others. In October, 1845, a national society convened in Philadelphia and elected as president George M. Dallas, who was also Vice-President of the United

67. *Journal of the Senate of the State of New Hampshire, November Session, 1844* (Concord, 1845), p. 19. Governor Steele made a strong speech against the decision. In 1842 an abolition bill had been rejected in the House by the narrow margin of 104 to 109, and a law had been passed empowering the governor to commute sentences of death. Public opinion was excited by a murder case at the time of the referendum, and Governor Steele, disregarding the popular verdict, commuted the prisoner's sentence. See my article, "Murder in New Hampshire," *New England Quar.,* XXVIII (June, 1955), 147–63.

68. Lee, *Capital Punishment* (n.p., n.d.), p. 9.

69. Post, "Capital Punishment in Pennsylvania," p. 45.

70. The magazine had begun in 1845 as a weekly paper, *The Hangman;* it was rechristened *The Prisoners' Friend* in 1846 and began as a monthly in 1848. Spear corresponded with British reformers and reprinted their articles; he listed Dickens, Elizabeth Pease, John Bright, Richard Cobden, and the Howitts as friends of the cause (*The Prisoners' Friend,* I [Mar., 1849], 317).

71. *Ibid.,* II (Feb., 1850), 281.

States.[72] By 1850 state societies were reported in Tennessee, Ohio, Alabama, Louisiana, Indiana, Iowa, Pennsylvania, New York, and Massachusetts.[73] In addition to this organizational activity, Theodore Parker thundered against the barbarity of executions at Boston's Melodeon, Horace Greeley supported the reform in the *Tribune,* and pamphlets and public letters by Rantoul and Charles E. Burleigh were distributed to legislative committees. By 1846 even the staid *North American Review* printed a long article which sought to chart a middle course between the extremes of Parker and Cheever but concluded with a stirring plea for abolition based on the uncertainty and inexpediency of executions.[74]

Yet the movement lacked the concentration of effort which characterized antislavery and temperance reform. Parker, Greeley, and Upham were mainly preoccupied with other causes. By the mid-1840's O'Sullivan was absorbed by extravagant dreams of manifest destiny, and Rantoul was to find western speculation more enticing than the fate of murderers. Even Charles Spear divided his energies between capital punishment and prison reform.[75]

Throughout the Northeast, however, an increasing number of people accepted the belief that executions were illegal and involved society in an unbearable guilt. In 1847 petitions bearing nearly 12,000 signatures flooded the Pennsylvania legislature. The previous year a select committee in New York reported signatures running 7,580 to 113 in favor of abolition,[76] but the efforts of New York reformers were unsuccessful in the constitutional convention of 1846 and again in 1847, when an abolition bill nearly passed in the Assembly.[77]

The memorable year for reformers was 1846, when, according to James H. Titus, leader of the movement in the New York legislature, the sun had risen in the West and its light had finally penetrated the darkness of the East.[78] It was in Michigan that the first success was staged. There

---

72. Post, "Capital Punishment in Pennsylvania," p. 49.

73. *The Prisoners' Friend*, II (Feb., 1850), 282.

74. "The Punishment of Death," *NAR*, LXII (1846), 42–44, 52. When the humane, rational tone of the article is compared with the radical Non-Resistants and romantic writers on the one hand, and with the almost hysterical defense of tradition on the other, it is clear how far the controversy had moved from the sober utilitarianism of the eighteenth century. The *Review* did not sympathize with reformers who denied the right of society to defend itself, but it was incensed by the doctrine of Old Testament retaliation.

75. Spear's first paper had been devoted solely to the abolition of capital punishment, but *The Prisoners' Friend* became increasingly concerned with prison reform, temperance, and romantic literature. Spear claimed a circulation of 3,000 for *The Hangman,* but by 1854 *The Prisoners' Friend,* despite its wider range of interests, had only 1,500 subscribers (*The Prisoners' Friend,* VI [Jan., 1854], 216).

76. *State of New York Assembly Doc. No. 213* (May 4, 1846), p. 2. Documents on both sides spoke of the increasing interest and active discussion of the subject in all parts of the state.

77. *Journal of the Assembly of the State of New York, 1847,* pp. 1618–19, 1687.

78. *State of New York Assembly Doc. No. 191* (Apr. 12, 1848), p. 53.

had been no execution in that state since 1830, but despite petitions and the efforts of a few reformers in the Michigan legislature, the majority of citizens seemed definitely opposed to abolition.[79] In 1843 a bill had passed in the House but had been defeated in the Senate. Throughout March and April, 1846, the issue continued to provoke violent debate. This time the House resisted a Senate bill substituting solitary confinement for the penalty of death. After an amendment had been added providing for hard labor in solitary confinement, the legislature voted in May to abolish capital punishment for first degree murder.[80] On March 1, 1847, when the law went into effect, Michigan became the first English-speaking state to adopt the reform.

In 1852 Rhode Island followed the example of Michigan,[81] and when Wisconsin adopted a similar law the next year, many believed that the gallows was doomed in the North.[82] Tobias Purrington proclaimed with confidence: ". . . it will not be long before capital punishment will be banished from every State of this great and glorious Union—the consummation of which is an event devoutly to be wished by every true christian, statesman, and philosopher."[83]

During 1849 and 1850 reformers were inspired by Michigan's success and by Sampson's phrenological writings. Public debates, such as one held at the Boston Latin School in 1849,[84] helped to arouse popular interest, and more people were becoming involved in the controversy. The orthodox clergy, however, were more and more successful in their effort to identify abolition with materialists, Unitarians, and Harvard intellectuals: "On a more noxious set of human beings the sun never shines; a company more accursed of the Lord, does not probably pollute the air. . . . Atheism is entitled to profound respect, in comparison with their insolent exhibitions of falsehood, in the name of religion."[85]

---

79. Post, "Michigan Abolishes Capital Punishment," *Michigan History Magazine*, XXIX (1945), 49.

80. *Journal of the Senate of the State of Michigan, 1846* (Detroit, 1846), pp. 241–357; *Journal of the House of Representatives of the State of Michigan, 1846* (Detroit, 1846), pp. 498–515, 548, 575, 599, 613.

81. Five years later Rhode Island's secretary of state reported that an increase in murder had aroused public opinion against the new law, and an effort to restore capital punishment had been defeated by a narrow vote (*State of New York Assembly Doc. No. 170* [Mar. 16, 1857], pp. 24–25).

82. William Tallack, *The Practical Results of the Total or Partial Abolition of Capital Punishment in Various Countries* (London, 1866), p. 20. Reformers thought that Maine and Louisiana had practically abolished the penalty, the latter by empowering juries to render verdicts of guilty "without capital punishment" (*The Prisoners' Friend*, IV [Apr., 1852], 160–62).

83. *Report*, p. 47.

84. *An Exercise in Declamation; in the Form of a Debate on Capital Punishment . . .* (Boston, 1849).

85. Timothy Alden Taylor, *The Bible View of the Death Penalty: Also, a Summary of the Webster Case* (Worcester, 1850), p. 23.

When in 1850 liberals and intellectuals protested the execution of Harvard's Professor John W. Webster, the identification was complete. Despite the growing number of famous and respectable men supporting the cause, the opposition could rely on a traditional current of anti-intellectualism and religious orthodoxy: "Thou College of the Puritans, begun in prayer, reared for the glory of Father, Son and Holy Ghost; dedicated to Christ and the Church; thou has greater cause of grief than that one of thy Professors has gone from the gallows to eternity; the blessed Redeemer is daily crucified in thee!"[86]

In Ohio the turning point came in 1850, when reformers were defeated at the constitutional convention. The agitation of Clement Vallandingham had produced close votes in the 1840's, but petitions and interest subsided after 1850.[87] A bill modeled on the Maine law missed enactment by one vote in the New York Senate in 1851, but in the following years there was a gradual ebbing of the reform tide.[88] In 1852 Massachusetts adopted a similar law delaying executions for one year and requiring the issuance of an executive warrant for each hanging. However, reformers were disheartened in 1854 when Governor John H. Clifford, backed by the Supreme Judicial Court, ruled that the statute did not modify an earlier law requiring the death of murderers. After ordering an execution the Governor justified himself at state expense in *The Prisoners' Friend,* claiming that he had been obliged by law to issue the order.[89] When accused of violating the spirit of the new law, he argued that the Commonwealth should follow the example of Rhode Island if the majority of citizens actually desired the abolition of capital punishment. In 1857, however, the General Court repealed the law altogether.[90] Thus, despite success in Rhode Island and Wisconsin, and despite the triumph of Tobias Purrington when he induced President Fillmore to commute the penalty of a condemned Marine,[91] there was a lessening of interest in capital punishment from 1852 to 1860.

However, a final burst of agitation stirred the New York legislature in 1860. Committee reports favorable to abolition had been made in 1857 and 1859, and the flow of petitions increased in 1860. After receiving encouraging letters from officials in Wisconsin and Michigan, the legislature passed a law on April 14 delaying executions for one year from date of sentence, when they could be carried out only upon

86. *Ibid.*, p. 34.
87. Post, "The Anti-gallows Movement in Ohio," pp. 109–11.
88. *Journal of the Senate, 1851,* pp. 688, 936.
89. VI (Feb., 1854), 273–78.
90. *Acts and Resolves Passed by the General Court of Massachusetts, in the Year 1857* (Boston, 1857), pp. 427–28.
91. Purrington, *Report,* p. 38.

receipt of an executive warrant.[92] The law also repealed previous sections of the criminal code which prescribed the mode of execution, thereby effectively abolishing the death penalty. But the 1860 law, which was greatly misunderstood and at best had struck an ambiguous compromise, was repealed the following year. For the duration of the Civil War there was no mention of capital punishment in the legislative journals.[93]

It was difficult for romantic poets to evoke sympathy for a few murderers when the attention of sympathetic people was focused increasingly on a different and more numerous group of oppressed aliens. It was difficult for rationalist reformers to preach against the violence of capital punishment when reformers themselves advocated the shedding of blood. At the height of the controversy over the death penalty in 1860, Martin H. Bovee, who had been primarily responsible for the Wisconsin law and who worked for reform in New York and Illinois, was struggling to complete what he hoped would be the definitive work against capital punishment. Drawing on arguments and statistics of earlier legislative reports, the book would present a final and unanswerable case against hanging, a case which could not fail to persuade reasonable men to follow the enlightened example of Michigan, Wisconsin, and Rhode Island. But the publication date had been set for the year 1861. As Bovee later confessed, explaining why his book had not appeared: "To have presented a work of this kind during the continuance of such a struggle, would have been 'ill-timed,' to say the least. . . ."[94]

After the Civil War, men's finer sensibilities, which had once been revolted by the execution of a fellow being, seemed hardened and blunted. In the 1870's and immediately prior to World War I, many states would at least temporarily abolish capital punishment, but the movement failed to recapture the widespread enthusiasm and evangelical fervor of the 1830's and 1840's.

92. *Journal of the Senate of the State of New York, 1860*, p. 876; *Journal of the Assembly of the State of New York, 1860*, pp. 1310, 1337.

93. *State of New York Senate Doc. No. 40* (Feb. 7, 1862), p. 2; *Journal of the Senate of the State of New York, 1862*, p. 12. In 1861 an act revived all provisions of the earlier statutes, but there remained great uncertainty about the effective date of the repeal. In 1862 a new law was passed which clarified this matter and provided instructions on the method of executions. In the later nineteenth and early twentieth centuries, many states abolished capital punishment, only to follow this example of repeal, usually after a sensational murder.

94. Bovee, *Reasons for Abolishing Capital Punishment* (Chicago, 1876), p. viii.

3

Violence in American Literature

For more than one hundred and sixty years American literature has shown
a peculiar fascination with homicidal violence. Charles Brockden Brown,
our first serious novelist, presents us with one character who is driven
by an irresistible impulse to kill, another who laughs ecstatically after
murdering his wife and children, and a third who attempts to rape a
heroine alongside the corpse of his latest victim. As one follows James
Fenimore Cooper through innumerable pursuits, escapes, and battles,
one soon loses count of the bodies of Indians and renegades strewn
behind. The tales of Edgar Allan Poe are a gallery of dark and ghastly
crime. George Lippard, a friend of Poe and the most popular American
writer of the mid-nineteenth century, managed to include six rapes and
a dozen murders in a single novel! The market Lippard helped to develop has been exploited even more callously in our own time by such
writers as James M. Cain and Mickey Spillane. But on a loftier level,
Melville's *Pierre* and *Billy Budd* both turn on acts of homicide. In Nathaniel Hawthorne's *The Marble Faun* we are told that when Donatello
kills Miriam's persecutor, the lovers are bound together in an intimate
union, closer than marriage, since they are now governed by a law created for them alone. Huck Finn is an eye witness to two of the most
unforgettable murders in American literature. *A Connecticut Yankee in
King Arthur's Court* ends in a cataclysm of mass slaughter. A theme of
raw, explosive violence runs through the works of Ambrose Bierce,

From *The Annals of the American Academy of Political and Social Science,* Philadelphia, Vol. 364
(March 1966), 28–36. © 1966, by The American Academy of Political and Social Science. All
rights reserved. Reprinted by permission.

Stephen Crane, and Jack London. It erupts with an almost predictable frequency in the novels of F. Scott Fitzgerald, Ernest Hemingway, William Faulkner, John Steinbeck, James T. Farrell, and Robert Penn Warren.

The significance of such literary motifs can easily be exaggerated. There has been considerable carnage, after all, in the world's great classics from *Oedipus Rex* and the *Song of Roland* to *King Lear* and *Crime and Punishment*. If the shootings, stabbings, lynchings, and fist-fights of American fiction present a different world from that portrayed by Jane Austen, Anthony Trollope, or C. P. Snow, there has been a strain of sadistic violence in English popular fiction from Matthew Gregory Lewis's *The Monk*, published in 1795, to Ian Fleming's recent *From Russia, with Love*. One might also compile a list of important American writers whose works contain little bloodshed—William Dean Howells, Henry James, Edith Wharton, Sinclair Lewis, J. P. Marquand, Saul Bellow, even Theodore Dreiser come to mind. Since literary fashions have almost a life of their own, and since much of the violence in American literature bears the imprint of Elizabethan drama, English Gothic romance, or Flaubertian realism, it would be naïve to conclude that the frequency of fighting and killing in American fiction is proof of an unusually violent society.

On the other hand, there can be no doubt that the treatment of violence in American literature reflects certain historical conditions and circumstances. Although we are handicapped by the absence of a fully developed sociology of the novel, we can make a number of tentative observations on the relations between fictional violence and American social patterns.

Perhaps the most obvious point is the sheer marketability of imagined violence. Literary historians have tended to ignore the prosaic fact that writers want to sell books and are usually sensitive to the tastes of their audience. This orientation may conflict with an artist's creative instincts or with the standards of his craft, but our greatest writers have usually established an equilibrium between the opposing forces. When we note that many of the themes and situations of the best twentieth-century fiction were anticipated in crude nineteenth-century potboilers which dealt with moral insanity, monomania, sex and sadism, the uninhibited violence of the South, and the dehumanizing effects of the Northern city, it is tempting to speculate on a "trickle up" process which refines literature from trash. Unfortunately, we know far too little about the influence of "subliterature" on serious writers. What does seem certain is the desire of the mass audience for a literature of violence. And this may be better explained by the limited attention span of the average reader than by theories of repressed aggression and vicarious release. As Alexis de Tocqueville suggested in the 1830's, at the very moment when American book production reflected a rapid increase in popular literacy, a mass market is not conducive to a literature of nuances, understatement, and delicate pleasures. Tocqueville misjudged America's capacity to produce a rich and diversified literature, but his theory that a democratic audience feeds on exaggeration, strong emotion, and striking effect helps to account for the violent sensationalism which today is so characteristic of mass media throughout the Western world. To hold the attention of the ordinary reader or even of the educated but fatigued mind in search of diversion, a story must be full of suspense, surprise, and startling contrasts. Violence is the cheapest means to a change of pace.

If the modern literature of violence has become as international as a James Bond movie, American writers have often been preoccupied with certain distinctive themes. Before the Civil War no genre was more popular than the historical romance of the American Revolution. To understand the significance of these highly standardized tales, one must recognize how much of our historical writing on the Revolution has been devoted to exorcising its radical spirit. Yet it has always been difficult to conceal the fact that the nation was conceived in violence, that its birth was accompanied by mobs and confiscations, and that a burden remained on the people collectively to validate their rebellion against lawful authority. For the first generations born after the event, there was a particular need to relate the violence of their nation's origin to their own experience and to affirm that a revolutionary heritage need not lead to a future of strife and anarchy. By the 1820's and 1830's young Americans professed unquestioning allegiance to the Founding Fathers, whom they saw as legendary demigods, and assumed that the cause of liberty lay not in further rebellion, but in fidelity to the true spirit of Washington and Jefferson. Anything that seemed to threaten the public welfare they pictured as a betrayal of tradition; change was justified as a removal of corruption and a restoration of former purity.

This mentality, which differed so markedly from that of European liberals who sought to throw off established privileges and powers, left a deep imprint on literary treatments of the Revolution. In the popular image, the War of Independence was not a challenge to sovereignty but rather a struggle between peers, usually symbolized by good and bad brothers, for the possession of land and women. The bad brother is the agent of an enemy power; the good brother often has the sanction of a Washington-type father, who gives legitimacy to the patriots' cause. But despite the effort to identify rebellion with a defense of tradition and lawful order, there is a tacit recognition that American society is characterized by a weakness of authority and an unregulated competition for power. And this literary view of the Revolution provided a model for later imaginary struggles for America's destiny, which usually involved conspiratorial brotherhoods linked, like the Tories, with the schemes of a foreign despot. The villains in early American fiction were seldom the bad father or wicked king figures so common in European literature. The hero's trimuph was not a blow against evil authority but rather a defeat of the Tory, the renegade brother, the ruthless competitor who defied the sacred rules of the compact. These conventions, one suspects, gave expression to a widespread fear of factionalism and anarchy, and to a desire to identify one's own interests with a tradition of self-sacrificing unity.

Yet the ideal of social unity might conflict with the ideal of the self-sufficient and omnipotent individual, who was celebrated in American popular culture from the Age of Jackson to the Age of the Robber Barons. One way of evading such a conflict was to project the image of the American hero into the vacant spaces of the West, where his aggressive self-reliance could be interpreted as a constructive and wholly natural force. "When the law of the land is weak," says Cooper's Ishmael Bush, "it is right the law of nature should be strong." And this meant, according to another of Cooper's characters, that when men lived beyond the law, they must be their own judges and executioners.

It was Cooper who inaugurated the great tradition of the American Western and who furnished the main ingredients for the American individualist hero. Leatherstocking and his countless descendents were isolated, solitary men. Far removed from the complexities of adult love, family relations, or vocation, they were the perfect wish-fulfillment of the preadolescent mind. Instead of shaping their lives to distant goals, they lived for the present moment and according to an understood code of natural justice and good-natured generosity. Their independent existence implied a repudiation of sexual and economic responsibilities; yet even their violence retained a certain innocence, since it was devoid of social consequence. There was also an element of primitivistic democracy in the physical heroism of the cowboy or forest scout, whose status was not enhanced by noble lineage or the loyalty of followers, but depended entirely on the exercise of natural abilities in a setting of unexpected dangers. If the European chivalric romance provided a model for testing character by the trial of combat, the American Western stripped the contestants of family ties or clan grudges and reduced their encounter to the most elemental struggle for survival.

As a young hunter who has not yet killed a man, Cooper's Deerslayer tells a hostile Indian that the world is large enough for both of them, but that if they meet fairly in battle, "the Lord will order the fate of each of us." In this archetype of Western combat, Cooper's hero is caught off guard when the treacherous Mingo suddenly raises his rifle to fire. Having caught only a glimpse of his peril, Deerslayer shoots with such lightning speed that the reports of the two rifles sound as one. The dying Mingo admires his killer's prowess, and gives him the new name of "Hawkeye," because "eye sartain—finger lightning—aim, death—great warrior soon." And though Deerslayer still believes it wrong to kill "a human mortal without an object," the West had provided an object, and in so doing had helped an undistinguished youth prove his manhood and win the esteem of his fellow frontiersmen. During the next sixty years the scene of combat moved from colonial New York to the deserts of Wyoming, but the formula changed very little. In Owen Wister's classic version, the Virginian faces an ultimatum from the bully, Trampas, and knows he must either flee and be thought a coward, or fight and risk the loss of his girl's love. As he confronts Trampas at sundown, "a wind seemed to blow his sleeve off his arm, and he replied to it, and saw Trampas pitch forward." The Virginian laconically informs the spectators that if anyone wants to see him about the shooting, he will be at the hotel. " 'Who'll want you?' asked Scipio. 'Three of us saw his gun out. . . . You were that cool! That quick!' " Unlike the ascetic Deerslayer, the Virginian can fulfill the boyish wish for triumph over all intimidating bullies, and also win the hand of Molly Wood. And yet in Wister's story the girl is really no more than a vehicle for adoring the hero and an instrument for revealing his conscience and manly tenderness. We know that in the next book or the next movie he will be married only to his faithful horse, and will be free to re-enact the drama of a quick draw and sudden death in the dusty streets.

When one thinks of cowboys one also thinks of Indians, and as we have just seen, Leatherstocking's first victim was a Mingo brave. The convention of Indian-killing as a kind of rite of passage goes back in American fiction at least to 1799, when Charles Brockden Brown's Edgar Hutley overcomes religious scruples and tomahawks an Indian in order to rescue a captive maiden. By 1837 a father in Robert Montgomery Bird's immensely popular *Nick of the Woods* can boast that his son had killed his first "brute" at the age of fourteen, and had then "blubbered" all night after realizing he might have killed two. Such tales did not shock a reading public thoroughly familiar with the treachery and inhumanity of Indians, and convinced of the need for exterminating them as if they were poisonous reptiles. When we recall that for some two centuries Americans were engaged in a continuing racial war, it is not surprising that so much fictional violence should center on the red man. To kill an Indian was a ritual that sealed one's claim to the rights and privileges of the white man's civilization; it was a symbolic acknowledgement that American freedom and wealth depended on the sacrifice of the aborigine's blood. Of course, American writers often drew upon the European stereotypes of the noble savage, and portrayed "good" Indians who served the white man's cause. But even the most faithful brave could not be assimilated into white society. He was always the last Mohican, the dying warrior whose self-sacrifice contributed in some vague way to a greater America.

If American expansion required the forcible dispossession of the Indian, the American economy was long dependent on a system of coerced labor which began with the violent seizure of native Africans and which led to a militant society dedicated to the preservation of white supremacy and terrorized by the fear of racial war. From colonial times, the American mind associated the Negro with violence. This can be seen in the privately expressed fears of Southern slaveholders, in the debates of legislatures, in the Constitutional Convention, in countless court records, tracts, and sermons. Yet the Negro in American fiction, at least before the Civil War, was a peculiarly nonviolent being. Because pro-Southern writers were acutely sensitive to abolitionist attacks, they sought to prove that slaves were content and loyal and that masters lived a life of serene security, disrupted only by an occasional meddler from the North. When a Negro in such literature is involved in violence, it is almost always in the defense of his master or mistress. At the other end of the spectrum, antislavery writers pictured the Negro as the embodiment of Christian charity, dignified and forgiving even in his suffering. He might flee his oppressors and even fight in defense of his wife's honor, but except under the most extreme provocation, he was incapable of revenge. It is true that both Melville and Poe left haunting images of Negroes in savage mutiny, of a black horror rising from beneath the decks of society. But during the slavery era most writers respected the convention of dissociating the Negro from the violence of sadistic planters or Yankee fanatics.

By the beginning of the twentieth century, a tightening of segregation and an increase in racial tension brought historic phobias to the surface of popular literature. The Negro Gus in Thomas Dixon, Jr.'s *The Clansman,* from which the movie, *The Birth of a Nation,* was made, is a far cry from Uncle Remus or Uncle Tom. The brave sons of the Ku Klux Klan know that Gus has raped a beautiful white girl. His image was frozen in the eyes of the girl's dead mother, after she had witnessed the event and had jumped with her daughter off a cliff to shield their disgrace. But the men of the "Invisible Empire" want to be sure of their justice, and force Gus to re-enact the crime:

> His thick lips were drawn upward in an ugly leer and his sinister bead eyes gleamed like a gorilla's. A single fierce leap and the black claws clutched the air slowly as if sinking into the soft white throat.

This is more than the calmest Southern man can take:

> "Stop him! Stop him!" screamed a clansman, springing on the negro and grinding his heel into his big thick neck. A dozen more were on him in a moment, kicking, stamping, cursing, and crying like madmen.

Needless to say, the battered monster is sentenced to death.

Curiously enough, the Negro is no less a creature of violence in Richard Wright's *Native Son*. Although Bigger Thomas does not rape a white girl, he kisses and fondles the drunken Mary Dalton as he takes her to her room and puts her to bed. He does not sink his fingers into her soft white throat, but he is panicked when her mother enters the darkened room, and he smothers the girl to death with a pillow. Fortunately, Mrs. Dalton is blind, so her eyes do not record the image of Bigger Thomas. But the white power structure soon discovers that he has dismembered and incinerated the corpse and has proceeded to murder his colored mistress, Bessie. At the end of the novel, as Bigger is about to be executed, he tries to explain:

> "What I killed for must've been good! . . . It must have been good! When a man kills, it's for something. . . . I didn't know I was really alive in this world until I felt things hard enough to kill for 'em."

Even earlier, Mr. Max, his heroic Communist lawyer, had tried to amplify the point:

> "Every time he comes into contact with us, he kills! . . . Every thought he thinks is potential murder. Excluded from, and unassimilated in our society, yet longing to gratify impulses akin to our own but denied the objects and channels evolved through long centuries for their socialized expression, every sunrise and sunset make him guilty of subversive actions. . . . He was impelled toward murder as much through the thirst for excitement, exultation, and elation as he was through fear! It was his way of living!"

In *Light in August* William Faulkner refrained from such sermons when he came to the agonizing fate of Joe Christmas, who is beaten, flogged, and castrated after he has killed his white mistress and set her house on fire. But, like Bigger Thomas, Joe Christmas tries to strike off the depersonalized mask of his Negrohood and rebels against both the white man's hatred and paternalistic sympathy. As Alfred Kazin has said, Christmas is an abstraction seeking to become a human being, and it is for this that he is crucified. If abolitionist and proslavery writers once agreed that the Negro was a pacific being, in twentieth-century fiction he has become a focal point of violence and a symbol of man's infinite inhumanity to man.

Thus far we have considered a number of themes which give a distinctive character to the treatment of violence in American literature and which reflect historic tensions in American values. But we should not forget that American literature is part of the literature of the Western world, and has echoed changes in intellectual climate that have usually originated in Europe. In the present century the role and meaning of violence in literature have been profoundly influenced by a complex shift in thought and values which, for want of a more precise term, may be called anti-rationalism.

When defending Bigger Thomas, Mr. Max refers to the murder of Mary Dalton as " 'an act of creation!' " This idea, if still incomprehensible to most people, has found wide expression in modern literature. Its antecedents go back to the romantic revolt against eighteenth-century rationalism, to the celebration of man's passions, fears, and irrationality as an antidote to the classic virtues of prudence, decorum, and moderation. When a mechanistic psychology threatened to deprive man of his moral autonomy, romantic writers increasingly turned to the spontaneous impulse as a source of truth, goodness, and beauty. In so doing, however, they tended to confuse virtue with desire, and freedom with revolt and struggle. Instead of thinking of violence as something to be suppressed, disciplined, or applied to rational ends, many of the early romantics became fascinated by Cain, Satan, and Dr. Faust, and showed undisguised sympathy for sublime murderers and amoral supermen who were moved by demonic urges. In American literature such tendencies came to their highest artistic fulfillment with Melville and Poe.

Another source of the idea of creative violence can be found in the great revolutionary thinkers of the nineteenth century, who attacked the bourgeois synthesis of utility, Christianity, and private property. In spite of their obvious differences, such figures as Karl Marx, Mikhail Bakunin, Friedrich Nietzsche, Jean Arthur Rimbaud, and Georges Sorel were united in their repudiation of the injustice and moral hypocrisy of bourgeois civilization, in their disgust with sentimentality and the cult of tender-hearted idealism, and in their view of violence as in some sense a regenerative, purifying force. As social radicalism merged with the more demonic strain of romanticism, one of the products was a literature designed to strip off pretensions and shock genteel sensibilities. The novel itself could be an instrument of aggression.

There were two sides to the new literature of violence. In an objective sense, it taught that all traditional ideals from God to Christian charity were either illusions or instruments of class oppression; when one tore off the shams and myths, it was clear that society as it existed was ruled by brute force. In a subjective sense, man was found to be an irrational animal, moved by deep, destructive impulses which were either irresistible or were self-expressive, and, therefore, creative. According to Sigmund Freud, this Thanatos was part of man's basic nature; one might sublimate or displace one's darker desires, but the death-wish remained. And such pessimistic views were reinforced by a brand of Social Darwinism which found violent struggle to be the main theme of life; they seemed to be confirmed by the "lessons" taught by the First World War and the rise of totalitarian regimes which used terror as an instrument of policy.

It is unnecessary to trace the influence of such diverse intellectual movements on modern literature. Nor are we concerned here with aesthetic evaluation or the artistic uses to which violence has been put. What needs to be emphasized is that in twentieth-century literature violence has come to be identified with the very quintessence of reality, as opposed to abstract ideals, myths, and institutions. It is for this reason that Mr. Max could call Bigger Thomas's murder " 'an act of *creation!*' "

The theme of violence as reality has taken a variety of forms in modern American literature. It can stand for the true nature of class struggle: in Steinbeck's *In Dubious Battle,* Mac and Jim interrogate a high school boy who has been aiding the strikebreakers, and who has been caught with a rifle; in order to send him back as a warning to other youth, Mac beats his face to a pulp and breaks his nose; later, Jim's face is blown off by a shotgun blast as he falls into the strikebreakers' trap. It can be man's spontaneous outrage at oppression: Tom Joad, in *The Grapes of Wrath,* crushes the head of a policeman who has just killed Casy with a pickhandle. It can make sentimentality seem more hard-boiled: in *Of Mice and Men* George talks to Lennie, the giant half-wit, about their plans for settling on a little farm, but then shoots him in the back of the head, because poor Lennie had unintentionally broken the neck of Curley's wife. It can represent the puncturing of dreams and illusions: Fitzgerald's Jay Gatsby lies on a pneumatic mattress in his gorgeous swimming pool, surrounded by leaves and little ripples from the gusts of wind. It can fulfill the design of history: in *All the King's Men* Adam Stanton learns that his revered father had been dishonest and that his sister has become the mistress of Willie Stark, and he proceeds to shoot the great boss and is cut down himself by Sugar Boy's bullets. It can be the way life really is, no matter what the priests and politicians say: in the orgiastic New Year's Eve party which ends Farrell's *The Young Manhood of Studs Lonigan,* Weary Reilley tackles the resisting and virginal Irene, rips off her dress, beats her unconscious, and leaves the bloody sheets in the bathtub. It can symbolize the brutality of a world to which one must be resigned: Hemingway's killers take over a lunch counter and prepare to ambush their victim.

But violence as reality can also stand for the supreme moment of art and truth: In *The Sun Also Rises,* Romero maintains a perfect purity of line in the bullring of Pamplona, only to be savagely beaten by a man who has no understanding of Hemingway's code of life. Or it can be a nightmarish burst of horror, as in Marc Chagall's painting of the falling angel or Pablo Picasso's "Guernica": in Faulkner's *Sanctuary* a lynch mob incinerates a man with gasoline, and the grotesque Popeye, who as a child cut up live birds and kittens, rapes Temple Drake with a corn-cob. And for some of our most recent writers, violence can be a vehicle of unrelieved dehumanization: Herbert Selby, Jr.'s amoral Tralala is raped by a mob in a vacant lot; her body is then abused and covered with filth by children, while her former companions roar with drunken laughter.

As we have suggested, there is nothing peculiarly American about such images of violence as reality. They arise from an international disenchantment with the view that life is essentially decent, rational, and peaceful. It would appear, however, that American writers have wrought a synthesis between such rebellious antirationalism and the older, native tradition of the individualistic hero who seeks to prove himself by violent acts. It may not be wholly farfetched to see an affinity between Cooper's Deerslayer and Hemingway's Robert Jordan, between Melville's Ahab and Faulkner's Joe Christmas, between Wister's Virginian and Spillane's Mike Hammer. Moreover, the theme of patriotic violence against conspiratorial Tories, which was first developed in the historical romances of the Revolution, seems to have been endlessly reworked in comic strips and popular fiction, the Tories, of course, having become Communist subversives. Critics who interpret violence in contemporary literature as a symptom of a sick society may be reassured to know that American writers have always been preoccupied with murder, rape, and deadly combat. Yet, in so far as the older themes have been assimilated to an antirationalist philosophy, and as the individualist hero has been moved from the open seas or prairies to a dense society in which only the most brutal survive, the treatment of violence in our literature has grown increasingly ominous for a people who profess to believe in peace and human brotherhood.

4

Stress-Seeking and the Self-Made Man in American Literature, 1894–1914

It is difficult to imagine a body of literature built on the model of man as a wholly rational creature who calmly defers pleasure, accepts temporary pain, and always chooses the most appropriate means to his end of maximum happiness. It would also be difficult to write an interesting novel about men who seek nothing but peace, contentment, and security. Even in utopian literature the most vivid scenes deal with cataclysms which precede the millennium. And who is to say whether the apocalyptic vision of Armageddon is a means of enhancing the value of a New Heaven and making man worthy of salvation, or whether the vision of final peace is a means of justifying a subversive delight in orgies of lust, clashing armies, seven-headed beasts, earthquakes, eclipses, fire, smoke, and brimstone? Whatever the reason, from the earliest times men have been fascinated by imaginative projections of danger, strife, terror, and violence.

Since Western literature has so often been preoccupied with man's demonic and aggressive impulses, one must be cautious in relating literary themes of stress-seeking to a supposed historical context. In the nineteenth century, for example, American tales of roving adventurers and border warfare probably owed more to Byron and Scott than to the conditions of frontier life. American writers have seldom portrayed a compulsive young truth-seeker without alluding to Hamlet, or an amoral and defiant rebel without suggesting Milton's Lucifer. Nevertheless, literature is not only the product of a culture, but may provide an imaginative illumination of its deepest tensions and conflicts. And there can be no doubt that literary conceptions of man's desire for stress and excitement often reveal significant historical shifts in interest, mood, and values. Thus the roving, lonely protagonists of Hemingway, Faulkner, and Thomas Wolfe bear a resemblance to the homeless Ishmaels and solitary Adams of the American literary tradition. Yet it is only after the First World War that we find such archetypal figures rendered impotent and hopeless by the trauma of past events, or in desperate search of stresses that can be manipulated and controlled in order to keep the self from being annihilated by waves of meaninglessness. According to Jack Burden, in Robert Penn Warren's *All the King's Men,* "the dream of our age" is that all life is "but the dark heave of blood and the twitch of the nerve." Although Jack is obviously a descendant of Hamlet, and discovers that truth always "kills the father," he also comes to see that the man of ideas, Adam Stanton, and the man of fact, Willie Stark, were doomed to destroy each other "because each was incomplete with the terrible divisions of their age." It is the lesson of Warren's masterpiece, which was written after the impacts of the Great Depression and the Second World War, that man is neither a free, rational agent who can make the world conform to his highest ideals, nor an irresponsible robot who responds to the strongest impulse or twitch of nerve. The conclusion that man must accept the burden of the past and the awful responsibilities of time—that he must, in short, "live in the agony of will"—is surely a reflection of the world of the mid-twentieth century.

With the perspective of time we are beginning to see that the period from 1890 to the First World War was not only marked by extraordinary scientific and artistic creativity, but also witnessed what John Weiss has recently termed "the origins of modern consciousness." In a stimulating essay on "The Reorientation of American Culture," which appears in Weiss' volume, [1] John Higham has shown that in the 1890's American popular culture was suddenly permeated with a sense of liberation from stifling norms and restrictions. From popular songs and fads to serious literature and even foreign policy there was a celebration of youth, vigor, ruggedness, and virility. The new ideal was defined at the end of the decade in a famous speech by Theodore Roosevelt on "The Stren-

---

1. In *The Origins of Modern Consciousness,* ed. by John Weiss (Detroit: Wayne State University Press, 1965), pp. 25–48.

uous Life.'' It found expression in a national enthusiasm for combative sports; in the bicycle craze and the physical culture movement; in the wilderness cult and the yearning for an outdoor life of fishing, hunting, and camping; in a fascination with military exploits; in a new contempt for sissies, stuffed shirts, and effete manners; in a glorification of the New Woman, who, if less sexually aggressive than Fleming's heroines, was nevertheless shockingly bold, vigorous, and athletic. Higham points out that the spirit of exuberance, restlessness, and rebellion extended to such intellectual innovators as William James, Frederick Jackson Turner, and Frank Lloyd Wright. In every sphere of culture there was a zest for new experience, an emphasis on man's unlimited energies and creative powers, and a joy in breaking through the confining walls of custom and routine to ''boundless space.''

Before turning to an analysis of stress-seeking in representative novels of the 1894–1914 period, we should consider the significance of this pervasive shift in attitudes and values. Why should strenuous activity take such precedence over sensual indulgence, domesticity, or intellectual discipline? One might answer that Americans had always been activists, that the task of clearning the wilderness and building a nation, coupled with the Protestant Ethic, had always made them value vigorous striving and a determination to overcome all obstacles. But this explanation does not account for the sudden obsession with virility, toughness, and combativeness, and the rejection of the ideal of tenderhearted sensibility, which had actually been most popular among the middle and upper classes when there was still a wild frontier to be won. Another possible answer might lie in the consequences of rapid industrialization.

By the 1890's there was a growing consciousness of the intensifying struggle for economic power, both among nations and between capital and labor. In his speech on the strenuous life, Roosevelt concluded that ''it is only though strife, through hard and dangerous endeavor, that we shall ultimately win the goal of true national greatness.''[2] There can be no doubt that Roosevelt envisioned a vigorous and manly middle class as an antidote to socialism and anarchism and as an indispensable support for advancing and protecting America's interests abroad. Just as the English had been prepared for greatness by their imperial responsibilites, so Americans had been toughened by their frontier experience to meet the challenge of world power.[3] Yet such pragmatic thoughts could not have been in the minds of the promoters of college football or of the Americans who were thrilled to read how Gentleman Jim Corbett

2. Theodore Roosevelt, *The Strenuous Life* (New York: Century Books, 1900).
3. David H. Burton, ''Theodore Roosevelt's Social Darwinism and Views on Imperialism,'' *Journal of the History of Ideas,* Vol. XXVI (January–March 1965), pp. 103–18.

knocked out John L. Sullivan in the twenty-first round. It is doubtful whether the cyclists and mountain climbers thought of toughening themselves for future combat against anarchists or foreign enemies. Even Roosevelt saw national greatness as only an indirect product of the strenuous life. If certain "virile qualities" were necessary to win in "the stern strife of real life," they were also goods in themselves. The important thing was manly character—"unselfishness, courage, devotion to duty, honesty"—and these were virtues threatened by the sloth and self-indulgence that comes with wealth.

In his misgivings over the effects of economic success Roosevelt revealed one of the most profound and complex sources of the cult of the strenuous life. That Americans have valued individual success is so much a truism that we have failed to appreciate the enormous tensions and conflicts entailed by the ideal of the self-made man.[4] What so many writers on the subject have been unable to see—and what Justin Kaplan so brilliantly documents in his recent biography of Mark Twain—is that an American could internalize the ideal of economic success and frantically pursue every opportunity to make money, and still know that wealth corrupts and despise a society in which money is the ultimate measure of human worth. This conflict could lead to self-punishing and self-defeating action; painful stresses seemingly endured for rational goals might be chosen for their own sake.

The origins of this paradox were deeply embedded in the religious past, especially in the Protestant rejection of salvation by good works, which meant that the moral risks and stresses of self-discovery must always transcend worldly goals and achievements. Originally the Protestant was free to pursue material rewards precisely because they were irrelevant to his spiritual pilgrimage. The crucial problem was the state of his soul in withstanding the tests of life. Even in nineteenth-century America, where the drama of salvation had been largely secularized in terms of individual success, the apostles of the self-made man warned against the sin of making wealth an end in itself. Young Americans were told to emulate the successful man not because he was rich but because he had proved his character by struggling with adversity.

Irvin Wyllie and John Cawelti have noted that the tracts, sermons, and manuals that preached self-help and the duty of economic success made little reference to practical skills or techniques for accumulating wealth. The emphasis was rather on such religious and moral virtues as faith, strength of will, self-discipline, and perseverance. Cawelti has

---

4. Some of these conflicts are imaginatively explored by John G. Cawelti in his *Apostles of the Self-Made Man* (Chicago: The University of Chicago Press, 1965).

also pointed out that in popular novels celebrating the self-made man, including those by Horatio Alger, Jr., the hero's rise from rags to riches is not due to his virtues of industry and self-reliance, but to the unexpected aid of a benevolent patron or some other providential force. The hero proves his worth and deserves success, but he is not directly responsible for it. Cawelti might have added that this device was obviously a vestige of the Protestant doctrine of election. Upward mobility could be justified only if it were untainted by egoism or by a desire for wealth and sensual gratification. The stresses that proved one's moral stamina could never be directly linked with material goals.

To be sure, the prophets of success always recognized a certain correspondence between moral character and worldly success. It was necessary to find some material corroboration for one's inner, spiritual progress. According to Ralph Waldo Emerson, for example, the American environment was a testing and liberating force which at once stimulated and rewarded self-reliance. Nevertheless, Emerson was deeply aware of the inadequacy of wealth and material success as goals in themselves. If one of the meanings of American opportunity was to give a material basis to free and unlimited grace, there were grave dangers in materializing spiritual goals. Material successes could easily absorb all other motives and stultify man's vision of life. And as too many business apologists were to show by the late nineteenth century, one could easily arrive at a simple equation of wealth and moral character.

Yet, in Western culture wealth had long been associated with sybaritic decay. In America the quest for material success was always balanced by traditional middle-class suspicions of aristocratic luxury and by ancient Christian denunciations of avarice, mammonism, and voluptuaries. The apostles of the self-made man make it clear that the second and third generations could expect no benefits from their fathers' struggles with adversity. John Cawelti has found that the novels of success are filled with rich snobs and lazy, arrogant youths who were born with the proverbial silver spoon in their mouths. One of the most frequently recurring figures in American literature is the effeminate, good-for-nothing son who breaks the heart of his otherwise omnipotent father. It was a major paradox of American life that the two forces of regeneration and progress—the frontier and economic success—were self-consumptive. By the end of the nineteenth century the crucial problem was how to retain the ideal of America as a material paradise offering unlimited opportunities for individual salvation, and yet keep success from polluting the very process of redemption. How could one cultivate the virtues associated with upward mobility without becoming enslaved to material goals or softened and corrupted by wealth? One answer might be the strenuous life.

The problems of wealth and success had long been felt with particular acuteness by American writers. The values most esteemed in the Western literary tradition—culture, wisdom, courage, honor, selflessness, martial vigor and prowess—were traits of nobility. It is significant that writers like Cooper and Parkman attacked both the *nouveau riche,* who were boorish and materialistic, and the effete New World gentry, who shrank from conflict and responsibility. The natural aristocrats of Cooper and Parkman, men like Leatherstocking and La Salle, were proved by extreme physical stress to be men of strength, courage, and fortitude, who could never be demeaned by petty goals.

But from the time of Cooper and Scott literature was itself an appealing route to material success. For writers like Mark Twain, Jack London, and Theodore Dreiser it was a means of spectacular upward mobility. American writers have been so personally committed to the ideal of success that they have been unable to treat the subject without great ambivalence.[5] By the end of the nineteenth century the mainstream of American literature had absorbed a hostile view of the conventional self-made man and a deep suspicion of the corrupting power of wealth. And one of the major themes of American novels from the 1890's to the First World War was a search for alternatives to material success in adventure, self-knowledge, social reform, loyalty, or the zest of youth for culture and experience. One should add that American writers from Stephen Crane and Frank Norris to Jack London and Ernest Hemingway have often been ardent stress-seekers themselves, and have tried to prove they are tough knowers-of-life by dashing off to foreign wars or other hazardous escapades.

If American writers never emancipated themselves from the popular dream of success, popular culture was itself eager to adopt strenuosity as an antidote to the debilitating aftereffects of wealth. Irvin Wyllie has concluded that, even on the popular level, Americans' faith in the traditional image of the self-made man was severely shaken between 1890 and 1914;[6] in the same period John Cawelti has traced a shift in the literature of self-help from an ascetic moralism to a new emphasis on willpower, initiative, personal magnetism, and a relish for competitive struggle. Money was less an end in itself or a sign of divine favor than a symbol of personal power. Economic failure was the result of weak-

5. See Kenneth S. Lynn, *The Dream of Success* (Boston: Little, Brown & Company, 1955).
6. *The Self-Made Man in America* (New Brunswick, N.J.: Rutgers University Press, 1954).

ness of character and failure of nerve. With the increasing impersonality and rationalized organization of an industrial and corporate society, it was essential to live at full throttle if one were to create a distinctive identity and preserve the immediacy of life. By the 1920's Bruce Barton could win fame by telling Americans that Christ was not a namby-pamby moralist but a man of magnetism and potency who imposed his will on history.

The need for preserving the immediacy and vitality of experience suggests another source of the American vogue of strenuosity, although this aspect of the subject is so immense that it can barely be mentioned here. For some time historians have recognized that at the turn of the century Western literary and philosophic thought was curiously divided between a delicious *Weltschmerz,* a *fin-de-siècle* savoring of decay, hopelessness, and degradation, and a fierce will to believe, a buoyant intoxication with the *élan vital,* a Dionysian joy in the throbbing intensity and passionate struggle of life. It seems fairly clear that both postures, which could be assumed at different times by a single man, were responses to what Robert Penn Warren later called the modern dream that all life is "but the dark heave of blood and the twitch of the nerve," to an uncompromising positivism and materialism that reduced human aspirations and consciousness to the mechanistic movement of individual particles of matter in a universe totally lacking in purpose and indifferent to the fate of man.

Of course, philosophic materialism has often been used as a weapon to liberate man from superstitious fears and ignorant submission to vested authority. In the early twentieth century many American writers embraced an eclectic and half-baked materialism as a refreshing alternative to the anemic idealism of the Genteel Tradition. Yet it was difficult to avoid moments of doubt and gloom as one contemplated the cold abstractions of mathematical science, the apparently certain dissipation of kinetic energy, the appalling waste and blind fortuity of the Darwinian system. In the eyes of Anatole France and Henry Adams life was an absurdity made tolerable only by lies and illusions. Even William James, who from youth was intensely alive to the wonder and beauty of life, experienced the crushing loss of purpose, the anomic failure of commitment, and the yearning for suicide that were so common among intellectuals of the late nineteenth century. Yet it was James, along with figures like Bergson and Nietzsche, who helped to provide a new faith for the generation that matured in the early twentieth century. Bergson was applauded by Theodore Roosevelt for restoring hope to philosophy. It was James who celebrated the spontaneity and exhilaration of life, who preached of the limitless energies of men, and who searched for moral equivalents of war that would create risks to challenge the human spirit. As young American rebels selected and blended elements from the thought of James, Bergson, Nietzsche, Herbert Spencer, and Ernst Haeckel, they arrived at a kind of misty vitalism that gave philosophic reinforcement to the strenuous life. For in this amalgamated world view life was to be stripped of abstract ideals and pretentious rhetoric, of mean calculations, dull routine, and bourgeois fears. Only then could man live joyously and dangerously, and open his soul to the full, rich immediacy of experience. Not surprisingly, Americans tended to envision this liberation in purely individualistic terms. If a Mussolini could later cite William James as one of his favorite philosophers, it is a gross distortion to see seeds of fascism in American vitalism, with its built-in bias against institutions.

As Americans of the 1890's pondered the meaning of success in a world transformed by industrialization, economic consolidation, and Darwinian notions struggle and natural selection, they often looked back to the great Civil War of their fathers' generation as a key to their national identity. From its beginning the war had been recognized as a crucial test; as America's great Passion, it was constantly reenacted in ritualistic ceremonies as well as in ponderous histories and memoirs, as if a vicarious participation in national suffering could mitigate the self-indulgence of the Gilded Age. Yet the meaning of the war was almost immediately obscured by sentimentality, high-flown rhetoric, and political or constitutional abstractions. It was for this reason that Stephen Crane, at the age of twenty-one, achieved such instantaneous success by recreating a psychological response to Civil-War combat in language perfectly tuned to the mood of his generation.

For Crane the Civil War was the agency of self-discovery; his tale was almost a parable of America's quest for identity and justification in a critical moment of stress, or in what young Henry Fleming calls "one of those great affairs of the earth." The overriding question in Fleming's mind, as in the mind of any soldier approaching combat for the first time, is how he will respond. Still enticed by literary images of heroism and Homeric struggles, which were so appealing to a middle-class, commerical society, Fleming knows that this is real life and not fantasy, and that no one can be certain how he will act. By mathematical calculation he tries to prove to himself that he will not run. But the "monster of fear" grows as the moment of judgment approaches.

Fleming's problem is total self-absorption. As an isolated, individualistic American he is on his own and must prove himself against the entire universe, without the comfort of genuine communion with his fellows. Each soldier is walled up within his own internal foxhole, where his fears feed upon themselves and generate autistic images of reality. In the first confusion of combat Fleming is swept by feelings of impotence, rage, and self-congratulation. Then suddenly the entire battle and war seem aimed at destroying his own being; annihilation threatens from all points. Fleming runs in wild and unashamed panic.

He is now not only alone but is overwhelmed by crushing guilt. Like a sinner who wishes that the entire human race might be damned, he momentarily hopes that the Union Army will suffer defeat so that his dishonor can be shared. Even nature offers no reassurance, for in the serene forest groves he stumbles upon a ghastly corpse. Wandering through the swirling chaos on the edge of battle, Henry Fleming seems a totally alienated soul in a purposeless void. But after experiencing pangs of self-hate and a wish for death, he suddenly forgets that he is "engaged in combatting the universe" as he comes upon panicked troops fleeing as he had done, from the front. Fleming tries to stop one of them to ask questions, and is crushed in the head with a rifle butt. The receipt of this wound, this "red badge of courage," is the turning point in Fleming's life. As Bernard Weisberger has noted, the wound had been wished for and might as well have been self-inflicted.[7] Fleming slowly realizes that it does not matter where the blow comes from or which side one is on. There is no purpose to war or life. Man has no control over his fate, which means that he is released from responsibility, guilt, and fear. Weisberger shrewdly observes that this is a perfect negation of Protestant faith. Yet the naturalist Stephen Crane was the son of a Methodist minister, and if Fleming's crisis was a "conversion in reverse," it nevertheless leads to a purging of egoism and to a discovery of life through a heedless risking of life.

Henry Fleming fights like a devil once he has been emancipated from guilt and fear. Temporarily he loses all sense of self-consciousness. He rushes forward, blind to the odds, with other men who are wild with the "enthusiasm of unselfishness." Like the others, Fleming is eager to show his willingness to take further risks. With no thought of heroics or of the meaning of the war, he fights with the reckless daring of a savage. Then suddenly the engagement is over. The men retire from "the place of blood and wrath" to momentary tranquillity. The battle had been blind and purposeless, but Henry Fleming has conquered his fear of death and has found his identity in a feeling of quiet self-confidence and sturdy manhood.

In a sense Henry Fleming was a self-made man who won success in

7. In *Twelve Original Essays on Great American Novels,* ed. by Charles Shapiro (Detroit: Wayne State University Press, 1958), pp. 96–123.

the meaningless strife of war. As an alternative to war, the Great West had long been regarded as a place where a man might prove his character without becoming tainted by avarice or the decadence of wealth. In the words of Owen Wister, who did much to shape the conventions of popular Western melodrama, the West was the realm of the "horseman, the cowpuncher, the last romantic figure upon our soil." Wister's *The Virginian* (1902) is wholly lacking in the psychological subtlety and impressionistic realism of *The Red Badge of Courage* (1894). But it is an interesting expression of the ethic of the strenuous life, and was appropriately dedicated to Wister's friend, Theordore Roosevelt.

The novel offers a forthright rejection of sentimental democracy. In the Virginian's words, "equality is a great big bluff." The true American creed is that all men should have equal liberty to find their own level, and "let the best man win, whoever he is!" Molly Stark Wood, the young heroine of the tale, comes from the natural aristocracy of New England. Her character has been formed by family pride and pluck, and by "struggling with hardship." This was all in line with the self-help manuals and the values of Horatio Alger, Jr. But by the 1870's America had begun to change. Despite their pride and natural merit, Molly's family had fallen on hard times and the girl was tempted to marry a man she did not love in order to help her family. In the South, the Virginian's lazy brothers sat around talking "hawgs and turkeys," and seemed unwilling to take chances. For men and women of ambition, the West was the only escape from decadence and vice. The Eastern narrator, who travels to Wyoming and follows the Virginian around in unembarrassed adoration, observes that the West sees more of death but less of vice than the East. He is entranced by the "wild and manly" faces of the cowboys, and by their "daring, laughter, [and] endurance."

The Virginian himself is a slim young giant who exudes strength and personifies the chivalric code of the West. Deferential and shy toward women, he is also a humorous prankster and a deadly realist in his attitude toward life and death. It should not bother anyone to have killed a man, he says, "when he'd ought to have been killed." He is a bit bothered, however, when he participates in the lynching of his friend Steve, because Steve is easygoing and "game" to the end. If it is only justice to hang a cattle rustler, the Virginian cannot help admiring a man who "took dying as naturally as he took living. Like a man should." But when the Virginian is plagued by nightmares of Steve, he is ashamed of being "that weak."

The drama of Wister's novel turns on an epic conflict of will between the Virginian and the bully Trampas. From the moment that Trampas first backs down, after the Virginian makes his now classic utterance—

"When you call me that, *smile!*"—it is inevitable that the two must meet in mortal combat. The Virginian courts trouble by humiliating Trampas with a practical joke and by refusing, as ranch foreman, to dismiss his enemy in order to avoid further conflict. Since the Virginian never knows the fear of a Henry Fleming, the only complicating factor is his love for Molly Wood. For it is on the day before their wedding that Trampas publicly slanders the Virginian and issues an ultimatum that he leave town before sundown. The sympathetic bishop advises the hero to observe the higher law of love, and to leave town with Molly. Molly flatly says that "fear of outside opinion" cannot justify killing in cold blood, and that therefore "if you do this, there can be no tomorrow for you and me." But the Virginian cannot resign his manhood. After he shoots Trampas, even Molly's New England conscience "capitulates to love," which is a good thing for her since the Virginian eventually becomes a prosperous man who is "able to give his wife all and more than she asked or desired." Presumably the Virginian, having once proved his selfless courage and manhood, could be perfectly satisfied with the wealth that came with railroads and the discovery of coal on his ranch.

But what of the later generations who could receive no moral benefit from the Civil War or the vanishing frontier? In 1895, while still in college, Frank Norris wrote a semi-autobiographical novel, *Vandover and the Bute,* about the sensitive, artistic son of a self-made man. Like his creator, Vandover is a shy and awkward lad, looked upon as a sissy by other boys and psychologically dominated by his immensely strong and upright father. Vandover's father had devoted his entire life to business, and though now a wealthy "old gentleman," he has reentered the sordid business world as the only escape from the "mortal ennui and weariness of the spirit" that had plagued him in a brief retirement. He has no capacity for enjoying anything but the challenge of competitive life, and in his new venture as a builder and real-estate developer is soon an enormous success. Nonetheless, the father is not lacking in sympathy for Vandover's artistic aspirations, and except for substituting Harvard for Paris as a more suitable moral environment, he encourages and supports his son's unconventional career. He continues to do so even after Vandover has left Harvard and has confessed to grave sexual sins which culminate in the suicide of a young girl.

Like Norris himself, Vandover associates virtue with success and social respectability, and yet is strangely drawn to vice. Norris places great emphasis on the fact that Vandover's mother had died when he was eight, which meant there was no feminine influence to counterbalance the perverse and vicious ideas, the "brute" that began stirring within him in his teens. Norris' later novels rely on powerful Amazons who, like Moran in *Moran of the Lady Letty,* are virginal superwomen who beat up villains and help the frail hero become a man. The one force within Vandover that keeps the libidinal brute from plunging him into total degradation is his hallowed respect for women. Nevertheless, "as the desire of vice, the blind, reckless desire of the male, grew upon him, he set himself to destroy this barrier." He deliberately tries to corrupt his impulse to idealize women, which has been his only saving grace.

In one sense Vandover is the very opposite of a stress-seeker. In the manner of Zolaesque determinism, Norris pictures him as simply a weak and pliable youth who, being unaccustomed "to doing hard, disagreeable things," submits to the strongest impulse and adjusts to the most sordid environment. Yet, as a student, he does not know why he gets drunk, since he enjoys drinking no more than his father enjoys leisure. Sleeping with a cheap girl does not bring pleasure but an agonizing repentance. Vandover continually hurts his father with confessions of sin, and is hurt in return by his father's kindly understanding. When his father dies and Vandover inherits the hard-earned fortune, there is no check to his idleness, self-indulgence, and decline. Ostracized by friends, he no longer fears the opinion of others and feels free to do anything he chooses. Needing violent and untried excitement, he develops a mania for gambling and finds that he must continually raise the stakes in order to maintain interest and excitement. His fortune dwindles and the brute within him grows, destroying first his artistic creativity and then his reason, until Vandover has hallucinations that *he* is the beast itself. A victim of lycanthropy, Vandover suffers a ghastly punishment which, Norris informs us, he brought upon himself: "His whole life had been one long suicide."

If Vandover's choices bring him to the point of imagining he is a wolf, his friend Charlie Geary is a wolf of another kind. Originally one of the youths who caroused with Vandover and helped to corrupt him, Geary is a pushing, ambitious, domineering figure who lives by the motto, "Every man for himself . . . the weakest to the wall, the strongest to the front." If this is only a Darwinian version of the Virginian's "let the best man win," Geary shows what success has come to mean in Vandover's generation: "anything to be a 'success,' to 'arrive,' to 'get there,' to attain the desired object in spite of the whole world . . . trampling down or smashing through everything that stood in the way." It is Geary who moves in voraciously to grab what he can of Vandover's property, and who finally hires the demented man to clean and scrub some filthy tenements on land he had formerly owned. It is as if Geary were the punitive agent of Vandover's father.

Vandover and the Brute contrasts the success of a ruthless strong man to the failure of a weak artist who is driven to dissipation and madness by the temptations of affluence and by internal compulsions that seem provoked by a father and a society wholly committed to material success. Theodore Dreiser's *The Financier* (1912) and *The Titan* (1914) chart the repeated successes of a man who possesses the same strength and ruthless code as Charlie Geary. One might assume that novels modeled on the career of a great tycoon, in this case Charles T. Yerkes, would present a man who calculates rational strategy to achieve his goals, and would thus be irrelevant to the theme of stress-seeking. But Dreiser's Frank Cowperwood is as much an artist as Vandover, and is a rational goal-seeker in only a superficial sense. If he pursues money, power, and sex, it is only because they provide means for releasing his titanic energies and for imposing his will on an otherwise impersonal and meaningless world.

Theodore Dreiser, who knew the taste of failure and came close to suicide in 1903, was always dazzled by the glamour of wealth. His articles on great Americans, written for the magazine *Success,* showed that the self-made man was not necessarily a cramped, bourgeois moneygrubber. Instead of looking for an alternative to the self-made man, Dreiser worked a transvaluation of values and pictured Cowperwood as a Nietzschean superman, as the strongest product of evolutionary struggle, as a modern counterpart to Lucifer, Don Juan, and the greatest of Renaissance princes.

Cowperwood's father represents the limits of success within the framework of traditional values. A moderately prosperous banker, he is content with his station in life. His vision is restricted by excessive caution and conventional morality. But his son Frank lives by the rule, "I satisfy myself," and knows no law except that imposed upon him by his inability to think. Completely free of the self-doubts of a Henry Fleming, the only thing he dreads is inactivity. Frank Cowperwood is at once an intellectual, an amoralist, and an egoist; he is a man of enormous will and personal magnetism whose hypnotic eyes overpower other men and captivate women. He can simultaneously manage a number of illicit sexual affairs while manipulating politicians and bankers, dealing with strikes and labor unions, bonding and equipping tunnels for his street railways, and mapping the grand strategy for his conquest of Chicago. When a stubborn property owner blocks the construction of a tunnel, Frank simply has the building demolished on a Saturday afternoon, knowing that a court will not act until the following week, when he can protect a *fait accompli* with legal delays. If a mayor is elected to combat corruption, Frank simply engineers his seduction by an attractive prostitute, and then threatens his supposedly respectable enemy with the exposure of love letters and a suit for breach of promise.

Frank's cool sense of strategy makes it appear that his behavior might be explained by a theory of games. For example, when he is confronted by a Mr. Sohlberg, who is suspicious of Frank's relations with Mrs. Sohlberg, Cowperwood first tries the gambit of threatening to reveal what he has discovered about Sohlberg's own love affairs. When this fails, Cowperwood escalates the conflict by asking what Sohlberg would do if his suspicions proved to be true. Sohlberg replies that he would kill Cowperwood. Prepared for this, Frank pulls out two small revolvers, flatly states that he has been sleeping with Mrs. Sohlberg, and says, " 'Now if you want to kill me here is a gun. . . . Take your choice. If I am to die you might as well die with me.' " This proposal, coupled with a look of cold steel, undermines Sohlberg's nerve, as Frank knew it would. Cowperwood now denies the affair and tells Sohlberg that he will be shot on sight if he says anything more, but that he will be amply rewarded if he gets out of town.

But game theory, while perhaps relevant to Cowperwood's strategic use of power, cannot explain why he gets into such positions in the first place. Even as a young man in Philadelphia, Cowperwood is not simply the shrewd, calculating financier that the bankers take him to be. He is so reckless in his risk-taking that a financial panic exposes him to enemies who are able to send him to prison. Two years after this punishment he is back in the same room at the stock exchange where he was once ruined, again taking chances in a time of crisis, and now triumphing. Upon arriving in Chicago, he boldly seeks out the president of the largest bank, and after impressing the man with his wealth and personal magnetism, coolly informs him of the conviction for embezzlement, the prison term, and a recent divorce. Although Cowperwood knows nothing about the manufacture and distribution of natural gas, he is attracted to the field because it presents the opportunity for a big fight and for bitter lawsuits, both of which Frank says he loves. Even in the social sphere Frank and his new young wife Aileen take the risk of plunging immediately toward the upper strata, although they know that by pitching a lavish party much will be at stake both for them and their suspicious guests. Neither prudence nor patience is among Frank's virtues. This is because he is attracted only by the "complications" of life: "Nature was beautiful, tender at times, but difficulties, plans, plots, schemes to unravel and make smooth—these things were what made existence worthwhile." Life was essentially a battle without ultimate purpose; the only meaningful question was "whether the world would trample him underfoot or no."

Cowperwood is a great admirer and collector of paintings, and achieves a certain aesthetic satisfaction from his financial manipulations. This "artistic" bent is also expressed in his passion for beautiful women. Nothing could have been more foolhardy than his decision to pursue Aileen Butler, the daughter of a Philadelphia contractor who had the political and financial power to crush him. Not only was Frank heavily dependent on Butler, but he was a married man in a society that put sexual transgression on an altogether different plane from simple graft and corruption. Cowperwood is "almost nervous" after his first over-ture to Aileen, and realizes he is contemplating "a very treacherous thing." Yet seduction has much the same appeal as some daring finan-cial challenge. He is thus thrilled to watch himself deliberately, calcu-latingly pump the bellows that heighten his flames of desire, "to feed a fire that might ultimately consume him—and how deliberately and re-sourcefully!" Later on, in Chicago, he repeats the performance by se-ducing the wives and daughters of some of his principal supporters. And if Cowperwood is a "buccaneer" on a "sea of sex," it is not because he really seeks either beauty or sex. He is not dissatisfied with Aileen in either way. Rather, he must continually test himself against the will of the very best women. He must respond to every challenge and every risk as he pursues an ultimate ideal of perfection and mastery that can never be found. Frank Cowperwood is, in short, an embodiment of the *élan vital* that can never find an object or goal commensurate with its unlimited energy. In the end, Cowperwood's powers are diffused and become self-destructive as they fail to find limits that can give them meaning.

Theodore Dreiser accepted both the American ethic of success and a pessimistic materialism. Yet he clearly identified himself with Frank Cowperwood, who, by seeking stresses that would test his own will and capacity for transcending the deterministic flux, defiantly challenged both the materialistic world view and the narrow equation of morality and success. The same intriguing pattern can be seen in the work of Jack London. Born in illegitimacy and destitution, hardened as a physical laborer, oyster pirate, hobo, and sailor, London made a fortune by writ-ing forty-three books in sixteen years, crowned his success by building a patriarchal estate and instructing his Korean servant to call him "Mr. God," and then committed suicide at the age of forty. London's uncer-tainty over the meaning of success was matched by his confusion in philosophy. His reputation as a Socialist speaker and writer was based on his indignation at the authority structure of a capitalistic society, especially at the so-called custodians of culture; but Marxist rhetoric could not conceal London's deep contempt for the masses. A self-professed disciple of both Spencer and Nietzsche, he was at once a materialist, a Social Darwinist, and a believer in the creative energy of a kind of elemental life-force. Essentially he agreed with the elitist philosophy of Frank Cowperwood, and held that the race is to the swift and the battle to the strong. But instead of looking to the strife of business or the vanishing frontier, he treated the themes of success and failure within a framework of decadent civilization and regenerative savagery. Writing at a time when even the Far West had settled into the dull and repressive routines of civilized life, London found the last life-restoring stresses in Alaska and the Pacific. His best-known character, Buck, the self-made dog, moves from the boredom and soft decay of the Santa Clara Valley to a fierce contest for survival in the Klondike, and finally finds a richer and freer life by responding to the call of the wild and becoming a leader of the wolves of the forest.

As we have seen, when Vandover became a wolf it was a sign of the ultimate moral degradation, the triumph of the "brute" over reason and sensibility. Yet Dreiser frequently described Cowperwood as a predatory animal. Jack London wanted people to call him "Wolf," and even named his mansion "Wolf House," presumably to justify its luxury with a primitivistic label. His most memorable protagonist, Captain Wolf Larsen of *The Sea Wolf* (1904), is a kind of Cowperwood in the rough. Like Cowperwood, his magnetic eyes fascinate and dominate women until they surrender. The very archetype of virility, he is a man of massive build and titanic strength, the savage, ferocious strength, we are told, that one associates with wild animals or with our own "tree-dwelling prototypes." He embodies the "potency of motion" that is the essence of life, the "elemental stuff of which life's forms are molded." Although only a sealer and a kind of pirate, Larsen has read widely in literature and philosophy. From Spencer he has learned that life is a struggle in which only the fit survive. But he has rejected Spencer's sentimental notions of self-sacrifice for the benefit of children or the human race. Life, he says, is yeasty and crawling, and totally without purpose. It is absurd to lose one crawl or squirm of life through self-denial or sacrifice. Larsen's version of "I satisfy myself" is more brutal than Cowperwood's. Since he thinks that might is right and weakness is wrong, he enjoys inflicting physical pain on others, and is totally indifferent to suffering and death.

If Wolf Larsen is a more primitive, sadistic Charlie Geary, his foil, Humphrey Van Weyden, is a more effete Vandover. But in London's tale, the brutalization of the sensitive artist is a process of regeneration. When "Hump" Van Weyden is taken aboard Larsen's hell ship, he is a bookish dilettante, a self-confessed "sissy." In Wolf Larsen's eyes he is "a miserable weakling" who allows himself to be bullied by the entire crew until he finally proves his nerve by sharpening his knife in preparation for a fight. It appears that London could not decide whether Larsen was an admirable figure whose amoral philosophy was essentially correct, or whether the ideal was some kind of synthesis between Larsen's brutal realism and the traditional values of humanity. Various members of the crew rebel against Larsen's tyranny, and in so doing represent the struggle of idealism against the view that life is "but the dark heave of blood and the twitch of the nerve." A sailor named Johnson, for example, says that he would die for what is right, if necessary, in order to be true to himself. Van Weyden sees this as a triumph of spirit and principle over flesh, as a refutation of Larsen's materialism. But Larsen tells Hump that Johnson is only "a bit of animated dust" that defies him, and succeeds in breaking the sailor's will by a savage beating. Hump is both toughened and enlightened by his contact with Wolf, and becomes a kind of admiring fag.

The crew's resistance and plotting are hardly an affirmation of the human spirit. For a time Van Weyden sees something "sublime" in the defiance of young George Leach, whose denunciations of Larsen recall the moral courage of the Hebrew prophets. But Leach, like other members of the crew, regresses more and more to the level of the snarling animal. Why, Hump asks, is Larsen content to beat Leach to a pulp, when the sailor has tried so often to kill him? "There seemed a certain spice about it, such as men must feel who take delight in making pets of ferocious animals. 'It gives a thrill to life,' he explained to me, 'when life is carried in one's hand. Man is a natural gambler, and life is the biggest stake he can lay. The greater the odds, the greater the thrill.' " Larsen adds that he is really doing Leach a favor: " 'The greatness of sensation is mutual. He is living more royally than any man for'ard, though he does not know it. For he has what they have not—purpose, something to do and be done, an all-absorbing end to strive to attain, the desire to kill me, the hope that he may kill me. . . . I doubt that he has ever lived so swiftly and keenly before.' "

Wolf Larsen thus defends a philosophy of pure stress-seeking as a means of responding to an amoral and materialistic world. He says that he would like Van Weyden more if he joined the crew in their murderous plots. It is only fear that keeps Van Weyden from trying to murder the Captain, and he is thus a hypocrite who sins against his "whole pitiful little code." Hump inwardly knows that this is true, but he is faced with a great moral dilemma. His contact with Larsen has hardened his mind and body to the world of brutal reality; in a storm he finds that he is no longer afraid of death, that he will risk his life to carry out the

Captain's orders. Yet, in accordance with Larsen's code he should try to kill Larsen, but finds he lacks the nerve.

Apparently London was unable to resolve this dilemma without ultimately endorsing Larsen's philosophy, and consequently he sought escape in an absurd fantasy which nevertheless illuminates his conceptions of culture and the strenuous life. At the most unlikely moment, the hell ship takes on board one Maud Brewster, who turns out to be a famous and beautiful writer. Maud represents wealth, manners, and genteel culture. She stands, we are told, at the opposite end of the evolutionary ladder from Wolf Larsen. Yet Larsen more than holds his own with her in philosophic discourse, and lectures her on the sins and hypocrisy of the leisure class. Hump Van Weyden lectures her on the utter futility of "moral courage" against Wolf Larsen, but then leaps to her protection when Larsen tries to rape her. The rest of the story is too silly to summarize, but two themes deserve mention. After fleeing the ship, Maud and Hump land on a deserted seal island where the two literati are purified and regenerated by a reversion to caveman existence. Hump finally becomes a man as he learns to club seals and protect his "mate"; Maud becomes a woman as she sews skins and blows up the fire for the evening meal. It should be added that, despite their deep love for each other, Maud and Hump lead ascetic lives and even build separate huts to sleep in! The second theme concerns the morality of killing, when Wolf Larsen's ship, with only the blinded Captain aboard, washes ashore. Wolf tries to keep Hump from repairing the damaged vessel, but calls him a slave to conventional morality for not daring to kill a blind, unarmed man. While Hump has learned to club defenseless seals, he resolves not to shoot Larsen unless Larsen attacks. It is finally the newly toughened Maud who knocks Larsen over the head when Hump has been trapped by deceit. And though Wolf later tries to kill them both, just "to be the biggest bit of the ferment to the end," Maud comes to admire him and to sympathize with him before he dies. The conflict between brutal impulse and culture, between id and superego, is resolved in sentimentality.

Wolf Larsen never had a chance to test his powers in the realms of business and culture, and for that reason the novel is more concerned with the implications of materialism than with the implications of success. But in Jack London's autobiographical *Martin Eden* (1908), a Wolf Larsen-type hero pursues success and confronts a Maud Brewster-type heroine on her own ground. Martin Eden is not a cruel sadist, but like Larsen he is a man of indomitable will, whose muscled body is a "mass of quivering sensibilities." A former sailor, cowboy, and oyster pirate, he is a rough man of the world who is cut off by the widest chasm from

Ruth Morse's world of wealth, polite manners, and formal education. Nevertheless, Martin knows that he is superior to the sailors, dock workers, and cheap cannery girls who have never understood him; his body sings with strength and vitality; he yearns for self-fulfillment and beauty. Although Ruth seems to be an ethereal spirit, untouchable and impossibly remote, Martin is confident that he can leap the gap to a higher sphere of culture. For her part, Ruth is moved by an unconscious instinct "to tame a wild thing," and is also drawn to Martin's virility by "a primordial force." Thus she coaches him in grammar and reads him Browning.

As Martin furiously pursues his self-education, he stumbles upon the unity of all knowledge in the works of Spencer. He is now desperate to write about "the stress and strain of life, its fevers and sweats and wild insurgences . . . to glorify the leaders of forlorn hopes, the mad lovers, the giants that fought under stress and strain, amid terror and tragedy, making life crackle with the strength of their endeavor." In 1908 Jack London was writing about just such things, and making over sixty thousand dollars a year from it. Martin tells Ruth that he wants to become famous, as part of the adventure: "It is not the being famous, but the process of becoming so, that counts." But unfortunately, the magazines are not interested in the stress and strain of life, but rather in glorifying "sordid dollar-chasers" and "commonplace little love affairs of commonplace little men and women." Martin Eden receives nothing but impersonal rejection slips, and has no one to turn to for advice. Even Ruth fails to understand the great creative force that moves within him. Her literary values are those of genteel society; her ideal of success is her businessman father.

But though Martin faces starvation, he knows that the world belongs to the strong and that he can eventually lick the editors just as he once licked a bully named Cheese-Face when he was a boy. In a powerful scene that is similar to the fight to the death between Buck and Spitz in *Call of the Wild,* Martin recalls the circle of bloodthirsty boys, "howling like barbarians," as he and Cheese-Face confronted each other in deadly combat. For eleven years Cheese-Face had beaten and bullied him. Now the two fought like Stone-Age savages, and Martin was glad that even after his arm had been broken, the gang let the battle go on until he finally pounded Cheese-Face to a senseless blob. Such an elemental struggle, in Jack London's eyes, was the basic reality of life. And for all his life Martin Eden would have to pit himself against a cosmic Cheese-Face, his "eternal enemy."

After studying and writing for nineteen hours a day, as Jack London himself had done, Martin begins to find that the culture represented by the Morses is shallow and pretentious. The lawyers, bankers, and army officers who gather at the Morses' have read very little and make pompous pronouncements about writers and ideas they do not understand. Martin's quest for knowledge and culture leads him into ever sharper conflicts. When he preaches Nietzsche to the dull Republicans at the Morses' dinners, they think he is a Socialist and are perplexed when he argues that they are closer to Socialism than he. When Martin denounces the ignorance of a judge who insults Herbert Spencer, Ruth tells him he is unbearable. Nevertheless, she comes to love him and he keeps up his furious but apparently hopeless pace of writing in order to prove himself to her.

Then suddenly Martin becomes a tremendous success. Editors clamor for his work, money keeps flowing in, his name is on everyone's lips. Seeking temporary escape from fame, he tries to return to his old crowd of drinking, dancing, fighting friends. But though he is exhilarated by a gang fight and is sentimentally touched by the love of a lowly girl, Martin finds that books and culture have exiled him from his former companions. On the other hand, he is crushingly disillusioned by the sudden adulation of the bourgeoisie. The same editors eagerly compete for the same stories they had once scorned. "Fawn or fang," it was all a matter of chance. He was the fashion of the hour, and even the Morses, who had broken off his tentative engagement to Ruth and had forbidden him to enter their house, try to woo him back because of his fame and wealth. Everyone wants to feed him, when before they would have let him starve. After struggling so hard to prove himself, Martin Eden is sickened by the symbols and consequences of success. His success, he feels, is invalid, since he is not really appreciated for either his work or his own being. He has become so much a public fad, a mere symbol, that he feels an acute sense of nonbeing.

The climax is when Ruth arrives on what she represents as a daring mission to declare her love, regardless of her family's feelings. Martin knows that she had liked him for himself; yet this simple human attraction had given way to her bourgeois standards of success. She had opposed his writing and had urged him to get a conventional job and work for conventional symbols of success. She had wanted to make him afraid of life, as she and her class were, and remold him in the image of timid, repressed, bourgeois respectability. When Martin confronts her with these truths and asks if love is so gross a thing that it must feed on publications and public notice, Ruth confesses her sins and begs forgiveness. She loves him now, for what he is; and in order to prove that she can liberate herself from the values of her class, that she can be a traitor, as she says, to all that had previously made her a traitor to love, she offers him her virginity in free love. Martin is impressed by this gesture and says that she has redeemed herself. Yet the nonbeing of success has drained him of all desire and aspiration. He knows now that he had never loved the real Ruth Morse but only an idealized Ruth of his own creation. His disillusion is hardened when he finds that Ruth had lied about coming to see him alone, and that she had really been brought by her brother, obviously with her family's consent.

Whereas Martin Eden had once grasped every moment of life in its maximum intensity, he now sees every day as a bright light that hurts his soul. Instead of begrudging the moments lost in sleep, he yearns for rest. On a voyage across the Pacific he quietly slips out a porthole and into the night sea. He is amused by the way his instinctive will to live checks his resolution to die. Finally, he takes a deep breath and dives as deeply as he can. He knows that death can bring no suffering, that the pain in his chest is the last blow that life can deal him. When he inhales the sea and his hands and feet churn the water, in a desperate, reflexive effort to lift his body to the air, he knows that he has fooled them.

Erik Erikson has said that a creative man "must court sickness, failure, or insanity, in order to test the alternative whether the established world will crush him, or whether he will disestablish a sector of this world's outworn fundaments and make a place for a new one."[8] We have seen that in American literature the cult of the strenuous life was linked with a desire to break out of the confining and demeaning patterns set by the equation of individual salvation with material success, and to bring to man's quest for identity some of the dangers and unpredictability of the unknown. This search for new challenges that would restore a sense of the immediacy and richness of experience was also a response to a materialistic philosophy that reduced spiritual values to the level of animal desires and impulses, and thus destroyed the traditional Protestant ideal of a balance between moral character and material success. Unfortunately, in America it was difficult to test one's will and character, in the sense of Erikson's statement, without resort to the conventional canons of success. There were so few institutional channels and boundaries that when a stress-seeking man, that is, an identity-seeking man, tried to move beyond success, he became an embodiment of sheer vitality in a limitless void, a Martin Eden beating his arms and legs in the depths of a dark sea.

8. Erik Erikson, *Young Man Luther* (New York: W. W. Norton & Company, Inc., 1962), p. 46.

II

THE REDEEMING WEST

5

Ten-Gallon Hero

In 1900 it seemed that the significance of the cowboy era would decline along with other brief but romantic episodes in American history. The Long Drive lingered only in the memories and imaginations of old cowhands. The "hoe-men" occupied former range land while Mennonites and professional dry farmers had sown their Turkey Red winter wheat on the Kansas prairies. To be sure, a cattle industry still flourished, but the cowboy was more like an employee of a corporation than the free-lance cowboy of old.[1] The myth of the cowboy lived on in the Beadle and Adams paper-back novels, with the followers of Ned Buntline and the prolific Colonel Prentiss Ingraham. But this seemed merely a substitution of the more up-to-date cowboy in a tradition which began with Leatherstocking and Daniel Boone.[2] If the mountain man had replaced Boone and the forest scouts, if the cowboy had succeeded the mountain man, and if the legends of Mike Fink and Crockett were slipping into the past, it would seem probable that the cowboy would follow, to become a quaint character of antiquity, overshadowed by newer heroes.

Yet more than a half-century after the passing of the actual wild and woolly cowboy, we find a unique phenomenon in American mythology. Gaudy-covered Western or cowboy magazines decorate stands, windows, and shelves in "drug" stores, bookstores, grocery stores and supermarkets from Miami to Seattle. Hundreds of cowboy movies and

1. Edward Douglas Branch, *The Cowboy and His Interpreters* (New York: D. Appleton & Company, 1926), p. 69.
2. Henry Nash Smith, *Virgin Land* (Cambridge: Harvard University Press, 1950), pp. v, vi.

From *American Quarterly*, Vol. 6 (Summer 1954), 115–25. Copyright 1954, American Studies Association. Reprinted by permission.

television shows are watched and lived through by millions of Americans. Nearly every little boy demands a cowboy suit and a Western six-shooter cap pistol. Cowboys gaze out at you with steely eye and cocked revolver from cereal packages and television screens. Jukeboxes in Bennington, Vermont, as well as Globe, Arizona, moan and warble the latest cowboy songs. Middle-age folk who had once thought of William S. Hart, Harry Carey, and Tom Mix as a passing phase, have lived to see several Hopalong Cassidy revivals, the Lone Ranger, Tim McCoy, Gene Autry, and Roy Rogers. Adolescents and even grown men in Maine and Florida can be seen affecting cowboy, or at least modified cowboy garb, while in the new airplane plants in Kansas, workers don their cowboy boots and wide-brimmed hats, go to work whistling a cowboy song, and are defiantly proud that they live in the land of lassos and sixguns.

When recognized at all, this remarkable cowboy complex is usually defined as the distortion of once-colorful legends by a commerical society.[3] The obvious divergence between the real West and the idealized version, the standardization of plot and characters, and the ridiculous incongruities of cowboys with automobiles and airplanes, all go to substantiate this conclusion.

However, there is more than the cowboy costume and stage setting in even the wildest of these adventures. Despite the incongruities, the cowboy myth exists in fact, and as such is probably a more influential social force than the actual cowboy ever was. It provides the framework for an expression of common ideals of morality and behavior. And while a commerical success, the hero cowboy must satisfy some basic want in American culture, or there could never be such a tremendous market. It is true that the market has been exploited by magazine, song, and scenario writers, but it is important to ask why similar myths have not been equally profitable, such as the lumbermen of the early northwest, the whale fishermen of New Bedford, the early railroad builders, or the fur traders. There have been romances written and movies produced idealizing these phases of American history, but little boys do not dress up like Paul Bunyan and you do not see harpooners on cereal packages. Yet America has had many episodes fully as colorful and of longer duration than the actual cowboy era.

The cowboy hero and his setting are a unique synthesis of two American traditions, and echoes of this past can be discerned in even the wildest of the modern horse operas. On the one hand, the line of descent is a direct evolution from the Western scout of Cooper and the Dime Novel; on the other, there has been a recasting of the golden myth of

3. Smith, *Virgin Land,* p. 111.

the antebellum South.[4] The two were fused sometime in the 1890's. Perhaps there was actually some basis for such a union. While the West was economically tied to the North as soon as the early canals and railroad broke the river-centered traffic, social ties endured longer. Many Southerners emigrated West and went into the cattle business, and of course, the Long Drive originated in Texas.[5] The literary synthesis of two traditions only followed the two social movements. It was on the Great Plains that the descendants of Daniel Boone met the drawling Texas cowboy.

Henry Nash Smith has described two paradoxical aspects of the legendary Western scout, typified in Boone himself.[6] This woodsman, this buckskin-clad wilderness hunter is a pioneer, breaking trails for his countrymen to follow, reducing the savage wilderness for civilization. Nevertheless, he is also represented as escaping civilization, turning his back on the petty materialsim of the world, on the hypocritical and self-conscious manners of community life, and seeking the unsullied, true values of nature.

These seemingly conflicting points of view have counterparts in the woodsman's descendant, the cowboy. The ideal cowboy fights for justice, risks his life to make the dismal little cowtown safe for law-abiding, respectable citizens, but in so doing he destroys the very environment which made him a heroic figure. This paradox is common with all ideals, and the cowboy legend is certainly the embodiment of a social ideal. Thus the minister or social reformer who rises to heroism in his fight against a sin-infested community, would logically become a mere figurehead once the community is reformed. There can be no true ideal or hero in a utopia. And the civilization for which the cowboy or trailblazer struggles is utopian in character.

But there is a further consideration in the case of the cowboy. In our mythology, the cowboy era is timeless. The ranch may own a modern station wagon, but the distinguishing attributes of cowboy and environment remain. There is, it is true, a nostalgic sense that this is the last great drama, a sad knowledge that the cowboy is passing and that civilization is approaching. But it never comes. This strange, wistful sense of the coming end of an epoch is not something outside our experience. It is a faithful reflection of the sense of approaching adulthood. The appeal of the cowboy, in this sense, is similar to the appeal of Boone,

4. Emerson Hough, *The Story of the Cowboy* (New York: D. Appleton & Company, 1901), p. 200.

5. Edward E. Dale, *Cow Country* (Norman, Okla.: University of Oklahoma Press, 1942), p. 15.

6. Smith, *Virgin Land*, p. v.

Leatherstocking, and the later Mountain Man. We know that adulthood, civilization, is inevitable, but we are living toward the end of childhood, and at that point "childness" seems eternal; it is a whole lifetime. But suddenly we find it is not eternal, the forests disappear, the mountains are settled, and we have new responsibilities. When we shut our eyes and try to remember, the last image of a carefree life appears. For the nation, this last image is the cowboy.

The reborn myth of the ante-bellum South also involves nostalgia; not so much nostalgia for something that actually existed as for dreams and ideals. When the Southern myth reappeared on the rolling prairies, it was purified and regenerated by the casting off of apologies for slavery. It could focus all energies on its former rôle of opposing the peculiar social and economic philosophy of the Northeast. This took the form of something more fundamental than mere agrarianism or primitivism. Asserting the importance of values beyond the utilitarian and material, this transplanted Southern philosophy challenged the doctrine of enlightened self-interest and the belief that leisure time is sin.

Like the barons and knights of Southern feudalism, the large ranch owners and itinerant cowboys knew how to have a good time. If there was time for work, there was a time for play, and the early rodeos, horse races, and wild nights at a cowtown were not occasions for reserve. In this respect, the cowboy West was more in the tradition of fun-loving New Orleans than of the Northeast. Furthermore, the ranch was a remarkable duplication of the plantation, minus slaves. It was a hospitable social unit, where travelers were welcome even when the owner was absent. As opposed to the hard-working, thrifty, and sober ideal of the East, the actual cowboy was overly cheerful at times, generous to the point of waste, and inclined to value friendly comradeship above prestige.[7]

The mythical New England Yankee developed a code of action which always triumphed over the more sophisticated city slicker, because the Yankee's down-to-earth shrewdness, common sense, and reserved humor embodied values which Americans considered as pragmatically effective. The ideal cowboy also had a code of action, but it involved neither material nor social success. The cowboy avoided actions which "just weren't done" because he placed a value on doing things "right," on managing difficult problems and situations with ease, skill, and modesty. The cowboy's code was a Western and democratic version of the Southern gentleman's "honor."

In the early years of the twentieth century, a Philadelphia lawyer who

7. Alfred Henry Lewis, *Wolfville Days* (New York: Strokes, 1902), p. 24.

affected a careless, loose-tied bow instead of the traditional black ribbon and who liked to appear in his shirt sleeves, wrote: "The nomadic bachelor west is over, the housed, married west is established."[8] In a book published in 1902 he had, more than any other man, established an idealized version of the former, unifying the Southern and Western hero myths in a formula which was not to be forgotten. Owen Wister had, in fact, liberated the cowboy hero from the Dime novels and provided a snythetic tradition suitable for a new century. *The Virginian* became a key document in popular American culture, a romance which defined the cowboy character and thus the ideal American character in terms of courage, sex, religion, and humor. The novel served as a model for hundreds of Western books and movies for half a century. In the recent popular movie, "High Noon," a Hollywood star who won his fame dramatizing Wister's novel, reënacted the same basic plot of hero rejecting heroine's pleas and threats, to uphold his honor against the villain Trampas. While this theme is probably at least a thousand years old, it was Owen Wister who gave it specifically American content and thus explicated and popularized the modern cowboy ideal, with its traditions, informality, and all-important code.

Of course, Wister's West is not the realistic, boisterous, sometimes monotonous West of Charlie Siringo and Andy Adams. The cowboy, after all, drove cattle. He worked. There was much loneliness and monotony on the range, which has faded like mist under a desert sun in the reminiscences of old cow hands and the fiction of idealizers. The Virginian runs some errands now and then, but there are no cattle-driving scenes, no monotony, no hard work. Fictional cowboys are never bored. Real cowboys were often so bored that they memorized the labels on tin cans and then played games to see how well they could recite them.[9] The cowboys in books and movies are far too busy making love and chasing bandits to work at such a dreary task as driving cattle. But then the Southern plantation owner did no work. The befringed hero of the forests did not work. And if any ideal is to be accepted by adolescent America, monotonous work must be subordinated to more exciting pastimes. The fact that the cowboy hero has more important things to do is only in keeping with his tradition and audience. He is only a natural reaction against a civilization which demands increasingly monotonous work, against the approaching adulthood when playtime ends.

And if the cowboy romance banishes work and monotony, their very opposites are found in the immensity of the Western environment. To

8. Branch, *The Cowboy and His Interpreters*, pp. 190 ff.
9. Philip Ashton Rollins, *The Cowboy* (New York: Charles Scribner's Sons, 1922), p. 185.

be sure, the deserts and prairies can be bleak, but they are never dull when used as setting for the cowboy myth. There is always an element of the unexpected, of surprise, of variety. The tremendous distances either seclude or elevate the particular and significant. There are mirages, hidden springs, dust storms, hidden identities, and secret ranches. In one of his early Western novels William MacLeod Raine used both devices of a secret ranch and hidden identity, while Hoffman Birney combined a hidden ranch, a secret trail, and two hidden identities.[10] In such an environment of uncertainty and change men of true genius stand out from the rest. The evil or good in an individual is quickly revealed in cowboy land. A man familiar with the actual cowboy wrote that "brains, moral and physical courage, strength of character, native gentlemanliness, proficiency in riding or shooting—every quality of leadership tended to raise its owner from the common level."[11]

The hazing which cowboys gave the tenderfoot was only preliminary. It was a symbol of the true test which anyone must undergo in the West. After the final winnowing of men, there emerge the heroes, the villains, and the clowns. The latter live in a purgatory and usually attach themselves to the hero group. Often, after the stress of an extreme emergency, they burst out of their caste and are accepted in the élite.

While the Western environment, according to the myth, sorts men into their true places, it does not determine men. It brings out the best in heroes and the worst in villains, but it does not add qualities to the man who has none. The cowboy is a superman and is adorable for his own sake. It is here that he is the descendant of supernatural folk heroes. Harry Hawkeye, the creator of an early cowboy hero, Calvin Yancey, described him as:

> . . . straight as an arrow, fair and ruddy as a Viking, with long, flowing golden hair, which rippled over his massive shoulders, falling nearly to his waist; a high, broad forehead beneath which sparkled a pair of violet blue eyes, tender and soulful in repose, but firm and determined under excitement. His entire face was a study for a sculptor with its delicate aquiline nose, straight in outline as though chiselled from Parian marble, and its generous manly mouth, with full crimson and arched lips, surmounted by a long, silken blonde mustache, through which a beautiful set of even white teeth gleamed like rows of lustrous pearls.[12]

While the Virginian is not quite the blond, Nordic hero, he is just as beautiful to behold. His black, curly locks, his lean, athletic figure, his

10. William MacLeod Raine, *Bucky O'Connor* (New York: Grosset & Dunlap, 1907); Hoffman Birney, *The Masked Rider* (New York: Penn, 1928).
11. Rollins, *The Cowboy*, p. 352.
12. Branch, *The Cowboy and His Interpreters*, p. 191.

quiet, unassuming manner, all go to make him the most physically attractive man Owen Wister could describe. Later cowboy heroes have
shaved their mustaches, but the great majority have beautiful curly hair,
usually blond or red, square jaws, cleft chins, broad shoulders, deep
chests, and wasp-like waists. Like the Virginian, they are perfect men,
absolutely incapable of doing the wrong thing unless deceived.[13]

Many writers familiar with the real cowboy have criticized Wister for
his concentration on the Virginian's love interest and, of course, they
deplore the present degeneration of the cowboy plot, where love is supreme. There were few women in the West in the Chisholm Trail days
and those few in Dodge City, Abilene, and Wichita were of dubious
morality. The cowboy's sex life was intermittent, to say the least. He
had to carry his thirst long distances, like a camel, and in the oases the
orgies were hardly on a spiritual plane.[14] Since earlier heroes, like the
woodsman, led celibate lives, it is important to ask why the cowboy
depends on love interest.

At first glance, there would seem to be an inconsistency here. The
cowboy is happiest with a group of buddies, playing poker, chasing
horse thieves, riding in masculine company. He is contemptuous of
farmers, has no interest in children, and considers men who have lived
among women as effete. Usually he left his own family at a tender age
and rebelled against the restrictions of mothers and older sisters. Neither
the Virginian nor the actual cowboys were family men, nor did they
have much interest in the homes they left behind. Thus it would seem
that courting a young schoolteacher from Vermont would be self-
destruction. At no place is the idealized cowboy further from reality
than in his love for the tender woman from the East. Like the law and
order he fights for, she will destroy his way of life.

But this paradox is solved when one considers the hero cowboy, not
the plot, as the center of all attention. Molly Wood in *The Virginian,*
like all her successors, is a literary device, a *dea ex machina* with a
special purpose. Along with the Western environment, she serves to
throw a stronger light on the hero, to make him stand out in relief, to
complete the picture of an ideal. In the first place, she brings out qualities in him which we could not see otherwise. Without her, he would
be too much the brute for a real folk hero, at least in a modern age. If
Molly Wood were not in *The Virginian,* the hero might seem too raucous, too wild. Of course, his affair with a blonde in town is handled

13. A Zane Grey hero is typical and is also seen through the eyes of a woman: "She saw a
bronzed, strong-jawed, eagle-eyed man, stalwart, superb of height." Zane Grey, *The Light of
Western Stars* (New York: Harper & Brothers, 1914), pp. 29-30.

14. Charles A. Siringo, *A Lone Star Cowboy* (Santa Fe: C. A. Siringo, 1919), p. 64.

genteelly; his boyish pranks such as mixing up the babies at a party are treated as good, clean fun. But still, there is nothing to bring out his qualities of masculine tenderness, there is nothing to show his conscience until Molly Wood arrives. A cowboy's tenderness is usually revealed through his kindness to horses, and in this sense, the Eastern belle's rôle is that of a glorified horse. A woman in the Western drama is somebody to rescue, somebody to protect. In her presence, the cowboy shows that, in his own way, he is a cultural ideal. The nomadic, bachelor cowboys described by Andy Adams and Charles Siringo are a little too masculine, a little too isolated from civilization to become the ideal for the settled community.

While the Western heroine brings out a new aspect of the cowboy's character, she also serves the external purpose of registering our attitudes toward him. The cowboy ideal is an adorable figure and the heroine is the vehicle of adoration. Female characters enable the author to make observations about cowboys which would be impossible with an all-male cast.[15] This rôle would lose its value if the heroine surrendered to the cowboy immediately. So the more she struggles with herself, the more she conquers her Eastern reservations and surmounts difficulties before capitulating, the more it enhances the hero.

Again, *The Virginian* is the perfect example. We do not meet Molly Wood in the first part of the book. Instead, the author, the I, who is an Easterner, goes to Wyoming and meets the Virginian. It is love at first sight, not in the sexual sense, of course (this was 1902), but there is no mistaking it for anything other than love. This young man's love for the Virginian is not important in itself; it heightens our worship of the hero. The sex of the worshiper is irrelevant. At first the young man is disconsolate, because he cannot win the Virginian's friendship. He must go through the ordeal of not knowing the Virginian's opinion of him. But as he learns the ways of the West, the Virginian's sublime goodness is unveiled. Though increasing knowledge of the hero's character only serves to widen the impassable gulf between the finite Easterner and the infinite, pure virtue of the cowboy, the latter, out of his own free grace and goodness recognizes the lowly visitor, who adores him all the more for it. But this little episode is only a preface, a symbol of the drama to come. As soon as the Virginian bestows his grace on the male adorer, Molly Wood arrives. The same passion is reënacted, though on a much larger frame. In this rôle, the sex of Molly *is* important, and the tradi-

---

15. No male character could observe that, " 'Cowboys play like they work or fight,' she added. 'They give their whole souls to it. They are great big simple boys.' " Grey, *The Light of Western Stars*, p. 187.

tional romance plot is only superficial form. Molly's coyness, her reserve, her involved heritage of Vermont tradition, all go to build an insurmountable barrier. Yet she loves the Virginian. And Owen Wister and his audience love the Virginian through Molly Wood's love. With the male adorer, they had gone about as far as they could go. But Molly offers a new height from which to love the Virginian. There are many exciting possibilities. Molly can save his life and nurse him back to health. She can threaten to break off their wedding if he goes out to fight his rival, and then forgive him when he disobeys her plea. The Virginian marries Molly in the end and most of his descendants either marry or are about to marry their lovely ladies. But this does not mean a physical marriage, children, and a home. That would be building up a hero only to destroy him. The love climax at the end of the cowboy drama raises the hero to a supreme height, the audience achieves an emotional union with its ideal. In the next book or movie the cowboy will be the carefree bachelor again.

The classic hero, Hopalong Cassidy, has saved hundreds of heroines, protected them, and has been adored by them. But in 1910 Hopalong, "remembering a former experience of his own, smiled in knowing cynicism when told that he again would fall under the feminine spell." [16] In 1950 he expressed the same resistance to actual marriage:

> "But you can't always move on, Hoppy!" Lenny protested. "Someday you must settle down! Don't you ever think of marriage?" "Uh-huh, and whenever I think of it I saddle Topper and ride. I'm not a marrying man, Lenny. Sometimes I get to thinkin' about that poem a feller wrote, about how a woman is only a woman but—" "The open road is my Fate!" she finished. "That's it. But can you imagine any woman raised outside a tepee livin' in the same house with a restless man?" [17]

The cowboy hero is the hero of the pre-adolescent, either chronologically or mentally. It is the stage of revolt against femininity and feminine standards. It is also the age of hero worship. If the cowboy romance were sexual, if it implied settling down with a real *girl* there would be little interest. One recent cowboy hero summarized this attitude in terms which should appeal strongly to any ten-year-old: "I'd as soon fight a she-lion barehanded as have any truck with a gal." [18] The usual cowboy movie idol has about as much social presence in front of the leading lady as a very bashful boy. He is most certainly not the

16. Clarence E. Mulford, *Hopalong Cassidy* (Chicago: A. C. McClurg & Company, 1910), p. 11.

17. Tex Burns, pseud. (Louis L'Amour), *Hopalong Cassidy and the Trail to Seven Pines* (New York: Doubleday, 1951), p. 187.

18. Davis Dresser, *The Hangmen of Sleepy Valley* (New York: Jefferson House, 1950), p. 77.

lover-type. That makes him lovable to both male and female Americans. There can be no doubt that Owen Wister identified himself, not with the Virginian, but with Molly Wood.

While some glorifiers of the actual cowboy have maintained that his closeness to nature made him a deeply religious being, thus echoing the devoutness of the earlier woodsman hero who found God in nature, this tradition has never carried over to the heroic cowboy. Undoubtedly some of the real cowboys were religious, though the consensus of most of the writers on the subject seem to indicate that indifference was more common.[19] Intellectualized religion obviously had no appeal and though the cowboy was often deeply sentimental, he did not seem prone to the emotional and frenzied religion of backwoods farmers and squatters. Perhaps his freedom from family conflicts, from smoldering hatreds and entangled jealousies and loves, had something to do with this. Despite the hard work, the violent physical conflicts, and the occasional debaucheries, the cowboy's life must have had a certain innocent, Homeric quality. Even when witnessing a lynching or murder, the cowboy must have felt further removed from total depravity or original sin than the farmer in a squalid frontier town, with his nagging wife and thirteen children.

At any rate, the cowboy hero of our mythology is too much of a god himself to feel humility. His very creation is a denial of any kind of sin. The cowboy is an enunciation of the goodness of man and the glory which he can achieve by himself. The Western environment strips off the artifice, the social veneer, and instead of a cringing sinner, we behold a dazzling superman. He is a figure of friendly justice, full of self-reliance, a very tower of strength. What need has he of a god?

Of course, the cowboy is not positively anti-religious. He is a respecter of traditions as long as they do not threaten his freedom. The Virginian is polite enough to the orthodox minister who visits his employer's ranch. He listens respectfully to the long sermon, but the ranting and raving about his evil nature are more than he can stand. He knows that his cowboy friends are good men. He loves the beauty of the natural world and feels that the Creator of such a world must be a good and just God. Beyond that, the most ignorant cowboy knows as much as this sinister-voiced preacher. So like a young Greek god leaving Mount Olympus for a practical joke in the interest of justice, the Virginian leaves his rôle of calm and straightforward dignity, and engages in some humorous guile and deceit. The minister is sleeping in the next room

19. Hough, *The Story of the Cowboy*, p. 199; Branch, *The Cowboy and His Interpreters*, p. 160; Rollins, *The Cowboy*, p. 84; Lewis, *Wolfville Days*, p. 216.

and the Virginian calls him and complains that the devil is clutching him. After numerous sessions of wrestling with his conscience, the sleepy minister acting as referee, morning comes before the divine finds he has been tricked. He leaves the ranch in a rage, much to the delight of all the cowboys. The moral, observes Wister, is that men who are obsessed with evil and morbid ideas of human nature, had better stay away from the cowboy West. As Alfred Henry Lewis put it, describing a Western town the year *The Virginian* was published, "Wolfville's a hard practical outfit, what you might call a heap obdurate, an' it's goin' to take more than them fitful an' o'casional sermons I aloodes to,—to reach the roots of its soul."[20] The cowboy is too good and has too much horse sense to be deluded by such brooding theology. Tex Burns could have been describing the Virginian when he wrote that his characters "had the cow hand's rough sense of humor and a zest for practical jokes no cow hand ever outgrows."[21]

Coming as it did at the end of the nineteenth century, the cowboy ideal registered both a protest against orthodox creeds and a faith that man needs no formal religion, once he finds a pure and natural environment. It is the extreme end of a long evolution of individualism. Even the individualistic forest scout was dependent on his surroundings, and he exhibited a sort of pantheistic piety when he beheld the wilderness. The mighty captain of industry, while not accountable to anyone in this world, gave lip-service to the generous God who had made him a steward of wealth. But the cowboy hero stood out on the lonely prairie, dependent on neither man nor God. He was willing to take whatever risks lay along his road and would gladly make fun of any man who took life too seriously. Speaking of his mother's death, a real cowboy is supposed to have said:

> With almost her last breath, she begged me to make my peace with God, while the making was good. I have been too busy to heed her last advice. Being a just God, I feel that He will overlook my neglect. If not, I will have to take my medicine, with Satan holding the spoon.[22]

While the cowboy hero has a respect for property, he does not seek personal wealth and is generous to the point of carelessness. He gives money to his friends, to people in distress, and blows the rest when he hits town on Saturday night. He owns no land and, in fact, has only contempt for farmers, with their ploughed fields and weather-beaten buildings. He hates the slick professional gambler, the grasping Eastern

20. Lewis, *Wolfville Days*, p. 216.
21. Burns, *Hopalong Cassidy*, p. 130.
22. Siringo, *A Lone Star Cowboy*, p. 37.

speculator, and railroad man. How are these traits to be reconciled with his regard for property rights? The answer lies in a single possession—his horse. The cowboy's horse is what separates him from vagabondage and migratory labor. It is his link with the cavalier and plumed knight. More and more, in our increasingly property-conscious society, the cowboy's horse has gained in importance. A horse thief becomes a symbol of concentrated evil, a projection of all crime against property and concomitantly, against social status. Zane Grey was adhering to this tradition when he wrote, "in those days, a horse meant all the world to a man. A lucky strike of grassy upland and good water . . . made him rich in all that he cared to own." On the other hand, "a horse thief was meaner than a poisoned coyote." [23]

When a cowboy is willing to sell his horse, as one actually does in *The Virginian,* he has sold his dignity and self-identity. It is the tragic mistake which will inevitably bring its nemesis. His love for and close relationship with his horse not only make a cowboy seem more human, they also show his respect for propriety and order. He may drift from ranch to ranch, but his horse ties him down to respectability. Yet the cowboy hero is not an ambitious man. He lacks the concern for hard work and practical results which typifies the Horatio Alger ideal. Despite his fine horse and expensive saddle and boots, he values his code of honor and his friends more than possessions. Because the cowboy era is timeless, the hero has little drive or push toward a new and better life. He fights for law and order and this implies civilization, but the cowboy has no visions of empires, industrial or agrarian.

One of the American traits which foreign visitors most frequently described was the inability to have a good time. Americans constantly appear in European journals as ill-at-ease socially, as feeling they must work every spare moment. Certainly it was part of the American Protestant capitalistic ethic, the Poor Richard, Horatio Alger ideal, that spare time, frivolous play, and relaxation were sins which would bring only poverty, disease, and other misfortunes. If a youth would study the wise sayings of great men, if he worked hard and made valuable friends but no really confidential ones, if he never let his hair down or became too intimate with any person, wife included, if he stolidly kept his emotions to himself and watched for his chance in the world, then he would be sure to succeed. But the cowboy hero is mainly concerned with doing things skillfully and conforming to his moral code for its own sake. When he plays poker, treats the town to a drink, or raises a thousand dollars to buy off the evil mortgage, he is not aiming at personal suc-

23. Zane Grey, *Wildfire* (New York: Harper & Brothers, 1917), pp. 10, 7.

cess. Most cowboy heroes have at least one friend who knows them intimately, and they are seldom reserved, except in the presence of a villain or nosey stranger.

Both the hero and real cowboy appear to be easy-going and informal. In dress, speech, and social manner, the cowboy sets a new ideal. Every cowboy knows how to relax. If the villains are sometimes tense and nervous, the hero sits placidly at a card game, never ruffled, never disturbed, even when his arch rival is behind him at the bar, hot with rage and whisky. The ideal cowboy is the kind of man who turns around slowly when a pistol goes off and drawls, "Ah'd put thet up, if Ah were yew." William MacLeod Raine's Sheriff Collins chats humorously with some train robbers and maintains a calm, unconcerned air which amuses the passengers, though he is actually pumping the bandits for useful information.[24] Previously, he had displayed typical cowboy individualism by flagging the train down and climbing aboard, despite the protests of the conductor. Instead of the eager, aspiring youth, the cowboy hero is like a young tomcat, calm and relaxed, but always ready to spring into action. An early description of one of the most persistent of the cowboy heroes summarizes the ideal characteristics which appeal to a wide audience:

> Hopalong Cassidy had the most striking personality of all the men in his outfit; humorous, courageous to the point of foolishness, eager for fight or frolic, nonchalant when one would expect him to be quite otherwise, curious, loyal to a fault, and the best man with a Colt in the Southwest, he was a paradox, and a puzzle even to his most intimate friends. With him life was a humorous recurrence of sensations, a huge pleasant joke instinctively tolerated, but not worth the price cowards pay to keep it. He had come onto the range when a boy and since that time he had laughingly carried his life in his open hand, and . . . still carried it there, and just as recklessly.[25]

Of course, most cowboy books and movies bristle with violence. Wild fist fights, brawls with chairs and bottles, gun play and mass battles with crashing windows, fires, and the final racing skirmish on horseback, are all as much a part of the cowboy drama as the boots and spurs. These bloody escapades are necessary and are simply explained. They provide the stage for the hero to show his heroism, and since the cowboy is the hero of the pre-adolescent, he must prove himself by their standards. Physical prowess is the most important thing for the ten- or twelve-year-old mind. They are constantly plagued by fear, doubt, and

24. Raine, *Bucky O'Connor*, p. 22.
25. Mulford, *Hopalong Cassidy*, p. 65.

insecurity, in short, by evil, and they lack the power to crush it. The cowboy provides the instrument for their aggressive impulses, while the villain symbolizes all evil. The ethics of the cowboy band are the ethics of the boy's gang, where each member has a rôle determined by his physical skills and his past performance. As with any group of boys, an individual cowboy who had been "taken down a peg," was forever ridiculed and teased about his loss in status.[26]

The volume of cowboy magazines, radio programs and motion pictures, would indicate a national hero for at least a certain age group, a national hero who could hardly help but reflect specific attitudes. The cowboy myth has been chosen by this audience because it combines a complex of traits, a way of life, which they consider the proper ideal for America. The actual drama and setting are subordinate to the grand figure of the cowboy hero, and the love affairs, the exciting plots, and the climactic physical struggles, present opportunities for the definition of the cowboy code and character. Through the superficial action, the heroism of the cowboy is revealed, and each repetition of the drama, like the repetition of a sacrament, reaffirms the cowboy public's faith in their ideal.

Perhaps the outstanding cowboy trait, above even honor, courage, and generosity, is the relaxed, calm attitude toward life. Though he lives intensely, he has a calm, self-assurance, a knowledge that he can handle anything. He is good-humored and jovial.[27] He never takes women too seriously. He can take a joke or laugh at himself. Yet the cowboy is usually anti-intellectual and anti-school, another attitude which appeals to a younger audience.[28]

Above all, the cowboy is a "good joe." He personifies a code of personal dignity, personal liberty, and personal honesty. Most writers on the actual cowboy represented him as having these traits.[29] While many of these men obviously glorify him as much as any fiction writers, there must have been some basis for their judgment. As far as his light-hearted, calm attitude is concerned, it is amazing how similar cowboys appear, both in romances and non-fiction.[30] Millions of American youth

26. Sam P. Ridings, *The Chisholm Trail* (Medford, Okla.: S. P. Ridings, 1936), 297.

27. The cowboy hero was judged to be "out of sorts when he could not vent his peculiar humor on somebody or something." Grey, *The Light of Western Stars*, pp. 118–19.

28. This anti-intellectualism in the Western myth is at least as old as Cooper's parody of the scientist, Obed Bat, in *The Prairie*. More recently, Will James took pride in his son's poor attitude and performance in school. Will James, *The American Cowboy* (New York: Charles Scribner's Sons, 1942), p. 107.

29. Ridings, *The Chisholm Trail*, pp. 278–94; Rollins, *The Cowboy*, p. 67; Dale, *Cow Country*, pp. 122, 153.

30. According to Alfred Henry Lewis, surly and contentious people were just as unpopular in Wolfville as they appear to be in fiction. Lewis, *Wolfville Days*, p. 217.

subscribed to the new ideal and yearned for the clear, Western atmosphere of "unswerving loyalty, the true, deep affection, and good-natured banter that left no sting."[31] For a few thrilling hours they could roughly toss conventions aside and share the fellowship of ranch life and adore the kind of hero who was never bored and never afraid.

Whether these traits of self-confidence, a relaxed attitude toward life, and good humor, have actually increased in the United States during the past fifty years, is like asking whether men love their wives more now than in 1900. Certainly the effective influence of the cowboy myth can never be determined. It is significant, however, that the cowboy ideal has emerged above all others. And while the standardization of plot and character seem to follow other commercial conventions, the very popularity of this standard cowboy is important and is an overlooked aspect of the American character. It is true that this hero is infantile, that he is silly, overdone, and unreal. But when we think of many past ideals and heroes, myths and ethics; when we compare our placid cowboy with, say, the eager, cold, serious hero of Nazi Germany (the high-cheekboned, blond lad who appeared on the Reichsmarks); or if we compare the cowboy with the gangster heroes of the thirties, or with the serious, self-righteous and brutal series of Supermen, Batmen, and Human Torches; when, in an age of violence and questioned public and private morality, if we think of the many possible heroes we might have had—then we can be thankful for our silly cowboy. We could have chosen worse.

31. Mulford, *Hopalong Cassidy,* p. 155.

6

The Deerslayer, A Democratic Knight of the Wilderness: Cooper, 1841

In the Leatherstocking series Fenimore Cooper hoped to create the Great American Epic. Like Cotton Mather and Joel Barlow in earlier generations, he was convinced that American history offered a theme equal, if not superior, to the themes of Homer and Virgil. For Cooper, as for many of his countrymen, there was no subject with greater drama and significance than the destiny of Christian morality in the American wilderness. More explicitly, he was concerned with the relation between Christian morality and the skills necessary in America for survival and exploitation, the skills esteemed and cultivated by the self-sufficient and individualistic woodsman hero. An attempt to combine Homeric heroism and Christian sainthood in the figure of the American pioneer was doomed to certain failure, but it was a magnificent failure, and, in a larger sense, America's failure. In spite of his serious faults as a convincing character, Leatherstocking stands as not only the greatest, but as the prototype, of American fiction heroes. With all his shortcomings as an artist Cooper must be taken as one of the few writers whose imagination gave form to American ideals, and whose plots, however juvenile, dealt directly with problems basic to the American experience.

Although *The Deerslayer* was the last of the Leatherstocking tales to be published (appearing in 1841, nineteen years after *The Pioneers*),

From *Twelve Original Essays on Great American Novels*, edited by Charles Shapiro (Detroit: Wayne State University Press, 1958). Reprinted by permission.

chronologically it is the first of the five romances which trace the history of Leatherstocking from the first test of manhood to the noble exploits of an aged Odysseus on the American prairies. Thus Cooper concluded the saga by returning to his hero's youth, to "the first war-path" (the subtitle of the romance), and we must not forget that the callow hunter who exclaims in wonder at the shimmering expanse of Lake Otsego was conceived in the light of a mature Leatherstocking, whose character had been fully developed in previous tales. As a result, *The Deerslayer* is not the story of a youth showing promise of future heroism, but is rather a portrayal of the fresh innocence, spontaneous honesty, and supreme courage of a famous hero's early manhood.

It is impossible to understand Cooper, or for that matter the mass of popular adventure fiction indebted to him, unless we recognize that his narratives were intended to reveal ideal modes of action. Cooper was primarily a moralist, that is to say, an expounder of a particular code of morality, not a philosopher seeking moral truth in the ambiguities of human experience. While he strove to arouse interest and suspense, his contrived episodes were but devices for conveying moral values in specific terms. The rather monotonous rhythm of capture and escape does not represent a genuine and unpredictable struggle between human beings. On the contrary, the intense concentration on physical action illustrates fixed differences in individual skill and morality. Cooper's characters are essentially unchanging, ideal types, and he was more interested in showing facets of each character as revealed by varieties of physical experience than in tracing the development or fulfillment of a given person. If his tales sacrifice psychological reality, they succeed in portraying the social significance of contrasting states of morality.

Before turning to the moral implications of the romance, however, we must first briefly summarize the action, for it is only in action that Cooper's characters reveal their fundamental differences. In his tale of the first war path Cooper's narrative covers only six days and the action is limited to the shores and surface of Lake Otsego, or the Glimmerglass. It is a summer in the early 1740's, and war has just broken out between the English and the French, leaving the Otsego country, though nominally British, a kind of no-man's land between hostile forces. Cooper incorrectly places the Hurons on the side of the French, while making the Delawares, who are supposed to be morally superior to the Iroquois, loyal to England. Deerslayer has been reared by the Delawares, but his Indian training in hunting and warfare has been softened somewhat by the Christian pietism of Moravian missionaries. Before the story opens, Deerslayer has set out alone through the forest for the Glimmerglass, where he plans a rendezvous with Chingachgook, an Indian friend. The purpose of the expedition is to help Chingachgook rescue his betrothed, the beautiful Delaware maiden, Wah-ta!-Wah (the Wild Rose), who has been kidnapped by a Delaware traitor and taken to a Huron camp.

Traveling toward the Glimmerglass, which he has never seen before, Deerslayer meets and accompanies Hurry Harry, a gigantic young hunter bound for the same country. Harry is returning to the lake to woo Judith Hutter, a coquettish, beautiful, and high-spirited girl who is visited frequently by hunters and English officers from the settlements, and who lives at the lake with her father and half-witted sister Hetty. Tom Hutter is not, however, the real father of Judith and Hetty, but a former pirate who took the girls, their mother, and a chest of booty to the Glimmerglass, where he traps muskrat and lives securely beyond the reach of the law. The three Hutters (for the mother died) live in a "castle" built on a shoal in the lake, but spend part of their time in a houseboat or "ark" which is used for trapping and which in war-time gives the family command of the Glimmerglass.

On the first day of the narrative Deerslayer and Harry arrive at the lake, Deerslayer is introduced to the Hutters, and a band of Hurons makes a surprise attack on the ark. The Hurons, who are returning to the Canadas from a hunting trip, have just learned of the war and hope to take scalps to the French for bounties. If the Hutters and their friends can protect themselves for a few days, and keep the Hurons from capturing a canoe and gaining access to the castle, they are sure to be saved by British soldiers from the settlements. But while the men succeed in securing all available canoes, Tom Hutter and Hurry Harry are captured by the Hurons when they foolishly launch a night scalping raid of their own. The British also offer bounties for scalps, and it is this official barbarism which arouses the woodsmen's greed, thereby igniting a chain reaction of violence.

On the second morning Deerslayer kills his first Indian. Left to defend the Hutter girls by himself, he attempts to retrieve a canoe which has drifted ashore, and is forced to shoot a Huron brave who attacks him. At sunset of the second day Chingachgook joins Deerslayer and helps him defend the castle and the Hutter girls. On the third day Deerslayer bargains with the Huron chief, who returns Tom and Harry in exchange for some ivory chess pieces which Judith and Deerslayer have taken from Hutter's pirate chest. But Deerslayer himself is captured by the hostile Indians when he helps Chingachgook rescue Wah-ta!-Wah. Although the Hurons already respect Deerslayer's prowess, they are furious over the loss of the Delaware maiden, and they become still more angered when Harry impulsively shoots a Huron girl. It seems only a matter of time, then, before Deerslayer will be tortured, killed, and scalped.

On the fourth day the Indians temporarily seize the castle and scalp Tom Hutter, but Hurry Harry escapes to the ark after a tremendous struggle. When Chingachgook, Harry, and the girls finally repossess the castle, Deerslayer arrives unexpectedly on a "furlough" granted him by his Huron captors. The Indians, knowing his reputation, accept his word that he will return by noon the following day. Harry, who has meanwhile been unsuccessful in courting Judith, leaves for the settlement, at once abandoning the Hutter girls and promising to send British troops as soon as possible. Judith has fallen in love with Deerslayer, but her provocative advances are either ignored or gently repulsed. At noon the next day he manfully returns to face torture and death at the Huron camp.

The Hurons, impressed by Deerslayer's courage and integrity, offer to spare him if he will marry the widow of the brave he killed. But he refuses to be adopted into the tribe, and, free from his pledge of honor, he escapes into the woods, only to be recaptured after an exciting chase. Even the most vindictive of the Hurons admire his cool bravery during the preliminary torture, yet death is delayed only by the arrival of the feeble-minded Hetty Hutter, who preaches Christian forgiveness to the Indians, and by Judith, who arouses stupified wonder among the savages when she poses as a queen, appearing in a magnificent brocaded gown taken from the pirate chest. But just as Deerslayer is finally about to be killed, Chingachgook, Harry, and the king's troops spring from the forest. Hetty is accidentally shot in the battle, and she dies urging Harry, whom she secretly loves, to be more like Deerslayer. In a final appeal Judith openly proposes marriage to the young hunter, but he loftily declines her offer. The first war path is over, and it is time for Deerslayer to move beyond the suspended and timeless arena where he has drawn his first human blood.

In the action we have just summarized, character types are differentiated according to moral adjustment to wilderness life and behavior toward the opposite sex. Judith Hutter represents the manners and values of civilization, isolated but essentially unchanged by the surrounding wilderness. Her beauty is entirely external and is thus divorced from natural moral purity. Indeed, before the story opens, her personal vanity and infatuation with fine clothes, gay parties, and handsome men had led to her seduction by Captain Warley, a British officer at the neighboring fort. Though deeply repentant, Judith can never escape the limitations of her own nature. Cooper hints at the close of the tale that she ultimately became Warley's mistress in England. Yet she prefers Deer-slayer's honesty to Harry's handsome physique, and would gladly for-sake the comforts of civilization to become the loyal wife of Leather-stocking. Chastened by her unhappy affair with Captain Warley, Judith is cautious, rational, and practiced in her handling of men. Her re-sourcefulness, her pragmatic intelligence, and her frank sexuality make her Cooper's strongest heroine. She seems to typify the American woman who is forever torn between her enviable freedom and power over men and her passionate yearning for the security of a passive and domestic role. But despite her genuinely feminine impulses, Judith is hopelessly tainted by the values of an artificial civilization. Regardless of her de-sire, she must remain alienated from the divine harmony of nature.

Hetty Hutter lacks both the intelligence and brilliant attractiveness of her sister, but her beauty and morality rest upon an inner harmony and not upon a rational adjustment to external experience. Of all the char-acters in *The Deerslayer,* Hetty is least capable of manipulating her environment, for she utterly lacks a sense of expediency and self-interest, and cannot distinguish the actual from the ideal. But if isolation from the world of physical reality leaves her impotent and inarticulate, for Cooper she suggests the nobility of mute nature itself. Her naïve pro-nouncements, however unrealistic, are revelations from a source so pure that even the Hurons respect and try to understand her words. Hetty loves Hurry Harry because her inexperience and feeble understanding prevent her from seeing his serious faults, but unlike her more percep-tive sister, she is saved from indiscretion by a simple devotion to moral principle. Adapted neither to civilized nor wilderness life, Hetty is hap-piest in the forest. At the Glimmerglass her inner perceptions of truth and beauty are reinforced by a closeness to nature, while her defective understanding is undistracted by the hypocrisies and artificial complex-ities of civilization.

Wah-ta!-Wah, the Delaware maiden, represents a third possibility of feminine nature. As with Hetty, her beauty is completely natural, and she is guided in love and war by a spontaneous and uncorrupted moral sense. Yet Wah-ta!-Wah is perfectly adapted to her wilderness environ-ment, in which she is highly efficient, intelligent, and resourceful. If Judith suggests at times a fallen Eve, cut off from the moral harmony of the American Garden, the Indian maiden and her betrothed enjoy the original, sinless love of Adam and Eve before the fall. Whenever Wah-ta!-Wah's moral principles seem to be compromised by her acceptance of aggression and violence, Cooper reminds us that she is an Indian, and that Indian values are determined by unique "gifts" granted by God to his savage children. Revenge, scalping, and torture are natural to an

Indian's way of life, but are forbidden to a white man, whose peculiar gifts impose an ideal of selfless love and forgiveness. Wah-ta!-Wah condones scalping, but Cooper escapes ethical relativism by making her outraged at Harry's wanton shooting of a Huron maiden. All races, according to Cooper, despite their differences in custom, admire courage, honesty, loyalty, and respect for deity, just as they condemn betrayal of honor, or heedless waste and destruction. Cooper's savages are noble in their lack of hypocrisy and in their fidelity to fixed natural principles, and if their unique gifts prevent them from reaching the supreme heights of Christian morality, they successfully harmonize the skills and values of physical combat with a respect for unchanging law.

Indians might be governed by custom and natural law, but in the wilderness white men found themselves removed from the laws and restraints of organized society. The aristocratic Captain Warley represents the corruption of European civilization, essentially unchanged on the American frontier. Whether stationed in the American forest or in a European town, the captain would be tough, worldly, and prepared to seduce girls of inferior rank. But Tom Hutter is not temporarily stationed at Glimmerglass, nor is his presence there fortuitous. Hutter is a fugitive from law who finds security and livelihood as an isolated trapper. He cannot, however, escape his dominant passion of greed, which had made him an outlaw to begin with, and which finally brings him death at the hands of a Huron brave. Unaffected by the beauty and moral sublimity of nature, Hutter is driven only by a desire for exploitation. Although he rebukes Harry for an impulsive and purposeless murder which endangers the security of all, he proposes an expedition to scalp women and children for sheer profit. Tom Hutter is an example of the greedy, exploitive squatter-pirate, a type often pictured by Cooper as the most dangerous threat to a virtuous republic. Such insensitive squatters, unchecked by law or custom on the frontier, swindled and killed Indians, despoiled forests, and slaughtered game. The avaricious trapper symbolizes one of the possible meanings of American democracy, one of the unhappy concomitants to continental expansion.

If Tom Hutter reminds us of later captains of railroads and industry, who were equally unprincipled and exploitive, Hurry Harry resembles the bigoted and aggressive pioneer of the hunter and farmer class. Harry is governed by principles, but his principles are based on frontier ignorance and prejudice. He is the vain, boisterous, and immensely strong gamecock of the wilderness. As opposed to Chingachgook, his combativeness is uncontrolled by racial ideals of honor and manhood, and his total selfishness prevents him from being either loyal or truly courageous. Harry is self-righteously intolerant of Judith's failings, since her sexual freedom insults his masculine vanity, yet he continues to court her, as well as to slander her reputation. He is dominated by a powerful and irrational hatred of Indians, whom he regards as monstrous reptiles fit only for extermination. Yet Harry himself has regressed to a state of moral savagery unmitigated by the customs of Indian society. For Cooper he represents the moral deterioration accompanying a rapid expansion of the frontier. Always fleeing the restrictions of encroaching civilizations yet corrupted by the inherent evils of society, the wild hunter sinks to the lowest level of animal existence but continues to destroy as only humans can destroy.

The characters we have described so far must be taken as generalized types of life and action in the American wilderness. We should note that Christian morality is upheld and practiced only by a feeble-minded girl who is incapable of realistic and efficient action. The question Cooper sought to answer was whether a Christian hero might be created from the materials of a democratic, frontier society. Or, to put it another way, was America capable of creating a hero who embodied democratic and Christian ideals without sacrificing the skills and physical prowess of the frontiersman? Folk literature would celebrate the fabulous strength and exploits of the mighty hunter and boatman, but Davy Crockett and Mike Fink were more like the boastful and swaggering Hurry Harry than like Roland or Galahad. Could the illiterate woodsman, whose distinction lay in his acute senses, his highly developed forest skills, and his astonishing marksmanship, become an appropriate hero for a Christian society? To understand Cooper's answer we must examine the hero's relationship to nature, his participation in war, and his response to the opposite sex.

We have said that Cooper, like the Puritans, was concerned with the destiny of Christian morality in the wilderness. We should add, however, that Cooper found the source of morality in the wilderness itself and not in the protection and preservation of European civil society. To give religious sanction to his American hero, Cooper was forced to convert the uncouth and desolate backwoods into the unspoiled and shimmering world of God's original creation. In *The Deerslayer* trees and lakes and hills are not simply objects to be perceived, or obstacles to be overcome by civilization; they are, Cooper emphasizes, the essentially unchanged creations of God, and behind their serenity and natural harmony lies the divine law of the universe. The American wilderness is the world of Genesis, fresh, dazzling, still emanating the divine spirit of its origin. Though Deerslayer's first war path takes place in a small area of New York, the timeless quality of the virgin forest, which stretches from the Hudson to the prairie, gives it a representative, even a cosmic, significance. The six days of action seem to echo the cycle of creation, and Cooper stresses the movement of the sun, earth, and heavens when describing the dawning and fading of light on the basin of the Glimmerglass. When Deerslayer first beholds the sparkling sheet of water, he is glad it has not yet been named. In the American wilderness man is free from rigid and meaningless conventions of traditional speech, from sterile logic and dry classification, and when lakes or warriors receive a name, it corresponds exactly with the thing. Cooper succeeds admirably in conveying the delight of man in intimate harmony with nature, beholding and naming creation for the first time.

If man is closest to the divine spirit in a virgin forest, it is because civilization distracts him from nature by accentuating his greed and selfishness. According to Deerslayer, people in the settlements think always of their own ends, and decay comes not as the natural cycle of life, but as the untimely consequence of waste and violence. Cooper makes it clear that previous contact with civilization is responsible for Hutter's avarice, for Harry's blind prejudice, and for Judith's vanity. Muskrat castle is a tiny point of civilization, a dissonance on the tranquil sheet of the Glimmerglass, and it is this single discordant note which breaks the peaceful harmony of nature. Throughout the tale violence revolves around this isolated and fortified castle which suggests the abrupt intrusion of civilization and the imminent corruption of natural creation.

Yet Hutter's residence is only partly a castle, for in the owner's absence on the first day, Deerslayer and Hurry Harry enter it as freely as if it were part of the landscape. A house in the American forest is never a permanent nor a truly private castle. It is always possible that such a dwelling will eventually be reclaimed by nature. On the other hand, the pirate chest is securely private and totally alien to nature. Even in an emergency Deerslayer will not touch it without Judith's permission. The buried sins and mysteries of the chest emphasize the contract between civilization and the American forest. Moreover, the contents of the chest, unlike the castle, can never be adapted for use in the wilderness. Deerslayer's reaction to the chest and its contents suggests both his identity with the forest and his freedom from contamination by society. He first denounces the chess men as idols, which they in fact become in the eyes of the Hurons. Both the chess pieces and the brocaded gown fail to bring peace, as Judith hopes they will, and Deerslayer warns the beautiful maiden that the dress was not meant for her, that it is an unnatural and even immoral garment in the American forest. We remember the warning when, at the end of the tale, Captain Warley's desire is reawakend by the sight of Judith in the magnificent dress. Even a pistol which Deerslayer takes from the chest explodes in his hand, a final symbol of the evil and decay resulting from a misuse of these articles of civilized life. Gowns, pistols, and chess pieces did not inherently embody an evil principle, but they easily distracted man's attention, and in the wilderness they were totally out of place.

At the core of Cooper's romanticism was the belief that human character is pure or corrupt according to its degree of harmony with nature. Nature in its true glory and divinity was a kind of Holy Grail which could be seen only by the purest of heart. But if harmony with nature was limited to the morally elect, it also sanctified the martial skills of the American knight. Cooper noted that European poets chose sunset as the hour of revery, when man reached a sad and ephemeral union with nature; yet in the American wilderness sunrise was a holier moment, for then the increasing clarity of light led the mind to sublime and far-reaching thoughts. In *Deerslayer* the most dramatic episodes occur at sunrise, when, according to Cooper, the senses recover their original powers of accurate and undistracted perception. In the almost liquid lucidity of morning air, certain men acquire an acuteness of sight and smell and perceive the true nature of physical objects, as well as the simplicity and beauty of moral truths. At dawn the sparkling and bewitching clarity of atmosphere brings a sharpening of aesthetic, moral, and physical senses, since man is at such moments in subtle harmony with the inner rhythms of nature. Yet Hurry Harry and Tom Hutter, whose *moral* senses have been stunted by civilization, are blind both to beauties and hidden dangers in the morning hours. Only Deerslayer and Chingachgook perform extraordinary feats at sunrise. By uniting the physical, moral, and aesthetic senses with nature, Cooper succeeded in relating physical prowess to moral perfection and an appreciation for beauty.

Images of the lake and forest dominate Cooper's descriptions. The forest is irregular, mysterious, and physical in an almost sexual sense (Cooper frequently dwells on the "matted and wild luxuriance of a virgin American forest"). Throughout the tale the forest is a place of danger and surprise, at one moment deathly silent and at the next moment swarming with murderous Indians. Cooper likened forest scenes to the tenebrous paintings of Salvator Rosa, and even the illiterate Deerslayer is sensitive to the fascinating contrasts of "the picturesque."

But despite his love for the dense and tangled forest, Deerslayer is truly inspired only at an open spot where an expansive view conveys the idea of God's majesty and man's creaturehood. It is the wide expansiveness of the Glimmerglass that evokes in Deerslayer a sentiment half-poetic, half-religious, which is something more than response to the picturesque. For example, when observing the picturesque and barbaric scene of Indians in the flickering light of campfires, Deerslayer is tensely fascinated, his excited senses alert for instant action; but suspended in a canoe on the calm sheet of the Glimmerglass, he experiences the repose and spiritual uplift of one in the presence of the sublime. The contrast of forest and lake, of picturesque and sublime, of sudden violence and peaceful solitude, tends to harmonize the hero's feats of physical skill and bravery with his Christian selflessness and humility before God's works. Thus nature insulates Deerslayer from the corruptions of civilization, and at the same time purifies his acts of violence by relating them to the natural rhythms and contrasts of the wilderness. Just as lake and forest merge into a harmonious unity when seen from a distance, so serenity and martial skills finally combine in the figure of the woodsman hero.

When we turn from Deerslayer's relationship with nature to his participation in war, we should perhaps remind ourselves that the Leatherstocking tales are dominated by the theme of killing Indians. In *The Deerslayer* Cooper was concerned with racial war beyond the boundaries of human justice, and with the circumstances and morality of a young American's first homicide. More than forty years before Cooper wrote, Charles Brockden Brown had described the ritual of a young man killing his first Indian victim, but in Brown's novel the act was a "loathsome obligation" followed by anguish and remorse. In the frontier tales of the 1830's and 1840's, however, it was almost necessary for the heroic youth to establish himself as a free American citizen by "killing his brute," as it was termed by Robert Montgomery Bird. Certainly many Americans had actually experienced the killing of an Indian as part of the process of maturity. Writers had a certain justification for dwelling upon the ritual, since it signified the free white man's possession of the rights and privileges of his civilization, a racial eucharist, granting secular freedom and wealth after the sacrifice of a red man's flesh and blood. But even a ritualistic slaying may involve guilt, especially when the victim represents a persecuted and dispossessed race.

In the opening pages of *The Deerslayer* we learn that the hero has never shed human blood, his unusual fame as a hunter notwithstanding, and that the loss of this innocence is to be one of the themes of the tale. Hurry Harry, the crude but experienced braggart, chides Deerslayer the same way an older soldier might tease an obviously virginal recruit. According to Harry, a man is not a man until he has killed and scalped an Indian. As a test of skill and training, Deerslayer looks forward modestly to his first combat, but he condones neither scalping nor wanton killing. As we have seen, Harry's lust for scalps nearly brings destruction to the company of white characters. Although he feels guilt after needlessly taking human life, he projects this guilt on the victims themselves, arguing that Indians are sub-human monsters who do not deserve to live. Blind to the glories of nature, Harry is consequently inferior to Deerslayer in both skill and morality. Living beyond the reach of human law, his brutal aggressiveness condoned by a government which offers bounties for scalps, Hurry Harry leaves a wake of evil and suffering behind him.

In contrast, Deerslayer approaches his first combat in the solitude and tranquility of daybreak. Drifting softly in a canoe toward a seemingly deserted point of land, he is in perfect harmony with the sublime rhythms of light, air, and mirror-like water. The combat itself is a lyrical movement of graceful and faultless skill against a background of singing birds and the shining sky of sunrise. Deerslayer is calm and gracious, yet his muscles and animal senses are prepared for instantaneous and deadly action. He is like a champion bullfighter who shows profound respect for his antagonist, but who gracefully and deliberately risks his life, in every way maximizing the danger to himself, while at the same time maintaining exquisite control over his dangerous enemy. Refusing to take advantage of the Huron, Deerslayer shoots only in self-defense, after the Indian has attacked him. The Huron dies in his conqueror's arms, rewarding Deerslayer with a new name, Hawkeye, and the hunter concludes in a melancholy mood that the brave's treachery, like his own marksmanship, is a racial gift, Deerslayer had not desired the Indian's death, and doubted the virtue of any killing, yet he reflects that he had acted only according to his training and his God-given nature.

In his sympathy and respect for the hostile savage, Deerslayer redeemed his less sensitive brothers. Even the Huron mistook him for a missionary at first, when the hunter observed that the world was large enough for both of them. But in spite of his Moravian ideals, Deerslayer had the power and skill to shoot a human being, and in one sense, this soft-hearted, musing hero was but America's gesture of apology to a vanquished foe. A sordid fact of American history was purified when the woodsman killed the noble savage in this idyll of death in the midst of unspoiled nature.

However, Deerslayer's aggression is justified not only by his intimacy with nature, but also by his relation to woman. On the second night, when Deerslayer and Chingachgook are alone for the first time, the Indian gazes intently at his young friend, obviously aware that the hunter is no longer the callow youth he had once known. Deerslayer finally confirms Chingachgook's suspicions, and admits that he has killed a brave. Previously, he had hoped for a chance to tell Chingachgook that he had not disgraced his Delaware training, and now Deerslayer is obviously pleased by the Indian's delight. Like one youth telling another of his first sexual conquest, Deerslayer is proud of his newly-won man-hood. But the hunter's pride in physical combat can be excused, for Cooper at least, only by a negation of true sexuality. If Deerslayer is partly a Homeric warrior, he is also a Christian saint whose sanctity requires an ascetic life.

Soon after the first combat Deerslayer is alone with Judith and Hetty, since the other male characters are still captives of the Hurons. When Judith asks him about the shots she has heard, he modestly admits that he has been true to his gifts and has fought and killed an Indian while defending the canoes. Judith, who has known Deerslayer for less than a day, caresses his hand and admires his bravery. After her bitter experi-ences with the flattery of smooth-voiced officers and predatory frontiers-men like Hurry Harry, she is much attracted by the unassuming bravery and soft-spoken honesty of Deerslayer. His tale of Chingachgook's pur-suit of the kidnapped Wah-ta!-Wah gives Judith a chance to talk of love. But when asked about his own sweetheart, Deerslayer replies that he loves only the soft rain in the forest, clouds floating in a blue sky, the dew of the morning, or the sweet water of natural springs. The wilder-ness he describes is a succession of water images, culminating in the sublime Glimmerglass itself. Despite Judith's free glances and forward manner, Deerslayer is unaware of either her subtle coquetry or genuine affection. His deepest love is reserved for mother nature herself, for the movement of bubbling brooks, for the rhythmic cycle of rain and dew, for the glistening expansiveness of lakes, and for water washing through the dark and tangled forest.

Later, when Deerslayer's "furlough" draws to a close and he pre-pares to return to the Huron camp, Judith tells him she would die for a husband who was stout-hearted, modest, sure on a hunt or war path, and above all, honest. Knowing that she is describing his own qualities, Deerslayer is for a moment tempted by the idea of marriage. Judith is the most beautiful woman he has ever seen, but his mind is not accus-tomed to being swayed by fancy or imagination. After scarcely a minute of hesitation, he smiles at his own weakness. At midnight he is alone on the ark with a sensuous woman, but he shows not a trace of even suppressed passion. As in so much American fiction, the "love" scenes are abstract arguments over ideal qualities in men and women. Love itself is a moral dialogue bringing, at best, a reserved sense of mutual understanding.

But Deerslayer's cold asceticism does not mean that his relation with Judith Hutter is unimportant. For six days he gently dominates her, breaks down her feeble resistance, and destroys her personal integrity, as well as her self-esteem. He exercises over her a total mastery and control similar to that which characterized his physical conflict with the Huron brave. At the same time, she glorifies and even worships him as a symbol of the chaste purity of nature. Cooper's heroines are sometimes merely objects to be rescued, but Judith is also a means for the glorification and purification of Leatherstocking. As with many of the dream girls in American fiction, her adoration proves to the reader that the hero, despite his deadly skills, is truly lovable. Through Judith Hutter we see Deerslayer's innocence, his purity of heart, and his rustic chivalry. If Leatherstocking, at least in his youth, had not been loved by a woman, he might well appear as a toughened killer instead of a romantic hero.

We have suggested that Deerslayer's first homicide was justified partly by his subsequent sexual innocence in the face of Judith's advances. Thus woman's love not only glorifies the hero, but also gives him an opportunity to prove his ascetic purity. Cooper emphasized this point at the end of the tale when Deerslayer kills a second Indian. As a captive he refuses to marry the widow of his first Huron victim, and her brother avenges the insult by hurling a tomahawk at the hunter's head. Deerslayer catches it, however, and following the natural law of retaliation, kills the Indian on a return throw. Soon afterwards, the Hurons are annihilated by soldiers, whereupon Judith openly proposes marriage to Deerslayer, suggesting that they live at the castle where they might enjoy the beauties of nature alone. Showing that she has been chastened by his earlier lectures on the dangers of feminine vanity, lectures which had sometimes brought her to tears, she promises to light the first fire in their hearth with the brocaded gown. But this time Deerslayer is not even tempted. He quietly rejects her offer, remarking that he could never love her as he once loved his parents and as he now loves the wilderness. He also indicates that his feelings are in part influenced by Hurry Harry's tales of her past misconduct. Cooper implies that Deerslayer's presence had brought forth gleamings of Judith's purer spirit, but her transgressions could never be excused.

Perhaps the most tender contact between the two lovers was when Judith gave Deerslayer her father's magnificent rifle, Killdeer. Unlike the pistol which nearly wounded Judith when it exploded, Killdeer is a safe and appropriate weapon for Leatherstocking, though after needlessly shooting an eagle he questions his right to possess so fine a rifle. Only after Deerslayer has proved his asceticism, his innocent purity, and his unity with nature, does he feel truly justified in carrying this symbol of masculine destructiveness.

Fifteen years after the end of the tale, Deerslayer and Chingachgook returned to the Glimmerglass, now deserted and hushed by the stillness of the primeval forest. On the eastern shore the Hutters' ark lay stranded, weather-beaten, and filled with water. We are told that Deerslayer's heart quickened when he found one of Judith's ribbons fluttering from a log. He had not loved her, Cooper adds, but he ''still retained a kind and sincere interest in her welfare.'' The ribbon recalled both her beauty and her failings, and Deerslayer knotted it to the stock of Killdeer as a souvenir. His triumph was now complete. He flew a lady's colors from his weapon as a sign of his tenderness and warmth of heart, but the American knight's strange purity was untainted by love.

In *The Deerslayer* the young Leatherstocking kills his first Indian, wins his reputation as a hero, and protects his chastity. The tale has about it the peculiar freshness and melancholy of a youth entering manhood, which in the American wilderness was signified by the first war path. Rejection of woman and unity with nature are fused in a heroic ideal which distinguishes Deerslayer from Hurry Harry, whose violence is unsanctified by either asceticism or the touch of sublime nature. Deerslayer's aggressive actions acquire moral sanction when he negates his sexuality and dedicates himself to a life in the maternal forest. If Cooper failed to convert the crude American hunter into a Homeric hero and Christian saint, he did invent a beautiful myth which embodied American fears, ideals, and values. In subsequent literature the American hero was, above all, a figure combining deadly skills with social innocence. Only harmony with the divine rhythms of uncorrupted nature could soften his terrifying efficiency at destruction and exploitation.

7

Marlboro Country

History of the Westward Movement
by Frederick Merk.
Knopf, 660 pp., $20.00

Like his great mentor Frederick Jackson Turner, the historian Frederick
Merk moved *eastward* from Madison, Wisconsin, to Cambridge, Massachusetts. Born in Milwaukee in 1887 (he died in 1977), Merk was
still a senior at the University of Wisconsin when in 1910 Turner packed
up his course on the history of the westward movement and struck out
for the wilds of Harvard. By that time Turnerism was beginning to sweep
the historical profession, transforming textbooks and reshaping the teaching
of American history. In 1916 Merk himself finally moved to Harvard
where under Turner's direction he wrote a prize-winning doctoral dissertation on Wisconsin history. At Turner's invitation Merk then delivered the lectures on western history during the spring terms when the
master was on leave. In 1924, when Turner retired, Merk took over the
course and was promoted, at age thirty-seven, to assistant professor.

Over the next thirty-three years Merk's "Cowboys and Indians" became a cherished Harvard institution. Merk himself, once described by
an admiring Harvard colleague as "a man of icy integrity," became
legendary, especially after the great blizzard of 1940 when he snow-
shoed five miles from his Belmont home to meet his morning class.
Like Turner, he trained a galaxy of distinguished and devoted graduate
students whose interests ranged far beyond western history.

More remarkable, however, were Frederick Merk's scholarly achievements after retiring at the age of seventy. Not content with revising two earlier books, he published six new monographs and collected essays including four major works on the ideology and diplomatic history of American expansion. Now a seventh book, his magnum opus, has been published posthumously. Consisting of sixty-four chapters and roughly 370,000 words, it begins with the prehistoric Indian migrations across the Bering Strait and ends with state land-use planning legislation enacted in 1975. Essentially this vast undertaking is an expansion of the lecture course bequeathed to Merk by Turner. Accordingly, in his acknowledgments Merk especially singles out his old mentor along with his collaborator-wife, Lois Bannister Merk, herself a professional historian.

An assessment of Merk's *Westward Movement* must begin with the Turner thesis, which like most fruitful paradigms is more complicated than the popular understanding suggests. Here it will be most useful to review the Turner thesis by noting a series of revealing paradoxes. First, having been trained in classical and medieval history, Turner was above all concerned with a macroscopic approach to the evolution of human institutions. He saw the westward movement as a variant on and continuation of the more general epic of European expansion. He also emphasized that "the real significance of western history is that it is national history."[1] Yet in his reaction against the reigning "germ theory" of history which ignored New World environment and which traced the origin of free institutions back to ancestral, Teutonic tribes, Turner stressed the uniqueness of the American West to an extent that encouraged parochialism if not outright xenophobia.

A second paradox arises from Turner's central premise: the influence on American development of "free" land in the West—"free" in the sense that the land itself was untitled and uncultivated and that forest, water, and mineral resources were untapped. In response to Malthusian concerns over Old World scarcity, typified by classical theories of rent and "return," writers had long invested the boundless expanses of the New World with the mythical associations of an ever-filled cornucopia. Turner's glowing vision of the West thus drew on ancient dreams of plenitude and satiation—myths of a western Arcadia of freshness, purity, and eternal fertility; of a new Eden of ageless youth; of an Earth

---

1. In addition to Turner's writings, I have especially drawn on Ray Allen Billington's two invaluable works: *Frederick Jackson Turner: Historian, Scholar, Teacher* (Oxford University Press, 1973) and *The Genesis of the Frontier Thesis: A Study in Historical Creativity* (The Huntington Library, 1971).

Goddess, both Giver and Redeemer, capable of undepleted nourish-
ment. Yet by definition Turner's frontier was a line dividing advancing
settlement from receding free land. If the virginal West was in some
sense a supernatural power precisely because, to borrow Marshall Sah-
lin's words, it was "beyond society, escaping its order," the power was
rapidly being subdued and assimilated.[2]

Even by 1890, as Turner emphasized in his famous speech in 1893
to the American Historial Association, the end was in sight. Whereas
various "primitive" peoples had tried to ensure good harvests by sacrificing and eating symbolic embodiments of godhood, Turner's frontier
consumed the Earth Goddess herself. The more this self-consuming frontier was viewed as crucial for America's regeneration, the more the
apparent message of universal salvation turned out to be a doctrine of
limited atonement, a sacrifice benefiting only the elect who were fortu-
nate enough to live during the colonizing and settlement phases of
American history. It is true that Turner later professed faith in "new
frontiers of unwon fields of science, fruitful for the needs of the race,"
and that Merk ultimately identifies all the virtues and infinitude of the
old frontier with the "open frontier" of science and technology. But
this is to shift one's reverence from the sacrificed god to the sacrificial
knife.

A third paradox is that Turner presented the frontier as a force of liberation, "a new field of opportunity, a gate of escape from the bondage
of the past . . . offering new experiences, calling out new institutions
and activities." Yet his argument also presupposed that ideas and culture are irresistibly reshaped by physical environment, an assumption
that seems to undercut the theme of liberation. Though Turner dis-
avowed the extreme geographic determinism of his day, his explanation
for America's mosaic of "sectional" differences suggested that even
diverse racial "stocks" were of less importance than the physiographic
environments to which they adapted.

A fourth paradox is that Turner was obsessed with finding scientific
verification for what was essentially a poetic vision of man's interaction
with nature. In his most inspired and influential passages Turner was
reformulating sentiments familiar to Emerson, Thoreau, and the Anglo-
American romantic tradition. But like so many thinkers of his day, Turner
looked to science as his model. Overcompensating for his lack of logical
rigor, he compulsively postponed writing his most ambitious book while

2. "Culture as Protein and Profit," *The New York Review,* November 23, 1978, p. 47.

slaving over the preparation of maps designed to correlate, county by county, physiographical conditions with political, economic, and social behavior.

A final paradox concerns the fate of the Turner thesis, which, as John Higham has written, "offered the only comprehensive, distinctive interpretation of the whole of American history."[3] Among scholars Turnerism provoked for several decades unusually fruitful debates, especially over such questions as mobility, the relation of labor systems to free land, and the role of the West as a "safety valve" for economic and political discontent. It is an interesting question why the most powerful and suggestive theory of American development should also have lent itself to essentially anti-intellectual popularizations.

One answer is that certain characteristics of the theory allowed it to become confused with its subject matter. This blurring of boundaries not only gave a heightened, miragelike significance to every artifact of western Americana, but often persuaded students of the frontier that they themselves were frontiersmen. Overt Turnerism declined after World War II not because the issues it raised had been settled or its main premises rejected, but rather because the writings of Turner's more parochial and chauvinistic disciples appeared jejune to a new generation of urbanites. Yet as early as 1928 Merle Curti, one of Turner's most brilliant students, observed that Turner had given new directions to diplomatic, intellectual, and cultural history, and quoted Arthur M. Schlesinger's remark that Turner's "chief importance to American historical thinking has, in the last analysis, been his elucidation of the part played by economic group conflicts in our history."[4] In fact, Turner's students were "pioneers" in the history of immigration and industrialization. The recent and fashionable community studies, which use quantitative techniques and interdisciplinary methods in an effort to reconstruct the social structure of an entire population, are a fulfillment of Turner's dreams.

Or at least of his scientific dreams. Turner's broader appeal is best understood when we realize that he offered an ingenious solution to the ancient problem of primitivism and progress. From the time of the ancient Cynics and Stoics, many philosophers and poets had contrasted the restraints, prejudices, and corrupting tastes of civilized life with either a former age of virtue or a simpler, more primitive state of society. This

---

3. "The Old Frontier," *The New York Review*, April 25, 1968, p. 10.
4. Billington, *Genesis*, pp. 265–270.

tendency was further fueled by reports of the New World from early explorers and Catholic missionaries.[5] Primitivism in various forms became a central theme of the romantic tradition from Rousseau to Thoreau. Yet the nineteenth century was preeminently committed to the doctrine of historical progress and to the global triumph of Christian civilization.

Increasingly, therefore, yearnings for pastoral or primitive simplicity, freedom, and authenticity were relegated to a separate aesthetic realm which had little relevance to the onward-and-upward struggles of history. Social Darwinism, which exerted such a powerful influence on Turner's generation, gave compelling support to the prevailing faith in temporal progress: the faith that each step on what Frederick Merk calls "the ladder of civilization"—from savage hunters and trappers to herdsmen, farmers, traders, and manufacturers—marked an evolutionary improvement. But Social Darwinism also added two disturbing implications to traditional fears of "overcivilization." First, paleontology proved that the evolution from simple to complex forms could lead to overspecialization and thus extinction. Second, even the human capacity for adaptation appeared to be limited if, as feared by sociologists like William Graham Sumner, we are propelled onward by a unilinear stream of time which dictates our thoughts, mores, and even scientific experiments.

Turner's most brilliant stroke was to argue that in America primitivism and progress intermeshed. Though agreeing with the Social Darwinists that democracy had evolved from the adaptation of certain "stocks" to the needs and opportunities of the environment, Turner insisted that in America this process had not been confined to a unilinear dimension of time. In the East institutions had evolved in the usual stages toward greater complexity and specialization. "But we have in addition to this," Turner wrote, "a recurrence of the process of evolution in each western area reached in the process of expansion. Thus American development has exhibited not merely advance along a single line, but a return to primitive conditions on a continually advancing frontier line, and a new development for that area."

Each frontier zone recapitulated the entire history of civilization. As a result, even the more "advanced" urban civilization of the East had

---

5. See especially Arthur O. Lovejoy, Gilbert Chinard, George Boas, and Ronald S. Crane, *A Documentary History of Primitivism and Related Ideas* (The Johns Hopkins University Press, 1935); Chinard, *L'Amérique et le rêve exotique dans la littérature française au XVIIe et au XVIIIe siècle;* Fredi Chiapelli, ed., *First Images of America: The Impact of the New World on the Old,* 2 volumes (University of California Press, 1976); Lois Whitney, *Primitivism and the Idea of Progress in English Popular Literature of the Eighteenth Century* (The Johns Hopkins University Press, 1934).

been continually purified and revitalized by the lifegiving frontier. It was this "perennial rebirth, this fluidity of American life" that had saved the East from decadence, class struggle, and from what Brooks Adams called "the law of civilization and decay." The notion that the primitive West can somehow redeem the sins of our civilization has remained one of our most potent myths. We are told that the crystal air of Marlboro Country can detoxify even cigarettes.

Despite some appearances to the contrary, Merk's *History of the Westward Movement* is a Turnerian book. It is an account of "one of the great migrations of mankind" which "replaced barbarism with civilization," unlocking "the bounties of nature," including rich soil, forests, water power, copper, lead, iron, coal, gas, and oil, making them "a blessing to mankind." Like Turner, Merk is interested in broad evolutionary forces, not in personalities (though, ironically, "individualism" becomes one of the central issues of the book). For Merk collective behavior and group identity ultimately owe less to cultural tradition than to the character of soil, glaciation, watersheds, rainfall, and such features as the Wisconsin drift and Shelbyville moraine.

Merk's occasional disavowal of geographic determinism and his acknowledgment of "other factors" are even less convincing than Turner's similar disclaimers. From the outset, when Merk considers the first seaboard colonies, it becomes clear that "in New England, as in Virginia, geography thus stamped its influence on the economy and on the political and religious views of society." Making much use of Turner's maps of voting patterns in presidential elections from Jackson to Lincoln, Merk triumphantly points out that in 1856, for example, the Republican area of the Middle West "corresponds with the area of glaciation." Ignoring the research of recent decades on the complexity of local politics and the importance of ethnocultural alignments, Merk interprets national elections in terms of geography and stereotyped images of various migrant groups.

In some respects an unreconstructed Turnerian, Merk even fails to follow revisionary leads that Turner suggested late in life. For example, while Merk curiously devotes a whole chapter to "Industrialization of the Great Lakes Region," he says virtually nothing about western urbanization. "Movement" and "migration," his governing themes, seldom apply to the momentous rural migration to towns and cities, to say nothing of the eastward drain of professionals like Merk himself. The Turnerian emphasis on adaptability and assimilation is linked to an ethnocentrism that can be understood only when one recalls that Frederick Merk was thirty years old when America entered the First World War.

Hence it is not surprising that he stresses the inability of the Indian "to effectively exploit his resources" or contrasts the Indian with the Negro, who "even while in a state of slavery, rose steadily on the ladder of civilization." The devastating mortality of California Indians, under the rule of Mexican missionaries, was not the result of "overwork or neglect." The blunt fact, Merk assures us, was that "the California Indians were unclean in their habits. Indians up and down the Pacific coast allowed filth to accumulate about their villages." An ascetic puritan when compared to Turner, Merk is especially stern when dealing with alcoholic consumption and sexual license. There is no conscious humor in his remark that for American sailors "the great attraction in the Hawaiian Islands was the Hawaiian maidens, whose ideas of modesty and virtue were the same as those of the sailors." The next paragraph begins: "After a generation of this trade the Hawaiian people were in need of missionaries."

It is Merk's imperviousness to all forms of primitivism that sets him apart most dramatically from Frederick Jackson Turner. His peroration seems to echo the old Turnerian faith: "The hope of the future is that all the optimism, all the indomitable will to overcome obstacles, all the love of freedom and of democratic process, and all the determination to make things better for the future, which the old frontier nourished and symbolized, will remain part of American thought and aspirations." But this passage refers specifically to the new frontier of science and technology, and the preceding six-hundred-odd pages barely mention any positive influences of the frontier on individual thought and aspiration. Merk's West is utterly devoid of romance. It is a West of often fascinating scientific detail described in the language of a hydraulic engineer.

Upon closer inspection, Merk seems to turn Turner on his head. For Merk feels an astonishing repugnance toward Westerners, especially frontiersmen of Southern origin. Again and again we encounter "semivagrant types"; crude, hard-drinking riffraff; Scotch-Irish squatters who are "pests" in "matters of land policy"; frontier rebellions led by "rash and inexperienced leaders"; border "traders, whiskey dealers, and other dregs of society" who prey on Indians; debtors who demand an expansion of paper currency and other "heresies" at variance with "sound fiscal policy." Above all, Merk unquestionably proves that the key to western settlement was rampant land speculation, often accompanied by wholesale theft and fraud. Obsessed with quick profit, buccaneering capitalists seized the most valuable tracts of timber and mineral lands while single-cropping "exploitive farmers" impoverished the soil. As the story moves on through timber wars and mining bonanzas, it adds up to a free-for-all rape of the nation's public domain.

For Merk the governing word is disorder. Through the first three-quarters of his book individualism, speculation, and wheeler-dealer prof-iteering continue to triumph over the rational plans of various central administrations. From the time that Crown authorities sold Virginia headrights "on a purely commercial basis," the great lesson of frontier history was "that the purposes of theoretically excellent land systems were defeated by the activities of land speculators."

It is a bit startling to realize that the speculators included George Washington among other leading patriots. But Merk's sympathies clearly lie with the early French and British regulations designed to protect Indians from the abuses of the fur trade and with later British plans to restrict land speculation and "to ensure an orderly occupation of the western wilderness." He applauds both the New England tradition of community planning and the rational goals of the 1785 Land Ordinance, but then describes the disintegration of all orderly programs with the exception of the "planned, united, and devoted" achievements of the Mormons in the Great Basin of Utah and the enlightened administration of the Hudson's Bay Company in the Oregon Country.

At one point, after contrasting the anarchy of the American mining camps with the orderly government of those in British Columbia, Merk explicitly asks "whether the local democracy of the frontier—informal squatter government—was the best government for a frontier society, or whether better results would have been obtained from executive govern-ment on the frontier." His only answer is that the British system, in-cluding "a very superior type of governor," would probably not have been "admitted on an American frontier." We are thus forced to con-clude that the characteristics of the American frontier were responsible for the dismal story of waste, swindle, violence, and self-indulgence which is only occasionally leavened by Turnerian assurances that west-ern settlement somehow kept the economy in vigorous health and cre-ated a great continental nation.

Merk's admiring treatment of the Mormons provides a clue to the book's central meaning. Under the Church's leadership, he writes, "Mormon-ism was an experiment in cooperation and in social planning, one of the most successful large-scale examples of it in American history, prior to the rural electrification cooperatives of the New Deal era." He also affirms that "among the elements accounting for the coherence and suc-cess of the Church one of the most important was the physiography of the Enclosed Basin." In other words the rich resources of the arid re-gions of the Far West could not be tapped by the individualistic methods of the earlier frontier. The Mormon achievements of the mid-nineteenth century point forward to Merk's highly informative chapters on the twentieth-century Colorado River, Columbia Basin, and Central Valley Projects; the TVA; soil conservation, and land-use planning.

Most of the *History of the Westward Movement* concerns the political, economic, and diplomatic history of America before the 1860s. Much of the detail has little specific relevance to the West. In contrast, the later chapters focus on modern agriculture and the use of natural resources, with little reference to larger political, economic, and diplomatic issues. The covert message, one begins to realize, is that the older Turnerian frontier fostered centrifugal forces of disorder, violence, and self-seeking that dominated politics and diplomacy and that culminated in the trauma which Merk barely mentions and which is not even listed in his index—the Civil War. After a painful interregnum, further penalties of planlessness "manifested themselves in the opening quarter of the twentieth century in a series of dramatic disturbances of nature in major areas." Flood, drought, erosion, depression—all contributed to a growing acceptance of land-use planning and regulation. In Merk's symmetrical vision, the later trend toward integration culminated not in sectionalism and war but in unifying projects like TVA, which was "comparable to the colonizing corporations of the early colonial period" (presumably before the serpent urged colonists to bite the apple of commercial speculation).

This is still Turnerism, but Turnerism socialized and purged by Progressive ideology of all traces of primitivism. Yet it is still the land, especially the fabulous resources hidden beneath the harsh surface of the Far West, that becomes America's regenerative force, "calling out new institutions and activities," as Turner had said, but now in the form of reclamation, resettlement, reforestation, and government planning. Indeed, Merk transfers to government agencies and experts much of the mythical aura of the West—the aura of clean plenitude, power, and ennobling purpose. In this respect Merk's book gives more insight into the mentality of the New Deal era than into the history of the westward movement. After the disillusion of viewing the rape and squandering of the public domain, Merk's bracing optimism reminds one of the ironic scene in Robert Penn Warren's *All the King's Men,* when Jack Burden, after hitting bottom in a Long Beach motel, concludes:

> "So there is innocence and a new start in the West, after all. If you believe the dream you dream when you go there."[6]

---

6. Harcourt, Brace and Company, 1946; Bantam Books, 1959, p. 311.

8

Secrets of the Mormons

America's Saints: The Rise of Mormon Power
by Robert Gottlieb and Peter Wiley.
Putnam's, 278 pp., $16.95

Mormonism: The Story of A New Religious Tradition
by Jan Shipps.
University of Illinois Press,
211 pp., $14.50

Joseph Smith and the Beginnings of Mormonism
by Richard L. Bushman.
University of Illinois Press,
262 pp., $17.95

Brigham Young: American Moses
by Leonard J. Arrington.
Knopf, 522 pp., $24.95

History has always been central to Mormonism as a foundation of faith, a source of group identity, and a vulnerable target for heretical and Gentile attack. The historical consciousness of the Mormons is wholly different from that of such relatively modern denominations as the Methodists, Unitarians, and Christian Scientists. For Mormons the visions and revelations received by Joseph Smith, Jr., beginning in 1820, opened a new dispensation in human history and ended ''the Great Apostasy'' of some fifteen centuries, during which Catholic and Protestant churches had deluded the world and blocked the way to Christian

From *The New York Review of Books*, August 15, 1985. Copyright © 1985 by NYREV, Inc. Reprinted by permission.

salvation. The sudden intrusion of sacred power into mundane history led in 1830 to the restoration of the only true Church of Christ, later renamed the Church of Jesus Christ of Latter-day Saints, and to the rebuilding of social and political institutions based on divine authority.

Traditionally, Mormon faith has rested on a belief in the literal historicity of sacred events. These include Joseph Smith's vision of God and Christ as physical beings in 1820, the subsequent appearances of the Angel Moroni to Joseph Smith, and Joseph's discovery and translation of buried golden plates containing lost books of holy scripture. According to Smith, the golden plates, after being translated into what later became the Book of Mormon, were taken up to heaven. The meaning of history was infinitely enriched by the great Mormon epic of persecution, the gathering of the Saints, the martyrdom of the Prophet, and the Mosaic-like exodus to a promised land. As Jan Shipps observes, "Today's Saints live out their lives in a corporate community that still stands squarely and securely in the presence of the past."

From the very beginning Mormon leaders saw the strategic importance of retaining control over their own history. Faced with doubt and skepticism even among his own followers, Smith sought divine assistance to persuade three disciples to bear testimony that they had seen the golden plates and heard the voice of God affirm that the translation was accurate. Soon thereafter Smith created another historical document in which eight witnesses testified that they had "seen and hefted" the golden plates. Oliver Cowdery, one of the three original witnesses and the scribe to whom Smith had dictated the last part of the Book of Mormon, became the Church's first record keeper and historian. Soon after the founding of the Church, apostates and anti-Mormons accumulated their own historical evidence to challenge Mormon claims. But in view of the number of defections and the divisive struggle for leadership after Smith's assassination by a mob in 1844, there were remarkably few leaks or recantations. Brigham Young, Smith's successor as "Prophet, Seer, and Revelator," was so fearful of the unauthorized use of a controversial text that he suppressed the first published edition of *Biographical Sketches of Joseph Smith, the Prophet,* recollections dictated by Smith's aged mother, which remains a prime source of information on the origins of the Mormon movement.

Authorized Mormon histories, including the indispensable seven-volume *History of the Church* attributed to Joseph Smith, have been written to propagate or reinforce Mormon belief. There has also been a continuing stream of anti-Mormon works, supplemented since the early twentieth century by many doctoral dissertations that have sought to apply to Mormonism the methods of social science. While outsiders have been eager to relate Mormonism to the social and intellectual environment of the Jacksonian period, they have seldom given serious attention to the movement as a distinctive religion. Mormon authorities, for their part, have been determined to prevent the records of God's dealings with his chosen people from being put to sacrilegious use. Access to Mormon archives has traditionally been restricted and we still have no scholarly editions of key Mormon texts.

During the 1940s and 1950s several prominent Mormon writers and intellectuals left the Church or, like the historian Fawn M. Brodie, were excommunicated. Encouraged by the cultural ferment of the mid-1960s, groups of intellectuals who were also practicing Mormons sought a middle ground between faith and humanistic values. Leonard J. Arrington, who in 1958 had met the highest professional standards with his landmark book, *Great Basin Kingdom,* was involved in launching both the Mormon History Association and *Dialogue: A Journal of Mormon Thought.* The new journal, which had no connection with the Church, proposed to bring Mormon faith "into dialogue with human experience as a whole" and to encourage artistic and scholarly achievement based on the Mormon cultural heritage. Richard L. Bushman, the young editor of its book review section, pointed out that Mormon college students were frequently "overpowered by a secular culture that dazzles them with its splendors and seemingly puts Mormon parochialism in the shade." A new intellectual dialogue would help young Mormons learn to live in the modern world.[1] The first issues of the journal promoted open critical discussion and debate. The lead article on Mormon history was written by Mario S. DePillis, a young Roman Catholic scholar who had been trained at Yale.

During these same years the Correlation movement started by a Mormon reformer, Harold B. Lee, had been engaged in reorganizing and centralizing the Latter-day Saints' bureaucracy. As Gottlieb and Wiley show in their new book, which is a useful and well-researched guide to the Mormon establishment (unfortunately written in the style of a journalistic exposé), this movement was basically a conservative reaction against secular erosion and was designed to strengthen the priesthood and above all the patriarchal family. But Correlation was also keenly attuned to public relations and professionalization. Lee and other leaders were eager to increase public respect for the Church and to place experts in specialized administrative positions.

In 1972 Leonard Arrington became the first professional historian to occupy the office of "Church Historian." Under Arrington's leadership,

---

1. *Dialogue: A Journal of Mormon Thought,* 1/1 (Spring 1966), p. 12.

the Church staffed a new historical department with professionally trained scholars, commissioned a sixteen-volume history of the Church, considered editing authoritative editions of key Mormon texts, and made the archives more accessible to non-Mormon scholars. During the "Arrington spring," as it came to be known, the historical department's numerous publications addressed a wider academic and professional audience as well as church members who had previously been restricted to "salvation history."

For Arrington and younger Mormon historians like Davis Bitton, Marvin S. Hill, and D. Michael Quinn, free scholarly inquiry could only strengthen faith among Mormon intellectual and professional groups exposed to the wider academic culture. Arrington himself had grown up outside the Mormon cultural community and had been deeply influenced by Santayana's *Reason in Religion* before he thought seriously about the historical meaning of Mormon miracles. He finally concluded that "ultimate truths are often, if not always, presented artistically or imaginatively in a way suited to the needs and exigencies of the living community of persons." Since God's will could be revealed only to "those prepared, by intellectual and social experience and by spiritual insight and imagination, to grasp and convey it," a "naturalistic" approach was not only valid but "makes more plausible" the truths that prophets attempted to convey. Arrington admitted in 1958 that a naturalistic method made it "difficult, if not impossible, to distinguish what is objectively 'revealed' from what is subjectively 'contributed' by those receiving the revelation."[2]

This moderating position raises fundamental problems for a church that has always been literal-minded and intolerant of ambiguity. The optimistic liberals of the 1970s misperceived the Church's aims and fears. The corrosive effects of naturalism had been all too evident in the writings of such ex-Mormons as Bernard DeVoto and Fawn M. Brodie. The Church harbors a deep suspicion of intellectuals; as the authorities concluded in 1983, there is "no need for innovation." Having withstood all the twentieth-century forces of secularization, Mormonism remains the fastest growing religion in America. Thanks to a high birth rate and the extraordinary success of foreign missions, especially in the third world, church membership by the early 1980s passed five million. A

2. Leonard J. Arrington, "Why I am a Believer," *Sunstone* 10/1 (January 1985), pp. 36–38; Arrington, *Great Basin Kingdom: An Economic History of the Latter-day Saints, 1830–1900* (Harvard University Press, 1958), p. ix. For a moving account of the "golden decade" from 1972 to 1982, see Davis Bitton, "Ten Years in Camelot: A Personal Memoir," *Dialogue*, 16/3 (Autumn 1983), pp. 9–13.

vast business empire is complemented by growing political power, most recently evidenced by the crucial lobbying pressures of the Mormon church in defeating the ERA. The Church was instrumental in mobilizing anti-ERA forces in the Rocky Mountain West and also helped to coordinate fund-raising and letter-writing campaigns concentrated on such pivotal states as Florida, Illinois, and Georgia. The main danger the Church faces, in the eyes of the leadership, is a "secular humanism" that would undermine faith, family unity, and obedience to authority.

In 1978 the Church began to demote Arrington and curtail the historical department's projects. As the purge progressed, the surviving historical activities were transferred to an institute at Brigham Young University, and in 1982 Arrington was discharged from his ecclesiastical and bureaucratic positions. Ultraconservatives, such as Ezra Taft Benson, secretary of agriculture in the Eisenhower administration, Boyd K. Packer, and Mark E. Petersen, tried to launch a campaign to identify and root out unorthodox intellectuals. According to Gottlieb and Wiley, this effort has recently been restrained by Apostle Gordon B. Hinckley, an expert at public relations and the dominating figure in the First Presidency since President Spencer W. Kimball became enfeebled by age and ill health. Even so, Mormon intellectuals were deeply shocked and saddened by Arrington's dismissal and by the new restrictive policies. Scholars who are also practicing Mormons continue to speak out courageously; they write critical essays in such journals as *Sunstone* and *Dialogue*. Their position is complicated, however, by the activities of such anti-Mormon zealots as Jerald and Sandra Tanner. The Tanners are apostate Mormons and Christian evangelicals who during the past quarter-century have printed a large number of Mormon and anti-Mormon documents, some of them smuggled from Church archives, in an effort to expose the fraudulence of Mormon religious claims. The Tanners have supplied Mormon historians with rare and inaccessible texts, but they have also endangered the assumption that free inquiry will strengthen and deepen Mormon faith. In the eyes of anti-intellectual traditionalists, the Tanners and Arrington's historical department were both responsible for a "New Mormon History" that subverted the faith. The discovery and publication of historical documents have been the battleground defining alignments both within and outside the Church.

This past spring the press has printed accounts of two important and recently discovered letters, one apparently written in 1825 by Joseph Smith, Jr., and the other in 1830 by Martin Harris, one of the original Mormon witnesses and a key figure in early Mormon history. While the Tanners originally suspected that the Harris letter was a forgery, it may well be authentic. Together, the letters confirm the view that Smith was deeply immersed in the folk magic of the early nineteenth century and was first regarded as a remarkably successful practitioner of occult arts, especially those dealing with underground spirits that guarded buried money and other treasure. The Harris letter, which describes Joseph's efforts to uncover the golden plates, makes no mention of angels or other divine figures but refers instead to a spirit that "transfigured himself from a white salamander in the bottom of the hole."

According to Harris, the spirit also insisted that Joseph bring along his older brother Alvin, who had recently died. There are reports that the Church possesses an early manuscript history written by Oliver Cowdery, who asserts that it was Alvin, not Joseph, who first found the golden plates and was prevented by a "taunting salamander" from digging them up. The Church, which originally denied ownership of the 1825 Smith letter, has refused to say whether the Cowdery history is locked within the First Presidency's vault. For Mormon historians the recent controversies raise two questions: How can one reconcile trickster spirits with traditional accounts of divine revelation? How can historians write confidently about Mormon beginnings if they are denied access to crucial sources? If the first question is resolved in a way that sustains faith, there may be hope that the "Arrington spring" set a precedent for freer access and open inquiry.

Richard L. Bushman interprets Joseph Smith's ties with necromancy in a way that should satisfy all but the most intractable Mormon fundamentalists. Bushman, a professor of history at the University of Delaware, is a highly respected American colonial historian and is also a devout Mormon. He shrewdly anticipates the unbeliever's amazement that a Harvard-trained scholar who is so obviously intelligent and well informed could believe that the Book of Mormon is the authentic word of God. One senses that Bushman's book, which covers only the first twenty-five years of the Prophet's life, is a personal testament designed to reconcile the author's secular profession with his strong faith. His attempt to address non-Mormons on the sensitive question of Mormon "beginnings" is an act of courage that commands respect.

Bushman avoids homilies and adopts the behaviorist approach of trying "to relate events as the participants themselves experienced them, using their own words where possible." But this technique leads to a curious combination, often within a single paragraph, of critical analysis of the socioeconomic details of early nineteenth-century life and an unquestioning acceptance of Mormon religious testimony and canonical texts. Because Bushman refuses to establish any critical distance between himself and his key sources, his voice and criteria for selection often merge with official Sunday school history. When he writes, concerning Joseph Smith's first vision in 1820, that "a new era in history began at that moment," he mixes his own assertion with Smith's later understanding of the event.

Yet Bushman vividly reconstructs the family and social background of the Mormon prophet. He can investigate objective social origins precisely because he assumes that God could be expected to work through various worldly instruments and to prepare the soil for a new revelation of his will. Bushman also implies that one should expect God to address the common people and to make use of vernacular culture, including occult representations of the supernatural. Recent students of Christian and Jewish history have shown that sublime conceptions of divinity were long intermixed with folk magic and cabalistic arts. It was Enlightenment rationalism, Bushman emphasizes, "with its deathly aversion to superstition," that leached official Protestantism of any respect for the miraculous except for the miracles that ceased with Christ's Apostles. As the mainline churches disdainfully dismissed witchcraft, visions, healing, and speaking in tongues, the occult was driven underground or lived on among plain farmers and mechanics who thirsted for some living contact with the supernatural.

Joseph Smith grew up within a rural culture that still combined magic with an unquestioning faith in the Bible as the revealed word of God. As Bushman skillfully shows, young Joseph's personal search for buried treasure and religious truth was part of a family quest for meaning and security that arose from two generations of uprootedness and economic adversity. These secular conditions, Bushman suggests, can be understood in two ways: for nonbelievers they help to explain Mormonism's "origins," a word Bushman eschews for the more neutral "beginnings"; for Mormons they can be studied as divinely contrived preparations for the dawning of a new era.

But Bushman, for all his strictures on Enlightenment rationalism, sees no glow of divinity in Joseph's occult arts. He is determined to show how Joseph, as the human vehicle of God's purpose, outgrew his culture and led the way to a wholly independent creation, a church that broke free from the corruptions of its secular preconditions. Bushman's book may help fellow Mormons come to terms with the worldly setting from which their church arose. But his portrait of young Joseph as a reluctant money-digger increasingly at odds with his father's superstitions conflicts with the evidence. Although Bushman presents useful criticism of the standard secular readings of the Book of Mormon, his study is not as challenging intellectually as some of the recent articles by younger Mormon historians. Ultimately he fails to find a common ground for addressing Mormon and non-Mormon readers.

On this score, Jan Shipps, professor of religious studies and history at Indiana University-Purdue University, who is not a Mormon, is far more successful. Bushman himself is quoted as saying that Shipps's short collection of essays "may be the most brilliant book ever written on Mormonism," a judgment I am inclined to share even though the essays are somewhat repetitive and lacking in overall coherence. Mormon intellectuals long ago adopted Shipps as an "insider/outsider" and "den mother" of historians, in part because of her political tact and in part because her efforts to fit Mormonism within a comparative religious scheme confirm Mormon claims to being a chosen, unique people. Without involving herself in the methodological problems that bedevil Bushman, Shipps feels free to compare Joseph Smith's religious experiences with those of Jesus and Paul and to discuss the Book of Mormon as an example of sacred literature.

Fawn Brodie pictured Mormonism as a new religious creation, departing as radically from Christianity as Christianity had departed from Judaism. Shipps develops this insight with admirable skill. Mormonism, she shows, did not seek to reform Protestant Christianity or to purify Christian traditions. Smith's divine revelations signified an abrupt break from the fraudulent churches of the past, a release from secular history and time. Although Mormonism in its early years contained elements of primitivist Christianity, resembling other contemporary movements to restore the original church of the Apostles, this New Testament emphasis on repentance and baptism was soon outweighed by Smith's claim of literally restoring ancient Israel.

Christianity had of course appropriated and transformed a Judaic heritage. But Mormonism, as Shipps points out, appropriated not only the Christian version of Judaism but also the Hebraic covenant of the Old Testament. The Mormons thought of themselves as reliving Old Testament events. The Prophet restored the priesthood of Aaron, and Melchizedek, reestablished the temple and secret temple ordinances, and enabled Saints to trace their lineage to ancient Hebrew tribes. The re-creation of Israel's patriarchal age, with such appropriate institutions as polygamy or plural marriage, overlapped moves to prepare the way for the political Kingdom of God. Shipps stresses that as the Mormons moved to Kirtland, Ohio, and then founded a city-state at Nauvoo, Illinois, they kept replicating "experientially" the stories of the Old Testament. Like the first Christians, they thought of themselves as fulfilling Hebrew prophecy, though in a far more literal way.

The strong drift toward preexilic Judaism increasingly alienated early converts who had wanted simply to restore the apostolic Christian church and who opposed such innovations as plural marriage, temple ordinances, baptism for the dead, and the political Kingdom of God. This intrachurch conflict exacerbated the struggle for succession after Smith's murder in 1844, a subject muted in official histories and even in Leonard Arrington's new biography of Brigham Young. The dissidents who refused to accept Young's leadership and to join him in the exodus to Utah finally gravitated for the most part to the Reorganized Church of Jesus Christ of Latter-Day Saints led by the prophet's son, Joseph Smith III. Shipps suggests that this division made the Utah Mormons even more literal-minded and committed to Old Testament precedents.

Between 1847, when Brigham Young led the main body of Mormons to the promised land, and 1890, when President Wilford Woodruff chose to repudiate polygamy in the interest of political survival, the Saints lived in a theocratic and corporate community that channeled all energies into "building a counterpart of the Hebraic kingdom with Solomon's temple at its center." Shipps sees 1890 as a crucial dividing line marking the Mormons' entrance into "linear, profane time." Responsibility for maintaining the boundary between Saints and Gentiles shifted from the corporate community to individuals, who were expected to internalize a distinctive code of behavior. Shipps dramatizes the differences between Saints of today and of a century ago. In the pioneer world, she writes, the sacred and not sacred were wholly merged and the essential worship "was building up the kingdom and inhabiting it." A Mormon of today returning to Utah in the 1880s would be "astonished to find so few Saints at Sacrament Meeting, because the twentieth-century Sacrament Meeting is a visible worship sign, whereas in the pioneer era more expressive worship signs were irrigation canals, or neatly built and nicely decorated houses, or good crops of sugar beets."

This last point becomes the central theme of Arrington's *Brigham Young: American Moses*. For Young there could be no separation between Church and state, between spiritual and temporal affairs, between material and immaterial being, or between Church funds and his own growing fortune. Beginning his career as an uneducated carpenter, printer, and glazier, Young found in Mormonism the divine energies that enabled him to develop his practical talents as a colonizer, territorial governor, entrepreneur, empire builder, and ruler, by the time of his death in 1877, of 125,000 brethren in his Great Basin kingdom. Under God's direct guidance, worship became fused with human exertion to build the Kingdom of God on earth. During the fall of 1856, for example, Brigham defined the "text" of his religion, when addressing several thousand Saints, as the duty to send out hundreds of teams carrying food, clothing, and blankets to assist before snowfall the Mormon emigrants who were trekking across the plains with handcarts. The Mormon mission tested what Brigham proudly called his "grit."

Long troubled by the religious uncertainty generated by America's competing sects, Young joined the Latter-day Saints only after a year and a half of study and investigation. All the members of his immediate family, including nine siblings, also became devoted Mormons. Young soon developed an intense loyalty to Joseph Smith, struggling within the Church against members who resisted the prophet's temporal innovations and dutifully leaving his destitute wife and four young children for a twenty-one-month mission to England. Although Young acquired increasing responsibilities, such as organizing the Mormon evacuation from Missouri in 1838 and 1839, there is little in his first forty-three years of life to suggest the kind of leader who could manage twenty-four plural wives and fifty-seven children while counseling thousands of followers on the most minute financial and marital problems and successfully colonizing a region extending from San Bernardino, California, to southern Idaho.

Arrington's subsidiary themes concern Young's efforts to separate God's chosen people from the corrupt Gentile world and to build a self-sufficient society based on economic cooperation, as opposed to the individualism and privatism of American society at large. The quest for self-sufficiency originated in Joseph Smith's revelation from the Lord that the children of Israel should "never do another day's work, nor spend another dollar to build up a Gentile city or nation." Savage persecution widened the breach between Mormons and American society, encouraging Young to think of himself as a new Moses delivering "the only true Israel" from bondage. Young was remarkably successful in colonizing and irrigating the desert, defying federal authority, and insulating Mormons from the corruptions of Babylon, even while he eagerly built railroads and agreed to construct the segment of the first transcontinental telegraph from Wyoming to the California border. Despite the influx of Gentile merchants and continuing federal harassment on the polygamy issue, Young preserved the distinctive cohesiveness of the Mormon community. He also promoted the ideal of highly organized communitarian settlements, built on the model of an expanded family. But he became increasingly frustrated by his failure to extend the cooperative system beyond a few communities like Brigham City, St. George, and Orderville. Mormons retained a certain spirit of communal enterprise but soon turned away from their own traditions of radical experiment and innovation.

In 1966 an English historian, writing for special issue of *Dialogue* edited by Arrington, predicted that a satisfactory biography of Brigham Young would never be written. Among the obstacles he cited was the difficulty of penetrating beneath Young's public image and gaining access to uncensored sources.[3] Arrington would like us to see his new book as evidence that the Church has "come of age" and is prepared for objective appraisal. Although even as Church historian Arrington was denied access to several key documents in the First Presidency's vault, he and his "associates in Camelot" cataloged an extensive collection of Young's diaries, office journals, letter books, speeches, and sermons that were mostly unavailable to previous scholars and that require seventy single-spaced pages even to list in a register. Arrington's prodigious research was aided by a large staff of scholars and encouraged by two presidents of the Latter-day Saints, though he insists that the Young biography was "a private, not a church project." The book is a considerable achievement that will doubtless stand for many years as the most objective and authoritative biography of Brigham Young.

Nevertheless, the biography is also disappointing. Except for interesting details, it adds surprisingly little to what we have learned from other works, including Arrington's masterful *Great Basin Kingdom*. Arrington describes Young's multifarious activities, but we seldom glimpse his interior motives, feelings, moods, anxieties, or aspirations. This limitation may be inherent in the records that have survived. But Arrington also glosses over numerous controversial subjects, avoids apostate and non-Mormon sources, and adopts in the later chapters especially an apologetic tone that blunts his insight into important issues, such as Young's challenge to democratic institutions. These faults are minor, however, when held against the model of professionalism that Arrington has set for Mormon historians. As Mormons achieve a clearer perspective on their own past, we will all learn more about the nature of American dissent, pluralism, and accommodation.

3. P.A.M. Taylor, "The Life of Brigham Young: A Biography Which Will Not Be Written," *Dialogue*, 1/3 (Autumn 1966), pp. 107–110.

III

PROBLEMS OF LOYALTY
AND IDENTITY

9

Patricide and Regicide

Patricide in the House Divided: A Psychological Interpretation of Lincoln and His Age
by George B. Forgie.
Norton, 308 pp., $14.95

In his brilliant analysis of Freud's *Interpretation of Dreams,* Carl E. Schorske uncovered a patricidal and deeply anti-political impulse at the very origin of psychoanalysis. The death of a father, Freud said, is "the most important event, the most poignant loss, of a man's life." As Schorske probed the implications of this statement as revealed in Freud's dreams, especially the "Revolutionary Dream" of 1898 (two years after the death of Freud's father), he discovered that Freud had subtly renounced earlier fantasies of political defiance and revolution. Of the dream that Freud termed "revolutionary," Schorske wrote, "patricide replaces politics," and the resolution of the dream—pointing to his pursuit of fame as a scientific investigator—connects Freud's "victory over his father with his victory over politics." For the scenario of the dream moves "from political encounter, through flight into academia, to the conquest of the father who has replaced Count Thun [the reactionary minister president of Habsburg Austria]. Patricide replaces regicide; psychoanalysis overcomes history. Politics is neutralized by a counterpolitical psychology."

Schorske goes on to argue that Freud sublimated Ferdinand Lassalle's "latent forces of national revolution," symbolized by the demonic fury,

Allecto, into a universal sexual instinct; and that by accentuating the sexual aspects of the Oedipus myth, Freud diverted attention from Oedipus' kingship and regal obligation to restore public order:

> By resolving politics into personal psychological categories, [Freud] restores personal order, but not public order. . . . By reducing his own political past and present to an epiphenomenal conflict between father and son, Freud gave his fellow liberals an ahistorical theory of man that could make bearable a political world spun out of orbit and beyond control.[1]

George B. Forgie's *Patricide in the House Divided* takes precisely the opposite approach from that of Schorske (whom Forgie acknowledges as an adviser but never cites). One of the most ambitious, ingenious, and sophisticated works of psychohistory yet to appear (it won the Allan Nevins Award of the Society of American Historians), *Patricide* is much indebted to Freud's *Totem and Taboo* but also draws on some of the best recent psychoanalytic literature. To put it briefly, Forgie holds that Lincoln's generation, having internalized a reverence for the founding fathers as inimitable exemplars of heroic virtue, could neither recognize nor resolve their own needs to destroy their parents. Instead of retreating from politics and projecting political symbols into the private sphere, as Freud apparently did, they affirmed the primacy of politics while projecting the symbols of family and domestic life into the public world:

> . . . as society preempted functions that once were monopolized by the family, it looked for ways to model its performance on that of an idealized family, and described what it was doing in sentimental language. The effect was arguably to make society seem like the family writ large, embracing the whole country.

For Forgie, this psychological process shaped "not only the mentality of mid-century leadership but also the structure and style of the long struggle to preserve the Union and hence the origins of the American Civil War." Indeed, Forgie argues that the sentimental flight from symbolic patricide prevented antebellum Americans from achieving cultural and political autonomy, and ultimately unleashed fratricidal impulses which a leader like Lincoln could exploit but not control. Although this approach enables Forgie to illuminate hidden levels of meaning in the debates that led to the Civil War, it also forces him to reduce public

---

1. "Politics and Patricide in Freud's *Interpretation of Dreams*," *American Historical Review*, vol. 78, 1973, pp. 328–347. To be reprinted in Schorske's forthcoming book *Fin-de-siècle Vienna: Politics and Culture* (Knopf, 1979).

issues to an "epiphenomenal status in relation to the primal conflict between father and son."

Forgie's most forceful theme concerns the antebellum Americans' own Revolutionary Dream—their virtual obsession with the "newness" of the experimental Republic, with the heroic sacrifices of the nation's founders, and with the need for renewing "the bonds of political brotherhood" by perpetuating a reverence for the fathers: "begin with the infant in the cradle," Rufus Choate exhorted his countrymen; "let the first lisps be 'Washington.'" Anyone familiar with the documents of the period will recognize the pervasiveness of this filiopiety even among Americans who were in no sense "sons" or "daughters" of the Revolutionary heroes. Forgie convincingly argues that the psychological boundaries defining this "post-heroic generation" were wider than the boundaries of any chronological generation. They included, for example, both Henry Clay, who was born in 1777; and Stephen A. Douglas, who was born in 1813. Both were born "too late to experience the Revolution, but in time to be raised by the generation that had fought it," or at least in time to acquire a deferential sense of "having been born with the Republic" and having inherited a "fortune of liberty" and the "duty to preserve it for those who come after us."

Forgie might well have added that in 1820 the median age of the American population was 16.7 (compared to 28.1 in 1970), and that one-third of the white population was under the age of ten. Since in 1820 barely 12 percent of the white population would have been older than six at the time of the Battle of Yorktown, one can understand the impression made by President Monroe when he appeared in his old Revolutionary War uniform; the shock created by the almost simultaneous deaths of Jefferson and Adams on July 4, 1826; and the desperate sense, in the 1820s, that only a concerted effort at patriotic indoctrination could preserve the immortality of America's immortals.

But preservation is a notably unheroic assignment, especially for youth imbued with classical ideals of winning immortal fame for themselves. Forgie slights this classical heritage—which was as important in the Europe of Wellington, Wilberforce, Palmerston, Mazzini, and Louis Napoleon as in the America of Clay, Lincoln, and Douglas. But he brilliantly elucidates the problem of ambition for America's "post-heroic generation." Unlike their European counterparts, these "good sons" had been taught to venerate a selfless achievement of their fathers that could never again be equaled. While other historians have drawn attention to this "everlasting presence" of the Revolutionary generation, Forgie is the first to show that the rituals of apotheosis carried a double message: "on the one hand, the fathers are gone, and a new generation has succeeded them to power; on the other, the fathers are immortal and they will always rule."

Forgie's thesis challenges an entire tradition of American historiography, derived in part from Tocqueville and Frederick Jackson Turner, which finds the key to early American experience in the freedom from traditional authority, social structure, and prescribed identities along European lines. For according to Forgie, the ubiquitous belief in America's boundlessness, fresh beginnings, and self-made men simply reinforced the illusion that the past was dead and that there was nothing to rebel against. Our motto, *novus ordo seclorum* ("a new order of the ages") has never been far removed, as Forgie might have added, from an image of the deified Washington. Our confident assertion that our history has been free from limits has always revealed "an at least half-acknowledged sense that these limits were still quite strong." As Forgie shrewdly points out, it was precisely this continuing dependence and sense of inferiority that had to be disguised: "The strange calculus of patricidal desires did not require that they remain repressed—only that they be understood and dealt with as anything but what they really were."

Unfortunately, serious difficulties arise with Forgie's second major theme, "sentimental regression"—by which he means more than the persistent exploitation of nostalgic impulses in antebellum society.[2] His use of this concept blurs and even equates two ideas: an emotional withdrawal from the responsibilities of mature public life, a narcissistic regression to the bosom of the mother; and the projection into the public sphere of family models, metaphors, and sentiments. No one can doubt that a blurring of domestic and political imagery was significant characteristic of the Victorian era—and Forgie is superb in his description of the campaign to preserve Mount Vernon as a symbol of the Union and as a "house" to which all Americans should "come home" on curiously Mecca-like pilgrimages.

But this question of sentiment and politics is too complex for the cruder instruments of Freudian surgery, especially when the surgeon becomes so absorbed with his American patient that he forgets that the British were equally inclined to merge politics with domestic sentiment, and to invoke the passage from Saint Mark: "If a kingdom be divided against itself, that kingdom cannot stand. And if a house be divided

---

2. In developing this theme, Forgie acknowledges his indebtedness to Ann Douglas, *The Feminization of American Culture* (Knopf, 1977).

against itself, that house cannot stand.'' It is symptomatic of Forgie's neglect of British sources that he attributes to Charles Eliot Norton a well-known line—about nature as being ''careless of the single life''— from Tennyson's *In Memoriam*.

Forgie bases much of his thesis on the conservatism of the second meaning of ''sentimental regression''—the ''enlargement of the family'' into the sphere of public life. But he never acknowledges the fact that only seasoned conservatives insisted on maintaining a sharp distinction between domestic and public life. In 1840, for example, Heman Humphrey, the neo-Calvinist president of Amherst College, quoted the ''house divided'' passage to support his appeal for a parental united front when dealing with ''little culprits'' who had misinterpreted political rhetoric ''about liberty and equality, and . . . how glorious it is to be 'born free and equal.' '' Like other American conservatives, Humphrey defended the patriarchal family as a divinely instituted model of government ''for all times and all places,'' a realm of unchanging order that should never be confused with the fluctuations of national governments and constitutions.

Forgie approvingly quotes Alexander Sims, who in 1845 protested against the widespread confusion of family government with civil government. The latter, Sims said, had been founded to secure justice within the ''stern reality of actual life'' and should never be contaminated by ''the feelings of the heart'' or ''the sickly dream of childhood recollections'' associated with the family. But it should be stressed that Sims was a Democratic congressman from South Carolina. Although the question at issue was the naturalization of immigrants, Sims was exploiting rhetoric that had been used for many decades against both British and American abolitionists.

That conservatives have often profited from an idealization of the family proves very little. Forgie forgets that Freud's political theory assumes that the primal family contains the psychological seeds for *all* political action—that the ''regressive'' quest to recover an ''oceanic feeling'' of harmony can be a source of creativity, experiment, and revolution as well as a motive for defensive retreat and rigidity. With regard to the actual historical record, Forgie never explains why the leading radicals between the 1830s and 1860s—the various utopian and communitarian socialists, the abolitionists, the pacifists, the left-wing artisans, the militant free blacks—all appealed at times to the ''sentimental'' feelings of the heart, to the values of hearth and home, and to the intimate, fraternal bonds that should somehow replace the ''stern reality of actual life.'' It is hardly convincing to label all Americans as ''conservative'' or to claim that "the arrested development" encouraged by "sentimentalist rhetoric" served "to infantilize Americans generally." If there is something regressive about nostalgia based on maternal, familial, and face-to-face relations, has it ever been absent from a "progressive" movement, or from any religious or secular revitalizing of moral vision?[3]

One can even argue, taking a cue from Schorske, that nothing could be more conservative or regressive than reducing to psychological categories the stern realities of Lincoln's age, particularly black slavery. The cult of sentiment, however distasteful to our own antiromantic prejudices against mixing love with justice, at least enabled Lincoln's generation to express outrage over a form of injustice that had long been protected by culturally imposed boundaries—the "spheres" appropriate for Caesar and Christ, for men and women, for hard-headed statecraft and "sickly" domesticity. Since Forgie bravely joins the perennial debate over the origins of the Civil War, it is not unfair to read his "psychological interpretation" as an imaginative reformulation of the old "revisionist" thesis that America's greatest historical trauma had less to do with objective and "irrepressible" conflicts than with psychological defects and cultural illusions. According to Forgie, these self-destructive impulses finally became personified in Abraham Lincoln, whose ambition required a contemptuous rejection of his own father; who covertly longed to supersede the founding fathers; and who successfully displaced his patricidal aggression onto Stephen Douglas, whom Lincoln stalked and ultimately "killed" as the long-awaited betrayer of the founding fathers' legacy: "To confront and defeat such a villain—to *save* the temple of liberty the fathers had built—would not that deed be rewarded with immortality?"

As befits the conservatism of their craft, historians have been wisely skeptical about attempts to use the terminology of individual psychology for the diagnosis of collective behavior. Yet Forgie's central argument, however marred by exaggeration, cannot be dismissed out of hand. Indeed, Schorske's seeming demolition of Freud's Oedipal concept may in fact provide clues for reformulating Forgie's thesis and for liberating Freud's heroic Complex from its imprisonment in the depths of individ-

3. See especially, Hans W. Loewald, *Psychoanalysis and the History of the Individual* (Yale University Press, 1978). In a footnote, Forgie quotes a psychoanalytic definition of "regression" as: "the *re-emergence* of modes of mental functioning which were characteristic of the psychic activity of the individual during earlier periods of development." In theory, such morally neutral "reemergence" could be creative. In practice, Forgie, like most Freudians, sees regression as a negative, retrograde movement which impedes normal growth; indeed, Forgie sees regression as the source of fratricidal violence in the Civil War. Similar ambiguities arise from Forgie's use of "conservative," which sometimes refers to the morally neutral conservation of any tradition, but which usually implies opposition to change, especially to "the centrifugal and atomistic tendencies of an amorphous and rapidly expanding democracy."

ual psychogenesis. The meaning at this point can only be suggested by three observations. First, Schorske's own analysis is wholly dependent on a "Freudian" mode of thought, which indicates that Freud's discovery dialectically transcends its individual "political" or psychological origins. Second, Schorske never explains why a theory arising from unique circumstances of Jewish life in late nineteenth-century Austria should have had such continuing resonance in modern Western societies. Finally, Schorske's analysis points to a possible multi-lane flow of influence—a complex interchange where political conflict is neutralized and reduced to personal psychological symbolism and where, as Freud argued, familial conflict is projected into the political world. In other words, one can argue that Schorske's "reduction" of Freud's Oedipal theory to particular historical and political circumstances opens the way to a new range of possibilities freeing the Oedipal concept from any rigid or universal dependence on individual psychogenesis.

Since Forgie is remarkably successful in interweaving Lincoln's personal history with the collective experience, needs, and mythology of the antebellum era—and there can be no doubt that Lincoln rebuilt his political career by casting Douglas, his arch rival, in the role of the patricidal son who had broken the fathers' sacred compact prohibiting the unlimited extension of slavery into the territories—two other criticisms are worth considering. First, the "cult of the fathers" was not nearly so monolithic and restrictive as Forgie suggests. The rebels and reformers who idolized the Declaration of Independence also found strategies for superseding the authority of the founding fathers. David Walker, the free black who in 1829 wrote a revolutionary *Appeal to the Colored Citizens of the World,* mocked and challenged Jefferson while appealing to the precedents Jefferson had established: "See your Declaration, Americans!!! Do you understand your own language?" Addressing whites, Walker asked whether their fathers' sufferings had been "one hundredth part as cruel and tyrannical as you have rendered ours under you?" In 1833, the American Anti-Slavery Society's "Declaration of Sentiments" exploited the same theme, insisting that the founding fathers' "grievances, great as they were, were trifling in comparison with the wrongs and sufferings of those for whom we plead." In a succession of declarations, antimasons, abolitionists, pacifists, communitarians, radical artisans, feminists, and anarchists submitted "to a candid world" their own "assemblage of horrors," their own histories of "repeated injuries and usurpations." However imitative, these were radical declarations of *sentiment* that rebuked the fathers for limited moral vision: not only had the fathers condoned Freemasonry, black slavery, alcoholic beverages, and male tyranny; they had sought to win their physical independence, as the Anti-Slavery Society put it, by spilling "human blood like water."

There was a patricidal element, overlooked by Forgie, in the widespread affirmation that a new moral era or "dispensation," had begun, one based on the historical promise of the Revolution but transcending the fathers' dependence on physical violence, much as the New Testament had supposedly transcended the Mosaic law. Thus in their 1833 "Declaration," the abolitionists claimed that their purpose, "for its magnitude, solemnity, and probable results upon the destiny of the world, as far transcends theirs [the founding fathers'], as moral truth does physical force." Lincoln himself, addressing the Springfield Washingtonian Temperance Society on Washington's birthday, 1842, said that while Americans were justly proud of their fathers' political revolution, they should remember that "it breathed forth famine, swam in blood, and rode in fire; and long, long after, the orphan's cry and the widow's wail continued to break the sad silence that ensued." In contrast, Lincoln was confident that the "temperance revolution" would result in "a stronger bondage broken, a viler slavery manumitted, a greater tyrant deposed. . . . By it no orphans starving, no widows weeping." Everyone could hail such a *moral* revolution leading to the happy day when "all appetites [would be] controlled, all poisons subdued, all matter subjected—mind, all conquering mind . . . monarch of the world."[4]

The second criticism is that Forgie remains curiously oblivious to Europe, the original paternal (and maternal) authority from which Americans claimed independence.[5] A number of historians have analyzed the British denunciation of the American rebels as ungrateful "parricides," and the colonists' condemnations of England as an unnatural parent "red with the blood of her children." Winthrop D. Jordan has described rituals of "political eucharist," during the Revolution, in which Americans symbolically killed and ate "the Royal Brute of Great Britain," the title Thomas Paine assigned to George III.[6] Extending this Freudian

---

4. *The Collected Works of Abraham Lincoln,* Roy P. Basler, ed. (Rutgers University Press, 1953), vol. 1, pp. 271–279. Forgie never mentions this immensely revealing speech.

5. For example, Forgie devotes much attention to the "Young America" movement of the 1840s, but never mentions Mazzini's earlier La Giovine Italia and "Young Europe," or the "Young England" movement associated with Disraeli and Lord John Manners. These transatlantic phenomena were obviously related, but Forgie never considers whether the differences or similarities support his thesis that the imagery of "Young America" was "post-Oedipal."

6. Winthrop D. Jordan, "Familial Politics: Thomas Paine and the Killing of the King, 1776," *Journal of American History,* vol. 60, Sept., 1973, pp. 294–308; Edwin G. Burrows and Michael Wallace, "The American Revolution: The Ideology and Psychology of National Liberation," *Perspectives in American History,* vol. 7, 1972, pp. 167–306; David Brion, *Homicide in American Fiction, 1798–1860: A Study in Social Values* (Cornell University Press, 1957), pp. 239–313.

view of "familial politics," one can see the nation's founders not as "fathers" but as the triumphant brothers of a fatherless "primal horde," who ritualistically establish a compact defining the rules—and taboos—governing their future exploitation of a virgin continent.

This version of the patricidal myth would help to explain the recurring fear of degeneration and anarchy; the obsession with the need to make sectional and other compromises that would reaffirm the "fathers' " compact. It would also help to explain the basic political style, which had emerged by the 1820s, of portraying opponents as a self-serving, privileged interest that had secretly consolidated power and had begun to shut off equal access to the rewards of national growth. To a striking degree, Americans when they backed a new coalition of interests sought to make it legitimate by picturing their opponents as heirs of the British and Tories—as an un-American elite whose systematic encroachments demanded, on the model of the Declaration of Independence, a proclamation of grievances proving "a long train of abuses and usurpations."

Forgie is surely wrong in dismissing Anglophobia as derivative, as "the language of sons who obscure conflict with their fathers by displacing it onto their fathers' enemies." From the 1790s to the Civil War, the Great American Enemy was always a renegade brother working either deliberately or unwittingly as an agent of Old World despotism, aiding a conspiracy to wreak retributive vengeance on a fatherless horde who had imperiled all patriarchal authority. As Burton Spivak has recently shown, Jefferson's own attitude

> toward the Federalist party and its patron—toward "anglomen" and England—was a dramatic reenactment of the fears, suspicions, and antagonisms of the American Revolution. . . . The Republican and Federalist were reincarnations of the domestic antagonists of the American Revolution: the loyal patriot and the apostate tory.[7]

Andrew Jackson was always convinced that the most dangerous renegades, whether Indian-lovers, bankers, or abolitionists, were in the service of English conspirators intent on enriching and containing what Jefferson had called America's "empire for liberty," and then fomenting sectional discord leading to disunion and civil war. Similar convictions underpinned the expansionist policy of James K. Polk and other Democratic leaders.

For abolitionists and even for Lincoln and his fellow Republicans, the southern Slave Power was no less alien to America's heritage and mission. Based on a system of labor originally imposed by British mercan-

7. *Jefferson's English Crisis: Commerce, Embargo, and the Republican Revolution* (University of Virginia Press, 1979), pp. 212–225.

tilists, sustained by the British demand for cotton, the Slave Power had spread like an evil fungus, blighting republican institutions in the South and threatening to kill the dream of equality, which Lincoln termed the *"central idea"* of America.[8] If Lincoln's determination to crush the southern "rebellion" was partly patricidal, as the Confederates in their own way claimed, it was also a reenactment and resolution of the "good brothers'" long struggle to purge America of the last remnant of Old World despotism. In other words, Forgie's argument that fratricide displaced patricide, neutralizing a psychological problem with a political and military holocaust, is too simple. It can be argued that, even psychologically, the Civil War was less the result of an unconsummated patricide than the completion of the uncertain regicide begun in 1776, the burial of fears, guilt, and contradictions that had haunted America since its proclamation of independence from the Old World.

8. G. S. Boritt, *Lincoln and the Economics of the American Dream* (Memphis State University Press, 1978), p. 158. In this unfortunately neglected study, Boritt illuminates Lincoln's understanding of "equality" as well as the meaning of the concept in Lincoln's political economy.

10

Some Themes of Counter-Subversion: An Analysis of Anti-Masonic, Anti-Catholic, and Anti-Mormon Literature

During the second quarter of the nineteenth century, when danger of foreign invasion appeared increasingly remote, Americans were told by various respected leaders that Freemasons had infiltrated the government and had seized control of the courts, that Mormons were undermining political and economic freedom in the West, and that Roman Catholic priests, receiving instructions from Rome, had made frightening progress in a plot to subject the nation to popish despotism. This fear of internal subversion was channeled into a number of powerful counter movements which attracted wide public support. The literature produced by these movements evoked images of a great American enemy that closely resembled traditional European stereotypes of conspiracy and subversion. In Europe, however, the idea of subversion implied a threat to the established order—to the king, the church, or the ruling aristocracy—rather than to ideals or a way of life. If free Americans borrowed their images of subversion from frightened kings and uneasy aristocrats, these images had to be shaped and blended to fit American conditions. The movements would have to come from the people, and the themes

From *The Mississippi Valley Historical Review*, Vol. XLVII, No. 2 (September 1960), 205–224. Reprinted by permission.

of counter-subversion would be likely to reflect their fears, prejudices, hopes, and perhaps even unconscious desires.

There are obvious dangers in treating such reactions against imagined subversion as part of a single tendency or spirit of an age.[1] Anti-Catholicism was nourished by ethnic conflict and uneasiness over immigration in the expanding cities of the Northeast; anti-Mormonism arose largely from a contest for economic and political power between western settlers and a group that voluntarily withdrew from society and claimed the undivided allegiance of its members.[2] Anti-Masonry, on the other hand, was directed against a group thoroughly integrated in American society and did not reflect a clear division of economic, religious, or political interests.[3] Moreover, anti-Masonry gained power in the late 1820's and soon spent its energies as it became absorbed in national politics; anti-Catholicism reached its maximum force in national politics a full generation later;[4] anti-Mormonism, though increasing in intensity in the 1850's, became an important national issue only after the Civil War.[5] These movements seem even more widely separated when we note that Freemasonry was traditionally associated with anti-Catholicism and that Mormonism itself absorbed considerable anti-Masonic and anti-Catholic sentiment.[6]

Despite such obvious differences, there were certain similarities in these campaigns against subversion. All three gained widespread support in the northeastern states within the space of a generation; anti-Masonry and anti-Catholicism resulted in the sudden emergence of separate political parties; and in 1856 the new Republican party explicitly condemned the Mormons' most controversial institution. The move-

1. For an alternative to the method followed in this article, see John Higham's perceptive essay, "Another Look at Nativism," *Catholic Historical Review* (Washington), XLIV (July, 1958), 147–58. Higham rejects the ideological approach to nativism and stresses the importance of concrete ethnic tensions, "status rivalries," and face-to-face conflicts in explaining prejudice. Though much can be said for this sociological emphasis, as opposed to a search for irrational myths and stereotypes, the method suggested by Higham can easily lead to a simple "stimulus-response" view of prejudice. Awareness of actual conflicts in status and self-interest should not obscure the social and psychological functions of nativism, nor distract attention from themes that may reflect fundamental tensions within a culture.

2. For a brilliant analysis of Mormon-Gentile conflict, see Thomas F. O'Dea, *The Mormons* (Chicago, 1958).

3. Freemasons were blamed for various unrelated economic and political grievances, but anti-Masonry showed no uniform division according to class, occupation, or political affliction. See Charles McCarthy, "The Anti-Masonic Party," American Historical Association, *Annual Report for the Year 1902*, Vol. I (Washington, 1903), 370–73, 406–408. I am also indebted to Lorman A. Ratner, whose "Antimasonry in New York State: A Study in Pre-Civil War Reform" (M.A. thesis, Cornell University, 1958) substantiates this conclusion.

4. For a detailed analysis of the issues and development of anti-Catholicism, see Ray A. Billington, *The Protestant Crusade, 1800–1860* (New York, 1938).

5. It should be noted, however, that national attention was attracted by the Mountain Meadows Massacre and by Albert Sidney Johnston's punitive expedition to Utah.

6. For anti-Catholic references in *The Book of Mormon*, see I Nephi 13:4–9; II Nephi 6:12, 28:18. Parallels between Masons and the "Gadianton robbers" have been frequently discussed.

ments of counter-subversion differed markedly in historical origin, but as the image of an un-American conspiracy took form in the nativist press, in sensational exposés, in the countless fantasies of treason and mysterious criminality, the lines separating Mason, Catholic, and Mormon became almost indistinguishable.

The similar pattern of Masonic, Catholic, and Mormon subversion was frequently noticed by alarmist writers. The *Anti-Masonic Review* informed its readers in 1829 that whether one looked at Jesuitism or Freemasonry, "the organization, the power, and the secret operation, are the same; except that Freemasonry is much the more secret and complicated of the two."[7] William Hogan, an ex-priest and vitriolic anti-Catholic, compared the menace of Catholicism with that of Mormonism.[8] And many later anti-Mormon writers agreed with Josiah Strong that Brigham Young "out-popes the Roman" and described the Mormon hierarchy as being similar to the Catholic. It was probably not accidental that Samuel F. B. Morse analyzed the Catholic conspiracy in essentially the same terms his father had used in exposing the Society of the Illuminati, supposedly a radical branch of Freemasonry,[9] or that writers of sensational fiction in the 1840's and 1850's depicted an atheistic and unprincipled Catholic Church obviously modeled on Charles Brockden Brown's earlier fictional version of the Illuminati.[10]

If Masons, Catholics, and Mormons bore little resemblance to one another in actuality, as imagined enemies they merged into a nearly common stereotype. Behind specious professions of philanthropy or religious sentiment, nativists[11] discerned a group of unscrupulous leaders plotting to subvert the American social order. Though rank-and-file

7. *Anti-Masonic Review and Magazine* (New York), II (October, 1829), 225–34. It was even claimed that Jesuits had been protected by Frederick the Great because they were mostly Freemasons and shared the same diabolical designs. See *Free Masonry: A Poem, In Three Cantos, Accompanied with Notes, Illustrative of the History, Policy, Principles, &c. of the Masonic Institution; Shewing the Coincidence of Its Spirit and Design with Ancient Jesuitism . . . By a Citizen of Massachusetts* (Leicester, Mass., 1830), 134.

8. William Hogan, *Popery! As It Was and as It Is: Also, Auricular Confession: and Popish Nunneries,* two books in one edition (Hartford, 1855), 32–33.

9. Jedidah Morse, *A Sermon Preached at Charleston, November 29, 1798, on the Anniversary Thanksgiving in Massachusetts* (Boston, 1799); Vernon Stauffer, *The New England Clergy and the Bavarian Illuminati* (New York, 1918), 98–99, 233, 246–48.

10. In Ned Buntline's *The G'hals of New York* (New York, 1850) the Jesuits seem to be connected with all secret conspiracies, and their American leader, Father Kerwin, is probably modeled on Brown's Carwin. George Lippard admired Brown, dedicated a novel to him, and was also fascinated by secret societies and diabolical plots to enslave America. In *New York: Its Upper Ten and Lower Million* (New York, 1853), the Catholic leaders are Illuminati-like atheists who plan revolutions, manipulate public opinion, and stop at no crime in their lust for wealth and power. These amoral supermen were clearly inspired by such characters as Brown's Ormond, as well as by the anti-Catholic writings of Eugène Sue and others.

11. Though the term "nativist" is usually limited to opponents of immigration, it is used here to include anti-Masons and anti-Mormons. This seems justified in view of the fact that these alarmists saw themselves as defenders of native traditions and identified Masonry and Mormonism with forces alien to American life.

members were not individually evil, they were blinded and corrupted by a persuasive ideology that justified treason and gross immorality in the interest of the subversive group. Trapped in the meshes of a machine-like organization, deluded by a false sense of loyalty and moral obligation, these dupes followed orders like professional soldiers and labored unknowingly to abolish free society, to enslave their fellow men, and to overthrow divine principles of law and justice. Should an occasional member free himself from bondage to superstition and fraudulent authority, he could still be disciplined by the threat of death or dreadful tortures. There were no limits to the ambitious designs of leaders equipped with such organizations. According to nativist prophets, they chose to subvert American society because control of America meant control of the world's destiny.

Some of these beliefs were common in earlier and later European interpretations of conspiracy. American images of Masonic, Catholic, and Mormon subversion were no doubt a compound of traditional myths concerning Jacobite agents, scheming Jesuits, and fanatical heretics, and of dark legends involving the Holy Vehm and Rosicrucians. What distinguished the stereotypes of Mason, Catholic, and Mormon was the way in which they were seen to embody those traits that were precise antitheses of American ideals. The subversive group was essentially an inverted image of Jacksonian democracy and the cult of the common man; as such it not only challenged the dominant values but stimulated those suppressed needs and yearnings that are unfulfilled in a mobile, rootless, and individualistic society. It was therefore both frightening and fascinating.

It is well known that expansion and material progress in the Jacksonian era evoked a fervid optimism and that nationalists became intoxicated with visions of America's millennial glory. The simultaneous growth of prosperity and social democracy seemed to prove that Providence would bless a nation that allowed her citizens maximum liberty. When each individual was left free to pursue happiness in his own way, unhampered by the tyranny of custom or special privilege, justice and well-being would inevitably emerge. But if a doctrine of laissez-faire individualism seemed to promise material expansion and prosperity, it also raised disturbing problems. As one early anti-Mormon writer expressed it: What was to prevent liberty and popular sovereignty from sweeping away "the old landmarks of Christendom, and the glorious old common law of our fathers"? How was the individual to preserve a sense of continuity with the past, or identify himself with a given cause or tradition? What, indeed, was to ensure a common loyalty and a fundamental unity among the people?

Such questions acquired a special urgency as economic growth intensified mobility, destroyed old ways of life, and transformed traditional symbols of status and prestige. Though most Americans took pride in their material progress, they also expressed a yearning for reassurance and security, for unity in some cause transcending individual self-interest. This need for meaningful group activity was filled in part by religious revivals, reform movements, and a proliferation of fraternal orders and associations. In politics Americans tended to assume the posture of what Marvin Meyers has termed "venturesome conservatives," mitigating their acquisitive impulses by an appeal for unity against extraneous forces that allegedly threatened a noble heritage of republican ideals. Without abandoning a belief in progress through laissez-faire individualism, the Jacksonians achieved a sense of unity and righteousness by styling themselves as restorers of tradition.[12] Perhaps no theme is so evident in the Jacksonian era as the strained attempt to provide America with a glorious heritage and a noble destiny. With only a loose and often ephemeral attachment to places and institutions, many Americans felt a compelling need to articulate their loyalties, to prove their faith, and to demonstrate their allegiance to certain ideals and institutions. By so doing they acquired a sense of self-identity and personal direction in an otherwise rootless and shifting environment.

But was abstract nationalism sufficient to reassure a nation strained by sectional conflict, divided by an increasing number of sects and associations, and perplexed by the unexpected consequences of rapid growth? One might desire to protect the Republic against her enemies, to preserve the glorious traditions of the Founders, and to help insure continued expansion and prosperity, but first it was necessary to discover an enemy by distinguishing subversion from simple diversity. If Freemasons seemed to predominate in the economic and political life of a given area, was one's joining them shrewd business judgment or a betrayal of republican tradition?[13] Should Maryland citizens heed the warnings of anti-Masonic itinerants, or conclude that anti-Masonry was itself a conspiracy hatched by scheming Yankees?[14] Were Roman Catholics plotting to destroy public schools and a free press, the twin guardians of American democracy, or were they exercising democratic rights

12. For a lucid and provocative discussion of this "restoration theme," see Marvin Meyers, *The Jacksonian Persuasion* (Stanford, 1957), 162–64.

13. Hiram B. Hopkins, *Renunciation of Free Masonry* (Boston, 1830), 4–7.

14. Jacob Lefever of Hagerstown appealed to regional loyalty and urged citizens of Maryland to forget their differences and unite against "foreign influence" from an area notorious for its "tricks and frauds." *Free-Masonry Unmasked: or Minutes of the Trial of a Suit in the Court of Common Pleas of Adams County, Wherein Thaddeus Stevens, Esq. Was Plaintiff, and Jacob Lefever, Defendant* (Gettysburg, 1835), pp. xiii–xiv.

of self-expression and self-protection?[15] Did equality of opportunity and equality before the law mean that Americans should accept the land claims of Mormons or tolerate as jurors men who "swear that they have wrought miracles and supernatural cures"? Or should one agree with the Reverend Finis Ewing that "the 'Mormons' are the common enemies of mankind and ought to be destroyed"?[16]

Few men questioned traditional beliefs in freedom of conscience and the right of association. Yet what was to prevent "all the errors and worn out theories of the Old World, of schisms in the early Church, the monkish age and the rationalistic period," from flourishing in such salubrious air?[17] Nativists often praised the work of benevolent societies, but they were disturbed by the thought that monstrous conspiracies might also "show kindness and patriotism, when it is necessary for their better concealment; and oftentimes do much good for the sole purpose of getting a better opportunity to do evil."[18] When confronted by so many sects and associations, how was the patriot to distinguish the loyal from the disloyal? It was clear that mere disagreement over theology or economic policy was invalid as a test, since honest men disputed over the significance of baptism or the wisdom of protective tariffs. But neither could one rely on expression of allegiance to common democratic principles, since subversives would cunningly profess to believe in freedom and toleration of dissent as long as they remained a powerless minority.

As nativists studied this troubling question, they discovered that most groups and denominations claimed only a partial loyalty from their members, freely subordinating themselves to the higher and more abstract demands of the Constitution, Christianity, and American public opinion. Moreover, they openly exposed their objects and activities to public scrutiny and exercised little discrimination in enlisting members. Some groups, however, dominated a larger portion of their members' lives, demanded unlimited allegiance as a condition of membership, and excluded certain activities from the gaze of a curious public.

Of all governments, said Richard Rush, ours was the one with most to fear from secret societies, since popular sovereignty by its very nature required perfect freedom of public inquiry and judgment.[19] In a virtuous

15. *The Cloven Foot: or Popery Aiming at Political Supremacy in the United States, by the Rector of Oldenwold* (New York, 1855), 170–79.

16. William Mulder and A. Russell Mortensen (eds.), *Among the Mormons: Historic Accounts by Contemporary Observers* (New York, 1958), 76–79. The quotation is from the minutes of an anti-Mormon meeting in Jackson County, Missouri, July 20, 1833.

17. John H. Beadle, *Life in Utah: or, the Mysteries and Crimes of Mormonism* (Philadelphia, [1872]), 5.

18. *Anti-Masònic Review*, I (December, 1828), 3–4.

19. Letter of May 4, 1831, printed in *The Anti-Masonic Almanac, for the Year 1832*, ed. by Edward Giddins (Utica, 1831), 29–30.

republic why should anyone fear publicity or desire to conceal activities, unless those activities were somehow contrary to the public interest? When no one could be quite sure what the public interest was, and when no one could take for granted a secure and well-defined place in the social order, it was most difficult to acknowledge legitimate spheres of privacy. Most Americans of the Jacksonian era appeared willing to tolerate diversity and even eccentricity, but when they saw themselves excluded and even barred from witnessing certain proceedings, they imagined a "mystic power" conspiring to enslave them.

Readers might be amused by the first exposure of Masonic ritual, since they learned that pompous and dignified citizens, who had once impressed non-Masons with allusions to high degrees and elaborate ceremonies, had in actuality been forced to stand blindfolded and clad in ridiculous garb, with a long rope noosed around their necks. But genuine anti-Masons were not content with simple ridicule. Since intelligent and distinguished men had been members of the fraternity, "it must have in its interior something more than the usual revelations of its mysteries declare." [20] Surely leading citizens would not meet at night and undergo degrading and humiliating initiations just for the sake of novelty. The alleged murder of William Morgan raised an astonishing public furor because it supposedly revealed the inner secret of Freemasonry. Perverted by a false ideology, Masons had renounced all obligations to the general public, to the laws of the land, and even to the command of God. Hence they threatened not a particular party's program or a denomination's creed, but stood opposed to all justice, democracy, and religion. [21]

The distinguishing mark of Masonic, Catholic, and Mormon conspiracies was a secrecy that cloaked the members' unconditional loyalty to an autonomous body. Since the organizations had corrupted the private moral judgment of their members, Americans could not rely on the ordinary forces of progress to spread truth and enlightenment among their ranks. Yet the affairs of such organizations were not outside the jurisdiction of democratic government, for no body politic could be asked to tolerate a power that was designed to destroy it. [22] Once the true nature of subversive groups was thoroughly understood, the alternatives were as clear as life and death. How could democracy and Catholicism

20. *Anti-Masonic Review*, I (December, 1828), 6–7; Lebbeus Armstrong, *Masonry Proved to Be a Work of Darkness, Repugnant to the Christian Religion; and Inimical to a Republican Government* (New York, 1830), 16.

21. *The Anti-Masonic Almanack, for the Year 1828: Calculated for the Horizon of Rochester, N.Y. by Edward Giddins* (Rochester, 1827), entry for November and December, 1828; Armstrong, *Masonry*, 14.

22. Hogan, *Popery*, 32–33.

coexist when, as Edward Beecher warned, "The systems are diametrically opposed: one must and will exterminate the other"?[23] Because Freemasons had so deeply penetrated state and national governments, only drastic remedies could restore the nation to its democratic purity.[24] And later, Americans faced an "irrepressible conflict" with Mormonism, for it was said that either free institutions or Mormon despotism must ultimately annihilate the other.[25]

We may well ask why nativists magnified the division between unpopular minorities and the American public, so that Masons, Catholics, and Mormons seemed so menacing that they could not be accorded the usual rights and privileges of a free society. Obviously the literature of counter-subversion reflected concrete rivalries and conflicts of interest between competing groups but it is important to note that the subversive bore no racial or ethnic stigma and was not even accused of inherent depravity.[26] Since group membership was a matter of intellectual and emotional loyalty, no *physical* barrier prevented a Mason, Catholic, or Mormon from apostatizing and joining the dominant in-group, providing always that he escaped assassination from his previous masters. This suggests that counter-subversion was more than a rationale for group rivalry and was related to the general problem of ideological unity and diversity in a free society. When a "system of delusion" insulated members of a group from the unifying and disciplining force of public opinion, there was no authority to command an allegiance to common principles. This was why oaths of loyalty assumed great importance for nativists. Though the ex-Catholic William Hogan stated repeatedly that Jesuit spies respected no oaths except those to the Church, he inconsistently told Masons and Odd Fellows that they could prevent infiltration by requiring new members to swear they were not Catholics.[27] It was

23. Edward Beecher, *The Papal Conspiracy Exposed, and Protestantism Defended, in the Light of Reason, History, and Scripture* (Boston, 1855), 29.

24. *Anti-Masonic Review*, I (February, 1829), 71.

25. Mulder and Mortensen (eds.), *Among the Mormons*, 407; Jennie Anderson Froiseth (ed.), *The Women of Mormonism: or, the Story of Polygamy as Told by the Victims Themselves* (Detroit, 1881–1882), 367–68.

26. It is true that anti-Catholics sometimes stressed the inferiority of lower-class immigrants and that anti-Mormons occasionally claimed that Mormon converts were made among the most degraded and ignorant classes of Europe. This theme increased in importance toward the end of the century, but it seldom implied that Catholics and Mormons were physically incapable of being liberated and joined to the dominant group. Racism was not an original or an essential part of the counter-subversive's ideology. Even when Mormons were attacked for coarseness, credulity, and vulgarity, these traits were usually thought to be the product of their beliefs and institutions. See Mrs. B. G. Ferris, "Life among the Mormons," *Putnam's Monthly Magazine* (New York), VI (August, October, 1855), 144, 376–77.

27. Hogan, *Popery*, 35.

precisely the absence of distinguishing outward traits that made the enemy so dangerous, and true loyalty so difficult to prove.

When the images of different enemies conform to a similar pattern, it is highly probable that this pattern reflects important tensions within a given culture. The themes of nativist literature suggest that its authors simplified problems of personal insecurity and bewildering social change by trying to unite Americans of diverse political, religious, and economic interests against a common enemy. Just as revivalists sought to stimulate Christian fellowship by awakening men to the horrors of sin, so nativists used apocalyptic images to ignite human passions, destroy selfish indifference, and join patriots in a cohesive brotherhood. Such themes were only faintly secularized. When God saw his "lov'd Columbia" imperiled by the hideous monster of Freemasonry, He realized that only a martyr's blood could rouse the hearts of the people and save them from bondage to the Prince of Darkness. By having God will Morgan's death, this anti-Mason showed he was more concerned with national virtue and unity than with Freemasonry, which was only a providential instrument for testing republican strength.[28]

Similarly, for the anti-Catholic "this brilliant new world" was once "young and beautiful; it abounded in all the luxuries of nature; it promised all that was desirable to man." But the Roman Church, seeing "these irresistible temptations, thirsting with avarice and yearning for the reestablishment of her falling greatness, soon commenced pouring in among its unsuspecting people hoardes of Jesuits and other friars." If Americans were to continue their narrow pursuit of self-interest, oblivious to the "Popish colleges, and nunneries, and monastic institutions," indifferent to manifold signs of corruption and decay, how could the nation expect "that the moral breezes of heaven should breathe upon her, and restore to her again that strong and healthy constitution, which her ancestors have left to her sons"?[29] The theme of an Adamic fall from paradise was horrifying, but it was used to inspire determined action and thus unity. If Methodists were "criminally indifferent" to the Mormon question, and if "avaricious merchants, soulless corporations, and a subsidized press" ignored Mormon iniquities, there was all the more reason that the *"will of the people* must prevail."[30]

Without explicitly rejecting the philosophy of laissez-faire individualism, with its toleration of dissent and innovation, nativist literature

28. *Free Masonry: A Poem,* 55–58.
29. Hogan, *Popery,* 7–8; *Auricular Confession,* 264–65.
30. Froiseth (ed.), *Women of Mormonism,* 285–87, 291–92.

conveyed a sense of common dedication to a noble cause and sacred tradition. Though the nation had begun with the blessings of God and with the noblest institutions known to man, the people had somehow become selfish and complacent, divided by petty disputes, and insensitive to signs of danger. In his sermons attacking such self-interest, such indifference to public concerns, and such a lack of devotion to common ideals and sentiments, the nativist revealed the true source of his anguish. Indeed, he seemed at times to recognize an almost beneficient side to subversive organizations, since they joined the nation in a glorious crusade and thus kept it from moral and social disintegration.

The exposure of subversion was a means of promoting unity, but it also served to clarify national values and provide the individual ego with a sense of high moral sanction and imputed righteousness. Nativists identified themselves repeatedly with a strangely incoherent tradition in which images of Pilgrims, Minute Men, Founding Fathers, and true Christians appeared in a confusing montage. Opposed to this heritage of stability and perfect integrity, to this society founded on the highest principles of divine and natural law, were organizations formed by the grossest frauds and impostures, and based on the wickedest impulses of human nature. Bitterly refuting Masonic claims to ancient tradition and Christian sanction, anti-Masons charged that the Order was of recent origin, that it was shaped by Jews, Jesuits, and French atheists as an engine for spreading infidelity, and that it was employed by kings and aristocrats to undermine republican institutions.[31] If the illustrious Franklin and Washington had been duped by Masonry, this only proved how treacherous was its appeal and how subtly persuasive were its pretensions.[32] Though the Catholic Church had an undeniable claim to tradition, nativists argued that it had originated in stupendous frauds and forgeries "in comparison with which the forgeries of Mormonism are completely thrown into the shade."[33] Yet anti-Mormons saw an even more sinister conspiracy based on the "shrewd cunning" of Joseph Smith,

31. *Free Masonry: A Poem*, 29–37; *Anti-Masonic Review*, I (June, 1829), 203–207. The charge was often repeated that higher degrees of Freemasonry were created by the "school of Voltaire" and introduced to America by Jewish immigrants. Masonry was also seen as an "auxiliary to British foreign policy."

32. This question was most troubling to anti-Masons. Though some tried to side-step the issue by quoting Washington against "self-created societies," as if he had been referring to the Masons, others flatly declared that Washington had been hoodwinked, just as distinguished jurists had once been deluded by a belief in witchcraft. Of course Washington had been unaware of Masonic iniquities, but he had lent his name to the cause and had thus served as a decoy for the ensnarement of others. See *Free Masonry: A Poem*, 38; *Anti-Masonic Review*, I (January, 1829), 49, 54; *The Anti-Masonic Almanac, for the Year of the Christian Era 1830* (Rochester, 1829), 32.

33. Beecher, *Papal Conspiracy Exposed*, 391.

who convinced gullible souls that he conversed with angels and received direct revelations from the Lord.[34]

By emphasizing the fraudulent character of their opponents' claims, nativists sought to establish the legitimacy and just authority of American institutions. Masonic rituals, Roman Catholic sacraments, and Mormon revelations were preposterous hoaxes used to delude naïve or superstitious minds; but public schools, a free press, and jury trials were eternally valid prerequisites for a free and virtuous society.

Moreover, the finest values of an enlightened nation stood out in bold relief when contrasted with the corrupting tendencies of subversive groups. Perversion of the sexual instinct seemed inevitably to accompany religious error.[35] Deprived of the tender affections of normal married love, shut off from the elevating sentiments of fatherhood, Catholic priests looked on women only as insensitive objects for the gratification of their frustrated desires.[36] In similar fashion polygamy struck at the heart of a morality based on the inspiring influence of woman's affections: "It renders man coarse, tyrannical, brutal, and heartless. It deals death to all sentiments of true manhood. It enslaves and ruins woman. It crucifies every God-given feeling of her nature."[37] Some anti-Mormons concluded that plural marriage could only have been established among foreigners who had never learned to respect women. But the more common explanation was that the false ideology of Mormonism had deadened the moral sense and liberated man's wild sexual impulse from the normal restraints of civilization. Such degradation of women and corruption of man served to highlight the importance of democratic marriage, a respect for women, and careful cultivation of the finer sensibilities.[38]

But if nativist literature was a medium for articulating common values and exhorting individuals to transcend self-interest and join in a dedicated union against evil, it also performed a more subtle function. Why, we may ask, did nativist literature dwell so persistently on themes of brutal sadism and sexual immorality? Why did its authors describe sin

---

34. Beadle, *Life in Utah*, 30–34.

35. *Ibid.*, 332–33. According to Beadle, religious error and sexual perversion were related "because the same constitution of mind and temperament which gives rise to one, powerfully predisposes toward the other."

36. *Cloven Foot*, 294–95.

37. Froiseth (ed.), *Women of Mormonism*, 113.

38. Though Horace Greeley was moderate in his judgment of Mormonism, he wrote: "I joyfully trust that the genius of the Nineteenth Century tends to a solution of the problem of Woman's sphere and destiny radically different from this." Quoted in Mulder and Mortensen (eds.), *Among the Mormons*, 328.

in such minute details, endowing even the worst offenses of their enemies with a certain fascinating appeal?

Freemasons, it was said, could commit any crime and indulge any
passion when "upon the square," and Catholics and Mormons were
even less inhibited by internal moral restraints. Nativists expressed horror over this freedom from conscience and conventional morality, but
they could not conceal a throbbing note of envy. What was it like to be
a member of a cohesive brotherhood that casually abrogated the laws of
God and man, enforcing unity and obedience with dark and mysterious
powers? As nativists speculated on this question, they projected their
own fears and desires into a fantasy of licentious orgies and fearful
punishments.

Such a projection of forbidden desires can be seen in the exaggeration
of the stereotyped enemy's powers, which made him appear at times as
a virtual superman. Catholics and Mormon leaders, never hindered by
conscience or respect for traditional morality, were curiously superior to
ordinary Americans in cunning, in exercising power over others, and
especially in captivating gullible women.[39] It was an ancient theme of
anti-Catholic literature that friars and priests were somehow more potent
and sexually attractive than married laymen, and were thus astonish-
ingly successful at seducing supposedly virtuous wives.[40] Americans were
cautioned repeatedly that no priest recognized Protestant marriages as
valid, and might consider any wife legitimate prey.[41] Furthermore, priests
had access to the pornographic teachings of Dens and Liguori, sinister
names that aroused the curiosity of anti-Catholics, and hence learned
subtle techniques of seduction perfected over the centuries. Speaking
with the authority of an ex-priest, William Hogan described the shocking result: "I have seen husbands unsuspiciously and hospitably enter-
taining the very priest who seduced their wives in the confessional, and
was the parent of some of the children who sat at the same table with
them, each of the wives unconscious of the other's guilt, and the hus-

39. It should be noted the Freemasons were rarely accused of sexual crimes, owing perhaps to
their greater degree of integration within American society, and to their conformity to the dominant
pattern of monogamy. They were sometimes attacked, however, for excluding women from their
Order, and for swearing not to violate the chastity of wives, sisters, and daughters of fellow
Masons. Why, anti-Masons asked, was such an oath not extended to include *all* women? David
Bernard, *Light on Masonry: A Collection of all the Most Important Documents on the Subject*
(Utica, 1829), 62 n.

40. Anthony Gavin, *A Master-Key to Popery, Giving a Full Account of All the Customs of the
Priests and Friars, and the Rites and Ceremonies of Popish Religion* (n.p., 1812), 70–72. Such
traditional works of European anti-Catholicism were frequently reprinted and imitated in America.

41. *Cloven Foot*, 224. The Mormons were also alleged to regard the wives of infidels "lawful
prey to any believer who can win them." Beadle, *Life in Utah*, 233.

bands of both, not even suspecting them."[42] Such blatant immorality was horrifying, but everyone was apparently happy in this domestic scene, and we may suspect that the image was not entirely repugnant to husbands who, despite their respect for the Lord's Commandments, occasionally coveted their neighbors' wives.

The literature of counter-subversion could also embody the somewhat different projective fantasies of women. Ann Eliza Young dramatized her seduction by the Prophet Brigham, whose almost superhuman powers enchanted her and paralyzed her will. Though she submitted finally only because her parents were in danger of being ruined by the Church, she clearly indicated that it was an exciting privilege to be pursued by a Great Man.[43] When Anti-Mormons claimed that Joseph Smith and other prominent Saints knew the mysteries of Animal Magnetism, or were endowed with the highest degree of "amativeness" in their phrenological makeup, this did not detract from their covert appeal.[44] In a ridiculous fantasy written by Maria Ward, such alluring qualities were extended even to Mormon women. Many bold-hearted girls could doubtless identify themselves with Anna Bradish, a fearless Amazon of a creature, who rode like a man, killed without compunction, and had no pity for weak women who failed to look out for themselves. Tall, elegant, and "intellectual," Anna was attractive enough to arouse the insatiable desires of Brigham Young, though she ultimately rejected him and renounced Mormonism.[45]

While nativists affirmed their faith in Protestant monogamy, they obviously took pleasure in imagining the variety of sexual experience supposedly available to their enemies. By picturing themselves exposed to similar temptations, they assumed they could know how priests and Mormons actually sinned.[46] Imagine, said innumerable anti-Catholic writers, a beautiful young woman kneeling before an ardent young priest in a deserted room. As she confesses, he leans over, looking into her eyes, until their heads are nearly touching. Day after day she reveals to him her innermost secrets, secrets she would not think of unveiling to her parents, her dearest friends, or even her suitor. By skillful question-

42. Hogan, *Auricular Confession,* 289.

43. Ann Eliza Young, *Wife No. 19: or, the Story of a Life in Bondage, Being a Complete Exposé of Mormonism* (Hartford, 1875), 433, 440–41, 453.

44. Maria Ward, *Female Life among the Mormons: A Narrative of Many Years' Personal Experience, By the Wife of a Mormon Elder, Recently Returned from Utah* (New York, 1857), 24; Beadle, *Life in Utah,* 339.

45. Ward, *Female Life among the Mormons,* 68, 106, 374.

46. The Mormons, for instance, were imagined to engage in the most licentious practices in the Endowment House ceremonies. See Nelson W. Green (ed.), *Fifteen Years among the Mormons: Being the Narrative of Mrs. Mary Ettie V. Smith* (New York, 1857), 44–51.

ing the priest fills her mind with immodest and even sensual ideas, "until this wretch has worked up her passions to a tension almost snapping, and then becomes his easy prey." How could any man resist such provocative temptations, and how could any girl's virtue withstand such a test?[47]

We should recall that this literature was written in a period of increasing anxiety and uncertainty over sexual values and the proper role of woman. As ministers and journalists pointed with alarm at the spread of prostitution, the incidence of divorce, and the lax and hypocritical morality of the growing cities, a discussion of licentious subversives offered a convenient means for the projection of guilt as well as desire. The sins of individuals, or of the nation as a whole, could be pushed off upon the shoulders of the enemy and there punished in righteous anger.[48]

Specific instances of such projection are not difficult to find. John C. Bennett, whom the Mormons expelled from the Church as a result of his flagrant sexual immorality, invented the fantasy of "The Mormon Seraglio" which persisted in later anti-Mormon writings. According to Bennett, the Mormons maintained secret orders of beautiful prostitutes who were mostly reserved for various officials of the Church. He claimed, moreover, that any wife refusing to accept polygamy might be forced to join the lowest order and thus become available to any Mormon who desired her.[49]

Another example of projection can be seen in the letters of a young lieutenant who stopped in Utah in 1854 on his way to California. Convinced that Mormon women could be easily seduced, the lieutenant wrote frankly of his amorous adventures with a married woman. "Everyone has got one," he wrote with obvious pride, "except the Colonel and Major. The Doctor has got three—mother and two daughters. The mother cooks for him and the daughters sleep with him." But though he described Utah as "a great country," the lieutenant waxes indignant over polygamy, which he condemned as self-righteously as any anti-Mormon minister: "To see one man openly parading half a dozen or more women to church . . . is the devil according to my ideas of morality virtue and decency."[50]

If the consciences of many Americans were troubled by the growth of red light districts in major cities, they could divert their attention to

---

47. Hogan, *Auricular Confession*, 254–55; *Cloven Foot*, 301–304.
48. This point is ably discussed by Kimball Young, *Isn't One Wife Enough?* (New York, 1954), 26–27.
49. *Ibid.*, 311.
50. Quoted in Mulder and Mortensen (eds.), *Among the Mormons*, 274–78.

the "legalized brothels" called nunneries, for which no one was responsible but lecherous Catholic priests. If others were disturbed by the moral implications of divorce, they could point in horror at the Mormon elder who took his quota of wives all at once. The literature of counter-subversion could thus serve the double purpose of vicariously fulfilling repressed desires, and of releasing the tension and guilt arising from rapid social change and conflicting values.

Though the enemy's sexual freedom might at first seem enticing, it was always made repugnant in the end by associations with perversion or brutal cruelty. Both Catholics and Mormons were accused of practicing nearly every form of incest.[51] The persistent emphasis on this theme might indicate deep-rooted feelings of fear and guilt, but it also helped demonstrate, on a more objective level, the loathsome consequences of unrestrained lust. Sheer brutality and a delight in human suffering were supposed to be the even more horrible results of sexual depravity. Masons disemboweled or slit the throats of their victims; Catholics cut unborn infants from their mothers' wombs and threw them to the dogs before their parents' eyes; Mormons raped and lashed recalcitrant women, or seared their mouths with red-hot irons.[52] This obsession with details of sadism, which reached pathological proportions in much of the literature, showed a furious determination to purge the enemy of every admirable quality. The imagined enemy might serve at first as an outlet for forbidden desires, but nativist authors escaped from guilt by finally making him an agent of unmitigated aggression. In such a role the subversive seemed to deserve both righteous anger and the most terrible punishments.

The nativist escape from guilt was more clearly revealed in the themes of confession and conversion. For most American Protestants the crucial step in anyone's life was a profession of true faith resulting from a genuine religious experience. Only when a man became conscious of his inner guilt, when he struggled against the temptations of Satan, could he prepare his soul for the infusion of the regenerative spirit. Those most deeply involved in sin often made the most dramatic conversions. It is not surprising that conversion to nativism followed the same pattern, since nativists sought unity and moral certainty in the regenerative spirit of nationalism. Men who had been associated in some way with

---

51. George Bourne, *Lorette: The History of Louise, Daughter of a Canadian Nun, Exhibiting the Interior of Female Convents* (New York, 1834), 176–77; Hogan, *Auricular Confession*, 271; Frances Stenhouse, *A Lady's Life among the Mormons: A Record of Personal Experiences as One of the Wives of a Mormon Elder* (New York, 1872), 77.

52. *Anti-Masonic Review*, I (December, 1828), 24 ff.; *Cloven Foot*, 325–42, 357–58; Froiseth (ed.), *Women of Mormonism*, 317–18; Ward, *Female Life among the Mormons*, 428–29.

un-American conspiracies were not only capable of spectacular confessions of guilt, but were best equipped to expose the insidious work of supposedly harmless organizations. Even those who lacked such an exciting history of corruption usually made some confession of guilt, though it might involve only a previous indifference to subversive groups. Like ardent Christians, nativists searched in their own experiences for the meanings of sin, delusion, awakening to truth, and liberation from spiritual bondage. These personal confessions proved that one had recognized and conquered evil, and also served as ritual cleansings preparatory to full acceptance in a group of dedicated patriots.

Anti-Masons were perhaps the ones most given to confessions of guilt and most alert to subtle distinctions of loyalty and disloyalty. Many leaders of this movement, expressing guilt over their own "shameful experience and knowledge" of Masonry, felt a compelling obligation to exhort their former associates to "come out, and be separate from masonic abominations."[53] Even when an anti-Mason could say with John Quincy Adams that "I am not, never was, and never shall be a Freemason," he would often admit that he had once admired the Order, or had even considered applying for admission.[54]

Since a willingness to sacrifice oneself was an unmistakable sign of loyalty and virtue, ex-Masons gloried in exaggerating the dangers they faced and the harm that their revelations supposedly inflicted on the enemy. In contrast to hardened Freemasons, who refused to answer questions in court concerning their fraternal associations, the seceders claimed to reveal the inmost secrets of the Order, and by so doing to risk property, reputation, and life.[55] Once the ex-Mason had dared to speak the truth, his character would surely be maligned, his motives impugned, and his life threatened. But, he declared, even if he shared the fate of the illustrious Morgan, he would die knowing that he had done his duty.

Such self-dramatization reached extravagant heights in the ranting confessions of many apostate Catholics and Mormons. Maria Monk and her various imitators told of shocking encounters with sin in its most sensational forms, of bondage to vice and superstition, and of melodramatic escapes from popish despotism. A host of "ex-Mormon wives" described their gradual recognition of Mormon frauds and iniquities, the anguish and misery of plural marriage, and their breath-taking flights over deserts or mountains. The female apostate was especially vulnera-

53. Armstrong, *Masonry*, 22.
54. *Free Masonry: A Poem*, p. iv.
55. *Ibid.*, pp. iii, 51; Hopkins, *Renunciation of Free Masonry*, 5, 9–11; *Anti-Masonic Almanac*, 1830, pp. 28–29; Bernard, *Light on Masonry*, p. iii.

ble to vengeful retaliation, since she could easily be kidnapped by crafty priests and nuns, or dreadfully punished by Brigham Young's Destroying Angels.[56] At the very least, her reputation could be smirched by foul lies and insinuations. But her willingness to risk honor and life for the sake of her country and for the dignity of all womankind was eloquent proof of her redemption. What man could be assured of so noble a role?

The apostate's pose sometimes assumed paranoid dimensions. William Hogan warned that only the former priest could properly gauge the Catholic threat to American liberties and saw himself as providentially appointed to save his Protestant countrymen. "For twenty years," he wrote, "I have warned them of approaching danger, but their politicians were deaf, and their Protestant theologians remained religiously coiled up in fancied security, overrating their own powers and undervaluing that of Papists." Pursued by vengeful Jesuits, denounced and calumniated for alleged crimes, Hogan pictured himself single-handedly defending American freedom: "No one, before me, dared to encounter their scurrilous abuse. I resolved to silence them; and I have done so. The very mention of my name is a terror to them now." After surviving the worst of Catholic persecution, Hogan claimed to have at last aroused his countrymen and to have reduced the hierarchy to abject terror.[57]

As the nativist searched for participation in a noble cause, for unity in a group sanctioned by tradition and authority, he professed a belief in democracy and equal rights. Yet in his very zeal for freedom he curiously assumed many of the characteristics of the imagined enemy. By condemning the subversive's fanatical allegiance to an ideology, he affirmed a similarly uncritical acceptance of a different ideology; by attacking the subversive's intolerance of dissent, he worked to eliminate dissent and diversity of opinion; by censuring the subversive for alleged licentiousness, he engaged in sensual fantasies; by criticizing the subversive's loyalty to an organization, he sought to prove his unconditional loyalty to the established order. The nativist moved even farther in the direction of his enemies when he formed tightly-knit societies and parties which were often secret and which subordinated the individual to the single purpose of the group. Though the nativists generally agreed that the worst evil of subversives was their subordination of means to ends, they themselves recommended the most radical means to purge the nation of troublesome groups and to enforce unquestioned loyalty to the state.

56. Stenhouse, *Lady's Life among the Mormons*, 142–43.
57. Hogan, *Auricular Confession*, 226–29, 233, 296–97.

In his image of an evil group conspiring against the nation's welfare, and in his vision of a glorious millennium that was to dawn after the enemy's defeat, the nativist found satisfaction for many desires. His own interests became legitimate and dignified by fusion with the national interest, and various opponents became loosely associated with the un-American conspiracy. Thus Freemasonry in New York State was linked in the nativist mind with economic and political interests that were thought to discriminate against certain groups and regions; southerners imagined a union of abolitionists and Catholics to promote unrest and rebellion among slaves; gentile businessmen in Utah merged anti-Mormonism with plans for exploiting mines and lands.

Then too the nativist could style himself as a restorer of the past, as a defender of a stable order against disturbing changes, and at the same time proclaim his faith in future progress. By focusing his attention on the imaginary threat of a secret conspiracy, he found an outlet for many irrational impulses, yet professed his loyalty to the ideals of equal rights and government by law. He paid lip service to the doctrine of laissez-faire individualism, but preached selfless dedication to a transcendent cause. The imposing threat of subversion justified a group loyalty and subordination of the individual that would otherwise have been unacceptable. In a rootless environment shaken by bewildering social change the nativist found unity and meaning by conspiring against imaginary conspiracies.

11

Some Ideological Functions of
Prejudice in Ante-Bellum America

Historians are generally tolerant and liberal-minded people They naturally deplore outbreaks of hostility toward minority groups. And it is
not my purpose to suggest that groups founded on hatred and prejudice
were morally better than they have usually been pictured. No one who
has read accounts of the burning of Catholic churches and convents, of
the massacre of Mormon women and children, of the persecutions of
Negroes and abolitionists, of the cries for blood vengeance against
Southern slaveholders, can fail to be appalled by the power of blind
prejudice and explosive aggression in America's Middle Period. In spite
of rhetoric deifying a rationally balanced Constitution, in spite of a façade of ordered symmetry in the houses and public buildings of the
Greek Revival, ante-bellum America was not ruled by a mild and tolerant spirit of reason.

We should not be content, however, with mere righteous indignation
or with the dismissal of hate groups as symptoms of social disease. Nor
can we assume that violent intolerance had the same meaning in the
period from 1825 to 1860 that it has today. There are two general approaches available to a historian interested in movements against such
groups as Masons, Catholics and Mormons. The first would be to examine the immediate sources of group conflict, such as ethnic rivalry,
economic competition and institutional disharmony. This approach would

From *American Quarterly*, Vol. 15 (Summer 1963), 115–25. Copyright © 1963, American Studies
Association. Reprinted by permission.

bring out important differences in the various movements and would doubtless suggest that as long as people are animated by strong hopes and allegiances, they will attack any group that seems to endanger their security or to disrupt their expectations. In the unpredictable and socially fluid environment of the Burned-over District, for example, the influence and solidarity of Freemasons must have seemed a genuine threat to equality of opportunity. In Illinois, Joseph Smith's attempt to establish a political Kingdom of God, his creation of a Mormon Legion and a secret, oligarchic Council of Fifty, naturally aroused hostility. The sudden influx of hundreds of thousands of Catholic immigrants presented a mounting challenge to the religious and political power structure of the Northeast. When we look closely at such historical situations, and at what the average man perceived and believed, we can find sufficient cause for fear and conflict.

But even the most careful analysis of concrete social and economic situations would not account for four distinctive characteristics of these movements of counter-subversion. Firstly, their literature reflected an anxiety that was greatly disproportionate to any actual conflict of interest. Secondly, there was a cultural continuity between such movements and the traditional European response to radical religious sects and secular brotherhoods; anti-Catholicism, of course, was as old as the Reformation, and its principal arguments and accusations changed very little over the centuries. Thirdly, Protestant ministers played a key role in these crusades against alleged subversion, which were related by ideology and joint membership to a number of reform movements, including those for temperance, improved education and protection of the Sabbath. Fourthly, images of the subversive group, while often borrowed from the ruling classes of Europe, were adapted to fit the fears and half-conscious yearnings of the American people. I have attempted elsewhere to show that the movements against Masons, Mormons and Catholics shared a common stereotype of the Great American Enemy, whose traits formed an inverted image of the ideals of popular democracy and the cult of the common man.[1] It would appear that the movements of counter-subversion of the Middle Period were a social phenomenon quite different from the more familiar pattern of prejudice as a mask for privilege, as an instrument for the exploitation of a powerless and downtrodden people.

We can perhaps gain a better understanding of the seeming paradox

---

1. "Some Themes of Counter-Subversion: An Analysis of Anti-Masonic, Anti-Catholic, and Anti-Mormon Literature," *The Mississippi Valley Historical Review*, XLVII (September 1960), 205–24.

of prejudice accompanying a desire for greater liberty and equality if we place these movements within the larger context of American ideology and culture. If we ask what values were thought to be threatened by supposedly subversive groups, and what parts of American society were thought to be vulnerable and insecure, we may find that prejudice provided a basis for defining and working out certain fundamental problems. This would not imply that prejudice was a good thing or that it contributed to the mental health of the nation, any more than neurotic or psychotic symptoms contribute to the mental health of an individual. But as is well known, an understanding of the particular functions of a neurotic symptom may lead to a better knowledge of the tensions with which an individual struggles.

The literature of these movements reveals a preoccupation with the problem of intellectual and moral diversity in a free society; with the role of organization in an individualistic society; and with the relation of tradition and change to America's destiny. Each problem, as we shall see, involves a dualism in thought that has often produced tension and anxiety. It seems probable, though here we must rely on inference, that such tension and anxiety were at least temporarily resolved by definition of a subversive group and by a call for action limiting its power. I do not mean to imply that this explains the motives of nativists—and for convenience I shall use that term for all Americans who thought of themselves as defending native traditions against essentially alien forces. I suggest only that certain ideological tensions magnified and gave added meaning to concrete conflicts with minority groups.

Let us look first at the question of intellectual and moral diversity in a free society. It was a cardinal tenet of Protestantism that if men were free to read the Bible on their own, with minimum guidance from clerical authority, they would have no excuse for not recognizing the Revealed Word and accepting their obligations to God and their fellow men. It was also a traditional tenet of secular liberalism that if men were free to read, think and speak as they chose, truth would ultimately prevail over error and superstition. A diversity of opinion, far from being cause for alarm, was a guarantee that eternal truths would not be shut off from view by the false authority of custom or transient prejudice. Yet the liberal ideology, as descended from Locke, also acknowledged the supreme importance of environment in training the habits and shaping the ideas of men. If all ideas derived from sensory experience, it was theoretically possible for a social engineer to construct an environment that would mold a particular type of man. The threat and promise of such behavioristic conditioning were recognized in the eighteenth century, and later fascinated nativist writers, who sometimes associated the psychology of sensation with the mysterious powers of mesmerism and phrenology.

The usual way of reconciling environmentalism with a faith in intellectual freedom and diversity was to assume that truth, when conveyed by the written and spoken word, and especially when aided by the Holy Spirit or the innate moral sense, would overcome the effects of the most repressive environment. The funereal images of the revivalist preacher, the polished rhetoric of the political orator, the eloquent appeals of missionaries and reformers, the sentimental scenes of the temperance tracts, would play upon the senses and emotions of the most indifferent public. Perhaps no people ever displayed such faith in the power of sheer communication as did the Americans of the Middle Period. So long as a man was confident that the truth of his own doctrines could not fail of acceptance, as soon as they won sufficient circulation, he would not fear diversity of opinion or even the freedom of others to propagate patent falsehoods.

But despite official faith in the compatibility of truth and freedom, Americans frequently expressed misgivings over the proliferation of sects and faddist groups, the spectacular success of prophets, demagogues, revivalists and hoaxers.[2] In a land without intellectual or moral authorities, the only arbiter was public opinion, which was slow and gullible at first, but which might be brought to ridicule the charlatan or to laugh at its own credulity. Yet this self-corrective principle could operate only where all citizens accepted the ultimate authority of public opinion, acknowledging its right to penetrate every sanctum of privacy.

Henry Dana Ward, a prominent anti-Mason, emphasized the virtue of benevolent associations and other corporate bodies, so long as their activities were open to publicity.[3] But as Joseph Smith himself wrote, in the *Book of Mormon,* ''the Lord worketh not in secret combinations.''[4] Secrecy, according to Georg Simmel, is one of man's greatest inventions, for it raises the possibility of a hidden world alongside the manifest world.[5] We might add that this possibility, like that of an ideal world or utopia, may give form and direction to manifest reality. Yet a secret creates tension because it can always be betrayed, its effects may disrupt normal expectations, and it always stands in the position of an

2. See esp. David Meredith Reese, *Humbugs of New York: Being a Remonstrance against Popular Delusion . . .* (New York, 1838).

3. *Anti-Masonic Review and Magazine* (New York), I (December 1828), 3–4.

4. Ether 8: 19.

5. *The Sociology of Georg Simmel,* ed. and trans. Kurt Wolff (Glencoe, Ill., 1950), pp. 330–33.

exception to the general or universal rule—particularly to the will of the majority.

What if a group was insulated from the cleansing currents of public opinion? What if cunning leaders developed a system of deluding and conditioning people, a system so effective that its victims were no longer accessible to conversion to the truth? What if the Bible, the single fixed anchorage in the shifting flow of opinions, was perverted to fit the designs of Freemasons and Mormons, or withheld from the laity by Catholic priests? The relative autonomy of such groups was a barrier to the probing and dissolving power of public opinion, and thus a challenge to the whole process by which truth was to be sifted and preserved in the midst of limitless diversity. Such a challenge aggravated tensions and awakened anxieties that were an integral part of American culture. The nativists' fascination with secret conspiracy, which was often seen as the hidden force responsible for sectional conflict and for otherwise baffling fluctuations in the government and economy, reflected a deep concern over both the ignorance of the common citizen and the lack of rational direction in public affairs.[6]

If Americans generally accepted the liberal doctrine that truth could be secured only by free communication and publicity, they also accepted the romantic belief that morality could be secured only by the sanctification of woman. As early as 1797 John Robison, a Scottish professor of natural philosophy, defined the themes that were to dominate the American literature of counter-subversion for the next century. Expressing horror over the sexual depravity of the ancients, he attributed the moral progress of Europe to the elevation of woman and to the increasing influence of her moral sentiment. The greatest threat to Christian civilization lay in the degrading and desexing of woman, a tactic common to both the Catholic Church and the atheistic Illuminati. In his fantasies of subversion Robison came close to anticipating the

6. Richard Rush, letter of May 4, 1831, printed in *The Anti-Masonic Almanac, for the Year 1832*, ed. Edward Giddins (Utica, N.Y., 1831), pp. 29–30; Lebbeus Armstrong, *Masonry Proved to Be a Work of Darkness, Repugnant to the Christian Religion; and Inimical to a Republican Government* (New York, 1830), pp. 4–16; *Anti-Masonic Review*, I, 6–9; Edward Beecher, *The Papal Conspiracy Exposed, and Protestantism Defended, in the Light of Reason, History, and Scripture* (Boston, 1855), pp. 24–29, 31, 133, 388; William Hogan, *Popery! As It Was and as It Is: Also, Auricular Confession: and Popish Nunneries* (Hartford, 1855), pp. 9–11, 29, 73–76, 503–4, 571–77; *Among the Mormons: Historic Accounts by Contemporary Observers*, eds. William Mulder and A. Russell Mortensen (New York, 1958), pp. 60–61, 71, 76–79, 101, 293–95, 350; John H. Beadle, *Life in Utah: or, the Mysteries and Crimes of Mormonism* (Philadelphia, [1872]), pp. 30–34, 299–300; Maria Ward, *Female Life among the Mormons: A Narrative of Many Years' Personal Experience, By the Wife of a Mormon Elder, Recently Returned from Utah* (New York, 1857), pp. 94–95.

later image of licentious, polygamous Mormons.[7] Nativists agreed with him that any deviation from the romantic ideal of marriage and respect for woman's sensibility, modesty and sanctity, which were seen as balancing forces to the hard necessities of the business world, undermined the very foundations of society. Thus the Masons were repeatedly condemned for being cut off from the ennobling influence of women; it was said that their rites were devised "to harden the heart, stupify the conscience, and to eradicate every degree of moral sensibility."[8] The same accusations were made concerning Catholics and Mormons.[9] The pretensions to divine knowledge of all three groups supposedly led directly to a forgetfulness of human fallibility, to a worship of sheer expediency and ultimately to a life devoid of moral principles and the fear of God. Because of their contempt for and corruption of women, there was no moral force to check this progressive decline.

By associating various dangers, such as secrecy, popular gullibility and the corrupting power of environment and ideology, with the American enemy, the nativist was apparently able to preserve his faith in the triumph of truth and morality in a free society. But his continuing concern with these dangers evinced an underlying tension over the meaning of intellectual and moral diversity in a land without ultimate authorities.

This brings us to the second problem, which concerns the role of organization in an individualistic society. According to Tocqueville, individuals and minorities in America could not appeal to authoritative opinion, independent of the majority, precisely because the country was free from hierarchies of rank, vested privilege and the corporate structure of Europe. Thus America's lack of social orders and fixed distinctions tended to force a conformity to the tastes and standards of the majority. In so fluid and amorphous a society, such groups as Masons, Mormons and Catholics acquired a special significance as self-contained organizations, relatively independent of the shifting currents of majority

---

7. John Robison, *Proofs of a Conspiracy Against all the Religions and Governments of Europe, Carried on in the Secret Meetings of Free Masons, Illuminati, and Reading Societies,* 3rd ed. (London, 1798), pp. 243–65.

8. *Free Masonry: A Poem, In Three Cantos, Accompanied with Notes, Illustrative of the History, Policy, Principles, &c. of the Masonic Institutions; Shewing the Coincidence of Its Spirit and Design with Ancient Jesuitism . . . By a Citizen of Massachusetts* (Leicester, Mass., 1830), p. 203.

9. *Among the Mormons,* eds. Mudler and Mortensen, pp. 327–28, 405–11; Beecher, *Papal Conspiracy,* p. 148; Hogan, *Popery,* pp. 229, 290–91, and *passim; The Cloven Foot: or Popery Aiming at Political Supremacy in the United States, By the Rector of Oldenwold* (New York, 1855), pp. 294–304; Kimball Young, *Isn't One Wife Enough?* (New York, 1954), pp. 2–5, 16–27, 311; Beadle, *Life in Utah,* pp. 304, 332–74; *The Women of Mormonism: or, the Story of Polygamy as Told by the Victims Themselves,* ed. Jennie Anderson Froiseth (Detroit, 1881–82), pp. 113–14, 191; *Fifteen Years among the Mormons: Being the Narrative of Mrs. Mary Ettie V. Smith,* ed. Nelson W. Green (New York, 1857), pp. 44–51.

will. This alone would have made them suspect. But Tocqueville also found that one of the chief forces counteracting the tyranny of the majority was the American proclivity to found voluntary associations, for civic, political and philanthropic purposes, whose functions were similar to those of powerful individuals or families in Europe. The salient traits of such groups were the legislative character of their deliberations, their attempt to mobilize a strong and vocal minority and their ultimate goal of winning over the majority. The same characteristics can be seen in organizations based on a common fear or prejudice. Like most other voluntary organizations, they presented a dual aspect: they promoted their own special interests, attempting to increase their opportunities for economic and political power; they also strove to reorient the majority will in the name of preserving or restoring cherished values.

In Europe it was class consciousness and fear of the conspiracy of an opposing class that increasingly provided a sense of identity and group solidarity. In America, identity and group solidarity were commonly achieved by associating oneself with the people and with the tradition of the Founding Fathers. But the American could well ask "who are we?" and "who is against us?"—for there was no certainty that his own interests would always be supported by the majority will. This uncertainty raised fundamental questions regarding loyalty. As David Potter has recently shown, loyalties in the period from 1820 to 1860 formed a pattern far more intricate than a simple division of nationalism and sectionalism.[10] Throughout the country there were multitudes of shifting groups and interests whose main ideological bond was a common allegiance to the principles of the Revolution; by the 1820s, as the Revolutionary generation passed away, this bond of a common cause against foreign tyranny changed from living memory to ceremonial tradition. In both North and South, Americans tried to co-ordinate their loyalties to special interests with loyalty to the nation and Constitution. Increasingly, however, this co-ordinating process was carried on by contrasting one's own unconditional loyalty to the nation with the essentially subversive character of some reference group. Adopting a categorical approach to the problem of loyalty and special interest, nativists could assume that American democracy sustained their own values and interests, and deny the possibility of national loyalty being compatible with the special allegiances of Masons, Mormons or Catholics. But while they tried to define their own loyalty in negative terms, as a lack of attachment to a coherent minority, nativists were as much troubled by

10. "The Historian's Use of Nationalism and Vice Versa," *The American Historical Review,* LXVII (July 1962), 924–50.

solidarity in the majority as by the disciplined effective-
nous groups. They played repeatedly upon the theme of
norant public, criminally indifferent to the progress of
iring power in political decision and disposal of re-
They simulated repeated crises—the moral equivalents of war—
in an attempt to simplify issues and dissolve religious and factional
alignments by uniting all patriots against a force imperiling religion and
democracy. It would thus appear that movements of counter-subversion
were symptomatic of a profound need for community and consensus,
and for personal dedication in a higher cause. We may suspect that local
economic and social conflicts exacerbated fundamental tensions over the
role of organization in a laissez-faire society, or rather, in a society that
accepted an ideology of laissez faire.

Morton Grodzins has pointed out that a democracy is built on an
integration of nonnational loyalties, whereas a totalitarian state tries to
absorb and eliminate all subloyalties.[12] We may ask, therefore, whether
the movements of counter-subversion pointed in the direction of totali-
tarianism? The suspicion becomes stronger at a later period, in the writings of Josiah Strong, for example, where the tradition of anti-Catholicism and anti-Mormonism was combined with a near deification of the
power of the state.[13] And after the Civil War, Congress passed a series
of discriminatory laws that deprived the Utah Mormons of their basic
civil liberties. But in the ante-bellum period, with its multitude of local
and sectional loyalties, it was not at all clear which minorities could
achieve harmony with the national interest. Nativists represented religious and economic factions that could not possibly win a majority suf-
ficiently strong to enforce their more radical aims. This was especially
true when anti-Masons associated the Masonic conspiracy with the power
of the Albany Regency over state banks and the Erie Canal; when Whig
politicians sought to link Catholicism with the growth of the Democratic
Party in eastern cities; and when Gentiles in Utah used anti-Mormonism
as a means for protecting their interests in mines and land. A proliferation of rival interests, combined with a loose attachment to places and
institutions, meant that no loyalty could be taken for granted. Nativists
often lost public favor when they were accused of masking selfish intentions behind a façade of specious patriotism. And their brief triumphs

---

11. See esp., Hogan, *Popery,* pp. 7–8; *Auricular Confession,* pp. 264–65; *Women of Mormonism,* ed. Froiseth, pp. 285–87, 291–92.

12. *The Loyal and the Disloyal: Social Boundaries of Patriotism and Treason* (Chicago, 1956);
see also, Edward A. Shils, *The Torment of Secrecy; the Background and Consequences of American Security Policies* (Glencoe, Ill., 1956).

13. *Our Country; its Possible Future and its Present Crisis* (New York, 1886).

in political life were notably unsuccessful in producing legislation in accord with their principles.

Furthermore, the challenge to Masons, Mormons and Catholics brought an immediate reaction, and forced each group to define its own role in American society. Freemasons pointed to the great patriots who had been members of their order. Various Catholic leaders endeavored to prove the compatibility of Catholic doctrine and American ideals. Brigham Young was led to draw a distinction between loyalty to the Constitution and to "the damned rascals who administer the government"; and even in the 1880s and 90s when the beleaguered Utah Mormons were challenged at home by a Gentile Liberal Party, they responded by forming a People's Party.[14] Significantly, all three groups turned to public opinion as a source of moral authority. It is therefore possible that nativists contributed, in the long run, to an integration of loyalties; to a conviction, that is, that by being a loyal Mason, Mormon or Catholic, one was also being a loyal American. The great exception, of course, was the slavery controversy, which slowly generated a polarization of loyalties that led to outright secession.

The third and final problem is the relation of tradition and change to America's destiny. From its beginning as a nation, the United States had been remarkably hospitable to change and diversity. This permissive tradition was related, on the ideological level, to the ideal of America as a land of promise whose very meaning lay in change and the process of becoming. But as recent studies have shown, there was an underlying tension between the American's image of himself as an adventurous risk-taker, an expansive pioneer, confident of his ability to improve himself and the world; and a contrary image of the American as the Happy Husbandman, a wise innocent in a terrestrial paradise, who is content to enjoy the serene blessings of a simple rural life, and is unencumbered by the fears and superstitions of a moldering civilization.[15] This contradiction was embodied in the liberal ideology inherited from the eighteenth century, when desires to overcome immediate restraints were transformed into an abstract ideal of restoring a supposedly original and pre-social freedom. The pattern persisted as frustrations from concrete rivalries and competition were projected into a hostility to institutions and associations, the products of mere history, which seemed

14. Young, *Isn't One Wife Enough?*, pp. 344–46.
15. Charles L. Sanford, *The Quest for Paradise: Europe and the American Moral Imagination* (Urbana, Ill., 1961); R. W. B. Lewis, *The American Adam: Innocence, Tragedy and Tradition in the 19th Century* (Chicago, 1955); Roland Van Zandt, *The Metaphysical Foundations of American History* (The Hague, 1959); Marvin Meyers, *The Jacksonian Persuasion: Politics and Belief* (Stanford, 1957); Henry Nash Smith, *Virgin Land: the American West as Symbol and Myth* (Cambridge, 1950).

to block the emergence of the unconditioned, self-contained individual. Thus Americans tended to promote change and at the same time to exaggerate the evils and virtues of particular changes. If they professed to see Satan fast at work in the New World Garden, it was because he was a force for change of which they were a part.[16]

America's destiny, then, was associated with a progressive liberation of the individual from all restricting conditions and antecedents; Europe was thought to be sinking under the cumulative weight of evil institutions. But which interests and institutions were of permanent value in furthering America's mission, and which were harmful vestiges from the past? In a famous sermon Theodore Parker attempted to distinguish the permanent essence of Christianity from its transient, historical forms.[17] A similar approach was often taken in defining the meaning of America, which was usually seen as an essentially negative freedom. The agencies and institutions of crucial importance were those that offered the individual a chance for self-expression or fulfillment: the jury, the ballot, the free press, the public school and the western frontier. All of these were thought to be threatened by subversive groups bent on capturing control of America, enslaving its citizens, crushing republicanism and preventing the realization of America's millennial glory.[18] Such groups as Masons, Mormons and Catholics could be taken as symbols of the subordination of the individual to authority. They could also stand for all corporate bodies whose purpose would not end at a given moment in time or with the accomplishment of some limited objective. The enemy's mission, like that of America itself, was universal in scope. As we have already noted, most voluntary associations at once strove to push the aims of special groups, and yet thought of themselves as preserving the idyll of an individualistic, laissez-faire society. Americans ordinarily united on the assumption that once they had achieved some pragmatic objective, they would relinquish their special status as reformers or agitators. By definition, the nativist movements were temporary unities. They would dissolve once they had exposed the secrets

16. Historians who tend to categorize the Middle Period as one unrestrained optimism fail to see that such traits as optimism and pessimism have usually been linked together, and that the historical or social situation which gives rise to an expression of extreme optimism may also produce despair and anxiety. This is apparent, for example, in the history of millennialism.

17. *A Discourse on the Transient and Permanent in Christianity* (Boston, 1841).

18. *Free Masonary: A Poem*, pp. 29–58; *Anti-Masonic Review*, I (September 1829), 293, 315; *The Anti-Masonic Almanack, for the Year 1828*, ed. Edward Giddins (Rochester, N.Y., 1827), entry for November and December; Beecher, *Papal Conspiracy*, pp. 14–17, 377–89; Hogan, *Popery*, pp. 123–25; *Auricular Confession*, pp. 264–65; *Among the Mormons*, eds. Mulder and Mortensen, pp. 76–79, 101, 407; Austin N. Ward, *Male Life among the Mormons; or, the Husband in Utah* (Philadelphia, 1863), pp. 224–25, 247–48; Maria Ward, *Female Life*, pp. 378–89; Beadle, *Life in Utah*, pp. 5–9, 78–79, 178, 307, 400–1; *Women of Mormonism*, ed. Froiseth, pp. 285–87, 367–68.

of the enemy to public scrutiny, and had mobilized the political power of the majority to liberate individuals trapped in the meshes of an un-American group. In the meantime, however, they provided a sense of identity, a sense of belonging.

Since this essay has been of a frankly speculative character, it may not be out of place to suggest in conclusion an even more tentative hypothesis. There are certain striking parallels between the mentality of the nativist and that of the radical sectarian of medieval and early modern Europe.[19] But the radical sectarian, while professing faith in liberty of conscience, in the moral autonomy of the individual and in the inevitability of the millennium, after a period of struggle with the powers of darkness, always stood in the position of a heretic condemned and persecuted by the established order. In America the sectarian ideals, which had been appropriated and secularized by the Enlightenment, were at least to some degree a part of the established ideology; the defenders of those ideals were therefore in the position of defending an establishment. By their very nature, however, the sectarian ideals were diffuse and anarchic, especially if pushed to their extremes. They could lead to a repudiation of all laws, mores and social norms which limited the self-affirmation of the individual. Traditionally, they had acquired social meaning and had served as forces for unity and cohesion when pitted against the opposing power of a vast institution or corporate body. The nativist movements may thus have been somewhat regressive ways of coping with fundamental tensions and contradictions in American culture, which were the result, to speak metaphorically, of a disharmony between certain infantile ideals of liberation from all restraining authority, and the necessity of developing the social meanings of freedom in a modern age. If there is any truth to this hypothesis, the movements of counter-subversion provide insight into a transitional stage in the development of the American character.

19. See esp., Norman Cohn, *The Pursuit of the Millennium* (London, 1957) and Rufus M. Jones, *Spiritual Reformers in the 16th and 17th Centuries* (New York, 1914).

12

The American Family and Boundaries in Historical Perspective

TOCQUEVILLE AS A FATHER FIGURE FOR AMERICAN CULTURE

Since the 1840s, and especially since the 1940s, many Americans have turned almost compulsively to Alexis de Tocqueville's *Democracy in America* as the authoritative fountainhead of historical self-understanding. Tocqueville's prestige, which admittedly has had its ups and downs, owes something to his refreshing departure from the English empirical tradition, or to what the 11th edition of *The Encyclopaedia Britannica* calls his "excess of the deductive spirit." As one of the founders of classical sociology, he was also the first European to apply systematic social theory to American institutions. But I suspect that Tocqueville's appeal to Americans rests mainly on his ability to portray the United States as the vanguard of a long-term and irresistible movement toward democratization and modernization and to explain this revolutionary process by continual contrast with a premodern and aristocratic European tradition. Though Tocqueville was only 26 when he toured America in 1831, he soon became a cultural father-figure. For not only did he serve as interpreter and spokesman for the aristocratic past, but he assumed the role of an enlightened parent who accepts the inevitability

From *The American Family: Dying or Developing,* edited by David Reiss, M.D., and Howard A. Hoffman, M.D. (New York and London: Plenum Press, 1979). Reprinted by permission.

of growth and change, who wants to understand, and who offers counsel designed to mitigate the excesses and hazards of freedom.

While Tocqueville could not conceal his nostalgia for the ordered past, he frankly acknowledged the justice of democracy and the moral benefits of expanding equality. For Americans, his image of fixed and hierarchical boundaries was not a goal to be recovered but a reference point for measuring their own anxieties and aspirations, a peak of the Old World still in view to confident but giddy voyagers. Thus Catharine Beecher, whose 1843 *Treatise on Domestic Economy* has been likened in impact to Dr. Benjamin Spock's *Baby and Child Care,* repeatedly invoked Tocqueville to justify the preeminent mission of American mothers. Tocqueville had shown, she wrote, that in aristocratic lands "all ranks and classes are fixed in a given position, and each person is educated for a particular sphere and style of living." The price of American equality had been a loss of direction and coherence. In a land of rampant change, fluidity, and self-seeking individualism, only the family remained as a stabilizing and regenerating force. Because Catharine Beecher agreed with Tocqueville that in America the shaping of character was "committed mainly to the female hand," she concluded that "to American women, more than to any other on earth, is committed the exalted privilege of extending over the world those blessed influences, which are to renovate degraded man."[1] Women, in other words, by accepting the duties of their household sphere, were the providential antidote for the ills of the modern world.

THE ILLUSION OF A GOLDEN AGE OF FAMILY STABILITY

As we shall see later on, both Tocqueville and Beecher, to say nothing of countless others, assigned to the family burdens that had once been dispersed through less functionally differentiated societies. But the Tocqueville device of measuring the present against a more stable and ordered past—or what Ferdinand Tönnies would eventually describe as a *Gesellschaft* versus a *Gemeinschaft* society—also suggested a certain fall from grace, a decline from a golden era of reciprocal rights and duties, of organic and harmonious unity, when everyone honored the elderly and when children derived wisdom and joy from grandparents, aunts, uncles, and other kin. In fact, it would appear that this idyllic image is a fantasy of modern times, that is, of the 18th and especially the 19th centuries, when the family acquired a new symbolic importance

1. Quoted in Sklar (1973).

as the embodiment of the past and as a refuge from and antidote to a world of bewildering change. It was not accidental that the idealization of the bourgeois family emerged in close association with the literary idealization of Laplanders, American Indians, South Sea islanders, and other allegedly primitive and innocent peoples. The two trends were closely tied to the so-called discovery of childhood as a distinct, almost continental sphere of being (Victor Hugo is credited with saying, "Christopher Columbus only discovered America: I have discovered the child"). These various quests for models of simplicity, spontaneity, and wholeness may well have been rooted in deep and perhaps universal psychological longings for a world without boundaries, for a global union of self with all being, or what Freud termed an "oceanic feeling." One may theorize that such universal human longings were cast adrift, so to speak, by the diminishing credibility of myth, ritual, magic, and belief in the supernatural, and were further accentuated by the growing rationalization and differentiation of life. But the immediate point at issue is the reality of an earlier golden age, not the reasons for its discovery or idealization.

During the past decade, the history of the family has undergone exciting and explosive growth. Because of the diversity and complexity of the evidence and because our knowledge is expanding so rapidly, it is extremely hazardous to generalize about broad trends that include various social classes and nationalities and that extend over several centuries. Nevertheless, there is good reason to doubt theories of abrupt change in the character and viability of the family. In a recent and illuminating review of the literature from various scientific disciplines, including anthropology, biosociology, and neuroendocrinology, Alice S. Rossi (1977) stresses the central parenting bond between mothers and small children, a bond whose genetic and evolutionary antecedents derive from the hunting-and-gathering societies that account for over 90% of human history. Quite apart from this biosocial continuity, historians have discovered that the supposedly "modern family"—that is, the nuclear family of two parents and their children living in an independent, private household—became predominant in western Europe several centuries before industrialization. At an early period, Western Europe also diverged from the rest of the world in a number of other respects: in the late age at which females married (mid- to late 20s); in the high proportion of women who never married or bore children; in a "planning mentality" geared to long-term advances in family wealth and status; and in the appearance, at least in 18th-century France, of conscious and effective efforts at contraception. It has been convincingly argued that these modern familial patterns may have been more the cause than the consequence of the process of "modernization."

Even more forceful objections have been raised against the picture of decline from a previous golden age of familial stability and harmony.[2] Because of heavy mortality, three-generation households were always rare until the late 19th century.(While growing up, the majority of children lost one parent.) By present-day standards, the proportion of people over 60 in any population was very small—in 17th-century England, no more than 8%—and the economic burden of supporting the elderly was correspondingly light. Nevertheless, respect for the elderly depended in large part on their retention and control of property. The elderly who had no property to be coveted by heirs or to be legally deeded in exchange for lifetime support might find themselves reduced to beggary or to a marginal existence on parish welfare.

The treatment of children also dramatizes the failure of religious and ethical norms to protect the powerless, although such norms were far more effective in America than in Europe. It now appears that a massive decline in infanticide was a major contributor to western Europe's population explosion of the 18th century (McKeown, 1977; Stone, 1974). The earlier prevalence of infanticide probably encouraged a degree of aggression and "carelessness" toward small children in general. In this respect, Christian nations may well have differed psychologically from societies where infanticide was a legal and unquestioned means of population control. Since in Europe infanticide was legally defined as murder, its practice, even as an "accepted custom," had to take the form of an "accident"—suffocation, "lying-over" in bed, neglect, or beating. Archaeological evidence indicates an appalling number of infants and small children who died from physical violence or who were maimed in various ways to enhance their success as beggars (as is still done in India today).

There can also be little doubt that children were often indefensible targets for adult sexual gratification. This is a subject about which we know too little, and a subject to which we shall return when considering the prudery of the "Victorian" family. Philippe Ariès (1965), who was the first to explore the question in some depth, warns us against imposing our own values on the 17th-century aristocrats, and their servants, who played sexual games with toddlers and who toyed with the penises of princes. Ariès and other scholars have shown that the very idea of children's sexual innocence is a realtively recent development. Yet this

2. See Stone (1977) and Thomas (1976). But for a contrary view see Fischer (1977).

early lack of inhibition should not be confused with modern ideals—some would say fantasies—of an unrepressed and Eden-like state of nature. Ariès's own evidence does not suggest sexual education and initiation, as in many premodern societies, but rather the impulsive exploitation of very young children who were hardly yet considered human beings. Admittedly such evidence is confined to the aristocracy and can hardly be taken as representative. But future research may well confirm Ariès's contention that "playing with children's privy parts formed part of a widespread tradition, which is still operative in Moslem circles."

There are still other grounds for questioning the idyllic image of preindustrial family nurture. In Europe and even in colonial America, the newborn infants of well-to-do families were commonly "put out" to wet nurses for a period of a year or two. In France, where the custom was especially prevalent, nurses were recruited from among the most debased and exploited class, and infant mortality was correspondingly high. Deprivation was the hallmark of such absentee and unsupervised child care—many wet nurses had just weaned their own children and because of a low-energy diet thus had a diminished supply of milk. And of course the children faced the conscious traumas of separation at age 1 or 2. For upper-class children, by the early modern period, adjustment to the natal home might be followed in a few years by banishment to a boarding school of some kind. Less affluent families regularly sent out children as apprentices or servants, often as early as age 7, at which point guidance and discipline shifted from parents to a nonkin family.

One must also picture the plight of the colonial New England mother who regularly gave birth to a new child every two years while cooking, spinning, weaving, baking, pickling and preserving, making candles and soap, bleaching, dyeing, cleaning, laundering, and gardening. Unlike many Europeans, New Englanders did not immobilize toddlers in tight swaddling clothes, and it is not surprising that many children were burned by fire, fell into wells, or were the victims of other accidents indicating a lack of adult supervision. In both Europe and America, the desperation of parents, nursemaids, and others charged with child care is suggested by the widespread use of opium, alcohol, and other sedating narcotics. But as John Demos (1971) has written, New Englanders began exercising their principal control in the child's second year, when they resolved to break or beat down inherent "willfulness" as soon as it began to appear. The Puritans were not alone in conceiving this to be *"the central task* of parenthood," or to regard it, as Demos says, "as involving a direct confrontation with 'original sin.' " In this battle against Satan, adults could employ an imposing arsenal that ranged from the exhibition of corpses to folktales of castration, witchcraft, and abandonment.

One can easily distort historical reality by dwelling on the horrors of the past, and at this point I should stress that the preindustrial family performed a variety of economic, religious, educational, and welfare functions that were eventually assumed, for good or ill, by other institutions. Although the so-called modern family appeared in *form* at a surprisingly early date—that is, in the formal structure of conjugal units living in independent households—the *functions* of the family continued to be varied and diffuse, particularly in times of emergency. Indeed, there is a certain irony in the fact that the stunning uprootings and dislocations of the early industrial era encouraged a return among laboring families to earlier patterns of mutual aid based on extended kinship and ethnicity. At a time when laissez-faire dogma discredited every surviving form of parish or state paternalism, the family filled the gap as the only agency of welfare and mutual assistance. This phenomenon, with many cultural variations, was particularly striking among black freedmen in the post-Civil War South and among industrial immigrants, who evolved new forms of extended family dependence as well as mutual-aid societies based on shared religious or ethnic background. But the history of social welfare legislation, carrying with it appalling records of the human costs of early industrialization, proves that the resiliency of the family could be no substitute for an abdication of social and political responsibility. Nor was the family then or earlier a haven of security, order, and mutual self-fulfillment.

I have quite deliberately applied our own standards to the past, in order to highlight the opposite fallacy of idealizing the past and of forgetting that the past two centuries have witnessed a momentous change in moral sensibility. This change has been obscured by continuing laments over the decline and impending disintegration of the family. For over three centuries, ministers, moral philosophers, and their modern counterparts have been warning that children are becoming more contemptuous of authority, parents more irresponsible, wives more selfishly independent, families more fragile and rootless. Seldom have these prophets of doom taken note of the subtle transformation in functions and expectations assigned to the family. As we have already briefly noted, the family has been stripped of many of its traditional functions; and as we shall see, it has acquired awesome new responsibilities for ensuring individual happiness and social salvation. As Philippe Ariès (1977) has recently pointed out, I think with some exaggeration, the feelings and emotions that were one diffused among various natural and supernatural objects, including saints, friends, horses, and gardens, have become "focused entirely within the immediate family. The couple and their children became the objects of a passionate and exclusive love that transcended even death." What both Ariès and less knowledgeable lamenters tend to forget is that the 18th century marked the first upsurge in history, and then in a few select societies in Western Europe and America, of a *collective* concern for the fate of helpless and vulnerable humans—children, the aged, slaves, the insane, the physically handicapped—for a fate, that is, apart from that determined by family or kin. And by post-18th-century standards, family and kin have seldom had the resources or goodwill to provide the warmth and security imagined in nostalgic retrospect. The rather priggish Victorians who ventured into what we now call the Third World, and who recoiled at the sight of infanticide, child maiming, child prostitution and enslavement, widow burning, and all the rest, would have been similarly shocked if a time machine had transported them backward in their own societies two centuries or more.

TOCQUEVILLE AND THE SIGNIFICANCE OF BOUNDARIES IN A DEMOCRATIC SOCIETY

Having questioned widespread assumptions about the nature of the preindustrial family, I return to Tocqueville for two reasons. He presented a perceptive if highly theoretical analysis of the American family before the onset of significant industrialization but after a half-century or so of profound socioeconomic change, especially in the status and economic role of women. Tocqueville also sensed that the family somehow exemplifies the restructuring and redefinition of boundaries in a democratic society. His major concern, it should be stressed, was how the irresistible movement toward equality could be "civilized," so to speak, by a voluntary acceptance of various restraints and limits. And such voluntary acceptance, in Tocqueville's view, depended on the nature and the future of the family.

Tocqueville's great insight, which was in no way diminished by his bias or his factual errors, is that the historical drift toward equality impinges on boundaries of every kind: psychological, social, political, religious, and territorial. Not only is the family itself shaped by the trend toward equality of condition, but it is at once a key source, amplifier, and stabilizer of egalitarian aspirations, of individualism, and of the restless pursuit of success. With a view to the themes I wish to develop in the rest of this paper, Tocqueville's paradigm provides us with useful concepts for relating sex-role changes to the larger process of modernization; for understanding the new burdens and expectations that were just beginning to be placed on the American family; and for identifying the long-term costs that were associated with the elevation of women and with a new parental concern over "child development."

The significance of interrelated boundaries can be seen in the way that Tocqueville first introduced the subject of the American family while discussing the stabilizing influence of religion on democracy. Because Americans universally accepted a generalized and nonsectarian Christian morality, Tocqueville (1955) wrote:

> every principle of the moral world is fixed and determinate, although the political world is abandoned to the debates and experiments of men. Thus the human mind is never left to wander over a boundless field; and whatever may be its pretensions, it is checked from time to time by barriers that it cannot surmount. Before it can innovate, certain primary principles are laid down, and the boldest conceptions are subjected to certain forms which retard and stop their completion.

In other words, religion provides an outer rim of unquestioned rules, limits and assumptions, but within this circle custom, tradition, and political authority are all open to debate and transformation. But how does a vague and generalized religion retain such influence, particularly when, as Tocqueville admits, it is "often unable to restrain man from the numberless temptations which chance offers; nor can it check that passion for gain which everything contributes to arouse"? Certainly the force of religion cannot be explained by the Church as an institution, since Christianity in America is fragmented into scores of competing sects; nor can it be explained by the power and patronage of the clergy, who "keep aloof from parties and from public affairs."

Tocqueville concluded, almost casually at this point, that Christian morality (which he rather carelessly equated with "religion") is rooted in the home and is somehow connected with the ideal of "conjugal happiness." Significantly he also claimed that in Europe, rebellions against authority—the kind of sweeping, nihilistic rebellions that he most feared—originate in the home, in the "irregularities of domestic life." Such "irregularities" appear to include both an Oedipal struggle against paternal despotism and a cavalier regard for marital fidelity. As a result of such contempt for what Tocqueville called "the natural bonds and legitimate pleasures" of the home, Europeans were inclined to *transfer* rebellions and lawless impulses outward:

> Agitated by the tumultuous passions that frequently disturb his dwelling, the European is galled by the obedience which the legislative powers of the state exact. But when the American retires from the turmoil of public

life to the bosom of his family, he finds in it the image of order and of peace. . . . While the European endeavors to forget his domestic troubles by agitating society, the American derives from his home that love of order which he afterwards carries with him into public affairs.

No doubt this contrast is overdrawn, but it offers intriguing possibilities for psychohistorical research, and perhaps more important, it reflects an emerging ideology that assigned new psychological responsibilities to the middle-class home and to American women. Almost in passing, Tocqueville observed, still regarding religion, that "its influence over the mind of woman is supreme, and women are the protectors of morals." Many chapters later he returned to his theme and admitted that if asked:

Now that I am drawing to the close of this work, in which I have spoken of so many important things done by the Americans, to what the singular prosperity and growing strength of that people ought mainly to be attributed, I should reply: To the superiority of their women.

This was the message, as I have already briefly noted, that was seized upon by Catharine Beecher and other champions of the so-called cult of domesticity. Recent studies have shown that during the first decades of the 19th century, the Protestant clergy devoted increasing attention to women, who formed a growing majority of their congregations. The mission prescribed for women was not one of passive holiness or spirituality but of active work, mainly as mothers and wives, in saving masculine America from the effects of materialism, dollar worship, and competitive struggle. Historians have only recently begun to see that this evangelical enlistment of middle-class women had vast multiplier effects extending beyond the household into virtually every movement for social reform.[3]

Before we pursue this momentous division between masculine materialism and feminine idealism, it is important to summarize Tocqueville's more detailed diagnosis of the democratic family. First, like most European observers, Tocqueville was struck by the weakness of paternal authority, which did not reside in a kinglike *office* but depended rather on "natural affection" and on temporary advantage of age and experience. The paternal bond was thus informal, permissive, and premised on the early independence of sons:

The father foresees the limits of his authority long beforehand, and when the time arrives, he surrenders it without a struggle; the son looks forward

3. See Cott (1977).

to the exact period at which he will be his own master, and he enters upon his freedom without precipitation and without effort.

Similarly, whereas siblings in an aristocratic family were bound together by tangible family interests, jealousies, and obligations, democracy "divides their inheritance, but allows their hearts and minds to unite." In short, democracy "destroys or obscures almost all the old conventional rules of society" but at the same time tightens the bonds of natural feeling and sympathy.

A second characteristic, which again drew comment from numerous Europeans, was the seeming paradox that "in America the independence of woman is irrecoverably lost in the bonds of matrimony. If an unmarried woman is less constrained there than elsewhere, a wife is subjected to stricter obligations." Parents, instead of trying to shelter their daughters from the vices and temptations of the world, trained them to rely on their own strength of character. Yet upon marriage the self-reliant American woman accepted "a constant sacrifice of her pleasures to her duties" and a role defined by public opinion that "carefully circumscribes woman within the narrow circle of domestic interests and duties and forbids her to step beyond it." We now know that many young women experienced what one historian has termed a "marriage trauma" while either making or recoiling from this difficult transition, but the evidence suggests that for the middle class, Tocqueville's description was essentially correct.

It must be stressed, however, that Tocqueville was describing "ideal types" that cannot be taken too literally but that point to important historical trends. For example, in discussing what he termed "the equality of the sexes" in America, Tocqueville overlooked, or as a male simply took for granted, the actual inequalities that seem so shocking in retrospect: the minimal educational opportunities for girls; the limited access to employment outside the home, and pay-scales of one-third that for males in similar jobs, the denial of political rights and, in the case of married women, of the right to own property, to make contracts, or even to make a will. Yet there can be no doubt that the long-range trends favored greater sexual equality. Moreover, as Tocqueville acutely saw, the immediate path toward equality did not imply similarity or a blurring of gender boundaries:

> In no country has such constant care been taken as in America to trace two clearly distinct lines of action for the two sexes and to make them keep pace one with the other, but in two pathways that are always different.

The familial patterns that Tocqueville described were part of a profound process of societal change, a process that can be vaguely termed *modernization* but that can best be understood as the destruction and compensatory reconstruction of boundaries of every kind. This leveling and reordering process had a long history and in 1831 was probably still confined, in its more extreme forms, to the Northeastern middle class. While industrialization would eventually accelerate the rate of change, the original and critical transformation of the American family was intermeshed with earlier historical developments that can be only briefly enumerated here.

First was the gradual imposing of voluntary limits on human reproduction. During the colonial period, a plentiful food supply had helped to remove the ancient and lethal balance between fertility and mortality, leading to a population that continued to double every 20-odd years. Although a similar growth rate persisted well into the 19th century, fertility began declining in the late 18th century. By the second quarter of the 19th century, long before any significant use of contraceptives, middle-class American women were consciously limiting the size of their families, the space between children, and the age at which their child-bearing would cease. The population as a whole was gradually aging, and in the Northeast, adult women increasingly outnumbered adult men.

A second set of developments was the so-called transportation revolution, increased agricultural productivity and specialization, the growth of towns and seaports, and the spread of a market-oriented economy. For the family, these changes brought a rapid decline in economic self-sufficiency and in household industries, such as spinning and weaving, where women and girls had predominated. The need for cash income for a time involved many households in various putting-out systems of production. But increasingly the place of work was removed some distance from the home, whether for a male "breadwinner" or for daughters who lived as boarders while teaching school or working in textile mills. Housework, to be sure, was hardly less arduous than before, but in male eyes, the chores of mothers and wives lost the status of "work" when divorced from household industries. Psychologically the home became radically separated from the alienating and dehumanizing pressures of "modern work," that is, work defined by market forces and by impersonal standards of maximum efficiency, production, and profit. Though growing numbers of women, especially young unmarried women, worked temporarily as wage earners, this simply reinforced the dominant expectation that women's true and permanent "sphere" was the home, a recuperative oasis in the midst of a warlike jungle of competitive self-seeking. Significantly, the image of the home as a preserver of the organic and cooperative values of the past presupposed traditional rhythms of time and responsibility. For example, if the wife was blessed with the supposedly transcendent calling of motherhood and household management, her labor was task-oriented, irregular, and unsupervised, yet unending. Unless exempted by illness, she was on call 24 hours a day.

It should be stressed, however, that this concept of a segregated domestic sphere was part of a broader and truly revolutionary redefinition of woman's role. Precisely because middle-class women could claim to be untainted by the amoral expediency of the business world, they could demand a public hearing in movements like temperance and antislavery. There were complex connections, which cannot be spelled out here, between the cult of domesticity and the emergence, by the 1830s, of militant feminism as a new force in history.[4] The discovery of new modes of feminine self-assertion was also a response to political democratization, since the enfranchisement of adult white males had the effect of accentuating barriers of race and sex in the name of a more open and egalitarian society. Finally, women turned ideals of domesticity against the proliferating clubs, fraternal lodges, and barrooms that provided for segregated male recreation. This long campaign, finally and decisively aided by the 20th-century flight to the suburbs, can be viewed as part of the process of converting the family into a consumer society's primary unit of consumption.

To sum up, a focus on changing and interrelated boundaries suggests that the 19th-century family was as much the agent as the victim of modernization. The wife who made a self-conscious vocation of motherhood was as much a force for change as the female employee of a textile mill. The hallmarks of modernization were increasing differentiation of roles and specialization of functions. By the mid-19th century, in addition to the all-important division between home and work, there was a far more rigid and uniform timing of life stages: the timing of childbearing in marriage; of the duration of formal schooling; of the entrance into employment; of the age at marriage; and of a lengthening period when spouses could expect to live together after children had ceased to be responsibilities. In the economic world, such differentiation and specialization were still primarily geared to increased productivity. The family, having lost its main functions as a productive unit, became the key institution for adapting to socioeconomic change. Hence its burdens were increasingly psychological and ideological, and in serving

---

4. See Cott (1977), which traces these connections and brilliantly elaborates the themes I have summarized in the preceding paragraph.

these needs, it became increasingly oriented to various ritualized forms of consumption.

EVALUATION AND OVERVIEW

The American family failed to meet Tocqueville's expectations as a source of order and morality counterbalancing the rampant self-seeking of the modern capitalist world. Tocqueville was blind to the material forces of history and could not foresee the commercial exploitation of what he termed "natural feeling and sympathy." But before we look at long-term costs, it is important to stress the genuine gains, when judged by democratic and humanitarian standards, that accompanied the modernizing conquest and redefinition of familial boundaries.

Only a confirmed misogynist could deplore the growing insistence of American women that marriage not necessitate childbirth at two-year intervals until menopause; and only a confirmed misanthrope could express misgivings over the decline in infant mortality that, coupled with fewer childbirths, allowed parents to invest more love with less risk in each individual child. Yet these triumphs over previous natural limits cannot be applauded as isolated demographic phenomena; they carried far-reaching implications. Parents who became deeply involved in the welfare and the future of each child easily gravitated toward the modern ideal of developing the best potentialities of every human being. This humanitarian ideal probably originated in changing familial relations and in a growing tendency to perceive children as embodiments not of Original Sin but of innocence and of inclinations that could be trained for good or ill. Even in the 18th century, the task of parenthood gradually shifted toward sympathetic nurture and guidance, although the latter by no means excluded physical punishment as a means of cultivating self-discipline.

The sexual repression and family prudery that we loosely term Victorian were closely related to the modern concern with child development, self-discipline, and social progress. In this respect, it is worth emphasizing that efforts to stamp out children's masturbation became a cultural obsession only in the 19th century. Feminist historians have recently suggested that middle-class wives achieved a degree of independence and moral autonomy by insisting on periods of sexual abstinence, and it can be similarly argued, though much more evidence is needed, that efforts to negate and deny childhood sexuality originated as means of protecting children from molestations by adults. In other words, children could be defined as innocent only if they were first

desexualized and hence kept from being Satan's tempters to various servants and adult relatives in the same household. Emphasis on self-
discipline and avoidance of "bad habits" also tied in with the all-
important temperance movement, which exemplified the ideal of nurturing individual character within scrupulously respected family boundaries. For not only was alcohol blamed for child abuse and molestation,
for male sexual tyranny over wives, and for the violation of domestic
peace and the squandering of family resources, but the child who had
avoided bad habits of so-called self-abuse was expected to have the
power of will to resist all forms of intemperance.

Unfortunately, the moral boundaries ensuring wives and children a
degree of protection and self-determination depended on symbols of internalized discipline and self-denial that entailed heavy costs. One such
cost was the classic 19th-century neurosis. And here let me note that
Freud, whose initial discoveries appeared toward the end of this walling-
off and walling-in era, concluded with astonishment that the childhood
seduction by fathers of his female patients was an intrapsychic event, or
fantasy. Yet historically it may have been a more common objective
event, and one may speak hypothetically of a progression from external
family interactions toward subjective or intrapsychic family relations, a
progression coinciding roughly with the appearance of truly private rooms
not only for sleeping parents but for their children. The development of
the Victorian model of superego, Oedipal conflict, and neurosis may
thus be conceived as a psychological variant on the historical process of
differentiation and specialization.

A second long-term cost came due with the rebellion, to which Freud
unintentionally contributed, against all forms of repression. Upholders
of what Tocqueville had called "Christian morality" warned that the
family could never survive the defeat of national prohibition, which had
culminated a century of temperance agitation, to say nothing of the license increasingly given to sexual relations outside the bond of marriage. And here we should note the peculiar fact that while the American family had long been deprived of various supportive institutions,
such as those found in more traditional, homogeneous societies, it continued to receive compensatory support from incredibly detailed and authoritarian laws governing sexual behavior. Indeed, although Americans
proclaimed themselves the freest people on earth, they passively assumed that state legislators could apply distinctions of legality and illegality even to the sexual conduct of husbands and wives within the
privacy of a bedroom. The absurdity of such laws became apparent only
with the rebellion against so-called puritanical or Victorian values. No
less important was the critical redefinition of liberty, in roughly the mid-

20th century, from the notion of being as free as everyone else to the notion of being free to be different (Potter, 1976). This revolutionary change had, significantly, little effect on the laws, which remained, in the eyes of progressives, as mere sops to reactionary tastes. For progressives, the failure to suppress the drinking of alcohol simple dramatized the inability of puritanical moralists to enforce their own standards on the vibrant, fun-loving community at large. What went unnoticed was the discrediting of law and the further privatizing of the family as an institution supposedly immune from society's legitimate interests.

The American family has shown a remarkable strength, continuity, and adaptability as it has acquired an overload of expectation, much like a lonely life raft after the sinking of an ocean liner. It was helped, at least until the 1930s, by the example of immigrants, blacks, and other subcultures for whom the family could never appear as a therapeutic and easily expendable luxury. Nevertheless, it seems undeniable that the family's increasing isolation has weakened its capacity to function as a unit or to resist the manipulation of its members by various outside forces, such as advertising and peer-group norms. The continuing need for conjugal unions, as a testing ground for intimacy and authentic feeling, has been partly met by less demanding and more narcissistic sexual relationships. The ethic of self-centered liberation and fulfillment may not be compatible with parenting that extends beyond the joyful production of babies or with the notion of a sanctuary where people may safely recuperate or express feelings that would have no hearing in the outside world. But as I have repeatedly tried to emphasize, the problems of the family can never be isolated from the problems of society at large. In fact, the failures of the middle-class family are less troubling than the realization that it has performed its extraordinary functions mainly as a unit of extravagant and wasteful consumption and that it is this economic role that has made the family indispensable for a capitalist society.

This point seemed innocuous so long as intelligent planners could count on increasing per capita product, and hence per capita consumption, as the solution for human ills. Only a few years ago, the American family appeared to be a model of innocent and carefree abundance— with its separate rooms for each child, its educational toys and travel, its music and swimming lessons, its grassy spaces and child-centered outlook—a model that any society could achieve with sufficient productivity and scientific modernization. The vision lives on, despite our dark glimpses of a new reality principle.[5] But without debating the options

[5] See Hirsch (1976) and Heilbroner (1977).

between various risky and even terrifying futures, I suggest that the crisis over energy and ecology sheds stunning light on the contradictions and sustaining dynamics of the modern middle-class family.

The contradictions arise from the history we have been examining. In a rootless democratic society, the home became the only agent of conservation, the only symbol of a tangible past, the only place where achievement gave way to bonds of affection and loyalty and where people were loved because of who they were. Yet increasingly the family as conservator merged with the family as consumer. During the 19th century, the affluent home could be maintained as a conservatory of culture only by forays into the outside world—forays to the theater and the art museum, forays of tourism and adventure that stocked the household with souvenirs, bric-a-brac, *objets d'art,* and "relics"—the latter term having been originally applied to the holy artifacts that Crusaders brought back from Palestine. Such trophies became embarrassingly standardized; the game of showmanship became more subtle. Twentieth-century homes are far less cluttered than were the family museums of the Victorian era. Yet the message, and the contradiction, is much the same. The family homestead, as an embodiment of historic values and as a refuge from the commercial world, has depended on a symbolic display that can be purchased only in the commercial market. What has changed is that the market has become dependent on encouraging such display.

As advertisers and developers have long sensed, the disruptions of the modern world have greatly enhanced the appeal of supposedly premodern family solidarity—a solidarity that can be achieved, in fantasy, in suburban tract houses that become ranches by virtue of wagon wheels flanking a driveway, or plantations by virtue of small statues of liveried slave boys reaching out to take your horse, or New England manses by virtue of stone walls and fake wells. These one-acre manors are commonly fenced off, are protected by fierce dogs or electronic alarms, and, in keeping with the old American adage that "a man's house is his castle," contain sufficient arms to repel any invader. They also contain washers, dryers, disposals, dishwashers, air-conditioning, color television, gasoline-powered lawnmowers, and central heating. They have been designed, in fact, to consume a maximum amount of the world's resources and energy and thus to create more jobs for the future occupants of similar but improved houses. No one has begun to calculate the overhead cost of establishing from scratch, for each generation, such independent households equipped with appliances and ready for the photo albums, movies, and vacation souvenirs that record the history of an American family.

Let me stress that I am not questioning the benefits of technology or mourning over our undeniable weakness, as human beings, for material possessions. The point is that the American family, which was long seen as a moral counterforce to competitive individualism, has for that very reason become vulnerable to commercial exploitation. For it has been in the name of strengthening the family and supporting its virtues and independence that public policy, since World War II, has encouraged the exodus from cities, the construction of commuter highways, the purchase of automobiles, and the so-called development, at enormous private profit, of track housing and suburban shopping centers— all of which have made the middle-class family an outlet for appalling waste and duplicated effort.

The ultimate question for us is the effect of such exploitation on the family. And here one must recall that the premodern family was governed by sordid calculations regarding doweries, family alliances, and the transmission or consolidation of power. It is surely no more sordid for children to aspire, in their own future families, to outstrip their parents as extravagant consumers. Whereas the authority of fathers was once reinforced by landed property or productive skills that could be transmitted to sons, what is transmitted now is a style and identity as consumer—a transmission and training marked off by such rituals as Christmas and family vacations, much as the child's progression as consumer is marked off by his readiness for a tricycle, a swing set, a television, or a car.

For several millennia at least the family has served as humanity's nurturing and socializing institution, even among slaves and similarly dispossessed peoples. Only within the past century or so, and only within privileged groups confined largely to the Western world, has the family become the combustion engine for an economic system that is rapidly burning itself out, a system characterized, in Jacob Epstein's (1977) words, by declining profits and by

> the constantly rising cost of an extravagant standard of living whose average quality was steadily declining—a decline that could be seen in the collapse of neighborhoods, the wreckage of the natural environment, and the compulsive production of generally useless and increasingly expensive goods while real needs went unmet.

Possibly the family will be strengthened as we ultimately become forced to adopt less wasteful and more cooperative modes of consuming limited resources. One suspects that some of the narcissistic pressures that have weakened the family, such as an apparently growing incapacity to express deep or sustained affect toward people and things, may be related to our instantly disposable and replaceable consumerism. Through premodern, modern, and postmodern periods, the family has shown great resiliency, especially in its parenting role; its role as a sanctuary for self-indulgence may thus be a briefly transitory stage in an enduring history.

REFERENCES

Ariès, P. *Centuries of Childhood: A Social History of Family Life*, tr. by Robert Baldick. New York: Vintage Books, 1965, pp. 100–127.

Ariès, P. The family and the city, *Daedalus*, 1977 (Spring), p. 229.

Cott, N. F. Bonds of Womanhood: Woman's Sphere in New England, 1780–1835 New Haven, Conn.: Yale University Press, 1977.

Demos, J. Development perspectives on the history of childhood. In T. K. Rabb & R. I. Rotberg (Eds.), *The Family in History: Interdisciplinary Essays*. New York: Harper Torchbooks, 1971, pp. 132–133.

Epstein, J. Capitalism and socialism: Declining returns. *New York Review of Books*, 1977 (February 17), p. 37.

Fischer, D. H. *Growing Old in America*. New York: Oxford University Press, 1977.

Heilbroner, R. L. The false promise of growth. *New York Review of Books*, 1977 (March 3), pp. 10–12.

Hirsch, F. *Social Limits to Growth*. Cambridge, Mass.: Harvard University Press, 1976.

McKeown, T. *The Modern Rise of Population*. New York: Academic Press, 1977.

Potter, D. M. *Freedom and Its Limitations in American Life*, ed. by D. E. Fehrenbacher. Stanford, Calif.: Stanford University Press, 1976.

Rossi, A. S. A biosocial perspective on parenting. *Daedalus*, 1977 (Spring), pp. 1–31.

Sklar, K. K. *Catharine Beecher: A Study in American Domesticity*. New Haven, Conn.: Yale University Press, 1973, p. 159.

Stone, L. Massacre of the innocents. *New York Review of Books*, 1974 (November 14), pp. 25–31.

Stone, L. Walking over grandma. *New York Review of Books*, 1977 (May 12), pp. 1–16.

Thomas, K. Age and authority in early modern England. *Proceedings of the British Academy, 62, 1976.*

Tocqueville, A. de. *Democracy in America*, tr. by Henry Reeve, rev. by Francis Bowen, ed. by Phillips Bradley. New York: Vintage Books, 1955, 2 volumes.

IV

STUDIES IN SLAVERY
AND ANTISLAVERY

13

Slavery, and the Post-World War II Historians

FIVE TURNING POINTS IN THE POSTWAR HISTORIOGRAPHY OF NEGRO SLAVERY

In the opening paragraph of *Slavery: A Problem in American Institutional and Intellectual Life* (1959), Stanley M. Elkins refers to "certain inhibitions" that had continued to govern discussions of American Negro slavery. He also speaks of "a painful touchiness in all aspects of the subject."[1] These words may puzzle young historians who have cut their academic teeth on Elkins' much-gnawed Sambo bone, and who have no memory of the awkwardness and embarrassment surrounding the study of slavery in the early 1950's.

The tension arose from two lines of conflicting pressure. On the one hand, however parochial their discipline, historians had by then become aware of the growing sociological literature on racial prejudice and "the Negro problem," a literature that had culminated in Gunnar Myrdal's *An American Dilemma* (1944). The postwar students who eagerly read Myrdal, Franz Boaz, Sinclair Drake, E. Franklin Frazier, John Dollard, and Melville Herskovits discovered that their parents' quiet convictions—the half-whispered "truths" about Negro character—were dangerous stereotypes that had no place in a nation that had crushed Nazi

---

1. Stanley M. Elkins, *Slavery: A Problem in American Institutional and Intellectual Life* (Chicago: University of Chicago Press, 1959), p. 1.

From *Daedalus,* Journal of the American Academy of Arts and Sciences, "Slavery, Colonialism, and Racism," Vol. 3, No. 2 (Spring 1974), Boston, Mass.

racism and committed itself to the defense of the free world. By 1950 it was an embarrassment to find a passage like the following in a popular history that had won acclaim from New Deal liberals:

> The slave system . . . did incalculable harm to the white people of the South, and benefited nobody but the negro, in that it served as a vast training school for African savages. Though the regime of the slave plantations was strict it was, on the whole, a kindly one by comparison with what the imported slave had experienced in his own land. It taught him discipline, cleanliness and a conception of moral standards.[2]

It was hardly less disturbing when the most prestigious and respected textbook of the early 1950's introduced the subject of slavery with the phrase, "as for Sambo," and then proceeded to describe the carefree, happy-go-lucky Negro.

On the other hand, if I may borrow Gene Wise's recent labels for models of historical explanation, the counter-Progressive mode had only begun to appear by the early 1950's; the Progressive mode still reigned.[3] The ghosts of Turner, Parrington, and Beard had by no means been slain. And for the Progressives, including the younger disciples of the school, slavery had always been peripheral to the major forces and struggles that explained the rise of American civilization. Indeed, in the Progressive view, the nineteenth-century obsession with slavery had obscured the fundamental cleavages in American society: the cleavages between labor and big business, between farmers and middlemen, between self-seeking conservatives and liberal men of vision. In the antebellum era, as in the later New Deal years, the children of light had included Southern white supremacists. The search for a usable past, like the search for progressive public policy, required a "realistic" view of America's racial burden. W. E. Woodward's *A New American History* (1936), from which I quoted the above defense of slavery, is simply a popularization, Southern style, of the dominant themes of Progressive historiography. It was not by accident that the Progressive school relinquished the subject of slavery to a Southerner and a disciple of Frederick Jackson Turner, Ulrich Bonnell Phillips. Nor was it accidental that Phillips helped to rehabilitate the South's progressive image by picturing slavery as a system of racial adjustment which had arisen in response to environmental pressures and human needs.

Although Phillips' *American Negro Slavery* appeared in 1918, it was

---

2. W. E. Woodward, *A New American History* (New York: Farrar & Rinehart, Inc., 1936), p. 412.
3. Gene Wise, *American Historical Explanations: A Strategy for Grounded Inquiry* (Homewood, Ill.: The Dorsey Press, 1973).

still the only comprehensive scholarly work on the subject when I attended graduate school some thirty-five years later. My teachers supplemented assignments in Phillips with Frederick Law Olmsted's eye-witness accounts of slavery in the South, apparently assuming that Olmsted's antislavery sentiments would balance some of Phillips' more blatant apologies. For the most part, however, the "inhibitions" described by Elkins helped to consign slavery to a marginal place in the curriculum. For example, a course on the history of religion in America never touched on the slaves' religion or on the religious controversies over slavery. We simply took note of the dates when the major Protestant denominations had divided along sectional lines. At best, slavery could be perceived as a variant on the history of immigration and ethnic conflict. After preparing for my Ph.D. orals in 1954, I remained totally ignorant of the work of such black historians as W. E. B. Du Bois, Carter Woodson, Charles H. Wesley, Benjamin Quarles, Eric Williams, C. L. R. James, and John Hope Franklin. I am confident that few graduate students had at that time encountered Herbert Aptheker's *American Negro Slave Revolts* (1943) or even Frank Tannenbaum's pioneering essay, *Slave and Citizen* (1946), which Stanley Elkins rescued from undeserved obscurity.

There is an astonishing contrast between the inhibitions of the 1950's and the scholarly saturnalia of the past few years. The institution of slavery has now been probed at every spot, often with passionate intensity, and the explosive debates have left few questions settled. Virtually no "fact" or opinion of the earlier scholarly wisdom has gone unchallenged. Phillips has been dethroned as a racist Progressive and then reenlisted in the armies of the Left. Kenneth M. Stampp has been hailed for resolving the tensions between Progressive historiography and postwar racial enlightenment—for recognizing "that one must know what slavery meant to the Negro and how he reacted to it before one can comprehend his more recent tribulations." Stampp has also come to symbolize the unwitting arrogance of white integrationists who assumed "that innately Negroes *are,* after all, only white men with black skins, nothing more, nothing less." [4] Stanley Elkins' calmly reasoned study, which promised to escape the "moral coercions" of a century-long debate, has provoked sufficient warfare to provide an entire volume of critical essays. [5]

4. Kenneth M. Stampp, *The Peculiar Institution: Slavery in the Ante-Bellum South* (New York: Alfred A. Knopf, 1956), pp. vii–viii. It should be emphasized that Stampp's words have often been interpreted out of context, and that even his harshest critics, including Robert W. Fogel and Stanley W. Engerman, have striven to correct the misinterpretation.

5. Ann J. Lane, ed., *The Debate Over "Slavery": Stanley Elkins and His Critics* (Urbana, Ill: University of Illinois Press, 1971).

Meanwhile, we have been offered new and often startling conclusions regarding the history of racial prejudice; the demographic patterns of the Atlantic slave trade and of various slave populations; the nature of slave occupations and the adaptability of slave labor to skilled or industrial employment; the relative efficiency of slave and free labor; the profitability of the institution and its relation to economic growth; the various forms of slave resistance, including insurrection; the place of slavery in American political and Constitutional history; the nature of slave subcultures, including religion, folklore, and various adapted forms of African culture; and above all, the similarities as well as the contrasts between the slave systems of the New World.

Looking back on the profusion of scholarship during the past eighteen years, I would identify five major turning points which have opened new lines of inquiry and have transformed the character of debate. First, Kenneth Stampp's *Peculiar Institution* (1956) ended the era of inhibition by insisting on the "peculiar urgency" of understanding the history of slavery as "a key to understanding the present." By issuing an authoritative answer to Phillips—and indirectly to the entire Progressive tradition of scholarship—Stampp sanitized the subject and thereby placed it on the profession's agenda. As Elkins later noted, Stampp's book was the "culmination and quintessence" of an anti-Phillips reaction which had been signaled as early as 1944 by a cautious and deceptively objective essay by Richard Hofstadter. Elkins shrewdly added that "the strategy of *The Peculiar Institution* was still dictated by Ulrich Phillips," suggesting that the book represented an end rather than a beginning. No doubt many historians greeted Stampp's long-awaited achievement with considerable relief, assuming that Phillips had at last been replaced. In addition, even for Elkins, Stampp opened the way for new and more dispassionate modes of inquiry. Never again, presumably, would it be necessary to debate the moral wrongs of slavery or to rehearse the evidence concerning food, shelter, working hours, police regulations, medical care and punishments.

The Peculiar Institution is a transitional work that exhibits both Progressive and counter-Progressive characteristics. Stampp expressed little of the Progressives' faith in continuing human betterment. He did not see the slave system as the creation of reactionary or self-serving groups. Rather, Southerners "built it little by little, step by step, choice by choice . . . and all the while most of them were more or less blind to the ultimate consequences of the choices they were making." He spoke of "irony," "paradox," and "tragedy," all key terms in the counter-Progressive vocabulary. Yet unlike the counter-Progressives, Stampp opposed "myths" to "facts," in this case the myths of inherent racial characteristics to the facts of postwar social science. His unmistakable theme is the conflict between the oppressed and oppressors, between the weak and the powerful, between the innocent and the guilty. And the prevailing mood of Stampp's book is ultimately optimistic. Even a brutal slave regime, reinforced by racist ideology, could not crush the human spirit. The slaves remained "a troublesome property," capable of resistance as well as endurance. Like the earlier Progressives, Stampp sought to resurrect a usable past, a past that could serve as the first step toward a kind of social therapy. If white Americans could understand the psychic and cultural traumas occasioned by generations of bondage, they would presumably experience the necessary sympathy and guilt to undo the wrongs of the past. The sympathy, it needs to be stressed, required some evidence of the slaves' resistance as proof of their persevering humanity.

Stanley Elkins, who can be credited with the second major breakthrough in historiography, represents the more conservative wing of the counter-Progressive school. It is significant that both Elkins and Stampp paid tribute to Richard Hofstadter, the virtual godfather of counter-Progressivism.[6] Hofstadter, who did not share Elkins' pious respect for ancient institutions, directed the doctoral dissertation which ultimately emerged as *Slavery*. Aside from Hofstadter's initial critique of Phillips, he himself shied away from the subject of slavery. The same can be said of one of Hofstadter's most distinguished senior admirers, Perry Miller. Indeed, the representative figures of the counter-Progressive school—Louis Hartz, Henry Nash Smith, Leo Marx, John William Ward, William R. Taylor, Cushing Strout, and Marvin Meyers—either avoided slavery or treated the subject as a peripheral and embarrassing misfortune. Curiously, the scholars of myth and symbol seemed to take slavery no more seriously than had their Progressive forebears. They recognized Stampp as the new official authority on empirical detail. But much as the Progressives had delegated the last word to Ulrich Phillips, so the counter-Progressives tended to acknowledge Stanley Elkins as their theoretician on slavery and antislavery. Initially, Elkins drew fire from Avery Craven, Oscar Handlin, and David Donald; John William Ward, Nathan Glazer, Eugene D. Genovese, and C. Vann Woodward applauded his originality and boldness. Later on, Elkins would receive his sharpest criticism from blacks, New Leftists, and Marxists.

If Phillips dictated the strategy of Stampp's rebuttal, Elkins dictated the framework of much of the ensuing debate. There is no need here to

6. Richard Hofstadter's counter-Progressive leadership culminated in his masterful critique, *The Progressive Historians: Turner, Beard, Parrington* (New York: Alfred A. Knopf, 1968).

review all the heated controversy over Sambo and the Nazi concentration camp. It is sufficient to note that a considerable amount of energy has been expended in attempts to refute Elkins on three fronts: to show that Latin American slavery was not necessarily more open, flexible, and humane than North American slavery; to show that North American slavery did not bring a fundamental personality change in its victims, reducing the typical bondsman to a childlike, submissive, carefree, and self-depreciating Sambo; and to show that American abolitionists were not irresponsible, guilt-obsessed antinomians, whose contempt for institutions precluded a rational solution to social problems. The latter debate is still in its early stages and is not central to a discussion of the recent historiography on slavery. The battles on the first two fronts appear to have been won, or rather to have shifted to new ground after the neutralization of Elkins' salient positions.

I have chosen the word "neutralization" with some care, since Elkins shielded his arguments from the possibility of refutation. His portraits of Latin American and North American slavery are essentially ideal models, illustrating the polar extremes of open and closed slave systems. The "Sambo thesis" is a corollary to Elkins' view of North American slavery as the creation of "unopposed capitalism," an exploitive impulse unmitigated by institutional safeguards or a balance of political and cultural interests. Numerous critics, among them Sidney W. Mintz, Arnold Sio, Marvin Harris, David Brion Davis, Orlando Patterson, Carl N. Degler, Roy Simon Bryce-Laporte, Herbert Gutman, and Franklin W. Knight, have marshaled empirical evidence which clashes with Elkins' paradigms. It has been demonstrated that the more humane provisions of Latin American slave law were often not enforced, and that North American slavery was more complex, varied, and open than the laws imply. We have also learned that the sugar boom in nineteenth-century Cuba and the coffee boom in nineteenth-century Brazil led to highly regimented, exploitive forms of plantation slavery which approximate Elkins' model of "unopposed capitalism" in the United States; that the Sambo stereotype was by no means confined to the United States; that slaves in the United States had considerably more psychological and cultural "space" than Elkins suggests, and that they maintained a surprising stability of family life and succeeded in creating and preserving their own religion and folklore.[7] On the other hand, empirical evidence

7. See Lane, ed., *Debate Over "Slavery,"* and also Franklin W. Knight, *Slave Society in Cuba During the Nineteenth Century* (Madison: University of Wisconsin Press, 1970); Robert Brent Toplin, *The Abolition of Slavery in Brazil* (New York: Atheneum, 1972); Robert Conrad, *The Destruction of Brazilian Slavery, 1850–1888* (Berkeley: University of California Press, 1972); John

by itself cannot disprove Elkins' arguments. If Latin American culture significantly modified men's response to human bondage, and there can be no doubt that it did, Elkins can dismiss a sugar boom or nonenforcement of laws as exceptions that merely qualify a model that he never intended to be taken literally. If slaves in the United States generally accommodated themselves to white dominion, and no one could deny that they did, then Elkins can leave open the question of "internalization" and express his willingness to settle for a "broad belt of indeterminacy between 'mere acting' and the 'true self.' "[8]

As conceptual categories, Elkins' models had the great merit of raising key questions that went beyond the earlier fruitless debate over the cruelty or humaneness of American slavery. The key questions centered on two points: the relationship between cultural heritage and the economic pressures of plantation agriculture, and the relationship between the slaves' accommodation and resistance. Both points have been most thoroughly and imaginatively examined by Eugene D. Genovese, who has proved to be Elkins' most effective critic. I shall have occasion to return to Genovese' work later in this essay, and will now simply emphasize Genovese's indebtedness to Elkins. If Genovese questioned the utility of Elkins' models, he also incorporated them into his own explanatory framework. He rightly complained that Elkins' models were too rigid, oversimplified, and deterministic. Elkins ignored large bodies of conflicting and often blurred the distinction between a hypothetical construct and historical reality. The Sambo thesis was objectionable "not because it fails to account for hostile behavior, but because it proves too much and encompasses more forms of behavior than can usefully be managed under a single rubric." Yet Genovese had little patience with Elkins' critics who had been content merely to point to instances of slave rebelliousness or to Latin American cruelty. Elkins had raised the more subtle challenge of conceptualizing contradictions. How could one explain the docile, childlike slave who becomes a Nat Turner or Toussaint L'Ouverture? How could cruelty and paternalism be expressions of the same class position? How did the master-slave relationship modify cultural heritage and Old World traditions of lordship and bondage? If the dominion and dependency of the master-slave relationship tended to gravitate toward certain universal norms, what was the effect of geography, ecology, population distribution, and economic organi-

---

W. Blassingame, *The Slave Community: Plantation Life in the Ante-Bellum South* (New York: Oxford University Press), 1972.

8. Lane, ed., *Debate Over "Slavery,"* pp. 350–359.

zation? It was Elkins' methodological breakthrough, and the ensuing controversy it provoked, that led Genovese to the ambitious task of encompassing all variables and contradications within a dialectical theory of class and ideology.[9]

In his first and rather unseasoned book, *The Political Economy of Slavery* (1965), Genovese cautiously took issue with Alfred H. Conrad and John R. Meyer, two economists who in 1957 had ushered in what is now termed "the Cliometric Revolution." The burden of Genovese's book was to prove that slavery had been disastrous for the South's economy, which could only be saved, within the exploitive framework of national capitalism, by territorial expansion.[10] According to Genovese, slavery led to soil exhaustion, low productivity of labor, technological retardation, a restricted market, and numerous other competitive disadvantages. Conrad and Meyer had used sophisticated mathematical and statistical models to show that the purchase of a slave in the ante-bellum South was a highly profitable investment which yielded rates of return comparable to those from investments in Northern manufacturing. Since Genovese was concerned with the larger social and ideological effects of slaveholding, the narrow question of profitability appeared to be a minor annoyance. Theoretically, slavery might be profitable for slave owners and still give rise to the values and attitudes of a "precapitalist class," values and attitudes antithetical to balanced economic growth. Genovese sought to give a Marxian reformulation to the traditional picture of the South's economic backwardness. Since the Cliometric Revolution has now challenged every point of that traditional picture, it is clear that the initial paper by Conrad and Meyer must be classed as a third major turning point.[11]

The swelling Cliometric literature culminates in Robert William Fogel and Stanley L. Engerman's *Time on the Cross: The Economics of Amer-*

---

9. Eugene D. Genovese's initial essays have been collected in *In Red and Black: Marxian Explorations in Southern and Afro-American History* (New York: Pantheon Books, 1971). His thesis on the varying relationships between cultural heritage and the pressures of plantation agriculture can be found in *The World the Slaveholders Made: Two Essays in Interpretation* (New York: Pantheon Books, 1969), Part One. Genovese's detailed explorations of slave accommodation and resistance will appear in *Roll Jordan Roll* (1974). I am indebted to Professor Genovese for allowing me to read the latter manuscript.

10. *The Political Economy of Slavery: Studies in the Economy and Society of the Slave South* (New York: Pantheon Books, 1965).

11. The essay, "The Economics of Slavery in the Ante-Bellum South," has been reprinted in Alfred H. Conrad and John R. Meyer, *The Economics of Slavery and Other Econometric Studies* (Chicago: Aldine Publishing Co., 1964). For a review of the literature on profitability, see Harold D. Woodman, "The Profitability of Slavery: A Historical Perennial," *Journal of Southern History*, 29 (August 1963), pp. 303–325, which has been reprinted, along with many other valuable selections, in Allen Weinstein and Frank Otto Gatell, *American Negro Slavery: A Modern Reader*, 2nd ed. (New York: Oxford University Press, 1973).

ican Negro Slavery (1974), a book which incorporates the previous work
of many economists and historians, and which rests on the quantification
of prodigious empirical research.[12] In their attempt to correct "past error," Fogel and Engerman go far beyond the question of profitable investment. They maintain that slaves were highly efficient and productive
workers; that slave agriculture was 35 percent more efficient than the
Northern system of family farming; that slave labor was successfully
adapted to urban and industrial conditions; that slave owners encouraged
the stability of slave families, and provided their workers with a material standard of life that compared favorably with that of free industrial
labor; that slavery did not retard economic growth; that between 1840
and 1860 per capita income increased more rapidly in the South than in
the rest of the nation; that slavery as an economic system had never
been stronger than on the eve of the Civil War, when slaveholders rationally anticipated an era of unprecedented prosperity. These startling
conclusions are bound to provoke continuing controversy, though most
skeptical historians are ill-equipped to dispute the Cliometricians' technical apparatus and procedures. I shall later take note of some of the
nontechnical implications of Fogel and Engerman's work, which is certain to influence discussions of slavery for a long time to come.

Like everyone else, the Cliometricians have been heavily indebted to
a fourth seminal study which has transformed our view of New World
slavery, Philip D. Curtin's *The Atlantic Slave Trade: A Census* (1969).[13]
Frank Tannenbaum and Stanley Elkins had helped to break the barriers
of provincialism that had long distorted perceptions of slavery in the
American South. Curtin not only put the demography of the slave trade
in a hemispheric setting, but came to the remarkable conclusion that
North America (excluding Mexico) received no more than 4.5 percent
of all the slaves imported into the New World. Curtin's breakdowns of
estimated slave imports were even more dramatic than his evidence that
previous studies had greatly exaggerated the total number of African
slaves brought to the New World. His careful assessments underscored
the importance of the natural increase of the black population in the
United States, of the net natural decrease of the slave populations in the

12. I am extremely grateful to Professors Fogel and Engerman for allowing me to read various
manuscript versions of their forthcoming book, which will be published early in 1974 by Little,
Brown and Company. Unfortunately, the deadline for this essay has prevented me from having
access to more than limited portions of the revised proof of *Time on the Cross*. Some of my
references therefore refer to manuscript. Although it is hazardous to offer judgments on a work
that has not yet been published in final form, it would be even more hazardous to ignore a work
which is bound to make 1974 a landmark in the historiography of slavery, and which in manuscript
has already evoked international respect and controversy.

13. Philip D. Curtin, *The Atlantic Slave Trade: A Census* (Madison: University of Wisconsin
Press, 1969).

sugar colonies and in Brazil, and of the long dependence of the latter regions on a continuing labor supply from Africa. Though Curtin modestly limited the scope of his inquiry, it opened the way for much-needed studies on regional mortality and morbidity rates, on the sex and age structure of slave populations, on African origins and changing patterns of slave-trading. Above all, Curtin demonstrated the significance of demography for any comparison of slave systems. For example, the relative independence of the United States from the Atlantic slavetrading system raises a host of unanswered political, social, and ideological questions.

The fifth turning point for the study of slavery is not a single work but is rather the availability in published form of the evidence of slaves themselves. Although a few white historians had earlier made use of the autobiographies of ex-slaves, such sources had commonly been regarded with extreme caution, on the assumption that fugitive slaves could not write and that their accounts were fabricated to fit the needs of abolitionist propaganda. It is only recently that John W. Blassingame and other scholars have subjected the autobiographies to critical scrutiny, and have found that many of the ex-slaves were not fugitives and that many had no abolitionist amanuenses. We now have a rich library of reprinted autobiographies, as well as critical criteria for their evaluation. An even richer mine of information is Greenwood Publishing Company's nineteen volume series, *The American Slave: A Composite Autobiography,* containing more than 2,000 WPA interviews with ex-slaves.[14] If allowances must be made for the biases of nineteenth-century autobiographies, allowance must also be made for the biases of WPA interviewers. Nevertheless, historians have begun to shed the prejudices which long defined as inadmissible the most revealing kinds of eye-witness evidence. One point on which the United States is indisputably unique among former slaveholding nations is in its abundance of documented slave testimony. The significance of that fact hast not yet received the attention it deserves. In any event, the future course of historical inquiry will be no less dependent on the personal reminiscences of ex-slaves than on the demographical and econometric calculations that flow from the pioneering work of Curtin, Conrad, and Meyer. And if Stampp and Elkins addressed themselves to issues which now see to have been superseded, it is only because the issues themselves have been incorporated into new frames of reference.

14. George P. Rawick has written a valuable introductory volume to the series, *From Sundown to Sunup: The Making of the Black Community* (Westport, Conn.: Greenwood Publishing Co. 1972). It should be stressed that various black historians and social scientists, including Carter Woodson and E. Franklin Frazier, had earlier made valuable use of the black autobiographies and WPA narratives.

THE REWARDS AND PERILS OF PRESENTISM

American historians often write with a message for the present, assuming that their subject has, as Kenneth Stampp put it, a "peculiar urgency." But historians have little say about the public's definition of "relevance." In the 1950's no one could have predicted the astonishing upsurge of interest in American Negro slavery. Neither Stampp or Elkins wrote for a bullish market. For some years specialists alone took note of their books. The research for most of the scholarly landmarks of the 1960's, such as Winthrop D. Jordan's *White Over Black* (1968), originated in an era of relative public indifference toward slavery and race. No doubt Little Rock, the lunch counter sit-ins, and the Freedom Rides all quickened a limited public interest in "historical background." But the true black studies boom commenced in 1963, fed by the unforgettable images of the Birmingham boycott; of Bull Connor's police and of the unconvictable Sheriff Lawrence Rainey; of Malcolm X exhorting Black Muslims; and of Martin Luther King electrifying the massed throngs in Washington.

How had America arrived at such a crisis? Where had the traditional assumptions and expectations gone astray? The presses churned out a small library of answers, flooding the literate public with paperbacks, essays, feature stories, scholarly monographs, and reprints of long forgotten works. If the modern reading public has generally abandoned history as a source of entertainment and edicification, it retains a spasmodic need for quick historical orientation to immediate crises. The questions of the early 1960's were ethnocentrically self-evident. Why had Negroes failed to "assimilate" like other immigrant groups? Had the old schoolbooks been wrong in portraying slaves as relatively happy and well-treated? Why had Negroes ever been brought to America in the first place? The more popular explanations were not the work of historians, but often drew on Elkins and other recently established authorities. By the mid-1960's black writers began raising strident voices of dissent. The crisis, they insisted, was not one "in black and white," or in "race relations." White scholars who studied "the Negro problem" were simply the intellectual heirs of slaveholders who had studied problems of slave management. Black history, when controlled by whites and when dominated by the psychological needs of whites, was simply another weapon to preserve the cultural hegemony of the dominant race. The black critics grasped a crucial point, but soon blurred it by silly disputes over whether whites could legitimately write or teach about the black experience.

This is not the place to review the violent clashes over black studies programs in colleges and universities, or to examine the complex effects of public pressure on historical scholarship.[15] I shall content myself with three observations. First, it is obvious that the racial concerns of the 1960's channeled public and private funds into various programs for the study of Afro-American life and culture. Many of these programs sought to collect and disseminate well-known information. But in England and South America, as well as in the United States, the renewed interest in slavery also led to scholarly symposia, conferences, and coordinated research. By the late 1960's, scholars working on various aspects of New World slavery were closely in touch with one anothers' work. They also enjoyed an apparently insatiable market, by academic standards, for their outpouring of books and articles. It needs to be stressed, however, that the fruits of historical research take long to ripen. The serious revaluation of slavery began long before the public demand for historical background. The faddishness of Afro-American studies has produced a shelf of fly-by-night books of questionable merit. The classroom and textbook market has long been saturated. By now many students must be weary of readings on slavery and racial conflict; the memories of CORE and SNICC are as remote and distantly heroic as were the memories of Bastogne and Iwo Jima to the early 1950's. Yet we still await the full harvest of a decade's seeding: for example, the publication of the Frederick Douglass papers, the completion of Louis Harlan's masterful biography of Booker T. Washington, Eugene Genovese's monumental study of slave-master relations, the fruition of the Cliometric Revolution, to say nothing of studies that begin to compare the Negro slavery of the New World with various other historical forms of slavery and involuntary servitude. In other words, the civil rights and Black Power movements gave an impetus, sometimes distorting, sometimes enriching, to a scholarly enterprise which really began with the pioneering work of C. L. R. James, Eric Williams, and Frank Tannenbaum, and which has hardly begun to reach its crest.

My second observation is that the urgency of the civil rights movement focused attention on white racial prejudice, particularly on its psychology and historical origins. Postwar historians, enlightened by the earlier environmentalist school of social science, have understandably been preoccupied with the origins of their forebears' Negrophobia. In a sense, their interest in slavery has been derivative. Was New World slavery a product of the colonizer's racial prejudice, or did the prejudice arise from a functional contempt for slaves? And is slavery the ultimate

15. I have expressed some thoughts on this subject in a collection of essays which also provides a sampling of the black critique of white scholarship, *Black Studies in the University: A Symposium,* ed. Armstead L. Robinson, Craig C. Foster, and Donald H. Ogilvie (New Haven, Conn.: Yale University Press, 1969).

source of America's continuing racial malaise? These and related questions have been fruitful guides to inquiry, and have perhaps been definitively explored in such works as Jordan's *White Over Black* (1968), Carl N. Degler's *Neither Black nor White* (1971), and George M. Fredrickson's *The Black Image in the White Mind* (1971). It is conceivable, however, that the racial focus has cropped out questions of equal importance. Degler and others have underscored the point. For example, the attention devoted to racial conflict and racial adjustment—problems easily consigned to the realm of group psychology—may well have obscured questions of class, culture, and power that lead to the structural foundations of America society. I think it is not improbable that future studies of slavery will be less concerned with race as the ultimate reality, especially as we more accurately locate slavery on a spectrum of labor systems. Similarly, I suspect that future historians will be less certain about the importance of slavery in explaining post-emancipation patterns of racial oppression. Thus far, we have no comparative studies of racism, but have defensively suggested that their own interpretation cropping in post-emancipation societies.[16] Nor has anyone ventured to explain why, in the years immediately following the Armistice of 1918, race riots erupted in Liverpool and other English cities as well as in the United States.[17]

My final and broader observation, in this connection, is that postwar historians have not only striven to dissociate themselves from any taint of racism, but that defensively suggested that their own interpretation of slavery is the only one free from racist implications. The antiracist protestations are laudable, but the game of dodge ball has led to considerable confusion. Thus Kenneth Stampp proved his faith in equality by arguing that slaves suffered unspeakable hardships and deprivations, but were never crushed in spirit. His readers could conclude (1) that the deprivations helped to account for later seeming incapacities; (2) that slave resistance, which for Stampp included lying, stealing, sabotage, and work slowdowns, gave cause for hope; (3) that since the nation had sanctioned a system that wrought private profit at such a heavy human cost, the aggrieved heirs of slavery deserved some form of restitution.

But according to Stanley Elkins, even Stampp underestimated the deprivations. The typical slave had been broken in spirit, or in Elkins' terms, psychologically "infantalized." Only the harshest and most

16. C. Vann Woodward has long been working on such questions, and provides intriguing suggestions of what his forthcoming studies may accomplish in *American Counterpoint: Slavery and Racism in the North-South Dialogue* (Boston: Little Brown, 1971).

17. For England, see James Walvin, *Black and White: The Negro and English Society, 1555–1945* (London: Allen Lane, the Penguin Press, 1973).

hopeless system of slavery could account for the American Negro's degradation—that is, for his servile dependence on whites, for his self-
depreciation, for his lack of family stability, for his irresponsibility, and
for his alienation from any cultural heritage or institutional identity. This
environmentalist thesis, presented as a rebuttal to theories of biological
inferiority, opened Elkins to the charge of racism in disguise. Black
critics, especially, sensed that Elkins had accepted the racist terms of
his presumed antagonists. Yet the black critics could not easily free
themselves from another bind. They hardly wished to minimize the sufferings of their ancestors; yet they clearly saw the hazards of being
Elkinized. Who, after all, would want to claim Sambo for his grand-
father? Yet who, in the 1960's would want to claim that slavery was
not as bad as Elkins said? In point of fact, Elkins provided two escape
routes. First, he insisted that Latin American slaves had not been reduced to Sambos. Hence the infantalization process could not be attributed to the African temperament or even to slavery per se. It may
have been little comfort for North American blacks to know that their
Latin neighbors had escaped the psychological traumas of slavery. But
Elkins also contended that the infantalization process had ended with
emancipation. After the closed system had been broken, progress was
possible. Time and therapy could heal. Unfortunately, the historical evidence—especially that accumulated by Herbert Gutman, Genovese, Fogel, and Engerman—suggests that American blacks had greater family
stability and access to skilled occupations prior to the Civil War than
afterwards. It is clear that Elkins intended his harsh portrait of slavery
to provide the grounds for continuing white patience and forebearance.
In the 1950's, at least, it appeared that a more sanguine image of slavery could only reinforce unenlightened complaints that enough allowances had been made, that enough time had elapsed for Negroes to
begin to behave like white men.

Genovese, in his earlier essays, attacked Elkins for underestimating
the slaves' capacity for resistance, the integrity of their separate culture,
and their sustaining ties with an African past. Genovese also frankly
acknowledged the corollary to his thesis: Southern slaveholders were not
SS guards, systematically intent on torture and human debasement. Indeed, they desired nothing more than the genuine loyalty and gratitude
of their slaves. Unlike the paid functionaries who managed the West
Indian plantations for absentee owners, the Southern proprietors had an
interest in creating a viable society. Genovese agreed with Elkins that
Southern planters were not content with labor discipline alone. They
could accept nothing less than total cultural hegemony, which required

psychological dominion and the shaping of slave personality. But to achieve these objectives, Genovese insisted, the planters relied far less on coercion than on paternalism—that is, on alternating acts of kindness and cruelty, on flattery and rebuke, on bribes and deprivations. In a sense, Genovese turned Elkins upside down. White paternalism posed a far more serious threat to black autonomy that did any coercive attempts at dehumanization. And the slaves' only hope for resisting total dominion lay not in self-defeating insurrections or even in petty acts of theft and sabotage, but rather in responding to paternalism on their own terms. That the slaves succeeded in transmogrifying their masters' paternalism is the thesis of Genovese's *Roll Jordan Roll* (1974), one of the crowning achievements of the entire postwar scholarship on race and slavery, a work which brings a rich empathy, warmth, and humor to the dialectic of accommodation and resistance, a dialectic both subtle in process and deadly serious in conflicting objectives.

The immense learning and human concreteness of *Roll Jordan Roll* may satisfy critics who have objected to the abstractness of Genovese's categories and to the fuzziness of his concept of paternalism. Yet his professed Marxism may no longer provide protective coloration against the charge of sentimentalizing or romanticizing slavery. There are still ideological risks in softening the conventional, neoabolitionist view of Negro slavery, notwithstanding Genovese's attempts to pay homage to the integrity of black culture and to assimilate racial conflict into a larger structure of class conflict. It remains to be seen whether radical credentials will allow Genovese to get away with his bold and brilliant rehabilitation of the black Mammy who ministers to the whites in the Big House, or of the black driver whose mediating role depends on a faithful execution of the master's discipline. Genovese has suggested that the unwitting racists are those who measure black religion and family life against white middle-class norms, who conclude that slaves were defenseless and emasculated victims, and who fasten the guilt for America's continuing racial oppression on a small group of malicious planters.[18] More than any other modern scholar, Genovese has defied the pressures and compromises of presentism, and has fought to lift historical scholarship above the irresponsible rhetoric of racial conflict. Yet Genovese's work is saturated with defenses against racial bias, defenses which have sometimes implied that only radical scholars can escape the liberals' typical condescension on race. And when unfairly accused of

18. I should stress, however, that Genovese has scrupulously avoided accusing other scholars of racism.

racism himself, Genovese has delivered shrill attacks on black students of "dubious political connections," who may well have been, as he asserts, "agents-provocateurs" bent on exploiting racial antagonisms for political purposes.[19]

My point is simply that even the bravest and most honest historians have not been able to escape the coercions of the times, and that each new interpretation of slavery has professed to be more antiracist than the ones it replaces. The supreme irony, in this curious pattern of protestation, comes with Fogel and Engerman's *Time on the Cross,* a work which in most respects would bring a smile of approval from the grim lips of John C. Calhoun.

Time on the Cross is at times a self-defeating book. Its critically important contributions, presented in the guise of scientific objectivity, are often muddied by an emotional style and animus which reflect two non-scientific compulsions of the age: first, the compulsion to replace the uncertainties of traditional, impressionistic history with "hard" scientific facts, verified by computers and mathematical techniques; second, the compulsion to prove that the findings of Cliometrics will not only "expose many myths that have served to corrode and poison relations between the races, but also help to put into a new perspective some of the most urgent issues of our day." Fogel and Engerman do not consider the possibility that the findings of supposedly impartial Cliometrics might further corrode and poison the relations between the races, or that the "new perspective" on the most urgent issues of our day might clash with their own personal values.

To be fair, the authors acknowledge the limitations of scientific history and profess the laudable goal of integrating Cliometrics with humanistic values. They contend that rigorous mathematical and statistical methods, combined with "formal behavioral models," will help to clarify moral issues and reduce the number of questions on which speculation is the only option. Fogel and Engerman also admit that they have not been entirely successful in expunging all ideology from their book (they define ideology as "an unverified proposition which is held to be true," as distinct from "knowledge" which has "been verified according to a set of objective criteria such as those employed in statistics or in various fields of science"). But despite the authors' homage to the humanities, despite their indispensable contributions to knowledge, their

---

19. Genovese, *In Red and Black,* p. vi. His reference was to the explosive conflicts at Sir George Williams University. It is a mark of the extreme pressures of presentism that Genovese felt it necessary to refer to such conflicts in dedicating a collection of historical essays. Although his phrasing gives the opposite impression, Genovese's mention of "agents-provocateurs" referred to whites, not blacks.

prose is redolent with the stale battlesmoke from the war of the Two Cultures. Their tone is both defensive and belligerent. They speak of their "passion for discovering the facts," of their unremitting search for "hard" evidence, of their disdain for the "easy solutions" evoked by ideological debate. In a lengthy appendix, which provides an invaluable analysis of "the traditional interpretation of the slave economy, 1865–1956," they nail Kenneth Stampp to the cross, taunting him for his statistical errors, his nonscientific methodology, and his failure "to effect a fundamental break with racist depictions of the antebellum Negro, despite his enormous desire to do so." To the quaking and besieged humanist, Fogel and Engerman speak casually of their legions of research assistants, of their mobile SAM computers, of their electronic weaponry, of their occupation of every hidden and unknown strategic site—in short, we are told that we are encircled, cut off, and cannot fight back unless we have weapons-systems equal to those of the Cliometricians.

Yet we are not told why objective scientists baptise their book with the evangelical title, *Time on the Cross,* or why they allow themselves the indulgence, for example, of accusing the abolitionists of helping "to fasten the spikes that have kept blacks in the agony of racial discrimination during their century of freedom." The tone of *Time on the Cross* is often similar to that of a modern sex manual. The scientific researchers not only promise to give us the inside dope, but candidly confess that they offer us a "disturbing book," one which requires the "forebearance" of its readers (presumably, mature adults). After the warning of X-rating, we learn that "some of the discoveries were at one time as unbelievable to the Cliometricians as they will be to the readers of this volume. Indeed, many of the findings presented in the chapters that follow were initially discounted, even rejected out of hand as being too absurd to be true." This sort of sensationalism whets the reader's appetite. Is it possible that heterosexuality or monogamous marriage are founded on unscientific data? Is it possible that slavery was a positive good, both for blacks and whites? Like most sex manuals, *Time on the Cross* startles us and then comes down on the side of righteousness.

The startling arguments would be unobjectionable if they had not been grouped as a series of revelations, if they had carried some sense of human meaning and of the individual personalities involved, if they had referred to specific situations and environments instead of to vague statistical aggregates, and if they had not been followed by antiracist protestations, which sound much like sermons on spontaneous sexuality after statistical tables on the incidence of orgasm. To be specific, Fogel and Engerman marshal considerable statistical evidence to show that

Southern masters encouraged the family stability and promoted the material welfare of their slaves. The typical field hand, we learn, received during his lifetime approximately 90 percent of the income he produced. The slave system in no way thwarted the economic development of the South; in material terms, the slaves were no worse off than contemporary unskilled free workers. The blacks' opportunities and well-being declined after emancipation. Hence the Cliometricians would seem to have resurrected the essential arguments of proslavery philosophy. Of course Fogel and Engerman quickly deny this conclusion. The capital mistake of Kenneth Stampp and other neoabolitionist historians, they claim, was to focus attention on treatment and physical welfare. Slaves did suffer cultural and psychological deprivations—such as the denial of education and of access to the higher professions (we have no comparisons on such matters with Irish immigrants or women). From one point of view, according to Fogel and Engerman, the slaves did suffer exploitation. The true beneficiaries of the remarkably profitable system were the consumers of cotton textiles, whose diffused and therefore attenuated gains could not be justified by the concentrated losses of the slave labor force.

Yet Fogel and Engerman say very little about the implications of exploitation or the long-term effects of cultural deprivation. Of all the variables they consider, it is slave productivity that emerges as the dominant theme. They tell us that they have "attacked the traditional interpretation of the economics of slavery not in order to resurrect a defunct system but in order to correct the perversion of the history of blacks." The disastrous flaw in the abolitionist and neoabolitionist argument was to denigrate blacks by depreciating their performance as slaves, even when attributing the cause to an economic system. Hence Fogel and Engerman assert their own antiracism by detecting a subtle and lingering racism in those historians who have attributed "stunted development" not to biological inferiority but to "unfortunate sociological circumstances." With *Time on the Cross* we thus come full circle. A sanguine view of slavery, including its economic viability and its relative lack of deprivation, becomes a weapon in defense of black capability—of capability, it must be stressed, as defined by the standards of capitalist economics.

CONVERGENCE?

The weakest sections of *Time on the Cross* rest on a naive moralism and on a conviction that scientific history can resolve moral issues by at last setting the record straight. Fogel and Engerman's statistical data may or may not be modified over time, but they have already shaken conventional assumptions on the economics of Negro slavery. The substantive conclusions of *Time on the Cross* will not be easily brushed aside. On the surface, at least, the work of the Cliometricians would seem to be directly at odds with the work of Genovese. Like Stampp and Elkins, Fogel and Engerman insist on the capitalistic character of Southern slavery but argue that the forces of the market and of individual self-interest protected the slave from dehumanization. For Genovese, on the other hand, it was precisely the noncapitalist character of slaveholding that gave blacks room for maneuver and for preserving a cultural identity of their own. And according to Genovese, it was the noncapitalist aspects of slavery that ultimately defined the ideology of the master class and the fatal weaknesses of Southern society.

Insofar as *Time on the Cross* and *Roll Jordan Roll* represent the historiographical trends of the 1970's, they promise continuing controversy and point to diverging lines of interpretation. Yet further commentators may also be struck by certain lines of convergence. Genovese, no less than the Cliometricians, stresses the excellence and diversity of the slaves' occupational skills. As a result of the pioneering and tragically unfinished work of Robert Starobin, no one has recently questioned the adaptability of slave labor to mining and industry.[20] Michael Craton and James Walvin have shown that the most prosperous sugar estates of Jamaica depended on a tapping of slave talent, on an encouragement of slave skills and managerial ability, and ultimately on a slave elite of "Head People" who received preferential treatment.[21] When Fogel and Engerman offer statistical evidence on the stability of American slave families, they simply add strength to the arguments of Genovese, John Blassingame, and a host of other scholars—scholars who have also stressed the persistence and adaptability of African folklore, religion, iconography, and linguistic forms. In short, we have come a long way from the 1950's, when Elkins' concentration camp analogy seemed to explain the anomic and cultural disorientation which probably had less to do with slavery than with the Negroes' later migration to the ghettos of racially volatile cities. It is now at least conceivable that the share-cropper's "voluntary" move to Chicago or New York was at least as traumatic as the original slave trade.

Yet we must always be wary of presentist influences. The Birming-

20. Robert Starobin, *Industrial Slavery in the Old South* (New York: Oxford University Press, 1970).

21. Michael Craton and James Walvin, *A Jamaican Plantation: The History of Worthy Park, 1670–1970* (Toronto: University of Toronto Press, 1970).

ham of 1963 now seems almost as remote as the Mississippi plantation
of 1853. Today the once intransigent South seems almost as benign as
did Brazil, in the 1950's, to North American eyes. We are less prone
to sectionalize our dilemmas and responsibilities, but thereby run the
risk of idealizing the preurban slavocracies. If the emerging interpretations of slavery mark an undoubted advance in complexity and sophis-
tication, we should also be suspicious of the interests they serve—the
desire to prove that American Negroes preserved a degree of cultural
autonomy; that they escaped the scars of psychic impairment; that a free
market economy does not produce insoluble social problems; that a precapitalist labor system allows for more honest human interaction than
does a wage-and-profit system; that our fundamental ills stem from urbanization and its accompanying lack of regional and familial identity.

To their credit, Fogel and Engerman refer constantly, if somewhat
hazily, to the psychological costs of Negro slavery. It is precisely this
realm which Stanley Elkins overdramatized, and which Eugene Genovese has sought to redefine in terms of class and ideology. The non-
measurable realm of human dominion and resistance, which the Cliometricians helplessly classify as moral and ideological, is for Genovese
the heart of the entire problem. If Genovese is right, and I think he is,
the fundamental insight does not lie in Marx, or in the history of abolitionist propaganda, but in some highly condensed and eternally relevant
passages "on lordship and bondage" in Hegel's *Phenomenology of the
Mind*.

14

Of Human Bondage

Slavery and Social Death: A Comparative Study
by Orlando Patterson.
Harvard University Press,
511 pp., $30.00

The founders of social science expressed a continuing interest in the origins and workings of human bondage. This interest can be traced from Montesquieu and John Millar in the eighteenth century to Tocqueville, Comte, Marx, Lewis Henry Morgan, Sir Henry Maine, Spencer, E. B. Taylor, Edward Westmarck, William Graham Sumner, and Max Weber. The ideology of moral and material progress, coupled with debates over the ''anomaly'' of chattel slavery in the New World, also led by the 1840s to the first systematic histories of Greco-Roman slavery and to theories explaining the institution's decline and disappearance from Western Europe. In the major European languages scholars and popularizers produced thick volumes on the history of slavery from antiquity to modern times. However superficial or filled with Christian moralizing, this nineteenth-century literature recognized the importance and puzzling variations of an institution that has appeared from the time of the first written and ethnographic records and in virtually every part of the world.

But from the First World War to the mid-1950s (a period that set new records for the mobilization, degradation, and extermination of millions of unfree workers), slavery almost disappeared as a subject of central theoretical and historical interest. As Igor Kopytoff has recently pointed out, anthropology "almost completely forgot slavery" in this period when "so much of its modern world view was being forged." According to the standard textbooks and general works, "the message has been that slavery is incomparably less important a phenomenon than *compadrazco* or the distinction between cross and parallel cousins."[1]

For non-Marxian economists slavery raised few promising questions until 1957, when Alfred H. Conrad and John R. Meyer applied to historical data modern mathematical models and statistical techniques.[2] During the interwar decades American history was largely dominated by disciples of the "Progressive historians"—notably Frederick Jackson Turner and Charles Beard—who held that slavery had always been peripheral to the major forces and struggles that explained the rise of American civilization. Black slavery became a branch of "Southern history," a field increasingly devoted to vindicating the Lost Cause, to exposing the imperialist motives of the capitalist North, and to reinterpreting the Civil War as an avoidable and calamitous American tragedy. Between 1918 and 1956 the monumental but frankly racist work of Ulrich B. Phillips, who was strongly influenced by Turner and was the star of the William A. Dunning school of pro-Southern historiography, remained the standard authority on American Negro slavery. The one sentiment shared by the historians who romanticized the antebellum South and the antiracist anthropologists who emphathized with "primitive" and often slaveholding peoples was a common antipathy toward the modernizing, moralistic "civilization" that had brought on the First World War and global depression.

Even critics of Phillips and other racist scholars tended to accept the premise that black slavery was an aspect of the essentially southern or West Indian "racial problem." The pioneering works of such scholars as Melville J. Herskovits, E. Franklin Frazier, John Dollard, and Gunnar Myrdal challenged the myths that helped to justify racial discrimination and segregation, but they were concerned only incidentally with the meaning of human bondage. Knowledge of the structure and dynamics of modern slavery thus depended to a large extent on Afro-American studies.

1. "Slavery," *Annual Review of Anthropology*, vol. 11 (1982), pp. 207–227. As Kopytoff acknowledges, a few social scientists of the interwar period did produce important empirical and theoretical studies of slavery. In addition to William C. MacLeod's articles on slavery among North American aborigines, one should especially note the work of H. Lévy-Bruhl, G. Landtman, A. A. Alwahed, and B. J. Siegel (in the 1940s).

2. Essays published in *The Economics of Slavery and Other Studies in Econometric History* (Aldine, 1964).

From 1916 to the 1960s *The Journal of Negro History*, published by the Association for the Study of Negro Life and History, provided the main forum for a small group of scholars who defined the issues and did much to start the great revival of interest in slavery during the past two decades. A magazine for such black historians as Carter G. Woodson, William M. Brewer, Charles H. Wesley, Benjamin Quarles, and Eric Williams, the *Journal* was also one of the few outlets for white scholars who like many of the blacks were interested not only in the consequences of slavery and emancipation throughout the Americas but also in the interrelationship of slavery and other institutions.[3]

As might be expected, Marxian writers took a leading part in attacking the plantation legend of southern racial harmony as well as in debating the periodization of slavery and serfdom in world history. It was not until the late 1950s, however, that they became less rigidly doctrinaire, adopting more flexible and subtle forms of Marxist theory, which opened new approaches to the history of slavery, from Japan and central Asia to precolonial Africa. This flexibility and diversification coincided with two developments in non-Marxian scholarship: the "desegregation" of southern and Afro-American history, actively promoted by such distinguished scholars as C. Vann Woodward, David Potter, and David Donald, and immensely accelerated by the civil rights movement; and the independent appearance in Europe of Charles Verlinden's extensive work on slavery in medieval Europe and the studies by Joseph Vogt and others on slavery in classical antiquity.[4]

These converging and often conflicting approaches have led during the past twenty years to a veritable explosion of books, articles, and international symposia on slavery. Two years ago the most comprehensive "teaching bibliography" (which excludes popularizations) listed 3,259 books and articles on slavery, almost all published since the mid-1950s. While over 60 percent of these works deal with the Atlantic slave trade or black slavery in the New World, only 26 percent of the titles are limited to North America and an increasing number pertain to Africa, Asia, and premodern Europe.[5] No doubt general readers, together with

3. Two early books that revolutionized the study of New World slavery and that became justly famous by the early 1960s were C. L. R. James's *The Black Jacobins: Toussaint L'Ouverture and the San Domingo Revolution* (written in 1938 and reissued in a revised edition in 1962), and Eric Williams's *Capitalism and Slavery,* published in 1944. Orlando Patterson dedicated his first book on slavery to James and has frequently paid tribute to Williams's brilliant and provocative study. I do not mean to imply that *The Journal of Negro History* ceased to be significant in the 1960s, but only that other scholarly journals began printing articles on similar subjects.

4. Only a small part of this work has been translated. See Charles Verlinden, *The Beginnings of Modern Colonization: Eleven Essays with an Introduction,* translated by Yvonne Freccero (Cornell University Press, 1970); Joseph Vogt, *Ancient Slavery and the Ideal of Man* (Harvard University Press, 1975).

5. Joseph C. Miller, *Slavery: A Comparative Teaching Bibliography* (Crossroads, 1977); J. C. Miller and D. H. Borus, "Slavery: A Supplementary Teaching Bibliography," in *Slavery & Abo-*

most social scientists, still identify "slavery" with the antebellum South. During the past few years, however, we have had four important books of essays dealing with slavery in Africa; Charles Verlinden's second volume on slavery in medieval Europe, a work of 1,000 pages; Richard Hellie's long study of slavery in Russia from 1450 to 1725; and A. C. de C. M. Saunders's history of black slaves and freedmen in Portugal from 1441 to 1555.[6] These are only a few of the recent works that should widen our still-parochial perspective.

Orlando Patterson's *Slavery and Social Death* is in many ways the crowning achievement of the numerous works of scholarship of the past quarter-century. A Harvard sociologist who has published several novels as well as a detailed analysis of slavery in his native Jamaica, Patterson has read a staggering amount of the economic, historical, ethnographic, demographic, and theoretical literature on slavery in all parts of the world. No previous scholar I know of has gained such a mastery of secondary sources in all the Western European languages. With the help of research assistants, Patterson has even digested texts in Chinese, Japanese, Korean, and medieval Welsh and Irish. From the systematic sample of 186 world cultures assembled by the anthropologist George P. Murdock, Patterson has selected sixty-six slaveholding societies on which a sufficient amount of historical or ethnographic data could be found. He has then coded and statistically analyzed the information on these societies, which range from ancient Babylonia to the Bella Coola of central British Columbia and the Tehuelche of Patagonia. In addition, Patterson has studied and collected data on all the "large-scale slave systems" from ancient Greece and precolonial Africa to early modern Korea and the New World. His attempt to view slavery as a global institution is thus far more ambitious and comprehensive than that of H.

---

lition: A Journal of Comparative Studies, vol. 1 (May 1980), pp. 65–110; J. C. Miller, "Slavery: A Further Supplementary Bibliography," *Slavery & Abolition,* vol. 1 (September, 1980), pp. 199–258; Kopytoff, "Slavery," p. 208. Miller's forthcoming supplement brings the number of titles to approximately 4,000. The most valuable and extensive bibliographical essay on slavery is Orlando Patterson, "Slavery," *Annual Review of Sociology,* vol. 3 (1977), pp. 407–449. See also David Brion Davis, "Slavery and the Post-World War II Historians," *Daedalus* (Spring 1974), pp. 1–16.

6. Claude Meillassoux, ed., *L'Esclavage en Afrique précoloniale* (Maspero, Paris, 1975); Suzanne Miers and Igor Kopytoff, eds., *Slavery in Africa: Historical and Anthropological Perspectives* (University of Wisconsin Press, 1977); Henry A. Gemery and Jan S. Hogendorn, eds., *The Uncommon Market: Essays in the Economic History of the Atlantic Slave Trade* (Academic Press, 1979); Paul Lovejoy, ed., *The Ideology of Slavery in Africa* (Sage, 1981); Charles Verlinden, *L'Esclavage dans l'Europe médiévale,* Tome deux: *Italie—Colonies italiennes du Levant, Levant latin—Empire byzantin* (Rijks-universiteit te Gent, 1977); Richard Hellie, *Slavery in Russia, 1450–1725* (University of Chicago Press, 1982); A. C. de C. M. Saunders, *A Social History of Black Slaves and Freedmen in Portugal, 1441–1555* (Cambridge University Press, 1982).

J. Nieboer, who in 1900 published the only exiting work faintly comparable to Patterson's.[7]

It should be emphasized that this is not a history of slavery. Patterson's objective is "to come to a definitive statement of the fundamental processes of slavery, to grasp its internal structure and the institutional patterns that support it." His abstract approach will doubtless irritate humanist historians who, in C. Vann Woodward's words, hold "a profound respect for the varied particularity of human experience and a jealous regard for the precise integrity of time and place in the remembrance of things past."[8] Within four or five pages, Patterson skips from the Third Dynasty of Ur to Icelandic warriors, the Margi of northern Nigeria, ancient Athens and Sparta, eighteenth-century Jamaica, and the American Civil War. Specialists in every field are bound to pounce on errors and dubious generalizations. Patterson is fully aware of this and has at least fortified his assertions by drawing on the assistance of an imposing group of experts.

More serious objections can be made to his disdain for the nuances of specific historical settings, chronological developments, and the ways institutions become diffused. The societies he discusses are discrete units that can be coded and categorized but seldom interact or evolve. For the historian there is an inevitable distortion in juxtaposing the abstract characteristics of scores of societies separated by the greatest reaches of time and space, and then discovering striking "parallels" and "similarities" that may well be the artifacts of a sociological method that owes so much to the work of structural anthropologists. But historians' methods involve distortions and fictions of a different kind, and Patterson should not be read with an eye to the "precise integrity of time and place." Histories of slavery largely rest on unexamined and muddled concepts of what the institution *is*. The great merit of *Slavery and Social Death* is to offer a coherent theory that challenges deeply rooted assumptions and presents new points of departure for further research.

The book should also bury stale debates on the relative harshness of North American slavery, which some historians have attributed to racial prejudice or the coercions of unmitigated capitalism. Racial or ethnic distinctions characterized most of the slave systems Patterson studied, but this trait seems to have had no distinctive influence on the treatment of slaves or on the laws protecting them. Indeed, Patterson finds no significant correlations between the harshness of legal codes and the

7. *Slavery as an Industrial System* (2nd edition, Nijhoff, The Hague, 1910).
8. C. Vann Woodward, ed., *The Comparative Approach to American History* (Basic Books, 1968), p. 16.

economic function of slaves, the material conditions of life, or the frequency of manumission. Patterson's analysis of such variables helps to identify some of the exceptional features of North American slavery but also underscores the danger of idealizing premodern forms of servitude or of making generalizations about the harshness or leniency of any slave system. No system was static; all involved "a constant struggle between master and slave in the effort of the former to gain as much as possible for himself with the least possible loss, including the self-defeating loss of his slave, and the effort of the latter to minimize the burden of his exploitation and enhance the regularity and predictability of his existence."

In view of the disparate institutions Westerners have classified as "slavery," the more skeptical anthropologists have questioned the validity of the term as a concept that can usefully be applied to diverse cultures, especially when it carries the connotations of the New World plantation model. Patterson is fully aware that slaves often occupied a highly privileged status; that slave elites were sometimes valued as professional soldiers, palace guards, and imperial administrators; and that fathers or other heads of free families have sometimes had the right to kill or sell their children and have commonly received a brides-price for what amounts to the transfer of dominion over a daughter. Patterson also acknowledges that black slaves in the nineteenth-century South generally enjoyed better material conditions than did contemporary industrial workers in Britain, and that although slavery is "one of the most extreme forms of the relation of domination," it is by no means the only such form. Nevertheless, for all the rich empirical detail illustrating the diversity of master-slave relations, Patterson's central purpose is to establish the "constituent elements" of the institution—the universal characteristics that distinguish slavery from other kinds of subordination.

For Patterson slavery is essentially a relation of human domination or parasitism (a term he introduces, unfortunately, only in the last pages of the book), which can best be understood as an intersecting personal and institutional process. In the archetypal model found in the mythology and ethnology of many peoples, the process begins with the subjugation of a captive whose life is spared in a kind of "gift exchange" in return for acceptance of permanent servitude. Whether, in the absence of such an exchange, actual death would have resulted from execution, starvation, or exposure is in a way irrelevant since the relationship is founded on violent coercion, and the slave who seeks to escape his mater's domination is always liable to death. Even the most privileged slave janizaries and grand viziers understood that their exemption from death or brutal punishment was contingent upon obedience or even a master's whim. "There is no known slaveholding society," Patterson claims, "where the whip was not considered an indispensable instrument."

As an institutional process, however, enslavement also depended on what Patterson calls an "idiom of power" that legitimized the master's authority. Borrowing imaginatively from the writings of symbolic anthropologists, Patterson describes the rituals that enlisted communal support in making the master's rights and the slave's duties part of "the normal order of things." Whether captured or purchased from the outside world or recruited from the native population, the slave acquired a new identity as a "genealogical isolate"—a nonperson formally alienated from ancestors, kin, and progeny. Such rituals as hair-shaving, branding, and renaming marked off the bondsman from the recognized classes or castes of the organized community.

Although slaves might be allowed and could seldom be prevented from shaping their own informal communities, Patterson insists that they could never exercise the rights and duties of social beings, such as protecting their kin. The consequence of this "natal alienation," a key concept which Patterson derives in part from M. I. Finley, was a state of social death—a dependence on the master for even temporary familial security and for mediation with the community at large. Patterson logically concludes that hereditary slavery was a byproduct of natal alienation, since no kin could lay legitimate claim to the offspring of slave women. He might have added that the original model for such alienation was probably the domestication of animals, as may be indicated by the continuing practice of pricing slaves according to their equivalent in cows, horses, camels, pigs, and chickens.

Patterson is most original in analyzing the degradation or "generalized dishonor" of slaves. In many premodern societies, including Islamic ones, the principal motive for acquiring slaves was to enhance the prestige, respect, and honor of people who craved power. The point often overlooked by writers who romanticize such paternalistic forms of servitude is that the master's claim to honor depended not only on his slave's objective debasement but on the slave's surrender of any aspiration to honor in his own right.

Drawing on the anthropological work of Julian Pitt-Rivers, Patterson accentuates the distinction between acting honorably and *being* honorable: "There have been slaves who have been honored or whose acts have been considered honorable, yet who have remained despised as persons without honor." Hence even privileged slaves have commonly been subject to abuse and ridicule from the nonslaveholding population; and according to A. M. Wergeland, the timocratic German tribes tolerated insults from slaves themselves because "the abusive language of a slave cannot injure anybody's honor." In some societies the dishonor of having been a slave has even stigmatized former captives redeemed from an enemy. Patterson concludes that the "Sambo" stereotype of the fawning, docile, childlike, and carefree bondsman has been "an ideological imperative of all systems of slavery, from the most primitive to the most advanced. It is simply an elaboration of the notion that the slave is quintessentially a person without honor."

In a brilliant discussion of "the ultimate slave," Patterson applies the themes of dishonor and natal alienation to what appear to be the most unslavelike slaves in history—the administrative servants of the Roman emperors, the Islamic Mamluks and janizaries, and the political eunuchs of the Byzantine and Chinese emperors. Since contemporaries often considered it a great honor to be the powerful servant of an emperor or sultan, these marginal examples pose a test to any theory of the internal and invariable structure of human bondage. But as Patterson proceeds to argue, the slave's natal alienation removed aristocratic and dynastic barriers to meritocracy and efficient administration, providing a corps of slave bureaucrats "ever ready to move physically, and occupationally, not only upward but laterally, downward, and out; ever ready to retrain for entirely new positions and to accept, without complaint, whatever was offered in remuneration." Always distinct from that of the patron-client relationship, the power of elite slaves depended solely on the will of the master and might coexist with humiliations no Roman citizen or free Arab would accept. In other words, it was precisely the slave's position outside the threshold and his lack of honor that allowed him to act as an impersonal surrogate. And for the absolute ruler in particular, the ideal surrogate was the anomalous court eunuch.

This figure, widely stereotyped as foul, cruel, loathsome, and obscene, is Patterson's "ultimate slave." Ultimate because his castration signified the ultimate dishonor while simultaneously preventing the reproduction of himself and his class. But why did so many absolute rulers in various parts of the world place trusted eunuch slaves between themselves and their subjects? For Patterson, Mary Douglas's works on dirt and pollution, coupled with Edmund Leach's theory of binary oppositions and symbolic mediation, provide the clue. As an androgynous being universally associated with filth and pollution, the eunuch alone could cross otherwise impassable boundaries between good and evil, the sacred and profane. If the Byzantine emperor was God's vice-regent on earth, his remoteness from his subjects could be mediated by a eunuch slave who symbolized the distance between the carnal and the divine:

> The pollution incurred by the emperor in crossing the line between the sacred and the profane could be explained as resulting from the dirtiness of his chief eunuch, who thus became a symbolic as well as political scapegoat. . . . The slave eunuch, the ultimate slave, was the incarnation of the emperor, even as the emperor was the incarnation of Christ.

What the imperial eunuch shared with the lowly field hand was his structural marginality.

Paradoxically, the effectiveness of the slave's marginality usually required as an incentive the reasonable hope of eventual manumission. One of the most valuable innovations of Patterson's study is the insistence that "it is not possible to understand what slavery is all about until we understand it as a process including the act of manumission and its consequence." Manumission was the final stage in an extended rite of passage that began with the exchange of physical life for social death and culminated with a symbolic rebirth marking the negation of the negated honor and social existence. Yet because even a fee paid for redemption can never be commensurate with the gift of freedom, the ex-slave was commonly bound to his former master by continuing ties of gratitude and dependency. Thus manumission might be imperative as a reward for faithful service, but it signified only the beginning of a gradual process of assimilation that might require generations of further parasitism as well as the easy availability of slave replacements. No one else has written with such illumination on the contradictory meanings of manumission or on the socioeconomic variables that governed the status of freed people.

The usefulness of Patterson's ingenious theories can only be tested by future comparative studies. Marginality is such an inclusive category that it tends to lose meaning when divorced from specific settings and content. For the most part, for example, Patterson portrays the marginal slave as wholly dependent on his master for mediation with the nonslave community; yet it is the marginal eunuch who mediates between his master and all free subordinates. Similarly, while Patterson repeatedly stresses that slaves craved honor and refused to internalize the contempt with which they were regarded, he concludes that "none of them [was] ever able to bestow honor or to confirm it, at least not to anyone who mattered."

This is a surprising statement from a scholar scornful of historians who have either minimized slave resistance or have, in his view, accommodated such resistance to an "equilibrium" model of paternalism. Surely the imperial eunuchs and other palatine slaves "mattered," and also had some part in defining the rules of "the honor game." (As Patterson admits, they often exercised a dominant influence over emperors and sultans.) In Patterson's book we never view honor through the eyes of eunuchs, women, or really through the eyes of *any* slaves. Dishonor, like natal alienation, is always defined from the vantage point of a master class. In view of the recent studies by such historians as Eugene D. Genovese, Herbert G. Gutman, and John W. Blassingame, it is astonishing how little attention Patterson pays to the slaves' subjective sense of lineage and honor.[9]

This omission is related to Patterson's inconsistency in portraying the fundamental contradiction of human bondage. Genovese has summed up the problems "inherent in the contradiction in the slave's legal existence as man and thing" by concluding that "Hegel was therefore right in arguing that slavery constituted an outrage, for, in effect, it has always rested on the falsehood that one man could become an extension of another's will."[10] In an uncharacteristic polemic, Patterson attacks historians who focus on a fundamental conflict "between the treatment of the slave as a thing and as a human being. The formula ends with some ringing piece of liberal rhetoric to the effect that human dignity is irrepressible: 'You may define a person as a thing,' goes the flourish, 'but you cannot treat him as one' (or some such pious statement). The whole formula is, of course, a piece of irrelevance." Yet far from endorsing the anthropological position of moral relativism, Patterson continually reaffirms the existential and historical contradictions of human bondage. Consider the following piece of liberal rhetoric:

> Against all odds he [the slave] strove for some measure of regularity and predictability in his social life. Because his kin relations were illegitimate, they were all the more cherished. Because he was considered degraded, he was all the more infused with the yearning for dignity. Because of his formal isolation and liminality, he was acutely sensitive to the realities of community. . . . Everywhere the slave's zest for life and fellowship confounded the slaveholder class; and in all slaveholding societies the existential dignity of the slave belied the slaveholder's denial of its existence.

9. For some of these points I am indebted to Yale graduate seminar papers by David H. Brown and Donna Dennis.

10. *Roll, Jordan, Roll: The World the Slaves Made* (Pantheon, 1974), p. 88.

In fairness it should be added that the polemic quoted above is directed against conventional legalistic theories that define the slave as the *property* of an owner-master. Patterson argues convincingly that there are many forms of human capital and that the "property element" is neither unique to slavery nor a fundamental ingredient of the master-slave relation. Similarly, he argues, definitions that stress the economic function of slaves or a slave "mode of production" confuse changeable historical circumstance, such as the merger of slavery and capitalism in the American South, with the basic structural conditions he emphasizes throughout his book: domination, natal alienation, and generalized dishonor. It is still unclear how this triad of conditions distinguishes slaves from other oppressed peoples, such as prostitutes, convicts, and contract migrant laborers. Nor is it clear from Patterson's account why in modern times slavery should have been separated out from other forms of oppression and regarded as an obstacle to progress and a crime against humanity. But there can be no doubt that this rich and learned book will reinvigorate debates that have tended to become too empirical and specialized. Patterson has helped to set out the direction for the next decades of interdisciplinary scholarship.

15

Out of the Shadows

The Image of the Black in Western Art
Ladislas Bugner, general editor.

Volume One: *From the Pharaohs to the Fall of the Roman Empire*
by Jean Vercoutter, Jean Leclant,
Frank M. Snowden, Jr.,
and Jehan Desanges,
translated by William Granger Ryan.
Morrow, 352 pp., 385 illustrations,
$65.00

Volume Two: *From the Early Christian Era to the "Age of Discovery"*
Part 1, *From the Demonic Threat to the Incarnation of Sainthood*
by Jean Devisse, with a preliminary
essay by Jean Marie Courtès,
translated by William Granger Ryan.
Morrow, 288 pp., 168 illustrations,
$70.00
Part 2, *Africans in the Christian Ordinance of the World*
(Fourteenth to the Sixteenth Centuries)
by Jean Devisse and Michel Mollat,
translated by William Granger Ryan.
Morrow, 336 pp., 264 illustrations,
$80.00

During the fifteenth century B.C., the Theban pharaohs of the Eighteenth Dynasty established an empire extending from the Euphrates to

---

From *The New York Review of Books*, November 5, 1981. Copyright © 1981, NYREV, Inc. Reprinted by permission.

the Fourth Cataract of the Upper Nile. The southern conquests brought Egyptians into direct contact with black populations who continued to resist and counterattack. In the previous millennium black warriors and captives had occasionally appeared in the art of Egypt, Crete, and Cyprus—their precise racial origins are a matter of debate among scholars still attuned to dolichocephalous and mesaticephalous physical types. But as the first volume of *The Image of the Black in Western Art* shows us, from the mid-fifteenth century to Tutankhamun's painted box depicting the slaughter of black tribesmen (ca. 1342-1333 B.C.), Egyptian art increasingly portrayed realistic and unmistakable Negroes, often as warriors, dancers, or captive slaves. The almost caricatured head of a Negro captive, his neck constricted by three tight ropes, carved in limestone in the late Eighteenth Dynasty, would have struck any European slave trader over more than three thousand years later as a contemporary illustration. (See Volume 1, figure 59.)

By coincidence, the fifteenth century A.D. marked an even more momentous turning point in the history of global expansion, racial exploitation, and the conventions of dominant art. Ottoman conquests cut off southern Europe's supply of Caucasian slaves and servants, mostly from the Black Sea and the Balkans, at a time when Europe was still recovering from the disastrous population losses of the Black Death. In Sicily and even in southern Italy and France, black slaves imported from northern Africa began to replace lighter-skinned "Moors," who were now differentiated by color as well as by religion.

Almost simultaneously, after the mid-fifteenth century, Portugal's dramatic explorations southward along the African Atlantic coast led to the shipment of black slaves to Madeira and the Iberian Peninsula. This sudden discovery of sub-Saharan Africa, coupled with increasing knowledge of Asia, added realistic detail to European artists' fascination with the exotic, the Other. On the one hand, a French illustration of the *Departure of the Argonauts,* painted about 1470, shows Negro workers loading and preparing for departure a ship that seems to be modeled on the vessels of the new African slave trade. On the other hand, Hans Memling's contemporary triptych of *The Last Judgment* includes a well-defined Negro among God's elect. Following the lead of his master, Rogier van der Weyden, Memling painted a number of magnificent Negro kings in scenes of the *Adoration of the Magi,* a tradition soon perfected in masterpieces by Albrecht Dürer and Hieronymus Bosch.[1] It is a remarkable fact that the first two centuries of the West African slave

---

1. (See the illustration in Volume II, Part 2, p. 181, or the detail of the illustration on the dust jacket.)

trade, which went virtually unnoticed in Western art, coincided with extraordinarily beautiful and dignified portraits of blacks by Dürer, Bosch, Veronese, Velázquez, Rubens, and Rembrandt.

Although historians of the past two decades have greatly enriched our understanding of the origins of New World slavery and of whites' prejudices toward blacks, they have generally ignored iconographic evidence.[2] By training they have been accustomed to look upon art as a mere reflection or illustration, as in a textbook, of "facts" established by recorded words and numbers. Literary evidence should have suggested that art can influence perceptions—one thinks, for example, of Richard Ligon writing in 1653, in *A True & Exact History of the Island of Barbadoes,* that the Negro men were shaped exactly in accordance with Dürer's rules on proportion and that even a Titian could not capture the supple movements of the young virgins.

But apart from the historians' traditional reluctance to take art seriously, ignorance has been the elemental problem. One can hardly claim that "the black image" has been a major preoccupation in Western art, and even veteran museum goers would have difficulty recalling more than an occasional image by Rubens, Géricault, Delacroix, or Winslow Homer. It was not until 1976, when the fruits of the Menil Foundation's vast research enterprise began to appear, that even specialists could recognize the extraordinary richness, variety, and complexity of iconographic themes that span some five millennia of Mediterranean and European art.

The Menil Foundation, which has promoted racial equality and has patronized the fine arts in Houston and elsewhere, launched this project over twenty years ago on the assumption that a systematic study of the Western image of blacks would improve racial understanding and help erode the prejudices that sustained racial segregation. "With such a naive approach," Dominique de Menil notes at the beginning of the first volume, "a serious enterprise was started." It was also a staggering enterprise that required extensive photographic expeditions in Europe, Egypt, and the Sudan; the scrutiny of some six million photographs in archives throughout the world; and scholarly excursions into such subjects as cartography, the meaning of Ethiopia in patristic literature, and the curious appearance of Negro heads on ancient Delphic coins and in the armorial bearings of medieval heraldry.

2. A notable exception is Frank M. Snowden, Jr., *Blacks in Antiquity: Ethiopians in the Greco-Roman Experience* (Harvard University Press, 1970). See also the pathbreaking essay by Ignacy Sachs, "L'image du Noir dans l'art européen," *Annales—Economies, sociétés, civilisations* (May–June 1969), 883-893.

Because so much of this terrain is still uncharted, Ladislas Bugner, the brilliant art historian who serves as general editor and supervisor, emphasizes the provisional and tentative character of the entire enterprise. It will be left to future scholars, for example, to explore the connections between alchemy, astrology, and Western conceptions of blackness, or the earlier possible influence of Gnosticism and various forms of Manichaeism. The most striking gap in the project—the abrupt and unexplained transition from the realistic portraiture of blacks during the late classical age to the black demons of early Christianity—became apparent only after thousands of representations had been assembled and ordered in accordance with the canons of art history.

We have, to be sure, considerable scholarship on the European image of the "wild man," *l'homme sauvage,* and exotic Asians and Amerinds.[3] While it is unfortunate that the themes of such literature are generally ignored by the authors of the volumes under review, the connection between blacks and other non-European peoples will presumably become a central focus of Volume Three, which will begin with the sixteenth century (a separate book is now planned for the nineteenth century). The importance of this point is illustrated by a fascinating example Bugner cites in his admirable but regrettably brief and undocumented introduction to Volume One, an introduction that can only fully be appreciated after one has read the two books of Volume Two.

Albert Eckhout, a painter patronized by John Maurice of Nassau-Siegen, who from 1636 to 1644 governed Dutch Brazil, produced a series of portraits of nomadic "Tapuya" or Tarairiu Indians which helped define European conceptions of the exotic savage.[4] Eckhout's paintings, some of which Maurice presented to Louis XIV, also included black slaves and a Congolese black dressed in the most elegant European attire, including a broad felt hat plumed with a red feather. From 1653 to

3. See especially Hugh Honour, *The New Golden Land: European Images of America from the Discoveries to the Present Time* (Pantheon, 1975); G. Gliozzi, *Adamo e il Novo Mondo: La Nascita dell' Antropologia come Ideologia Coloniale: dalle genealogie bibliche alle teorie razziali* (Florence, 1977), U. Bitterli, *Die "Wilden" und die "Zivilisierten": Die europaischübersseeische Begegnung* (Munich, 1976); F. Tinland, *L'Homme Sauvage: Homo Ferus et Homo Silvestris* (Paris, 1968); *The Wild Man Within: An Image in Western Thought from the Renaissance to Romanticism,* edited by E. Dudley and M. E. Novak (University of Pittsburgh Press, 1972); B. Keen, *The Aztec Image in Western Thought* (Rutgers University Press, 1971); J. H. Elliott, *The Old World and the New, 1492–1650* (Cambridge University Press, 1970); and the essays by Charles Trinkaus, Wayland D. Hand, Aldo Scaglione, A. Bartlett Giamatti, Harold Jantz, and Hayden White in *First Images of America: The Impact of the New World on the Old,* edited by Fredi Chiapelli (two volumes, University of California Press, 1976).

4. I am indebted to Dr. E. van den Boogaart for calling my attention to essays published on the tercentenary of Maurice's death, *Johan Maurits Van Nassau-Siegen, 1604-1679,* edited by E. van den Boogaart in collaboration with H. R. Hoetink and P. J. P. Whitehead (The Johan Maurits van Nassau Stichting, The Hague, 1979); and the superb catalogue of the related exhibition. *Zo wijd de wereld strekt* (Mauritshuis, The Hague, 1979–1980).

1663 Eckhout introduced Brazilian scenes to Dresden, at the court of Frederick William, elector of Brandenburg. Although direct evidence is still lacking, Bugner suspects there is a connection between Eckhout's "documentary" ethnography and Dresden's magnificent but highly mannered *Grüne Gewölbe* of the early eighteenth century—ornate statuettes of Negroes and other exotic non-Europeans encrusted with gold and precious stones. Ethnographic discovery and curiosity gradually removed the African from the realm of demonic and religious symbolism to the "fairyland world" of little black pages and hussars, popular, as Bugner points out, "in all the princely courts" from Madrid to St. Petersburg.

One can understand the necessity of limiting such an ambitious enterprise to white perceptions of blacks, or as Bugner puts it, to "the plastic expression by which the white man has marked the state of difference, of 'otherness,' in which he situates the black man in relation to himself," excluding "any preliminary definition of the 'Negro' based on anthropological or ethnological data." This flexible approach illuminates the ambiguities of blackness and of racial definition, and also suggests as Frank M. Snowden, Jr., maintains, that racial intermixture increased in late antiquity.

But the Menil project also dramatizes the need for even broader and more comparative studies of ethnic (and class) iconography. How do Eckhout's Brazilian scenes compare with the somewhat earlier Japanese screen paintings that depict long-nosed Portuguese giants who are fanned or shaded from the sun by barefoot black slaves?[5] Can cartoons and caricatures of Negro faces be understood without reference to caricatures of European peasants or to a tradition of grotesques designed to illustrate "humours," emotions, and the plasticity of human expression? What are we to make of the ancient Greek vases and aryballoi that juxtapose a white head, often that of a god, with the head of a thick-lipped and woolly-haired Negro? (See Volume I, figures 160 and 193.) Is it significant that similar janiform black and white faces appear in representations of ancient Khmer and other Asian deities as well as in the folk art of West Africa? If art has its own internal history, can one think of a purely aesthetic formula extending from janiform vases of the sixty century B.C. to Jules Robert Auguste's juxtaposition of sensuous black and white female nudes in the early nineteenth century?

5. Late in 1980 there was a striking exhibit of such Japanese screens at the Musée Cernuschi, Paris.

The continuity and imaginative adaptation of artistic conventions can mislead any reader who simply assumes that art reflects social reality. For example, the casual viewer who encounters the extraordinary prevalence within the old Holy Roman Empire of a negroid St. Maurice could easily conclude that from the thirteenth to the fifteenth centuries the eastern Germanic marches were guarded by black knights in armor. In view of the racist stereotypes of the nineteenth century, it is also easy to assume that grotesque lips and exaggerated prognathism reflect similar contempt in Greco-Roman times, even when carved in garnets and gold intended for female adornment. (See Volume I, figure 244.) This is not to deny the possible presence of racial prejudice in classical antiquity or the more remote possibility that a wandering Negro warrior served as a model for the magnificent thirteenth-century statue of St. Maurice that decorates the Cathedral of Magdeburg. (See Volume II, part 1, figures 114 and 116.) The point is that iconography gives no answers to such questions. In Bugner's view art "brings us the fundamental quality of a presence. . . . It states but does not reason."

Yet Bugner also dreams of eventual synthesis of artistic and literary evidence that "would be the only guarantee of the soundness of the iconographic approach." Although Snowden and Jean Devisse are more sensitive than their co-authors to changing historical settings, *The Image of the Black* never seriously confronts the methodological problems of synthesizing art with social and intellectual history.[6] The text, while indispensable for an understanding of the superb illustrations, is often desultory and preoccupied with technical detail. It never develops Bugner's intriguing insights or his glimpses of a larger theoretical pattern that might explain the popularity of the black St. Maurice and Wise Man in northern Europe (the British Isles, unfortunately, are seldom mentioned); the virtual absence, before the nineteenth century, of paintings of black laborers, of the slave trade, or even of "the suffering Negro," except for a few Spanish representations of the Miracle of the Black Leg, to which we shall return in a moment. One hopes that Bugner himself will take the risk of expanding his ideas in a longer essay that will be more accessible to non-specialists.

Even now, however, the published volumes transform the standard view of Europe's response to Africa. If art does not reason, it still can tell the historian important things. Until the eighteenth century, for ex-

---

6. Any such synthesis must take account of the place of slavery and manumission in religious and political thought, a subject curiously ignored in *The Image of the Black in Western Art*, despite the detailed information provided by Piero A. Milani's *La schiavitù nel pensiero politico dai Greci al basso medio evo* (Milan, 1972).

ample, blacks were not automatically categorized as slaves. Except in
Greece, few Europeans had the opportunity to see sculptures of the
"Ethiopian" or Kushite kings of Egypt's Twenty-fifth Dynasty. But in
the late Middle Ages artists tended to picture Egyptians as black and to
include recognizable Negroes in scenes from the Old Testament. Consider the portrayals of the king of Mali, based on accounts of Mansa
Musa's pilgrimage to Mecca; of a black Prester John and Queen of
Sheba; and above all, the introduction of Negro attendants in thirteenth-
century scenes of the Adoration of the Magi and the gradual acceptance,
by the early fifteenth century, of a black Magus or Wise Man. All these
contradicted the common belief that Noah's curse of Canaan had subjected Africans to perpetual servitude and degradation. This ecumenical
approach was encouraged by the Church's desire to win military allies
on the flanks of the Ottoman empire, a strategy that led to Ethiopian
and Coptic delegations at the Council of Florence in 1441, and to the
Pope's futile efforts to communicate with "Prester John, illustrious emperor of the Ethiopians."

But if one accepts the reasonable but unprovable assumption that European racial attitudes were gradually shaped by the iconographic environment—by church paintings, sculptures, and stained-glass windows
as well as by maps, armorial bearings, illustrated books, wall paintings,
and tapestries—the fusion of art and religion was in some ways cata-
strophic. During the earlier Hellenistic and Roman periods skilled
craftsmen clearly took delight in presenting Negroes in a variety of roles,
moods, and postures—as musicians, dancers, jugglers, actors, acrobats,
jockeys, charioteers, and soldiers.

The popularity of such motifs, which spread far beyond the probable
physical presence of any blacks, may have derived from the fashion-
ableness of Alexandrian styles and ornamentation. The beauty and vitality of such figures do not preclude the possibility that living models,
usually young males, were often slaves and were subjected to physical
and sexual abuse. The fact remains that such individualized and humanistic representations would have been inconceivable in later slave societies founded on the premise of racial inferiority. In late antiquity the
image of the black was one expression of the infinite diversity of a
common human nature. It was not associated with the powers of darkness or with a pagan world to be redeemed by Christian light.

Volume Two explores the allegorical and anagogical interpretations of
blackness in early Christian thought, the complexities of which can
only be intimated here. Despite Augustinian cautions against identifying
color or physical appearance with spiritual realities, blackness was a

precondition for Christian cosmology and eschatology: the symbol of
death, sin, ignorance, idolatry, the synagogue, the devil, and the Church
before it was cleansed of heresies. Eventually it would symbolize Islam
and the dark-skinned Muslims who threatened to overrun Christendom.
While St. Matthew's legendary conversion of Ethiopia prefigured the
ultimate evangelizing of the world's most distant nations, patristic writers stressed that the Ethiopian was "born of the Devil and wished to
serve his evil designs. He is assumed to be black because of the darkness in which his ignorance of God and his perversity establish him."
Therefore, he could be admitted to the glorious city of God only after
he had been "wounded by Him who says these words and [has] given
up [the] Ethiopian way of life," and has been washed clean and made
whiter than snow.

It is true, as Jean Devisse points out, that Byzantine illustrations of
Biblical scenes included realistic blacks as a matter of course, "on a
footing of complete equality," without any suggestion of sin or culpa-
bility. It is also true that until the twelfth century the more hostile iconography in Western Europe was characterized by demonic fantasies that
lacked the specific ethnic connotations of written Biblical commentary.
As Ladislas Bugner shrewdly observes:

> Only the Devil is totally black. The whole dialectic of the black-white
> symbolism was developed out of an unrealism based upon the sense of
> salvation which allowed the possibility of passing from black to white as
> well as that of falling back from white to black. The black Ethiopian
> illustrated the state of sin insofar as the literary metaphor supported the
> image of an Ethiopian turned white by the grace of repentance and bap-
> tism. Could art follow the concept? . . .Was not the only way to render
> the image of the black Ethiopian, the figure of sin, to deny him any sort
> of human face in order to recognize in him the horned, fantastic creature
> of the Devil?
>
> On the other hand an Ethiopian purified by conversion and relieved of
> his blackness would no longer be distinguished from a white man. The
> sarcophagi of the early Christian centuries show us the Ethiopian Eunuch
> converted by Philip without any distinctive ethnic feature, whereas, in a
> parallel way, the images of demons eliminate all precise reference to a
> particular human type. In this case we would have the invisible "Negro"
> at the center of the debate, but passed over and denied from either side
> by the white man, in function of his idealized image on the one hand and
> his phantasmal image on the other.

From the twelfth to the mid-fourteenth century, however, the iconography of Western Europe became stocked with images of unmistakable Negroes as torturers, tempters, and executioners, often in scenes of

the Passion. Although our knowledge is limited to works that have survived, fortuitously, for five centuries or more, it seems probable that most Europeans got their first subliminal impressions of Negroes in the local church or cathedral—the image of death squads serving the devil. This ethnic realism was doubtless related to the expansion of Europe, the gradual reconquest of Spain, increasing contact with Africa, and the xenophobia and incipient racism exemplified by militant anti-Semitism. On the other hand, the ecumenism and relative tolerance of Byzantine iconography suggests that geographic proximity and relations with dark-skinned peoples did not necessarily lead to such results.

But it is easy to exaggerate the contrast between "positive" and "negative" iconography, as the authors of *The Image of the Black* tend to do. Unlike the terrifying beaked and horned demons that swarm through medieval visions of the apocalypse, the Negro executioner carved in stone at Chartres Cathedral is an altogether human youth, pensive, and perhaps even reticent as he is about to draw his sword. He is hardly distinguishable from the sculpture from the main portal of the Cathedral of Notre Dame in Paris (now at the Musée de Cluny) of a young black rising from his coffin at the trumpeting of the Last Judgment. As Devisse points out, the Negro scourger who dominates Giotto's *Mocking of Christ* in the Arena Chapel in Padua conveys a sense of impassivity and "formal beauty" that defies analysis. In a sense, the supposedly "positive" image of St. Maurice, the black knight who symbolized the Holy Roman Empire's crusade against the pagan Slavs, was simply a transmutation of the earlier Negro warrior and executioner. In both cases, the black image was an ambiguous and somewhat frightening presence, and hence a challenge to the artistic imagination.

What seems important here is a transmutation of one identity into another—or more precisely a transitional state between two identities—the African warrior and sainted knight; the exotic king or magus who merges his African physiognomy with the splendor of Oriental attire; the Ethiopian Eunuch who, having lost the potency to transmit his blackness, can safely be baptized as a kneeling supplicant—a possible model, as Bugner suggests, for the abolitionists' icon of the kneeling slave who pleads, "Am I Not a Man, and a Brother?" The most revealing image of transmutation was the Miracle of the Black Leg, a legend in which two saints replace the gangrenous leg of a white man with the limb of a dead or dying Negro.

The psychological implications of this theme deserve more careful analysis, but it is noteworthy that the subject was especially popular in Spain, where iconography was generally more hostile to blacks and where black-white interactions were far more frequent than in the rest of Europe. It is also noteworthy that representations of the "miracle" assumed no sympathy for the amputated Negro, whether pictured in agony or as a cadaver. Blackness seems to have been equated with a spiritual "gangrene" that could be cured only by merger with a white body; yet in this case it is by an African's sacrifice that a European is saved.

One concludes from these pioneering volumes that artistic representations were historical "events" that eventually helped to shape a mentality that justified the enslavement of millions of Africans as well as later attempts to Christianize and liberate their descendants. The pictorial image of blacks tells us little about social reality in the period from the Egyptian pharaohs to Emperor Charles V. What is most impressive, however, are the overriding interest and delight in diversity, the dignity with which most blacks were portrayed, and the enduring capacity of artists for empathy and human expression. Regardless of the complexities and ambiguities of the black image, the artistic heritage from Egyptian and Hellenistic times to the great portraits by Memling, Bosch, and Rembrandt presents an unanswerable challenge to the later racist societies that have relied on dehumanizing caricature as an instrument of social and economic oppression.

16

New Sidelights on Early Antislavery Radicalism

Sixty years ago Russell P. Jameson published a masterful study of Montesquieu's influence on French antislavery thought. Quite rightly, he singled out the Chevalier Louis de Jaucourt's article, "Traite des Nègres," published in the *Encyclopédie* in 1765, as a forceful and trenchant extension of Montesquieu's antislavery arguments, and as the most important statement on the subject until the later 1770s.[1] In a recent study of my own, I observed that "de Jaucourt was able to rise above the qualifications engendered by Montesquieu's tolerance for institutional differences," and after quoting the central passage, I termed the argument "one of the earliest and most lucid applications to slavery of the natural rights philosophy . . . [which] succeeds in stating a basic principle which was to guide the more radical abolitionists of the nineteenth century."[2] Neither Jameson nor I suspected that Montesquieu's ideas had earlier been refracted by the Scottish Enlightenment, or that de Jaucourt had merely copied someone else's words.

In an article on Montesquieu and English antislavery opinion published in 1933, F. T. H. Fletcher briefly mentioned a "brilliant pre-Blackstonian" jurist, George Wallace, whose massive tome, *A System of the Principles of the Law of Scotland,* quoted extensively from Book

---

1. Russell Parsons Jameson, *Montesquieu et l'esclavage: étude sur les origines de l'opinion antiesclavagiste en France au XVIIIᵉ siècle* (Paris, 1911), 345-346.
2. David Brion Davis, *The Problem of Slavery in Western Culture* (Ithaca, N. Y., 1966), 416.

From the *William and Mary Quarterly,* Third Series, Vol. XXVIII, No. 4 (October 1971). Reprinted by permission.

XV of the *Esprit des lois* and applied Montesquieu's antislavery arguments to Scotland. Fletcher said nothing about the nature of Wallace's arguments, adding merely that the treatise was expensive, weighted down with legal abstractions, and thus little read.[3] Wallace never carried the work beyond "Volume I," published in Edinburgh in 1760. This lone volume, now very rare, apparently had no influence on Scottish jurisprudence.

Nevertheless, a comparison between Wallace's text and de Jaucourt's influential article in the *Encyclopédie* reveals astonishing similarities. Following Montesquieu, Wallace denied all the classical grounds for justifying enslavement and asserted that no man has a right to purchase Africans or any other human beings: "Men and their liberty are not *in commercio;* they are not either salable or purchaseable." De Jaucourt mentioned an unidentified Englishman, "full of humanity and enlightenment," who had demonstrated that human beings cannot be the objects of trade and cannot be bought or sold at any price. This premise led to the following radical conclusions:

<table>
<tr><td align="center">WALLACE</td><td align="center">DE JAUCOURT</td></tr>
<tr><td>For these reasons, every one of those unfortunate men, who are pretended to be slaves, has a right to be declared to be free, for he never lost his liberty; he could not lose it; his prince had no power to dispose of him. Of course, the sale was *ipso jure* void. This right he carries about with him, and is entitled every where to get it declared. As soon, therefore, as he comes into a country, in which the judges are not forgetful of their own humanity, it is their duty to remember that he is a man, and to declare him to be free.</td><td>Il n'y a donc pas un seul de ces infortunés que l'on prétend n'être que des esclaves, qui n'ait droit d'être déclaré libre, puisqu'il n'a jamais perdu la liberté; qu'il ne pouvoit pas la perdre; et que son prince, son pere, et qui que ce soit dans le monde n'avoit le pouvoir d'en disposer; par conséquent la vente qui en a été faite est nulle en elle-même: ce negre ne se dépouille, et ne peut pas même se dépouiller jamais de son droit naturel; il le porte partout avec lui, et il peut exiger par-tout qu'on l'en laisse jouir. C'est donc une inhumanité manifeste de la part des juges de pays libres où il est transporté, de ne pas l'affranchir à l'instant en le déclarant libre, puisque c'est leur semblable, ayant une ame comme eux.[4]</td></tr>
</table>

It is clearly a mistake to attribute this radical antislavery position to the rationalism or secular humanitarianism of the French Enlightenment. Montesquieu may have prepared the way for Wallace's uncompromising

3. F. T. H. Fletcher, "Montesquieu's Influence on Anti-Slavery Opinion in England," *Journal of Negro History,* XVIII (1933), 416–417.

4. George Wallace, *A System of the Principles of the Law of Scotland,* I (Edinburgh, 1760), 95–96; *Encyclopédie, ou dictionnaire raisonné des sciences, des arts et des métiers . . . ,* XVI (Neufchâtel, 1765), 532.

argument, but his own position on colonial slavery was shrewdly ambiguous.[5] But who, then, was George Wallace, and why should he have
asserted the universal illegality of slavery in a scholarly treatise on Scottish law?

Unfortunately, Wallace remains a curiously obscure figure, although
he gained local prominence in Edinburgh at a time when the city flourished as one of the most culturally exciting centers of Europe. His father, the Reverend Robert Wallace, left a far more indelible impression.
The elder Wallace was the author of *A Dissertation on the Numbers of
Mankind in Ancient and Modern Times . . .* (1753), which was translated into French within a year of its initial publication; this and a later
work, *Various Prospects of Mankind, Nature and Providence* (1761),
were said to have anticipated and influenced Thomas Malthus.[6] Robert
Wallace belonged to an urbane, latitudinarian group that was gaining
power and patronage in the Church of Scotland, in opposition to the
evangelicals. He was also a prophet of modernity and a member of
Edinburgh's literary and social elite. It is hardly surprising that his son
should have become a member of the Scottish bar (the Faculty of Advocates) and of such organizations as the Rankenian Club, the Select
Society, and the Revolution Club. George evidently admired and respected his father, since he referred, in his discussion of slavery, to
"the learned, the ingenious, and the virtuous Author of a 'DISSERTATION
ON THE NUMBERS OF MANKIND.' " But a few years before George Wallace published his treatise on the laws of Scotland, when he was not yet
thirty, he became embroiled in the bitter *"Douglas* affair"—a controversy over the staging of a play, *Douglas,* which the evangelical party
angrily denounced. Whatever else contributed to Wallace's later obscurity, this scandal had complex political consequences and apparently
made him a victim of the rising and powerful Dundas family.[7]

The section on slavery in Wallace's *Law of Scotland* seems out of
step with the rest of the work. A book which sought to place Scottish
law within a broad theoretical framework derived from Montesquieu,

5. See Fletcher, "Montesquieu's Influence," *Journal Negro Hist.,* XVIII (1933), 414–426;
Jameson, *Montesquieu et l'esclavage,* 306–307, 340–347; and Davis, *The Problem of Slavery,*
394–396, 402–409.

6. Edinburgh, 1753; London, 1761. It is said in Robert Wallace's biographical sketches that
his *A Dissertation on the Numbers of Mankind* was translated under the personal supervision of
Montesquieu; Elie de Joncourt was the actual translator of the 1754 edition of *Essai sur la différ-
ence du nombre des hommes dans les tems anciens et modernes* (London). Marc-Antoine Eidous
translated a 1769 edition, *Dissertation historique et politique sur la population de l'ancien tems
comparée avec celle du nôtre* (Amsterdam). I have found no evidence of a French translation of
George Wallace's *A System of the Principles of the Law of Scotland.*

7. For information on George Wallace I have relied heavily on Mr. Nicholas Phillipson, of the
University of Edinburgh, whose detailed knowledge of 18th-century Scotland has richly supplemented the lean accounts of Wallace in standard reference works.

Kames, and Hume had no obvious need for a lofty digression on American slavery. Wallace's attack may have had some bearing on local political conflicts, especially if he knew that some of his orthodox opponents had interests in the slave colonies. Yet the *Esprit des lois* had set a precedent for such rhetorical excursions on slavery as a means of defining barbarous custom, natural law, and historical progress. Moreover, Wallace related his seeming digression to three specific goals.

First, he was concerned over the probability that colonial masters would bring slaves to Scotland and appeal to Scottish courts to uphold their rights as owners of human property. Well over a decade before the Somerset and Knight cases resolved this problem in England and Scotland by denying slaveholders any legal claim, Wallace insisted that human bondage could find no protection from the law of Scotland. That law had either abolished or had never recognized the institution. Judges, therefore, were "in *no case,* to adjudge one to be the slave of another."[8]

But Wallace found the question of slavery important and "interesting to humanity" for even broader reasons. As a disciple of the Enlightenment, he took it as axiomatic that "all that inequality, which is to be found among the individuals of human race, is derived from political and arbitrary institutions alone." From the principles of natural liberty and equality, it followed "that all inequality, all dependence, all servility, all superiority, all subjection, all pre-eminence, which is not *necessary* to the welfare of Society, is unnatural; and that, if it could, it ought to be destroyed." Unlike most of his contemporaries, Wallace doubted whether the necessities of social welfare could ever be permanently defined, since history showed "that many unexpected revolutions have happened, and that things have existed so contrary to all expectation, that he would, indeed be a rash man, who should pronounce decisively, any thing, which is not naturally to be absolutely impossible."

---

8. Wallace, *Law of Scotland,* 88–89, 95–96. In a footnote, p. 97, Wallace mentioned a 1757 case: "One *Montgomery Shedden,* a niger boy, being in Edinburgh, refused to return to his master, because he said he was, like every other British subject, a free man in Britain. Council were ordered to argue the point both in writing and *viva voce.* But during the very time when the Court of Session was *hearing* them plead at the bar, notice came, that the boy was dead. So Judgment was not pronounced." Wallace anticipated some of the main issues and arguments of the Somerset case of 1772 and the Knight case of 1777. Though he admitted that slavery was part of the ancient written law of Scotland, he also pointed out that "it may have been the case, that any thing like slavery, such as it is described in these ancient books, never took place in Scotland." In any event, laws, Wallace held, "may be repealed by Custom. The same principles, which seem to have determined us to abolish servile tenures, oppressive jurisdictions, and lawless attachments, have induced us totally to abolish the inhuman usage of slavery. So far as I have been able to learn, no vestige of it remains in Scotland. Indeed, it has been disused, and has been unknown for several generations past. So that there is not any remembrance of the establishment of it now remaining among us." (p. 89)

Wallace could even entertain the possibility, though hardly the probability, of an eventual abolition of private property, "that bane of human
felicity," and of the emergence of a society of perfect and universal
equality, like that described in Thomas More's *Utopia*. By emphasizing
man's capacity for change and by elevating the goal of possible perfectibility, Wallace opened the way for more imm~diate and tangible improvement: "But, tho the condition of human affairs may never arrive
at ideal perfection, we ought not to abandon them out of peevishness or
out of despair. We ought to use our endeavours to make them approach
as near it as possible. In the same manner, we ought not, because we
cannot reduce mankind to an *absolute* equality, therefore to abandon
them; but ought to do all, which we can do, to reduce them as near it,
and to make them as independent of one another, as may be. From
hence it follows, that an institution, so unnatural and so inhuman as that
of Slavery, ought to be abolished."[9]

For Wallace, then, colonial slavery symbolized an extreme of social
inequality which was the precise antithesis of the ideal toward which
mankind should strive: "It makes the bulk of mankind dependent on the
few; and that not only for their bread and for life, but for the enjoyment
of it, for ease, for tranquillity, and for a momentary felicity." He recognized, of course, that like any institution, lawful or unlawful, slavery
might be "attended with some accidental advantage." Alarmists would
warn that any tampering with slavery would ruin the colonies. Wallace's
initial response was virtually the same as that of the Abbé Raynal a
decade later: "Be it so; would it from thence follow, that the bulk of
mankind ought to be abused, that our pockets may be filled with money,
or our mouths with delicates? The purses of highwaymen would be empty,
in case robbery were totally abolished. Let, therefore, our colonies be
ruined, but let us not render so many men miserable."[10]

But this moral rhetoric merely prefaced Wallace's third major point,
which was a prediction of the material blessings that abolition would
entail. Clearly Wallace was not thinking of a gradual emancipation. "It
might," he admitted, "occasion a stagnation of business for a short
time. Every great alteration produces that effect." Yet slavery itself had
inhibited the growth of population and civilization in the New World:
"Set the Nigers free, and, in a few generations, this vast and fertile
continent would be crowded with inhabitants; learning, arts, and every

---

9. *Ibid.*, 89–91.
10. *Ibid.*, 91, 96. De Jaucourt copied these passages in the *Encyclopédie*, which may have been
the source for Raynal's rhetorical outburst in Book X of *Histoire philosophique et politique des
établissemens et du commerce des Européens dans les deux Indes* (Amsterdam, 1770), a work
which was actually the collaborative effort of several *philosophes*.

thing would flourish among them.'' After acknowledging that the great reformation might damage British commerce, Wallace drew on his father's work, which had supposedly demonstration ''that a nation may be more populous, more wealthy, more virtuous, and more happy without than with an extensive foreign trade.'' Wallace's antislavery views were thus linked with a hostility toward the old colonial system and with Hume's doctrine that '' 'Tis industry, which is the real source of wealth. As long as a nation continues to be industrious, it need not be afraid of poverty.'' For some reason Wallace failed to develop his economic arguments against slavery, which anticipated those of the Physiocrats, and abruptly concluded his chapter with long quotations, in French, from the *Esprit de lois*.[11]

Wallace's attack on slavery deserves more attention than it has received, not only because of its influence on the Encyclopedists, and perhaps on the Abbé Raynal, but because of its vision of Negro emancipation as a first and practicable step toward the ideal of human equality. While Wallace's arguments were too radical to play a major role in the later British antislavery movement, they had an immediate impact in America, where Anthony Benezet incorporated crucial passages from the *Law of Scotland* in his developing compendium of antislavery literature.

Given the obscurity of Wallace's tome, one is tempted to ask whether de Jaucourt lifted the antislavery argument from Benezet's *A Short Account of That Part of Africa, Inhabited by the Negroes . . . and the Manner by Which the Slave Trade is Carried On,* a pamphlet published in Philadelphia in 1762. It would be a nice irony of international communications if Montesquieu's influence, radicalized by George Wallace, returned to the *Encyclopédie* by way of an American publication. Unfortunately, textual discrepancies rule out this possibility.[12] Yet Benezet, unlike de Jaucourt, identified Wallace as the author of the doctrine that ''every one of those unfortunate men, who are pretended to be slaves, has a right to declared to be free, for he never lost his liberty.''

11. Wallace, *Law of Scotland,* 96–98. Although de Jaucourt's translation seldom changed Wallace's meaning, the following deviations should be noted: Wallace argued that after the Negroes had been set free, the American continent, ''instead of being inhabited by wild beasts and by savages . . . would be peopled by philosophers and by men.'' De Jaucourt changed the latter phrase to ''hommes industrieux,'' which presumably omitted philosophers. He also added ''liberté'' to Wallace's ''industry'' as the real source of wealth. *Encyclopédie,* 533.

12. Benezet omitted a few lines from Wallace which de Jaucourt translated. As I have already noted, Robert Wallace's writings were known in France as early as 1754, and it is possible that George's volume reached France through his father's literary contacts or by way of an enlightened traveler like Adam Smith. De Jaucourt was a latitudinarian Protestant who knew English well. No doubt Wallace's passages on slavery were a happy find for an encyclopedist burdened with the task of writing a multitude of short articles on a large variety of subjects.

And Benezet further disseminated Wallace's words in 1766, in his *A Caution to Great Britain and her Colonies, in a Short Representation of the Calamitous State of the Enslaved Negroes in the British Dominions*. In 1767 this pamphlet was reprinted in England and translated into French. Benezet was also an indirect source for the antislavery sentiment of the *Ephémérides du citoyen*, which in 1769 heaped praise upon the Pennsylvania Quakers for supposedly emancipating their slaves.[13]

It was as an anthologist and collator of scattered material that Benezet made his major contribution to the early antislavery movement. Many of his pamphlets are little more than hastily compiled collections of quotations and extracts regarding West African culture, the slave trade, and the injustice and inhumanity of Negro slavery. The juxtaposition of such testimonials was novel, and in the 1760s and 1770s many influential Englishmen and Americans first grasped the full horrors of the Atlantic slave system after stumbling upon a Benezet tract. In 1767, for example, Granville Sharp discovered Benezet's *A Short Account* in a London bookstall, and the next year had the work reprinted for further distribution.[14] In 1772 John Wesley encountered Benezet's *Some Historical Account of Guinea* (1771) which helped inspire him to write his own *Thoughts Upon Slavery* (1774), plagiarizing liberally from Benezet's pages.[15]

Benezet, then, acted as a kind of middleman of ideas who was led by antislavery zeal to collect and disseminate a radical, secular philosophy. But for a devout Quaker, this role had its hazards. Although

---

13. There was no French translation of Benezet's *A Short Account*, although on p. 487 of *The Problem of Slavery* I erroneously said that "even before Sharp had reprinted Benezet's tract in England, it had been translated into French." Evidently I confused *A Short Account* with Benezet's *A Caution to Great Britain*, which was translated in 1767. A related error is to be found in Joseph Sabin, *Bibliotheca Americana*, II (New York, 1869), 63, who repeated a mistake made in Joseph-Marie Quérard, *La France littéraire, ou dictionnaire bibliographique des savants, historiens et gens de lettres de la France, . . .* (Paris 1827–1839), in which Benezet's *Relation historique de la Guinée, avec une recherche sur l'origine et les progrès de la traite des nègres . . .* (London, 1788), is given an original publication date of 1762, the year of *A Short Account*, instead of the correct date of 1771. *A Short Account* was translated into German in 1763 as *Eine kurtze vorstellung des theils von Africa*, but this edition, printed at Ephrata, Pa., was designed only for the German-speaking inhabitants of Pennsylvania. Although Benezet was not well known in France until the Marquis de Chastellux and Brissot de Warville engaged in a literary controversy over his character in the late 1780s, there had been French translations of two of his antislavery pamphlets as well as his *A Short Account of the People Called Quakers* (Philadelphia, 1780). For the place of the Quakers in French thought, see Edith Philips, *The Good Quaker in French Legend* (Philadelphia, 1932).

14. However, in 1774 Sharp wrote to Benjamin Rush: "When I reprinted Mr. Benezets acco't. of Africa in 1768, so few Copies were sold that I gave away, by degrees, almost the whole impression being determined to make it as publick as I cou'd; for many well meaning people will read, (and some worthy talk of) Books that are given them, who will not put themselves to the trouble and expence of buying." London, Feb. 21, 1774, in George S. Brookes, *Friend Anthony Benezet* (Philadelphia, 1937), 447.

15. Philadelphia, 1771; London, 1774.

American Quakers were gradually absorbing a rationalistic vocabulary of natural rights, Benezet remained an intensely pious, self-effacing man. He held little hope for human happiness or perfectibility in this world. In 1752, for example, he warned that "the only end for which thou wast created in this world is, that by living in a state of obedience, by constant watching and prayer, thy soul may, with the assistance of divine grace, become so purified, as to be fitted to dwell with God for ever." Five years later, after exclaiming over "the weakness, the instability, the Self, the remains of a subtle Pride that hangs about human nature," he wrote Samuel Fothergill that "I hope I am cured from any more dependance and expectation from man." [16] It is noteworthy that he refrained from quoting Wallace on "the superior wisdom and civility of the present age," or on the ideal that "men ought to be reduced to a level [of equality] as much, that is, they ought to be as free, and as independent of one another, as is consistent with the good of Society." At that point in the text where de Jaucourt continued quoting Wallace (and Hume) on industry as the real source of wealth—"As long as a nation continues to be industrious, it need not be afraid of poverty. Industry, like necessity, is inventive, and falls on a thousand ways of employing itself to the profit of the industrious"—Benezet concluded the selection with his own appeals to God and piety, subjects notably absent from Wallace's argument.

Benezet was, in fact, highly selective in his use of radical antislavery literature. Aside from his handling of Wallace, a most interesting instance of this is his treatment in *A Short Account* of "a large extract from a pamphlet, lately published in London, on the subject of the slave trade." The anonymous pamphlet, now exceedingly rare, was entitled *Two Dialogues on the Man-Trade.* [17] It contained, although one would not know this from Benezet's long extract, the most radical antislavery doctrine that I have found in any publication that appeared before the French Revolution.

The mysterious author was well informed on the details of the English slave trade. He had read William Snelgrave and other traders' accounts, and had apparently conversed with sailors back from the Guinea coast. Even his estimate of thirty-five thousand blacks transported annually by

---

16. Benezet to a Schoolmaster, ca. 1752, and to Samuel Fothergill, Philadelphia, Oct. 17, 1757, in Brookes, *Friend Anthony Benezet,* 210, 223.

17. Benezet, *A Short Account of That Part of Africa,* 2nd ed. (Philadelphia, 1762), 37–63; J. Philmore [pseud.], *Two Dialogues on the Man-Trade* (London, 1760). The name "J. Philmore" appears only at the end of the pamphlet. I have been unable to trace the identity of the author, but perhaps some specialist in anonyms and pseudonyms will be able to solve the mystery. The pamphlet was printed "for J. Waugh in Lombard Street, W. Fenner in Paternoster Row, G. Woodfall at Charing-Cross, W. Owen at Temple Bar, and Mrs. Kingham at the Royal Exchange."

British ships is not far off the mark.[18] An educated man, the author could sprinkle his text with Latin quotations and draw on the authority of Cicero, Seneca, Juvenal, Locke, and Pufendorf. Although Benezet omitted the "dialogue" format, in the original the arguments were presented in the form of a friendly debate between "J. Philmore," who had all the logic and knowledge on his side, and "Mr. Allcraft," who was financially involved in the slave trade, but whose moral doubts made him a suitable candidate for conversion.

Benezet reprinted most of Philmore's arguments with obvious delight. The devout Quaker might bridle a bit at the statement that man is a "noble Creature, made but a little lower than the Angels, and crowned with Glory and Honour." [19] But he could welcome the assertions, long familiar to Quakers, that enslavement is equivalent to "manstealing," and that the receiver of stolen goods is as guilty as the original thief. He could endorse the ringing statement, which he later repeated as if it were his own, that "no Legislature on Earth, which is the Supreme Power in every civil Society, can alter the Nature of Things, or make that to be lawful which is contrary to the Law of GOD, the Supreme Legislator and Governor of the World." [20]

But this ancient doctrine's revolutionary potential lay in its direct application to an institution sanctioned by custom and statute. Although Philmore emphasized moral guilt and atonement ("How can you, as some of you do, go to the Sacrament of the Lord's Supper? How can you lift up your guilty eyes to Heaven?"), he also called for physical retribution. George Wallace had exhorted judges to free Negroes illegally and unjustly held down by force. Philmore said that the slaves could rightfully free themselves.

Here are the passages which Benezet, as a peace-loving Quaker, felt constrained to omit:

> And so all the black men now in our plantations, who are by unjust force deprived of their liberty, and held in slavery, as they have none upon earth to appeal to, may lawfully repel that force with force, and to recover their liberty, destroy their oppressors: and not only so, but it is the duty of others, white as well as blacks, to assist those miserable crea-

18. Philip D. Curtin estimated the "possible volume exported by the English slave trade, by coastal region of origin in Africa," at an annual average of 23,100 for the decade 1751–1760, and at 27,200 for the decade 1761–1770. However, the volume of trade varied greatly from year to year, and 18th-century estimates of British slave exports for separate years range from 42,560 in 1759 (this was the calculated capacity of ships sent out) to 53,100 in 1768. *The Atlantic Slave Trade. A Census* (Madison, Wis., 1969), 150, 146. It should be added that Philmore thought that the 35,000 estimate might be too low.

19. Philmore, *Two Dialogues,* in Benezet, *A Short Account of That Part of Africa,* 33.

20. *Ibid.,* 41.

tures, if they can, in their attempts to deliver themselves out of slavery, and to rescue them out of the hands of their cruel tyrants.[21]

To justify this uncompromising approval of slave violence, Philmore appealed to the "higher law" doctrine of Cicero. And he was prepared to carry the argument still further. Any nation, he affirmed, would be justified in demanding that England should free all her slaves. If England refused, the other could legitimately go to war to liberate the colonial slaves by force:

> They would be so [justified], Mr. Allcraft, as, in that case, we might justly be considered as the aggressors; for in truth we are now at war (we Englishmen, we christians, to our shame be it spoken) and have been for above a hundred years past, without any cessation at all, at war and enmity with mankind in general, and in this war we have destroyed every year, at least for some years past, near as many of the human race, who never did us any injury, as have been destroyed in the same time, by the war now carried on in Europe [the Seven Years' War].[22]

Needless to say, this was revolutionary doctrine in 1760, as it would be in America in 1860 (or 1970). But it was also a logical extension of Wallace's doctrine that "every one of those unfortunate men, who are pretended to be slaves, has a right to be declared free, for he never lost his liberty." Though Philmore called on England to set an example to other nations by proclaiming immediate liberty to "those captives now in our plantations," he broke new ground by condemning England and other slave trading countries as aggressor nations that had long been "at war and enmity with mankind in general." This view would never become a part of accepted antislavery doctrine, though it has reappeared in different forms in more recent times. Its open avowal in the mid-eighteenth century might either have inhibited the growth of antislavery movements, or have made them into truly revolutionary forces. But there was, we can see, a screening element in the gathering and transmission of early antislavery pronouncements. While the higher law doctrine would live on in the mainstream of antislavery literature, often in a muted or half-suppressed form, the names of George Wallace and "J. Philmore" were soon forgotten.

21. Philmore, *Two Dialogues*, 54. This revolutionary utterance came in response to Allcraft's fear of the danger of slave insurrections, evidenced by the timely discovery of a plot for rebellion among the blacks of Antigua.
22. *Ibid.*, 57.

17

The Emergence of Immediatism
in British and American
Antislavery Thought

In the history of reform few slogans have brought forth such confusion and controversy as "immediate emancipation."[1] To the general public in the 1830's the phrase meant simply the abolition of Negro slavery without delay or preparation. But the word "immediate" may denote something other than a closeness in time; to many abolitionists it signified a rejection of intermediate agencies or conditions, a directness or forthrightness in action or decision. In this sense immediatism suggested a repudiation of the various media, such as colonization or apprenticeship, that had been advocated as remedies for the evils of slavery. To some reformers the phrase seemed mainly to imply a direct, intuitive consciousness of the sinfulness of slavery, and a sincere personal commitment to work for its abolition.[2] In this subjective sense the word

1. For the dispute over which American abolitionist had been the first to preach the doctrine, see George W. Julian, "The Genesis of Modern Abolitionism," *International Review* (New York), XII (June, 1882), 538, 542; A. T. Rankin, *Truth Vindicated and Slander Repelled* (Ironton, Ohio, 1883), 2–15; and the Parker B. Osborn Papers (Ohio Historical Society, Columbus).
2. This was essentially the doctrine of the American Anti-Slavery Society in the 1830's. According to Gilbert H. Barnes, New York philanthropists borrowed the phrase from British abolitionists and interpreted it as meaning an honest and prompt beginning to gradual emancipation; but such jesuitical "gradualism in a British cloak" injured the cause, in Barnes's view, for many critics pointed out that the abolitionists must either be gradualists, in which case the slogan was meaningless, or favor instant and unconditional liberation of the slaves, which would be sheer madness.

From *The Mississippi Valley Historical Review*, Volume XLIX, No. 2 (September 1962), 209–230. Reprinted by permission.

"immediate" was charged with religious overtones and referred more to the moral disposition of the reformer than to a particular plan for emancipation. Thus some reformers confused immediate abolition with an immediate personal decision to abstain from consuming slave-grown produce; and a man might be considered an immediatist if he were genuinely convinced that slavery should be abolished absolutely and without compromise, though not necessarily without honest preparation.[3] Such a range of meanings led unavoidably to misunderstanding, and the antislavery cause may have suffered from so ambiguous a slogan. The ambiguity, however, was something more than semantic confusion or the unfortunate result of a misleading watchword. The doctrine of immediacy, in the form it took in the 1830's, was at once a logical culmination of the antislavery movement and a token of a major shift in intellectual history.

A belief in the slave's right to immediate freedom was at least implicit in much of the antislavery writing of the eighteenth century. If Negro slavery were unjust, unnatural, illegal, corrupting, and detrimental to the national interest, as innumerable eighteenth-century writers claimed, there could be no excuse for its perpetuation.[4] Several of the *philosophes* held that since masters relied on physical force to impose their illegal demands, slave revolts would be just;[5] Louis de Jaucourt went so far as to argue that slaves, never having lost their inherent

---

Yet the antislavery agents from Lane Seminary found in the doctrine a way of emphasizing the sin of slavery and making their cause "identical with religion." See Barnes, *The Antislavery Impulse, 1830–1844* (New York, 1933), 48–49, 66–67, 102–104, 248; Gilbert H. Barnes and Dwight L. Dumond (eds.), *Letters of Theodore Dwight Weld, Angelina Grimké Weld, and Sarah Grimké, 1822–1844* (2 vols., New York, 1934), I, vii-x. While Barnes shows that Americans were mainly preoccupied with the sin of slavery, he tends to overemphasize the British origins of immediatism and ignores the historical development of the doctrine in both countries. This criticism applies also to Stanley M. Elkins, *Slavery: A Problem in American Institutional and Intellectual Life* (Chicago, 1959).

3. In both England and America immediatists denied that they opposed careful preparation for full freedom. See, for example, the influential speech of Joseph Sturge at the Society of Friends' London Meeting of 1830, printed in Henry Richard, *Memoirs of Joseph Sturge* (London, 1864), 87–88.

4. Frank J. Klingberg, "The Evolution of the Humanitarian Spirit in Eighteenth Century England," *Pennsylvania Magazine of History and Biography* (Philadelphia), LXVI (July, 1942), 261–65; Klingberg, *The Anti-Slavery Movement in England* (New Haven, 1926), 25–69; Wylie Sypher, "Hutcheson and the 'Classical' Theory of Slavery," *Journal of Negro History* (Washington), XXIV (July, 1939), 263–80; Edward D. Seeber, *Anti-Slavery Opinion in France during the Second Half of the Eighteenth Century (Johns Hopkins Studies in Romance Literatures and Languages,* Extra Volume X, Baltimore, 1937), *passim;* Thomas Clarkson, *The History of the Rise, Progress and Accomplishment of the Abolition of the African Slave-Trade by the British Parliament* (2 vols., London, 1808), I, 83–126, 185–89, 461–67.

5. Seeber, *Anti-Slavery Opinion,* 71–72; F. T. H. Fletcher, "Montesquieu's Influence on Anti-Slavery Opinion in England," *Journal of Negro History,* XVIII (October, 1933), 414–26; Shelby T. McCloy, *The Humanitarian Movement in Eighteenth-Century France* (Lexington, Ky., 1957), 86–92.

liberty, should be immediately declared free.[6] Anthony Benezet advanced a similar argument, asking what course a man should follow if he discovered that an inherited estate was really the property of another: "Would you not give it up immediately to the lawful owner? The voice of all mankind would mark him for a villain, who would refuse to comply with this demand of justice. And is not keeping a slave after you are convinced of the unlawfulness of it—a crime of the same nature?"[7]

In England, Granville Sharp denounced slavery as a flagrant violation of the common law, the law of reason, and the law of God. After exhorting Lord North to do something about the plight of the slaves, he warned: "I say immediate redress, because, *to be in power,* and to neglect . . . even a day in endeavoring to put a stop to such monstrous injustice and abandoned wickedness, must necessarily endanger a man's *eternal* welfare, be he ever so great in *temporal* dignity or office."[8] Sharp, who argued that "No Legislature on Earth . . . can alter the Nature of Things, or make that to be lawful, which is contrary to the Law of God,"[9] secured a judicial decision outlawing slavery in England. Americans like James Otis, Nathaniel Appleton, and Isaac Skillman took a similarly uncompromising stand before the Revolution;[10] by the 1780's the doctrine of natural rights had made the illegality of slavery an established fact in Vermont and Massachusetts.[11]

6. Louis de Jaucourt, "Traite des Negres," *Encyclopédie, ou Dictionnaire Raisonné des Sciences, des Arts et des Métiers, par une Société de Gens de Lettres* (Neufchâtel, 1765), XVI, 532–33. De Jaucourt was simply developing the antislavery principles of Montesquieu to their logical conclusion. After arguing that Negro slavery was contrary to all natural law and human rights, he wrote: "Il n'y a donc pas un seul de ces infortunés que l'on prétend n'être que des esclaves, qui n'ait droit d'être déclaré libre, puisqu'il n'a jamais perdu la liberté; qu'il ne pouvoit pas la perdre; et que son prince, son pere, et qui que ce soit dans le monde n'avoit le pouvoir d'en disposer; par conséquent la vente qui en a été faite est nulle en elle-même. . . .C'est donc une inhumanité manifeste de la part des juges de pays libres ou il est transporté, de ne pas l'affranchir à l'instant en le déclarant libre, puisque c'est leur semblable, ayant une ame comme eux."

7. [Anthony Benezet], *An Address to the Inhabitants of the British Settlements in America, upon Slave-Keeping* (Philadelphia, 1773), 20–21.

8. Granville Sharp to Lord North, February 18, 1772, printed in Prince Hoare, *Memoirs of Granville Sharp, Esq., Composed from His Own Manuscripts* (London, 1820), 79. See also Granville Sharp, *A Representation of the Injustice and Dangerous Tendency of Tolerating Slavery; or of Admitting the Least Claim of Private Property in the Persons of Men, in England* (London, 1769), 15–16, 23, 41; Sharp, *Extract of a Letter to a Gentleman in Maryland; Wherein Is Demonstrated the Extreme Wickedness of Tolerating the Slave Trade* (London, 1793), 4–14.

9. Granville Sharp, *An Appendix to the Representation* (London, 1772), 25. In 1776 Sharp argued that it was not sufficient to get slavery outlawed in England when the "abominable wickedness" persisted in the colonies. See *The Just Limitations of Slavery in the Laws of God, Compared with the Unbounded Claims of the African Traders and British American Slaveholders* (London, 1776), 2.

10. Mary S. Locke, *Anti-Slavery in America from the Introduction of African Slaves to the Prohibition of the Slave Trade* (Boston, 1901), 19–20; Lorenzo J. Greene, "Slave-Holding New England and Its Awakening," *Journal of Negro History,* XIII (October, 1928), 523–25; Herbert Aptheker, "Militant Abolitionists," *ibid.,* XXVI (October, 1941), 440.

11. In Vermont, slavery was effectually prohibited by the state constitution; in Massachusetts the courts supported the claims of liberty of individual Negroes.

But the natural rights philosophy was not the only source of immediatism. Officially, the Society of Friends showed extreme caution in
encouraging emancipation, but from the time of George Keith a latent
impulse of moral perfectionism rose to the surface in the radical testimony of individual Quakers, who judged slavery in the uncompromising
light of the Golden Rule. For such reformers, slavery was not a social
or economic institution, but rather an embodiment of worldly sin that
corrupted the souls of both master and slave; emancipation was not an
objective matter of social or political expediency, but a subjective act
of purification and a casting off of sin.[12]

Immediatism, in the sense of an immediate consciousness of the guilt
of slaveholding and an ardent desire to escape moral contamination, is
similarly evident in the writings of men who differed widely in their
views of religion and political economy. John Wesley's combined attack
on the opposite poles of Calvinism and natural religion could also be
directed against slavery, which some defended by arguments similar to
those that justified seeming injustice or worldly evils as part of God's
master plan or nature's economy. In 1784 Wesley's antislavery beliefs
were developed into a kind of immediatism in the rules of American
Methodists: "We . . . think it our most bounden duty to take immediately some effectual method to extirpate this abomination from among
us."[13] A related source of immediatism can be traced in the development of the romantic sensibility and the cult of the "man of feeling,"
which merged with Rousseau and the French Enlightenment in the writings of such men as Thomas Day and William Fox.[14]

In the light of this evidence we may well ask why immediatism appeared so new and dangerously radical in the 1830's. The later abolitionists charged that slavery was a sin against God and a crime against
nature; they demanded an immediate beginning of direct action that would

12. Samuel W. Pennypacker, "The Settlement of Germantown, and the Causes Which Led to
It," *Pennsylvania Magazine of History and Biography,* IV (1880), 28–30; George Keith, "An
Exhortation & Caution to Friends Concerning Buying or Keeping of Negroes," *ibid.,* XIII (1889),
265–70; Society of Friends, Philadelphia Yearly Meeting, *A Brief Statement of the Rise and Progress of the Testimony of the Religious Society of Friends, against Slavery and the Slave Trade*
(Philadelphia, 1843), 21–24, 44–56; Letters Which Passed Betwixt the Meeting for Sufferings in
London and the Meeting for Sufferings in Philadelphia (MSS in Friends House, London): Philadelphia to London, February 1, 1759; London to Philadelphia, August 22, 1766; London to Philadelphia, September 4, 1795; Philadelphia to London, March 17, 1796; Thomas Drake, *Quakers
and Slavery in America* (New Haven, 1950), 14–15, 68–83.

13. Lucius C. Matlack, *The History of American Slavery and Methodism from 1780 to 1849*
(New York, 1849), 15–20.

14. Ronald S. Crane, "Suggestions Toward a Genealogy of the 'Man of Feeling,' " *English
Literary History* (Baltimore), I (December, 1934), 205–206, 216, 225, 229–30; Wylie Sypher,
Guinea's Captive Kings; British Anti-Slavery Literature of the XVIIIth Century (Chapel Hill, 1942),
10, 77–85, 193–98; Thomas Day and John Bicknell, *The Dying Negro* (London, 1773); William
Fox, *An Address to the People of Great Britain, on the Consumption of West India Produce*
(London, 1791).

eventuate in general emancipation. Yet all of this had been said at least a half-century before, and we might conclude that immediatism was merely a recurring element in antislavery history.

But if immediatism was at least latent in early antislavery thought, the dominant frame of mind of the eighteenth century was overwhelmingly disposed to gradualism. Gradualism, in the sense of a reliance on indirect and slow-working means to achieve a desired social objective, was the logical consequence of fundamental attitudes toward progresss, natural law, property, and individual rights.

We cannot understand the force of gradualism in antislavery thought unless we abandon the conventional distinction between Enlightenment liberalism and evangelical reaction. It is significant that British opponents of abolition made little use of religion, appealing instead to the need for calm rationality and an expedient regard for the national interest. Quoting Hume, Lord Kames, and even Montesquieu to support their moral relativism, they showed the principles of the Enlightenment could be easily turned to the defense of slavery.[15] A belief in progress and natural rights might lead, of course, to antislavery convictions; but if history seemed to be on the side of liberty, slavery had attained a certain prescriptive sanction as a nearly universal expression of human nature.[16] Men who had acquired an increasing respect for property and for the intricate workings of natural and social laws could not view as an unmitigated evil an institution that had developed through the centuries.

Though evangelicals attacked natural religion and an acceptance of the world as a divinely contrived mechanism in which evils like slavery served a legitimate function, they nevertheless absorbed many of the assumptions of conservative rationalists and tended to express a middle-class fear of sudden social change.[17] Despite the sharp differences be-

---

15. [Edward Long], *Candid Reflections upon the Judgment Lately Awarded by the Court of King's Bench* (London, 1772); [Gordon Turnbull], *An Apology for Negro Slavery; or the West-India Planters Vindicated from the Charge of Inhumanity* (2nd ed., London, 1786); [Robert Norris], *A Short Account of the African Slave Trade* (Liverpool, 1787); Lord Rodney to Lord Hawkesbury, March, 1788, British Museum, Additional MSS, 38, 416, fols. 72–76; A Few Conjectural Considerations upon the Creation of the Human Race, Occasioned by the Present Quixottical Rage of Setting the Slaves from Africa at Liberty, by the Reverend Dr. Lindsay (1788), Add. MSS, 12, 439; [Anon.], *Considerations upon the Fatal Consequences of Abolishing the Slave Trade* (London, 1789). For one of the sources for the doctrine of Negro inferiority, see David Hume, "Of National Characters," in *Essays Moral, Political, and Literary* (2 vols., London, 1889), I, 244–58.

16. This was a problem recognized by Montesquieu and Burke, among others. See Fletcher, "Montesquieu's Influence," *Journal of Negro History,* XVIII, 422; Seeber, *Anti-Slavery Opinion,* 14–16, 28–33.

17. For the influence of naturalism and the idea of progress on English theology in the eighteenth century, see Ronald S. Crane, "Anglican Apologetics and the Idea of Progress, 1699–1745," *Modern Philology* (Chicago), XXXI (February, 1934), 281–306, 349–79; Leslie Stephen,

tween evangelicals and rationalists, they shared confidence, for the most part, in the slow unfolding of a divine or natural plan of historical progress. The mild and almost imperceptible diffusion of reason, benevolence, or Christianity had made slavery—a vestige of barbarism—anachronistic. But while eighteenth-century abolitionists might delight in furthering God's or nature's plan for earthly salvation, they tended to assume a detached, contemplative view of history, and showed considerable fear of sudden changes or precipitous action that might break the delicate balance of natural and historical forces.[18]

There was therefore a wide gap between the abstract proposition that slavery was wrong, or even criminal, and the cautious formulation of antislavery policy. It was an uncomfortable fact that slavery and the slave trade were tied closely to the rights of private property, the political freedom of colonies and states, and the economic rewards of international competition. Yet from the 1790's to the 1820's British and American reformers were confident that they understood the basic principles of society and could thus work toward the desired goal indirectly and without infringing on legitimate rights or interests. Frequently they seemed to think of slavery as a kind of unfortunate weed or fungus that had spread through the Lord's garden in a moment of divine inattention. As expert horticulturalists they imagined they could gradually kill the blight without injuring the plants. The British reformers focused their attention on the slave trade, assuming that if the supply of African Negroes were shut off planters would be forced to take better care of their existing slaves and would ultimately discover that free labor was more profitable. In America, reform energies were increasingly directed toward removing the free Negroes, who were thought to be the principal barrier to voluntary manumission. Both schemes were attempts at rather complex social engineering, and in both instances the desired reform was to come from the slaveowners themselves. Antislavery theorists assumed that they could predict the cumulative effects and consequences of their

---

History of English Thought in the Eighteenth Century (2 vols., New York, 1949), I, 70–91; James Stephen, *Essays in Ecclesiastical Biography* (4th ed., London, 1860), 440–45.

18. For the connection between gradualism and the idea of progress, see John Millar, *The Origin of the Distinction of Ranks* (3rd ed., London, 1781), 304, 320–47; William Paley, *The Principles of Moral and Political Philosophy* (London, 1785), 197–98; James Ramsay, A MS Volume, Entirely in Ramsay's Hand, Phillipps MSS, 17,780 (Rhodes House, Oxford). For the conservative approach of the Church of England to slavery, see Edgar L. Pennington, *Thomas Bray's Associates and Their Work among the Negroes* (Worcester, Mass., 1939), 10–12; J. Harry Bennett, Jr., "The Society for the Propagation of the Gospel's Plantations and the Emancipation Crisis," in Samuel C. McCulloch (ed.), *British Humanitarianism* (Philadelphia, 1950), 16–29. For cautious gradualism in America, see "The Appeal of the American Convention of Abolition Societies," *Journal of Negro History*, VI (April, 1921), 200–201; "American Convention of Abolition Societies Documents," *ibid.*, VI (July, 1921), 323–24, 363–64.

limited programs, and since they never doubted the goodness or effectiveness of natural laws, they sought only to set in motion a chain of forces that would lead irresistibly to freedom.[19]

This gradualist mentality dominated antislavery thought from the late eighteenth century to the 1820's. Though French thinkers had been among the first to denounce slavery as a crime, the emancipation scheme which they pioneered was one of slow transformation of the slave into a free laborer.[20] Even the *Amis des Noirs* feared immediate emancipation; and the French decree abolishing slavery in 1794, which was the result of political and military crisis in the West Indies, seemed to verify the ominous warnings of gradualists in all countries.[21] The years of bloodshed and anarchy in Haiti became an international symbol for the dangers of reckless and unplanned emancipation.

British abolitionists were particularly cautious in defining their objectives and moving indirectly, one step at a time. When outlawing the slave trade did not have the desired effect on colonial slavery, they then sought to bring the institution within the regulatory powers of the central government by limiting the extension of slavery in newly acquired islands and by using the crown colonies as models for gradual melioration;[22] and when these efforts failed they urged a general registration of slaves, which would not only interpose imperial authority in the colo-

19. [William Belsham], *Remarks on the African Slave Trade* (London, 1790), 14–15; Thomas Clarkson, *History*, I, 282–89; II, 195, 586–87; [James Ramsay], *An Inquiry into the Effects of Putting a Stop to the African Slave Trade, and of Granting Liberty to the Slaves in the British Colonies* (London, 1784), 32–33, 40; [Joseph Woods], *Thoughts on the Slavery of the Negroes* (London, 1784), 31–32; *The Debate on a Motion for the Abolition of the Slave-Trade . . . the Second of April, 1792* (London, 1792), 12–17; *Society Instituted in 1787 for Effecting the Abolition of the Slave Trade* [Report] (London, 1788), 1–2; James Anderson, *Observations on Slavery* (Manchester, 1789), 11–23; Henry Brougham, *A Concise Statement of the Question Regarding the Abolition of the Slave Trade* (London, 1804), 57–60; Thomas Clarkson, *Three Letters (one of which has appeared before) to the Planters & Slave-Merchants, Principally on the Subject of Compensation* (London, 1807), 14–15; "Gustavus," letter to *Connecticut Courant* (Hartford), August 21, 1797; Joseph Parrish, *Remarks on the Slavery of the Black People* (Philadelphia, 1806), 40–42; *The Emancipator* (reprint, Nashville, 1932), ix; "Appeal of the American Convention," *Journal of Negro History*, VI, 332; "American Convention . . . Documents," *ibid.*, VI, 324–26; American Convention for Promoting the Abolition of Slavery, *An Address to the Free People of Color and Descendants of the African Race* (Philadelphia, 1819), 4–5. It is true, of course, that American reformers also devoted considerable attention to the slave trade.

20. For the economic considerations behind French gradualism, see Gaston Martin, "La doctrine coloniale de la France en 1789," *Cahiers de la Révolution française* (Paris), III (1935), 25, 38–39; Martin, *Histoire de l'esclavage dans les colonies françaises* (Paris, 1948), 130–42, 164–65, 189–90, 251–59.

21. Martin, *Histoire de l'esclavage*, 190, 209–26; McCloy, *Humanitarian Movement*, 114–25. Abolition became associated with the worst excesses of the French Revolution. See *Parliamentary History of England*, XXXI (House of Lords, 1794), 467–70; Clarkson, *History*, II, 208–12; Robert I. Wilberforce and Samuel Wilberforce (eds.), *The Correspondence of William Wilberforce* (2 vols., London, 1840), I, 89–90; Lafayette to Clarkson, January 27, 1798 (photostat in Rhodes House, Oxford); Louis Gottschalk, *Lafayette between the American and French Revolution* (Chicago, 1950), 380–81.

22. Wilberforce, *Correspondence*, I, 328–29; Robert I. Wilberforce and Samuel Wilberforce, *The Life of William Wilberforce* (5 vols., London, 1838), III, 30–33, 198–200; [James Stephen],

nies but provide a mechanism for protecting the Negroes' rights.[23] By 1822 these methods had proved inadequate and the British reformers began agitating for direct parliamentary intervention. Even then, however, and for the following eight years, British antislavery leaders limited their aims to melioration and emancipation by slow degrees. [24]

Between British and American antislavery men there was a bond of understanding and a common interest in suppressing the international slave trade and finding a home in Haiti or western Africa for free Negroes.[25] But in America the antislavery movement was given a distinctive color by the discouraging obstacles that stood in the way of even gradual emancipation. While states like New York and Pennsylvania provided tangible examples of gradual manumission, they also showed the harsh and ugly consequences of racial prejudice.[26] Americans, far more than British, were concerned with the problem of the emancipated slave. Even some of the most radical and outspoken abolitionists were convinced that colonization was the inescapable prerequisite to reform. Others stressed the importance of education and moral training as the first steps toward eventual freedom.[27]

The Crisis of the Sugar Colonies: or an Enquiry into the Objects and Probable Effects of the French Expedition to the West Indies (London, 1802), 121–28, 151–95; *Report of the Committee of the African Institution . . . July, 1807* (London 1807), 15; *Fifth Report of the Directors of the African Institution . . . March, 1811* (London, 1811), 1–2; Thomas Morton Birtwhistle, "The Development of Abolitionism, 1807–1823" (M.A. thesis, University of London, 1948), 19–30.

23. This had been proposed in 1788 by the Reverend F. Randolph, *A Letter to the Right Honourable William Pitt . . . on the Proposed Abolition of the African Slave Trade* (London 1788), 44–46. The scheme was later championed by James Stephen. See [James Stephen], *Reasons for Establishing a Registry of Slaves in the British Colonies* (London, 1815); letter of James Stephen, April 14, 1815, Add. MSS, 38,416, fols. 364–71; Lowell J. Ragatz, *The Fall of the Planter Class in the British Caribbean, 1763–1833* (New York, 1928), 389–94.

24. The gradualism, however, was combined with a sense that slavery was the ultimate of all evils. See Society for the Mitigation and Gradual Abolition of Slavery Throughout the British Dominions, *Prospectus* (London, 1823), v–vii; James Cropper, *A Letter Addressed to the Liverpool Society for Promoting the Abolition of Slavery* (Liverpool, 1823), 31–32.

25. *Twelfth Report of the Directors of the African Institution . . . April, 1818* (London, 1818), 35–37, 130–40; *Fourteenth Report of the Directors of the African Institution . . . May, 1820* (London, 1820), 33–37, 84–97; *Fifteenth Report . . . March, 1821* (London, 1821), 39–41; Wilberforce, *Correspondence*, I, 118; William Allen, *Life of William Allen, with Selections from his Correspondence* (3 vols., London, 1846), I, 114–15, 136–40. Thomas Clarkson to James Monroe, March 18, 1817 (photostat in Rhodes House, Oxford); Earl Leslie Griggs and Clifford H. Prator (eds.), *Henry Christophe and Thomas Clarkson: A Correspondence* (Berkeley, 1952), 124–25, 141–42; Zachary Macaulay to Mrs. Clarkson, March 31, 1823, Add. MSS, 41,267A, fols. 134–35.

26. Edward R. Turner, *The Negro in Pennsylvania* (Washington, 1911), 143–68; Charles H. Wesley, "The Negroes of New York and the Emancipation Movement," *Journal of Negro History*, XXIV (January, 1939), 65–103; Wesley, "The Concept of Negro Inferiority in American Thought," *ibid.*, XXV (October, 1940), 540–60; Thomas Branagan, *Serious Remonstrances, Addressed to the Citizens of the Northern States* (Philadelphia, 1805), *passim;* Branagan, *Political and Theological Disquisitions on the Signs of the Times* (Trenton, 1807), *passim.*

27. *Emancipator* (reprint), vii, ix–x; "Appeal of American Convention," *Journal of Negro History*, VI, 215–18; Drake, *Quakers and Slavery*, 114–15; Turner, *Negro in Pennsylvania*, 210–12; [William Griffith], *Address of the President of the New Jersey Society for Promoting the Abolition of Slavery* (Trenton, 1804), 8–9.

In America the gradualist frame of mind was also related to the weakness and limitations of political institutions. British abolitionists could work to enlist the unlimited power of a central Parliament against colonies that were suffering acute economic decline. But slavery in America was not only expanding but was protected by a sectional balance of power embodied in nearly every national institution. A brooding fear of disunion and anarchy damped down the aspirations of most American abolitionists and turned energies to such local questions as the education and legal protection of individual Negroes. Antislavery societies might call for the government to outlaw slavery in the District of Columbia or even to abolish the interstate slave trade, but in the end they had to rely on public opinion and individual conscience in the slave states. While British abolitionists moved with the circumspection of conservative pragmatists, their American counterparts acted with the caution of men surrounded by high explosives. For many, the only prudent solution was to remove the explosives to a distant country.

But if British and American abolitionists were gradualist in their policies and expectations, they did not necessarily regard slavery as simply one of many social evils that should be mitigated and eventually destroyed. The policy of gradualism was related to certain eighteenth-century assumptions about historical progress, the nature of man, and the principles of social change; but we have also noted a subjective, moral aspect to antislavery thought that was often revealed as an immediate consciousness of guilt and a fear of divine punishment. During the British slave trade controversy of the 1790's the entire system of slavery and slave trade became identified with sin, and reform with true virtue.[28] Though antislavery leaders adopted the gradualist policy of choosing the slave trade as their primary target, they bitterly fought every attempt to meliorate or gradually destroy the African trade. It was the determined opponents of the slave trade who first gave popular currency to the slogan, "immediate abolition," which became in the early 1790's a badge of moral sincerity.[29] When uncompromising hostility to the slave trade became a sign of personal virtue and practical Christianity, the rhetoric of statesmen acquired the strident, indignant tone that we associate with later American abolitionists. Charles James Fox made scathing attacks

28. Clarkson, *History*, I, 1-29, 158-66; II, 119-20, 347, 581-86; *Society Instituted in 1787* [Report], 2; [William Belsham], *Remarks on the African Slave Trade* (London, 1790), 18-19; Granville Sharp, *Serious Reflections on the Slave Trade and Slavery* (London, 1805), 8-38; Sharp, "*The System of Colonial Law*" *Compared with the Eternal Laws of God* (London, 1807), 13; Stephen, *Crisis in Sugar Colonies*, 174-76.

29. William Wilberforce, *A Letter on the Abolition of the Slave Trade* (London, 1807), 301-302; Wilberforce, *Life*, I, 345-46, 351; *Debate on the Motion for Abolition of Slave Trade . . . 1792* (Wilberforce speech), 47-48.

on those who pled for moderation; he even said that if the plantations could not be cultivated without being supplied with African slaves, it would be far better for England to rid herself of the islands. "How shall we hope," asked William Pitt, "to obtain, if it is possible, forgiveness from Heaven for those enormous evils we have committed, if we refuse to make use of those means which the mercy of Providence hath still reserved to us for wiping away the guilt and shame with which we are now covered?"[30]

This sense of moral urgency and fear of divine retribution persisted in British antislavery thought and was held in check only by a faith in the certain and predictable consequences of indirect action.[31] Whenever the faith was shaken by unforeseen obstacles or a sense of crisis, there were voices that condemned gradualism as a compromise with sin. Granville Sharp, who interpreted hurricanes in the West Indies as supernatural agencies "to blast the *enemies* of *law* and *righteousness*," called in 1806 for direct emancipation by act of Parliament, and warned that continued toleration of slavery in the colonies "must finally draw down the Divine vengeance upon our state and nation!"[32] When William Allen, Zachary Macaulay, and James Cropper became disillusioned over the failure to secure an effective registration scheme and international suppression of the slave trade, they pressed for direct though gradual emancipation by the British government.[33] The British Anti-Slavery Society remained officially gradualist until 1831, but individual abolitionists, particularly in the provinces, became increasingly impatient over the diffidence of the government and the intransigence of colonial legislatures.[34] From 1823 to 1832 the British Caribbean planters violently attacked the government's efforts to meliorate slavery. They not only

---

30. *Debate on the Motion . . . 1792*, pp. 116–17, 132–34, 164–65.

31. Granville Sharp, *The Case of Saul, Shewing that His Disorder was a Real Spiritual Possession* (London, 1807), preface to 1807 ed., iii–iv; [Anon.], *The Horrors of the Negro Slavery Existing in Our West Indian Islands* (London, 1805), 4–5, 36; James Stephen, *A Defence of the Bill for the Registration of Slaves* (London, 1816), 36–55; Wilberforce, *Correspondence*, II, 495–96.

32. Sharp, *Serious Reflections*, 38; Sharp, "*Systems of Colonial Law*," 13.

33. For the formation of the British Anti-Slavery Society, see David B. Davis, "James Cropper and the British Anti-Slavery Movement," *Journal of Negro History*, XLV (October, 1960), 241–58.

34. MSS Minutes of the Society for the Mitigation and Gradual Abolition of Slavery Throughout the British Dominions (Rhodes House, Oxford), I, 34–36, 133–35, 139, 141; II, 1–8, 18–21, 49–52, 81, 132–41; III, 4–6, 20–27; Society for the Mitigation and Gradual Abolition of Slavery, *Second Report* (London, 1825), *passim; Anti-Slavery Monthly Reporter* (London), I (January 31, 1826), 80; I (May 31, 1826), 185–88; III (June, 1830), 239–63. In the 1830's American abolitionists claimed that the British Anti-Slavery Society had adopted the principle of immediatism in 1826, and later historians have repeated the same error. It was only in 1831 and 1832 that immediatism gained widespread support, and even then the more conservative leaders looked to the government for an effective but gradual working plan.

devised schemes to nullify effective reform but threatened to secede from the empire and seek protection from the United States.[35] Though the evils of West Indian slavery were probably mitigated in the 1820's, the planters' resistance convinced many abolitionists that gradual improvement was impossible.

The most eloquent early plea for immediate emancipation was made in 1824 by a Quaker named Elizabeth Heyrick, who looked to the women of Great Britain as a source of invincible moral power, and who preached a massive consumers' crusade against West Indian produce. The central theme in Mrs. Heyrick's pamphlet, *Immediate, Not Gradual Abolition,* was the supremacy of individual conscience over social and political institutions. Since antislavery was a *"holy war"* against "the very powers of darkness," there was no ground for compromise or for a polite consideration of slaveholders. Like the later American immediatists, she excoriated gradualism as a satanic plot to induce gradual indifference. It was a delusion to think that slavery could be gradually improved, for "as well might you say to a poor wretch, gasping and languishing in a pest house, 'here will I keep you, till I have given you a capacity for the enjoyment of pure air.' "[36] For Mrs. Heyrick the issue was simple and clearcut: sin and vice should be immediately exterminated by individual action in accordance with conscience and the will of God.

In 1824 such views were too strong for British antislavery leaders, who still looked to direct government action modeled on the precedent of the Canning Resolutions, which had proposed measures for ameliorating the condition of West Indian slaves as a step toward ultimate emancipation.[37] Abolitionists in Parliament continued to shape their strategy in the light of political realities, but by 1830 several prominent reformers had adopted the uncompromising stand of Elizabeth Heyrick. The shift from gradualism to immediatism is most dramatically seen in James Stephen, who possessed a mind of great clarity and precision and who, having practiced law in the West Indies, had acquired direct experience with slavery as an institution. For a time Stephen adhered to the principle of gradualism, transferring his hopes from the slave registration scheme to a "digested plan" of abolition by stages, beginning

35. Ragatz, *Fall of the Planter Class,* 287, 332, 412–48; Claude Levy, "Barbados: The Last Years of Slavery, 1823–1833," *Journal of Negro History,* XLIV (October, 1959), 316–22.

36. Elizabeth Heyrick, *Immediate, Not Gradual Abolition; or, An Inquiry into the Shortest, Safest, and Most Effectual Means of Getting Rid of West Indian Slavery* (London, 1824), 8, 14–18.

37. But on June 8, 1824, the General Committee of the Anti-Slavery Society instructed its secretary to procure a dozen copies of the Heyrick pamphlet for distribution to interested members; and some of the Society's members were reported at the same time to favor immediate abolition. Minutes, I, 111–12.

with domestic servants. By 1830, however, he was convinced that debate over alternative plans merely inhibited action and obscured what
was essentially a question of principle and simple moral duty. It would
be a tragic mistake, he felt, for the abolitionists to propose any measure
short of a "general, entire, immediate restitution of the freedom wrong-
fully withheld." Lashing out at the moral lethargy of the government,
he denounced the principle of compensation to slaveowners and rejected
all specific gradualist measures such as the liberation of Negro women
or the emancipation of infants born after a certain date. Stephen's immediatism was based ultimately on a fear of divine vengeance and an
overwhelming sense of national guilt. "We sin remorselessly," he said,
"because our fathers sinned, and because multitudes of our own generation sin, in the same way without [public] discredit." [38]

On October 19, 1830, the Reverend Andrew Thomson, of St. George's
Church in Edinburgh, delivered a fire-and-brimstone speech that provided an ideology for George Thompson and the later agency Committee. [39] Beginning with the premise that slavery is a crime and sin, Thomson dismissed all consideration of economic and political questions. When
the issue was reduced to what individual men should do as moral and
accountable beings, there was no possibility of compromise or even
controversy. The British public should "compel" Parliament to order
total and immediate emancipation. With Calvinistic intensity he exhorted the public to cut down and burn the "pestiferous tree," root and
branch: "You must annihilate it,—annihilate it now,—and annihilate it
forever." Since Thomson considered every hour that men were kept in
bondage a repetition of the original sin of man-stealing, he did not shrink
from violence: "If there must be violence, . . . let it come and rage its
little hour, since it is to be succeeded by lasting freedom, and prosperity, and happiness." [40]

Taking its cue from men like Stephen, Thomson, and Joseph Sturge,
the Anti-Slavery Society reorganized itself for more effective action and
focused its energies on raising petitions and arousing public feeling against
slavery. [41] While Thomas Fowell Buxton sought to make the fullest use

38. James Stephen, *The Slavery of the British West India Colonies Delineated* (2 vols., London,
1824–1830), II, 387, 390–401; Minutes, III, 132–33.
39. Raymond English, "George Thompson and the Climax of Philanthropic Radicalism, 1830–
1842" (unpublished dissertation, Cambridge University), 33. I am indebted to Mr. English for
lending me a copy of his manuscript.
40. Andrew Thomson, *Immediate Emancipation: Substance of a Speech Delivered at the Meeting of the Edinburgh Society for the Abolition of Slavery* (Manchester, 1832), 4, 11, 24.
41. Many historians have been misled by Sir George Stephen's *Antislavery Recollections* (London, 1854), which states that the Agency Committee was an independent body formed by the
democratic "young England Abolitionists" after the conservative Anti-Slavery Society had vehemently rejected the plan of employing itinerant agents (pp. 128–29). Actually, the Society had

of public opinion to support his campaign in Parliament, he found himself under mounting pressure from abolitionists who refused to defer to his judgment. People's principles, he told his daughter, were the greatest nuisance in life.[42] When the government finally revealed its plan for gradual and compensated emancipation, the Anti-Slavery Society committed itself to vigorous and aggressive opposition.[43] But once the law had been passed, the antislavery leaders concluded that they had done as well as possible and that their defeat had actually been a spectacular victory. They had achieved their primary object, which was to induce the people to support a tangible act that could be interpreted as purging the nation of collective guilt and proving the moral power of individual conscience.

In America the developing pattern was somewhat similar. Despite the conservatism of most antislavery societies, a number of radical abolitionists branded slaveholding as a heinous sin, which, if not immediately abandoned, would bring down the wrath of the Lord. A few early reformers like Theodore Dwight, David Rice, Charles Osborn, and John Rankin, were well in advance of British antislavery writers in their sense of moral urgency and their mistrust of gradualist programs. As early as 1808, David Barrow, although he denied favoring immediate abolition, anticipated the later doctrine of the American Anti-Slavery Society by refusing to recognize the lawfulness of slavery or the justice of compensation. Holding that slavery was the crying sin of America, he urged a prompt beginning of manumission in order to avert the retribution of God.[44] Three years earlier Thomas Branagan, who opposed "instanta-

---

accepted the plan in principle in 1828. In large meetings of May 25 and June 1, 1831, the Society unanimously approved the Agency program and appointed a subcommittee which included such outsiders as George Stephen, Emmanuel Cooper, and Charles Stuart (Minutes, III, 93–100). Dissension did not arise over the wisdom of arousing public opinion, as Stephen claimed, but over the control of such efforts and the co-ordination of policy by a central authority. The Agency subcommittee remained a part of the parent society until July 4, 1832, when a rupture came over the General Committee's assertion of its right to inspect all antislavery documents prior to publication (*Ibid.*, 142–52). While many members of the parent society favored immediate emancipation, it was the Agency Committee that popularized the doctrine. See *The Tourist: A Literary and Anti-Slavery Journal* (London), I (1832–1833), 16, 94, 108, 124, 173, 231, 266, 308; *Report of the Agency Committee of the Anti-Slavery Society* (London, 1832), 3–4; Charles Stuart, *The West India Question* (London, 1832), 4–6; George Thompson, *Three Lectures on British Colonial Slavery, Delivered in the Royal Amphitheatre, Liverpool* (Liverpool, 1832), 57–64, 76–77.

42. Frank Carpenter Stuart, "A Critical Edition of the Correspondence of Sir Thomas Fowell Buxton, Bart., with an Account of his Career to 1823" (2 vols., M.A. thesis, Institute for Historical Research, London, 1957), II, 24–29, 45–46, 244.

43. Society for the Abolition of Slavery Throughout the British Dominions [Circular Letter to Provisional Organizations], April 4, 1833, pp. 1–2; [Anon.], *Some Remarks on Mr. Stanley's Proposed Bill for the Abolition of Colonial Slavery* (n.p., 1833), 1–7; Minutes, IV, 54–55, 61; Richard, *Joseph Sturge*, 106–107.

44. David Barrow, *Involuntary, Unmerited, Perpetual, Absolute, Hereditary Slavery, Examined; on the Principles of Nature, Reason, Justice, Policy and Scripture* (Lexington, Ky., 1808), 13–14, 42.

neous emancipation" if the freed Negroes were to remain within the United States, contended that his plan for colonization in the West would bring a speedy end to slavery and avert the divine judgment of an apocalyptic racial war.[45] In 1817 John Kenrick showed that colonization could be combined with a kind of immediatism, for though he proposed settlement of free Negroes in the West, he went so far as to suggest that the powers of the central government should be enlarged, if necessary, in order to abolish slavery. "If slavery is 'a violation of the divine laws,' " Kenrick asked, "is it not absurd to talk about a gradual emancipation? We might as well talk of gradually leaving off piracy—murder—adultery, or drunkenness."[46]

The religious character of this radical abolitionism can best be seen in the writings of George Bourne, an English immigrant who was to have a deep influence on William Lloyd Garrison. In 1815 Bourne condemned professed Christians who upheld the crime of slavery. "The system is so entirely corrupt," he wrote, "that it admits of no cure, but by a total and immediate, abolition. For a gradual emancipation is a virtual recognition of the right, and establishes the rectitude of the practice." But while Bourne associated slavery with the very essence of human sin, his main concern was not the plight of Negroes but the corruption of the Christian church:

> Had this compound of all corruption no connection with the church of Christ; however deleterious are the effects of it in political society, however necessary is its immediate and total abolition, and however pregnant with danger to the *Union,* is the prolongation of the system; to Legislators and Civilians, the redress of the evil would have been committed. But *Slavery* is the *golden Calf,* which has been elevated among the Tribes, and before it, the Priests and the Elders and the *nominal* sons of Israel, *eat, drink, rise up to play, worship and sacrifice.*[47]

Thus for Bourne "immediatism" meant an immediate recognition of the sin of slavery and an immediate decision on the part of Christians to purge their churches of all contamination. He was far more interested in the purification of religion than in slavery as an institution.

45. Thomas Branagan, *Serious Remonstrances,* 35, 64; Branagan, *Buying Stolen Goods Synonymous with Stealing* (2nd ed. [printed with *The Penitential Tyrant*], Philadelphia, 1807), 233–39.

46. John Kenrick, *Horrors of Slavery* (Cambridge, Mass., 1817), 38–39, 58–59.

47. George Bourne, *The Book and Slavery Irreconcilable: With Animadversions upon Dr. Smith's Philosophy* (Philadelphia, 1816), 7–8, 16–19, appendix. Bourne's appeal for unconditional emancipation attracted the attention of William Allen, the English philanthropist who was later instrumental in founding the British Anti-Slavery Society. See William Allen (ed.), *The Philanthropist: or Repository for Hints and Suggestions Calculated to Promote the Comfort and Happiness of Man* (London), VI (1816), 334–50.

In 1825 the Boston *Recorder and Telegraph* published a long correspondence that further clarifies the origins of immediatism. After arguing that slavery was unlawful and suggesting that slaves might have a
right to revolt, "Vigornius" [Samuel M. Worcester] asserted that *"the
slave-holding system must be abolished;* and in order to the accomplishment of this end, immediate, determined measures must be adopted for
the ultimate emancipation of every slave within our territories."[48] This
was the position of the later Kentucky and New York abolitionists, but
Vigornius combined it with strong faith in the American Colonization
Society. He was bitterly attacked by "A Carolinian," who accused him
of believing in "an entire and immediate abolition of slavery." "Philo,"
the next contributor, said he opposed immediate emancipation on grounds
of expediency, but recognized the right of slaves to immediate freedom;
he advocated, therefore, "immediate and powerful remedies," since "We
are convinced, and if our Southern brethren are not convinced, we wish
to convince them, and think with a little discussion we could convince
them, that to postpone these prospective measures a day, is a great crime
. . . and moreover, we wish to state directly, that this postponement is
that, in which we consider the guilt of slavery, so far as the present
proprietors are concerned, to consist."[49]

A Southerner, who called himself "Hieronymus," defended Vigornius and tried to avoid the ambiguities that were later to cloud discussions of immediate abolition. Vigornius, he wrote,

> pleads, it is true, for *speedy* emancipation, and immediate preparatory
> steps. But immediate and speedy are not synonimous [*sic*] expressions.
> One is an absolute, the other a relative or comparative term. An event
> may in one view of it be regarded as very speedy, which in another might
> be pronounced very gradual. If slavery should be entirely abolished from
> the United States in 30, 40, or even 50 years, many . . . will readily
> admit, that it would be a speedy abolition; while every one must per-
> ceive, that it would be far, very far, from an immediate abolition. In a
> certain sense abolition may be immediate; in another, speedy; and in
> both, practicable and safe. There are not a few blacks now at the South,
> qualified for immediate emancipation, if Legislatures would permit, and
> owners would confer it.[50]

Hieronymus, who had read and been impressed by Elizabeth Heyrick's
pamphlet, agreed with Vigornius that colonization was the only practicable solution to the nation's most critical problem.

These ardent colonizationists believed that slavery was a sin that would

48. [Samuel M. Worcester], *Essays on Slavery: Re-Published from the Boston Recorder &
Telegraph, for 1825, by Vigornius, and Others* (Amherst, 1826), 24–25.
49. *Ibid.*, 32–33.
50. *Ibid.*, 46–47.

increase in magnitude and danger unless effective measures were adopted without delay. Yet by 1821 Benjamin Lundy and other abolitionists had come to the opinion that the American Colonization Society was founded on racial prejudice and offered no real promise of undermining slavery. Lundy thought that slavery could not be eradicated until his fellow Americans in both North and South were willing to accept the free Negro as an equal citizen.[51] But in the meantime the institution was expanding into the Southwest and even threatening to spread to such states as Illinois. In the face of such an imposing problem, Lundy called for the swift and decisive use of political power by a convention of representatives from the various states, who might devise and implement a comprehensive plan for emancipation.[52]

The American antislavery organizations absorbed some of this sense of urgency and mistrust of palliatives. The Pennsylvania Society for the Abolition of Slavery was cautious in its approach to the national problem, but in 1819 it approved a declaration that "the practice of holding and selling human beings as property . . . ought to be *immediately* abandoned."[53] In 1825 the Acting Committee of the American Convention for Promoting the Abolition of Slavery advocated the "speedy and entire" emancipation of slaves, a phrase later used by the British Society.[54] The Convention showed little confidence in any of the specific proposals for gradual abolition but at the same time rejected direct emancipation by act of Congress as an impossibility. Alert always to the need for conciliating the South and remaining within the prescribed bounds of the Constitution, the Convention considered every conceivable plan in a rationalistic and eclectic spirit.[55] In the South, however, there was an increasing tendency to see the most conservative antislavery proposals as immediatism in disguise.[56] By 1829 the gradualist approach of the American convention had reached a dead end.[57]

51. *Genius of Universal Emancipation* (Greeneville, Tenn.), I (September, 1821), 33; (October, 1821), 49–52.

52. *Ibid.,* I (September, 1821), 35; (February, 1822), 118–20; (March, 1822), 135. Lundy favored colonization at public expense of Negroes wishing to leave the country, but he also called on the North to receive emancipated slaves without restriction, and exhorted the South to repeal laws discriminating against free Negroes.

53. Turner, *Negro in Pennsylvania,* 216. In 1819 the Pennsylvania Society sent a message to the American Convention, calling for the "total and most early abolition of slavery, consistent with the interest of the objects of your care." American Convention, *Minutes of the Sixteenth Session of the American Convention* (Philadelphia, 1819), 6–8.

54. American Convention, *Minutes of the Nineteenth Session of the American Convention* (Philadelphia, 1825), 30.

55. "Appeal of American Convention," *Journal of Negro History,* VI, 235–40; "American Convention Documents," *ibid., passim.*

56. Glover Moore, *The Missouri Controversy, 1819–1821* (Lexington, Ky., 1953), 303–304; [Worcester], *Essays on Slavery,* 29; William S. Jenkins, *Pro-Slavery Thought in the Old South* (Chapel Hill, 1935), 67–80.

57. This is perhaps most clearly seen in the memorial drawn up by a committee of the American Convention on December 11, 1829. See "American Convention Documents," *Journal of Negro*

It is a striking coincidence that both the British and American anti-slavery movements had come to a crucial turning point by 1830.[58] In both countries the decline of faith in gradualism had been marked in the mid-1820's by enthusiasm for a boycott of slave produce, a movement which promised to give a cutting edge to the moral testimony of individuals.[59] In both countries the truculence and stubborn opposition of slaveholders to even gradualist reforms brought a sense of despair and indignation to the antislavery public. To some degree immediatism was the creation of the British and American slaveholders themselves. By accusing the most moderate critics of radical designs and by blocking the path to many attempted reforms they helped to discredit the gradualist mentality that had balanced and compromised a subjective conviction that slavery was sin.[60] The sense of crisis between 1829 and 1831 was also accentuated by an increasing militancy of Negroes, both slave and free.[61] In 1829 David Walker hinted ominously of slave revenge; groups of free Negroes openly repudiated the colonization movement; and in 1831 bloody revolts erupted in Virginia and Jamaica. In that year a new generation of American reformers adopted the principle of immediatism, which had recently acquired the sanction of eminent British philanthropists.[62] But while American abolitionists modeled their new societies and techniques on British examples, the principle of immediatism had had a long and parallel development in both countries.

In one sense immediatism was simply a shift in strategy brought on by the failure of less direct plans for abolition. Earlier plans and programs had evoked little popular excitement compared with parliamen-

History, VI, 351–57. Also, Drake, *Quakers and Slavery*, 134–39; Alice Dana Adams, *The Neglected Period of Anti-Slavery in America* (Boston, 1908), 116–17, 154–57, 175–76.

58. This parallel development of British and American antislavery movements was recognized by Benjamin Lundy. See *Genius of Universal Emancipation*, New Series (Baltimore), III (November, 1832).

59. *The Philanthropist: A Weekly Journal* (Mount Pleasant, Ohio), II (August 21, 1819), 297–99; II (September 4, 1819), 324–25; Norman B. Wilkinson, "The Philadelphia Free Produce Attack upon Slavery," *Pennsylvania Magazine of History and Biography*, LXVI (July, 1942), 297–99; Adams, *Neglected Period*, 127, 149–51; Minutes of the Society for the Mitigation and Gradual Abolition of Slavery, II, 1–52; James Cropper, *The Support of Slavery Investigated* (London, 1824); Heyrick, *Immediate, Not Gradual Abolition, passim*.

60. William B. Hesseltine, "Some New Aspects of the Pro-Slavery Argument," *Journal of Negro History*, XXI (January, 1936), 8–13; *Philanthropist, A Weekly Journal*, VII (April 20, 1822), 353–55.

61. Aptheker, "Militant Abolitionists," *Journal of Negro History*, XXVI, 444–48; Wesley, "Negroes of New York," *ibid.*, XXIV, 68–81; Bella Gross, " 'Freedom's Journal' and the 'Rights of All,' " *ibid.*, XXVII (July, 1932), 241–62; Herbert Aptheker, *The Negro in the Abolitionist Movement* (New York, 1941), 33–36, 40–42. The crisis was also intensified by the tariff and nullification controversy in America and by the mounting pressure for political reform in Britain.

62. Barnes, *Antislavery Impulse*, 32–33, 42–44; Roman J. Zorn, "The New England Anti-Slavery Society: Pioneer Abolition Organization," *Journal of Negro History*, XLII (July, 1957), 159–73; David. M. Ludlum, *Social Ferment in Vermont, 1791–1850* (New York, 1939), 142–44.

tary reform or Catholic emancipation in England, or with tariff or land policies in the United States. As a simple, emotional slogan, immediate abolition would at least arouse interest and perhaps appeal to the moral sense of the public. As a device for propaganda it had the virtue of avoiding economic and social complexities and focusing attention on a clear issue of right and wrong.[63] If the public could once be brought to the conviction that slavery was wrong and that something must be done about it at once, then governments would be forced to take care of the details.

But immediatism was something more than a shift in strategy. It represented a shift in total outlook from a detached, rationalistic perspective on human history and progress to a personal commitment to make no compromise with sin. It marked a liberation for the reformer from the ideology of gradualism, from a toleration of evil within the social order, and from a deference to institutions that blocked the way to personal salvation. Acceptance of immediatism was the sign of an immediate transformation within the reformer himself; as such, it was seen as an expression of inner freedom, of moral sincerity and earnestness, and of victory over selfish and calculating expediency.[64] If slaveholders received the doctrine with contempt and scathing abuse, the abolitionist was at least assured of his own freedom from guilt. He saw the emergence of immediatism as an upswelling of personal moral force which, with the aid of God, would triumph over all that was mean and selfish and worldly.[65]

There are obvious links between immediate emancipation and a religious sense of immediate justification and presence of the divine spirit that can be traced through the early spiritual religions to the Quakers, Methodists, and evangelical revivals.[66] The new abolitionism contained

63. See, for example, the letter in *The Liberator* (Boston), I (January 22, 1831), 13, suggesting that a special juvenile department would help correct prejudice in adults: "For there is, perhaps, no better way of removing error, than by leading the mind back to the first simple view of a subject, which you would present to a child." Also, Barnes and Dumond (eds.), *Weld-Grimké Letters*, I, 95–97, 100, 118, 125–28; *Report of the Agency Committee* (London), 2–3; Letter of James Stephen to Anti-Slavery Society, April 3, 1832, Minutes, III, 131–35.

64. Barnes and Dumond (eds.), *Weld-Grimké Letters*, I, 97–103, 116, 132–35, 140–46; *Liberator*, I (January 8, 1831), 7; *Philanthropist, A Weekly Journal* (Mount Pleasant, Ohio), II (September 4, 1819), 324–25; *The Philanthropist* [an earlier journal published by Charles Osborn] (Mount Pleasant, Ohio), I (December 5, 1817), 114; Bourne, *The Book and Slavery*, 20–21, 58, 74–75, 139–40, Appendix; Heyrick, *Immediate, Not Gradual Abolition*, 34–36.

65. "Letters of William Lloyd Garrison to John B. Vashon," *Journal of Negro History*, XII (January, 1927), 36–38; Thompson, *Three Lectures on British Colonial Slavery*, 4–5, 7; *Tourist*, I, 84, 124; William Allen to Charles Babbage, December 1, 1832, Add. MSS, 37,187, fols. 255–56.

66. Rufus M. Jones, *Spiritual Reformers in the 16th and 17th Centuries* (Boston, 1959 [1st ed. 1914]), xviii–xlvii, 44–45, 234, 288–98; William C. Braithwaite, *The Beginnings of Quakerism* (London, 1955 [1st ed. 1912]), 449–50; Rufus M. Jones, *The Later Periods of Quakerism* (2 vols.,

attern of intense personal anxiety, rapturous freedom, eager-
crifice, and mistrust of legalism, institutions, and slow-working
for salvation. It was no accident that from the late seventeenth
he boldest assertions of antislavery sentiment had been made
by the who were dissatisfied with the materialism and sluggish formal-
ity of institutionalized religion, and who searched for a fresh and assuring meaning of Christian doctrine in a changing world.[67] To the extent
that slavery became a concrete symbol of sin, and support of the anti-
slavery cause a sign of Christian virtue, participation in the reform became a supplement or even alternative to traditional religion.[68] As a
kind of surrogate religion, antislavery had long shown tendencies that
were pietistic, millennial, and anti-institutional. By the 1830's it had
clearly marked affinities with the increasingly popular doctrines of free
grace, immediate conversion, and personal holiness. According to Amos
A. Phelps, for example, immediatism was synonymous with immediate
repentance: "All that follows is the carrying out of the new principle of
action, and is to emancipation just what sanctification is to conversion."[69]

Immediate emancipation was also related to a changing view of history and human nature. Whereas the gradualist saw man as at least partially conditioned by historical and social forces, the immediatist saw
him as essentially indeterminate and unconditioned. The gradualist, having faith in the certainty of economic and social laws, and fearing the
dangers of a sudden collapse of social controls, was content to wait until
a legal and rational system of external discipline replaced the arbitrary
power of the slaveowner. The immediatist, on the other hand, put his
faith in the innate moral capacities of the individual. He felt that unless
stifling and coercive influences were swept away, there could be no

London, 1921), I, 23–37, 78, 81–83; Wade C. Barclay, *Early American Methodism* (2 vols., New York, 1949–1950), I, xxii–xxiii; William G. McLoughlin, *Modern Revivalism* (New York, 1959), 103–105. It should also be noted that the issue of gradual versus immediate emancipation followed a long religious controversy over gradual versus immediate, instantaneous conversion.

67. For an expression of the religious motives of antislavery, see Wilberforce, *Life*, V, 156–59. There is a clear relationship between antislavery and religious anxiety in the lives of many abolitionists. Obviously, most religious anxiety found other outlets than antislavery; but the writings of abolitionists in both Britain and America show that the cause satisfied religious yearnings that could not be fulfilled by the traditional institutions of the church.

68. This point is made convincingly by Barnes, *Antislavery Impulse*, 104–107. See also, Granville Sharp, *The Law of Retribution* (London, 1776), 250–52; Locke, *Anti-Slavery in America*, 59–60; Branagan, *Political and Theological Disquisition*, 22–30; Kenrick, *Horrors of Slavery*, 40; Parrish, *Remarks*, 2–9, 34–36; Branagan, *Penitential Tyrant*, vi–xi; Bourne, *Book and Slavery*, 135–41.

69. Amos A. Phelps, *Lectures on Slavery and Its Remedy* (Boston, 1834), 179. For the relation between antislavery and revivalism, see Barnes and Dumond (eds.), *Weld-Grimké Letters*, I, 40–52, 94–97; McLoughlin, *Modern Revivalism*, 23–31, 53–54, 86, 107–12; Charles C. Cole, *The Social Ideas of the Northern Evangelists, 1826–1860* (New York, 1954), 101–25, 196, 231–38.

development of the inner controls of conscience, emulation, and self-respect, on which a free and Christian society depended.[70] His outlook was essentially romantic, for instead of cautiously manipulating the external forces of nature, he sought to crate a new epoch of history by liberating the inner moral forces of human nature.[71]

It falls beyond the scope of the present essay to show how immediatism itself became institutionalized as a rigid test of faith, and how it served as a medium for attacking all rival institutions that limited individual freedom or defined standards of thought and conduct. It is enough to suggest that immediatism, while latent in early antislavery thought, was part of a larger reaction against a type of mind that tended to think of history in terms of linear time and logical categories, and that emphasized the importance of self-interest, expediency, moderation, and planning in accordance with economic and social laws. Immediatism shared with the romantic frame of mind a hostility to all dualisms of thought and feeling, an allegiance to both emotional sympathy and abstract principle, an assumption that mind can rise above self-interest, and a belief that ideas, when held with sufficient intensity, can be transformed into irresistible moral action.[72] If immediate emancipation brought misunderstanding and violent hostility in regions that were charged with racial prejudice and fear of sectional conflict, it was nevertheless an appropriate doctrine for a romantic and evangelical age.

70. For the rise of new values concerning work, authority, and the development of inner disciplinary controls, see Reinhard Bendix, *Work and Authority in Industry: Ideologies of Management in the Course of Industrialization* (New York, 1956), 34, 60–62, 72–73; Adam Smith, *An Inquiry into the Nature and Causes of the Wealth of Nations* (Modern Library ed., New York, 1937), 364–66.

71. See Hoxie Neale Fairchild, *The Noble Savage; a Study in Romantic Naturalism* (New York, 1928), 404–405; Lois Whitney, *Primitivism and the Idea of Progress* (Baltimore, 1934), 21–22, 82–85; Margaret T. Hodgen, "The Negro in the Anthropology of John Wesley," *Journal of Negro History*, XIX (July, 1934), 308–23; Branagan, *Serious Remonstrances*, 32–35; Sharp, *Just Limitation*, 36–37, 65–67; William Roscoe, *The Wrongs of Africa* (London, 1787), 9–12; James Anderson, *Observations on Slavery* (Manchester, 1789), 3–5; New York City Anti-Slavery Society, *Address to the People of the City of New York* (New York, 1833), 3–12; George Allen, *Mr. Allen's Report of a Declaration of Sentiments on Slavery* (Worcester, Mass., 1838), 10–11; Barrow, *Involuntary . . . Slavery*, 45. For the relation between this romantic anthropology and the liberal theology of men like Nathaniel W. Taylor and Albert Barnes, see McLoughlin, *Modern Revivalism*, 45–69. Stanley Elkins correctly discerns the anti formal and anti-institutional character of immediatism (*Slavery*, 189–92), but he relates it to the fluid social structure in the United States; the same characteristics had been present in British and French antislavery literature from the eighteenth century, and their accentuation by the 1830's would seem to have been part of a major ideological development.

72. Walter J. Bate, *From Classic to Romantic* (Cambridge, Mass., 1946), 176–77; Walter E. Houghton, *The Victorian Frame of Mind* (New Haven, 1957); Meyer H. Abrams, *The Mirror and the Lamp* (New York, 1953).

18

James Cropper and the British Anti-Slavery Movement

I: 1821–1823

Studies of the British anti-slavery movement have usually treated James Cropper as a minor figure whose personal interests in East Indian sugar raised disturbing questions of motive and considerably embarrassed his more altruistic friends.[1] The wealthy Liverpool importer is either ignored or given the briefest mention by R. Coupland, W. L. Mathieson, Frank Klingberg, and W. L. Burn, though the latter apparently confuses him with Joseph Cooper. Cropper's economic arguments against slavery and bounties on West Indian sugar receive more attention from L. J. Ragatz, G. R. Mellor, and Eric Williams, who nevertheless differ widely in their estimates of the man. Ragatz concludes that Cropper "was one of those occasional cases in which conduct is not primarily influenced by self-interest though they may accidentally coincide." Williams, who sees Cropper as far more interested in West Indian monopoly than West Indian sugar, decides that his support "did untold harm to the cause of humanitarianism." Mellor suggests that the union of antislavery and East Indian interests may be best explained as rationalization.[2] But none

1. For making this research possible, I wish to express my gratitude to the John Simon Guggenheim Memorial Foundation and to the Librarian of Bodleian Library, Oxford.
2. Lowell Joseph Ragatz, *The Fall of the Planter Class in the British Caribbean, 1763–1833* (New York, 1928), pp. 435–436; Eric Williams, *Capitalism and Slavery* (Chapel Hill, 1944), pp. 186–187; George R. Mellor, *British Imperial Trusteeship, 1788–1850* (London *1951*), p. *421*.

From *The Journal of Negro History*, Part I, Vol. XLV, No. 4 (October 1960); Part II, Vol. XLVI, No. 3 (July 1961). Reprinted by permission.

of these writers makes reference to Cropper's correspondence, which casts considerable light on his motives and philosophy; and none of these studies gives any hint of Cropper's actual part in the formation and history of the Anti-Slavery Society.

James Cropper was born in 1773 of Quaker parents on a farm at Winstanley. His father was a small proprietor of land and steward for various estates in the neighborhood. The elder Cropper expected his son to succeed him on the farm, but James, having little taste for physical labor, longed to seek his fortune in the exciting port of Liverpool. After securing his father's permission, he was soon apprenticed to the American import firm of Rathbone and Benson. A dutiful and conscientious lad, James shortly pleased his parents with accounts of his growing worth. His extraordinary ability at figures won him respect and rapid promotion.[3]

Cropper's early success should not be taken, however, as evidence of a wholly acquisitive mind bent entirely to questions of profit and sumptuous living. Like many merchants and entrepreneurs of his generation, he held conflicting attitudes toward wealth and worldly success. If he considered thrift, diligence, and perseverance as disciplining virtues that would best protect a man from the sins of sloth and waste, he also feared the corrupting tendency of worldly affairs and yearned for the peace and spiritual security of a secluded life. This latter ideal was at least partly the result of his mother's powerful influence. Rebecca Cropper, an invalid confined to bed for a large potion of her life, became for her son a kind of model of saintliness, conveying a message of peace and perfect serenity in the face of suffering.

When James at seventeen was beginning his career in Liverpool, his mother wrote him long and affectionate letters. The world, she told him, seethed with terrible evils and temptations that might easily overwhelm a "natural man"; yet a man whose moral foundations were secure could retreat within his own inner refuge where, resigned to the divine will, he might see failure and suffering as opportunities for a renewed sense of dependency upon God's love. Rebecca Cropper saw her affliction as an occasion for increased piety and wonder at God's mercy; and some years later Cropper wrote that he believed with Edward Young, whose *Night Thoughts* had profoundly influenced him, that affliction is "Heaven's *last* effort of good will to man, its *last* & not its *first.*"[4]

3. Obituary in *Liverpool Times*, March 3, 1840; Extracts from letters of the late James Cropper, transcribed for his grandchildren, fols. 2–8 (British Museum)

4. Extracts, fols. 4–6, 14–15. Cropper named a son after Young, who also greatly influenced James Stephen. Rebecca Cropper's letters convey much of the Quietist spirit which had been developing in Quakerism. See Rufus M. Jones, *The Later Periods of Quakerism* (London, 1921), I, 57–103.

As Cropper became increasingly successful, he brooded over his absorption in commercial affairs and relative neglect of spiritual duty. He was confident that happiness even in this world awaited the man who strictly conformed his life to the will of God, cheerfully laboring for the good of his fellow-creatures. But he soberly noted his soaring profits and concluded that it was a "serious thing" to be doing so much business, especially in time of war. Nearly all trade was implicated in the war; yet Quaker principles were obviously weakened when a member sold or transported objectionable articles.

Now Cropper's mind returned to the course originally planned for him by his father; he longed to retire to a life of farming, a "useful activity" more consistent with the wise designs of God than commerce and business, which stimulated the vices and follies of mankind. Cropper admitted he would find inducements for staying in business and acquiring additional wealth if he were convinced there was no hereafter or that he would live forever. But having already approached financial independence, he dreamed of retiring to a simple cottage in his father's field where he might provide healthy employment for poor boys, laying up treasure in heaven by devoting himself to useful and benevolent activity. Cropper's partners, however, were not happy about his proposed retirement, and out of deference to them he agreed to continue working for another year.[5]

But as time passed, he found it difficult to withdraw from the worldly maze of commercial capitalism. He continued to dream of a life of peace, simplicity, and self-denial, and his letters expressed occasional distaste for business and uneasiness over profits. His religious ideals were strongly tinged with a Quietist desire for freedom from the natural self and utter dependence on God's will. But his parents had exhorted him to be diligent, and his mind, running naturally to accounts and balances, was equally quick to perceive opportunities for gain. Despite his early resolutions, Cropper went on to head the prosperous house of Cropper, Benson and Company, Liverpool's largest importers of East Indian sugar. Eventually he was to become an active promoter and director of the Liverpool and Manchester Railroad.

Cropper's doubts over the compatability of Christianity and capitalism were largely resolved by his discovery of Adam Smith's *Wealth of Nations*. The book became for him a second Bible, whose doctrines were a faith to live by and whose laws were to be no more questioned than the basic precepts of religion.[6] No doubt the reason for his passion-

5. Extracts, fols. 10–11. Cropper had married in 1796 and was also motivated by the hope that his family's health would improve in the country.
6. No date is given for his reading of Smith, but it was evidently in the 1790's.

ate allegiance to Smith's philosophy was that it provided a nearly cosmic justification for business enterprise and reconciled duty with profit. If still acutely aware of the corrupting power of wealth, Cropper now saw the great hand of God in the flow of goods toward their natural markets, in the interplay of capital, labor, and resources, and in the beneficient results of unhindered self-interest. Adam Smith supplied an ideology that ennobled and gave purpose to commercial activity, harnessing the petty exertions of an individual to the irresistible march of human progress. Instead of retreating to a life of contemplation in a country refuge, Cropper began attacking commercial restrictions with the zeal of a missionary. Believing fervently in the divinely-appointed union of moral progress and commercial expansion, he worked vigorously for the repeal of the Orders in Council restricting trade with America.

In 1816 he attended the Quaker Yearly Meeting in London and dined afterwards with William Allen and Thomas Clarkson, who aroused his interest in Sierra Leone. Cropper saw in Africa "an immense field for speculation" as civilization advanced, but he was alert to risks involved in sending a vessel to Sierra Leone, especially if his firm could not spare the capital.[7] Nevertheless, Allen supplied him with detailed information on both the colony and the slave trade. Cropper began to see important relations between slavery and free trade, between economic expansion and human progress toward universal freedom. Above all, he began to perceive that his own personal interest in East Indian sugar might contribute to the destruction of slavery in the Caribbean.

By 1821, despite continuing economic decline in the West Indies, the British anti-slavery movement seemed moribund. Britain's abolition of the slave trade had not had its expected effect of greatly meliorating the slaves' condition or preparing the way for emancipation. The scheme of a colonial slave registry, conceived by James Stephen and proposed by Wilberforce to establish direct parliamentary intervention in colonial affairs, had been so modified at the hands of colonial legislatures that its author considered it a total failure.[8] Though a few men like Allen and Wilberforce had secretly considered pressing for emancipation, there was a general conviction that any such move must be preceded by international agreement to extinguish the slave trade.[9] Thus the African Institution continued to collect information on the slave trade, not feeling authorized even to discuss the explosive issue of emancipation.

7. Extracts, fol. 17. Since at least 1809 Cropper had been contributing generously to the African Institution.

8. James Stephen, *The Slavery of the British West India Colonies Delineated, As It Exists Both in Law and Practice* . . . (London, 1824, 1830), I. xxiii–xxvii, lxi, 420.

9. R. I. Wilberforce and S. Wilberforce, *The Life of William Wilberforce* (London, 1838), IV, 368.

By 1821, however, the West Indian interests were moving for increased duties on East Indian sugar, and James Cropper's views on the economics of slavery were rapidly maturing. On May 3, 1821, he wrote to Wilberforce, introducing himself frankly as an East Indian trader and advancing the theory that slavery was an archaic institution that could not compete with free labor without the support of artificial bounties. According to Cropper, free labor meant "fair competition" in prices and low prices made slavery unprofitable.[10] Wilberforce may not have been impressed by Cropper's arguments; certainly his speeches gave little emphasis to the economic aspect of slavery. Yet it should be noted that Cropper proposed abolition of slavery, as well as the slave trade, by economic means. Twenty-one days later, Wilberforce wrote his famous letter to Thomas Fowell Buxton, requesting him to act as partner and successor in a great crusade for gradual emancipation.[11]

On September 3 Cropper again wrote to Wilberforce, this time calling for a full investigation of the economic support of slavery. To Cropper the decline in West Indian slave population was certain proof of an inattention to correct self-interest, an inattention fostered by protective bounties. In America, where the slave population had increased some 29% from 1810 to 1820, the institution was apparently more humane, because governed by a due regard for profits in a competitive market. Cropper thus came very near to saying that American slavery was better because more profitable. This dubious conclusion was the result of his unshakable conviction that slavery could not survive in a free and expansive economy in which wages and prices fell as production increased.[12]

When Cropper published these letters in 1822 he was well aware that his motives would be seriously questioned by critics. In a preface he frankly presented his case to the public, trusting that those who believed that God's laws worked through individual and national interest would not accuse him of hypocrisy. Yet in a private letter written at the same time, he revealed his sad astonishment upon discovering that even friends had questioned his motives:

> Even supposing this were my motive, and that I had, from the most sordid views, kept out of all things likely to be contrary to the laws of my Creator, because I thought that to act in accordance with his will was

---

10. James Cropper, *Letters Addressed to William Wilberforce* . . . (Liverpool, 1822), pp. 1–5.

11. Charles Buxton, ed., *Memoirs of Sir Thomas Fowell Buxton, Baronet* (London, 1848), pp. 117–118.

12. Cropper, *Letters to Wilberforce*, pp. 22–39.

the surest road to prosperity—even then my motives would not alter the nature of the truth. But this is not the state of the case. I have neither wish nor intention ever to add one more shilling to my property. I have already much more than I can ever feel justified in spending on myself; and by increasing my property I should only increase my responsibility.[13]

That Cropper was sincere we may not doubt. He had stayed in commercial business only reluctantly and with considerable misgivings; yet when he finally committed himself to a life of trade, he endowed his calling with something approaching holy sanction. There was not a doubt in his mind that enlightened self-interest and a free interchange of goods were divinely-appointed means for moral and spiritual progress. If some questioned the sincerity of his anti-slavery sentiment, merely because it formed a part of a larger vision of international progress and prosperity, this was a sacrifice he was prepared to accept. He had been taught that capacity to withstand affliction was a true sign of holiness, and he would not go out of his way to avoid suspicion or calumny.

Early in 1822 the West Indian interests began working for measures in Parliament to relieve their growing economic distress. On June 24, 1822, they obtained the right to export Caribbean produce directly to Continental markets and also succeeded in partially opening certain colonial ports to the American trade. Though these measures brought no immediate relief to the colonies, they removed one of the principal excuses for preferential sugar duties and thus roused East Indian merchants into action.[14]

As early as February 5, 1822, Cropper wrote his friend Zachary Macaulay, who was a stockholder in the East India company, urging him to unite friends of the slave against West Indian monopoly. He argued that even if foreign powers should declare the slave trade piracy, this would only reduce the world's production of sugar, raise prices of both sugar and slaves, and consequently aggravate the Negroes' suffering and stimulate smuggling of slaves. Only if abolitionists understood the economic side of the question would they stand a chance of success.[15]

Probably at Macaulay's instigation, Cropper was invited to the annual meeting of the African Institution.[16] On May 10, just before the meeting, he sought to relieve any doubts Macaulay might have about the influence of his private interests:

13. Extracts, fols. 19–20.

14. Ragatz, *Planter Class*, pp. 354–361.

15. Cropper to Zachary Macaulay, February 5, 1822, British Museum Add. MSS, 41, 267A, fols. 102–103.

16. Cropper to Macaulay, May 10, 1822, Add. MSS, 41, 267A, fols. 104–106. By 1821 Cropper was annually giving £51–10 to the African Institution.

As a matter of individual Interest I care comparatively little about the East India sugar questions, but believing as I do that it is the means which an allwise Creator has in the nature of things appointed for the destruction of this abominable system whether of slave trade or slave cultivation, I am most anxious that the African Institution should take the thing up as it deserves.

Cropper added that all the work expended toward abolishing the slave trade would be rendered meaningless unless followed up by the destruction of slavery itself. If the African Institution desired this, "it must embrace the obvious means."

Cropper conferred privately with Macaulay and William Allen, and actively participated in the general meeting whose changed tenor must have greatly pleased him. The bulk of speeches and reports still dwelt on the slave trade, but Wilberforce and Lord Calthorpe hinted at the duty of turning to slavery itself. James Stephen was more explicit. Instead of talking of destroying the slave trade as a necessary preliminary to emancipation, he warmly applauded Colombia and other Latin American republics for striking at the heart of the evil.[17] And the *Sixteenth Report* of the African Institution advanced ideas closely parallel to those of Stephen and Cropper. It charged that despite the colonies' refusal to enact an effective system of slave registry, the Government was about to relieve them of extensive trade restrictions, while already the nation helped maintain slavery by protecting West Indian sugar from competition. Without directly calling for emancipation, the *Report* pointed repeatedly to the evils of slavery and twice stressed the lack of measures "with a view to ameliorate the condition of Colonial Slavery, or promote its gradual and final extinction."

For the time being, however, any initiative would have to come from outside Parliament. Wilberforce soon decided it was an inauspicious year for action, largely because West Indian distress had received so much publicity. Moreover, he felt his energy and health ebbing and had little taste for leading an attack against powerful West Indian interests. Buxton, to whom he looked for leadership, had not yet decided to assume such responsibility.[18]

But since the meeting of the African Institution, James Cropper had been absorbed with the subject of slavery. On July 12, a little over two weeks after the West Indians had won their free trade measures, he wrote Macaulay that he was determined to form an anti-slavery society

17. African Institution, *Sixteenth Report of the Directors of the African Institution . . . 10th Day of May, 1822* (London, 1822), pp. xli–xliii.
18. Wilberforce, *Life*, V, 125–129; Buxton, *Memoirs*, pp. 119–122.

to promote the objectives defined in the African Institution's *Report*. He naturally saw such an organization as an agency for diffusing information on the divinely-ordained connection between humanitarianism and East Indian sugar. He had already written to friends in America asking for detailed proof of the comparative cheapness of free labor. But Cropper emphasized, disclaiming any radical intentions, that such irrefutable facts should be presented to the planters for their consideration, and "if possible without any Laws to force them see their own true interests by sweeping away all artificial into it." Yet the Government should help slave-holders to remove all barriers to the "natural course of things." Hence an anti-slavery society should regularly make use of the daily press, launching a vast campaign of propagating correct information.[19]

Even Cropper, however, did not wish to stand alone against the fury of unenlightened interest. Before organizing a society in Liverpool he wanted the approbation of Macaulay, Stephen, Wilberforce, and, he wrote, apparently as an afterthought, of Buxton. Similar societies, he said, might well be formed in other parts of the country, for the time was ripe. Only recently Cropper had seen William Allen, whose powerful influence extended through a vast array of benevolent associations, and had pressed upon him the necessity of forming such a society in London itself.

These suggestions were not without effect. On August 5 Cropper informed Clarkson that he had led a Liverpool deputation to London to present the case for East Indian sugar before a parliamentary commission. Although he found the commission prejudiced in favor of the West Indians, his time in London had not been wasted. The Friends Yearly Meeting considered the subject of slavery and authorized the Meeting for Sufferings to petition Parliament, which Cropper hoped they would do early in the next session. He also met with leading abolitionists, who now decided to promote the formation of anti-slavery societies over the entire kingdom. It was concluded, Cropper wrote, "that Wilberforce should at some proper time in this Session declare fully his opinions on Slavery, which I rejoice to hear that he has done, but the newspapers seem at present to be sealed against us."[20] Macaulay would therefore try to publish a pamphlet containing the speeches of Wilberforce, Buxton, and William Smith, which would provide an excellent foundation for a new society. Cropper sent Clarkson a letter from Elias Hicks, "an old & steady advocate of the cause," on the necessity of attacking slavery itself.

19. Cropper to Macaulay, July 12, 1822, Add. MSS, 41, 267A, fols. 108–109.
20. Cropper to Thomas Clarkson, August 5, 1822, Add. MSS, 41, 267A, fols. 110–111. In his speech of July 25 Wilberforce said that opponents of the slave trade had looked from the beginning toward ultimate emancipation.

On the same day, August 5, Cropper wrote Macaulay that the time had arrived for "the most open avowall of our sentiments. . . ." Since the enemies of slavery had no wild schemes for immediate emancipation, they had nothing to fear from presenting their case frankly to the public. But so long as reformers confined themsevles to the slave trade, West Indians could deny all complicity, and the public would fail to recognize the true nature of slavery and the price they paid to support it. "Our cause is great," Cropper wrote,

> we only seek to second or to remove impediments out of the way of the free operation of the Laws which the Creator has fixed in the nature of things,—I wish however not to go ahead of those who have so long laboured in this great cause, but I am more than ever convinced that we cannot have the public voice unless we do openly attack the System of Slavery. . . .[21]

If Cropper still sought moral support from the London group, he had helped lay a foundation for future organizations. He was still at work organizing a society at Liverpool; his pamphlets were beginning to excite interest; and his friend Adam Hodgson was busily writing letters to America. What was more imortant, Cropper had begun investigating possible financial sources for the support of an anti-slavery movement. Unfortunately, he told Macaulay, many East Indian merchants had opposing interests and would not contribute to anti-slavery. It was therefore best to have one fund "for the commercial part of the question," and a separate one "for those who take the subject up on the grounds of humanity. . . ."[22] Evidently not all East Indian merchants saw the sugar question in the cosmic proportions that Cropper did. But with the aid of William Allen, he had already located the fund that was actually to become the mainstay, especially in times of distress, of the London Anti-Slavery Society. This was a special fund raised by the Society of Friends for the total abolition of the slave trade.[23]

In October, when most abolitionists turned their attention to the Congress of Verona and prayed for strong international agreements to end the slave trade, Cropper succeeded in founding his Liverpool Society for the Amelioration and Gradual Abolition of Slavery.[24] In a circular

21. Cropper to Macaulay, August 5, 1822, Add. MSS, 41, 267A, fols. 112–113.

22. *Ibid.*

23. *Ibid.* The Anti-Slavery Society operated on a slender budget and frequently found itself deeply in debt. Both individually and as a religious body Quakers bore the main financial burden of the anti-slavery movement, a fact not generally recognized. MSS Minutes of the Anti-Slavery Society (Bodleian Library), I, 128–132; II, 8, 67; III, 13, 82.

24. The name was soon changed to the Liverpool Society for Promoting the Abolition of Slavery.

sent out to friends of the cause, he tried to divert interest from the slave trade to slavery itself. He mailed a copy to Clarkson, hinting that the latter might use his influence to form a similar society.[25]

Impatient at the London group's caution, Cropper kept forwarding information on American slavery to Macaulay, hoping that more interest might be aroused as people realized that emancipation helped raise the value of land. Although he felt that Christianity had aided emancipation in the northern states, the basic cause had been a reduction in the value of slaves as a result of competition with free labor. Cropper had been so carried away by evidence of the incompatibility of slavery and low prices that he told Clarkson no American would buy slaves for cotton cultivation, since the price of cotton was so low![26] Blinded by the importance he attached to his own interest, Cropper concluded that only sugar cultivation could be responsible for the high price of slaves in the South.

The precise origins of the London Anti-Slavery Society are not clear. It certainly was not, as some historians have implied, the result of a single historic meeting of Buxton, Macualay, and Wilberforce at Cromer Hall in the autumn of 1822. As we have seen, a decision had been reached in July to promote the formation of anti-slavery societies; by September Macaulay was writing to old warriors of the slave-trade campaign, and plans were under way for raising funds, recruiting members, collecting and publishing information.[27] The principal agents of this activity would seem to have been Allen, Cropper, Clarkson, and Macaulay. Clarkson himself gave credit only to Allen and Macaulay, but that was twenty-two years later, and after he had been publicly censured by Cropper for supporting the American Colonization Society. He then thought it was Allen who had first approached Macaulay on the matter, and was certain the first meetings to organize an anti-slavery committee were held in Allen's house.[28] Cropper's letters also refer to meetings in Allen's house and show that the two Quakers worked closely together.

25. Printed circular and letter sent to Clarkson, October 12, 1822, Add. MSS, 41, 267A, fols. 126–127.

26. Cropper to Clarkson, September 11, 1822, Add. MSS, 41, 267A, fol. 116. It is reasonable to question Cropper's sincerity on this point, since he had himself handled consignments of American cotton. He was, however, much disturbed and confused by the whole question of American cotton. A few months after this he recognized the importance of slave-grown cotton, explaining its expansion by the scarcity of labor in the South. In 1823 he publicly acknowledged his previous involvement with slave-grown cotton and convincingly defended his motives. It is probable that the views he expressed to Clarkson were simply wishful thinking concerning a problem that not only bore on his personal conduct, but threatened to undercut his entire philosophy of prices, profit, competition, and economic expansion.

27. George Harrison to Macaulay, September 30, 1822; Richard Phillips to Macaulay, September 24, 1822, Add. MSS, 41, 267A, fols. 120–122.

28. Clarkson to John Beaumont, January 22, 1844, Bodleian C 107/99.

Although Allen and Macaulay were doubtless the leading organizers in London, they must have been influenced by Cropper's urgent pleas and by the example of his existing society in Liverpool. On October 21 Cropper wrote Macaulay that his experience in Liverpool indicated support might come from unexpected directions; and he repeated his earlier request: "If you can form an association if ever so small in London it will be a very great help to me but I know its difficult to make a beginning."[29]

Macaulay and Wilberforce had visited Buxton at Cromer Hall in late September. Although others joined the conference, it is doubtful whether any detailed plans or strategy were decided upon. In early December Wilberforce wrote Buxton proposing "a secret cabinet council" a little before the opening of Parliament to consider what course to pursue.[30] He reproached himself for having so long postponed efforts to help the slaves; but far from leading others into battle, he began responding only in January 1823, to the pleas of friends for a manifesto on West Indian slavery.[31]

Cropper was not present at the initial meeting of the London Anti-Slavery Society held on January 31, 1823 at King's Head Tavern; but he stayed in London during April and May, regularly attending meetings of the Committee and cooperating in work that supported the first Parliamentary campaign.[32] He was appointed to the important subcommittees on publication, home correspondence, and periodical press; he took responsibility for arranging with booksellers for advertising and distribution of approved tracts. And on April 23 the London Committee officially recognized Cropper's Liverpool Society, not as an auxiliary but as an equal body, whose jurisdiction for correspondence and distributing pamphlets extended to Cheshire, Lancashire, Yorkshire, Ireland, and the United States.[33] The two societies were to exchange information regularly.

But if Cropper had won considerable power in the London organization, he found himself in an increasingly difficult position. His economic arguments were echoed by the East Indian party, yet many of

29. Cropper to Macaulay, October 21, 1822, Add. MSS, 41, 267A, fols. 128–129.
30. Wilberforce, *Life*, V. 157.
31. *Ibid.*, 158–159, 161–162.
32. Minutes, I, 1–20. Organization did not really begin until April 9, at which date Cropper was elected a member. Curiously, though Macaulay attended the initial meeting, he was not elected a member until April 9.
33. *Ibid.*, I, 21, 31. Cropper referred often to his correspondence with friends in America. He was listed as an agent for Benjamin Lundy's *Genius of Universal Emancipation*, and apparently sent reports on the British anti-slavery movement to Garrison and Lundy. See W. P. Garrison and F. J. Garrison, *William Lloyd Garrison . . . the Story of his Life Told by his Children* (New York, 1885), I, 146.

these merchants shied away from the slavery issue. Many anti-slavery leaders feared the taint of commercial interest and some doubtless regarded Cropper, whose motives were difficult to defend, as a liability to the cause.[34] The London Committee, while not unreceptive to all works with an economic approach, did not sanction his militant *Letter to the Liverpool Society for Promoting the Abolition of Slavery,* which stressed the futility of any measures for mitigating slavery so long as slave-holders received support from bounties and preferential duties.[35]

On May 15 the anti-slavery leaders in Parliament were outmaneuvered by Canning, who followed the strategy of the Society of West India Planters and Merchants by proposing certain palliative reforms that were only to be recommended to the charter colonies.[36] One week later the House of Commons voted down a motion advanced by the East Indian group to investigate sugar duties. Cropper had expected that Buxton's motion of May 15 would be lost (it was actually withdrawn), but thought a defeat might well advance the anti-slavery cause. If Buxton were unsuccessful, he thought hopefully, abolitionists would abandon time-consuming ameliorative measures and turn immediately to the sugar question, which held promise for swift and certain emancipation.[37] When Parliament adopted the Canning Resolutions and turned its back on the sugar question, Cropper saw the need for a decisive shift in policy. Instead of merely deferring to parliamentary leadership and publishing occasional tracts, the Anti-Slavery Society should take the initiative by actively arousing and organizing public opinion.

With this in mind, he hurried from London to Playford Hall, where he presented a bold plan to Thomas Clarkson. On June 9 the Anti-Slavery Committee met to consider Cropper's proposal, elaborated in a long letter sent from Clarkson's home. The Committee had previously agreed, when Cropper was present, that it might be advantageous to send one or more agents into parts of the country that had produced few if any petitions against slavery. But no resolutions to this effect had been adopted, and Cropper had clearly consulted Clarkson on his own initiative. Clarkson, said Cropper, was obviously the best man for the job; he would be quite willing to begin traveling if the Committee should agree to the plan.[38]

Cropper urged the Committee to make a major effort to supply Clark-

---

34. Cropper took notice of the objection to commercial considerations in his *Letter Addressed to the Liverpool Society for Promoting the Abolition of Slavery . . .* (Liverpool, 1823), p. 23.
35. Minutes, I, 9–10, 22–23.
36. Ragatz, *Planter Class,* pp. 413–420.
37. Extracts, fols. 21–22.
38. Minutes, I, 34.

son with an extensive list of names obtained from correspondence and from the Bible Society, the Church Missionary Society, and the Wesleyan Methodists. After mapping out a tentative itinerary for his friend, Cropper dealt bluntly with the matter of finances. Clarkson's trips should be at the Society's expense. If some feared that sufficient funds could not be obtained, Cropper was himself prepared to advance credit for £500. He also offered his own services to the Committee, suggesting that he might be most useful traveling at his own expense to areas where societies had already been formed in order to provide them with detailed information. Cropper's evident purpose was to have Clarkson stimulate new anti-slavery feeling, while he enlightened exiting groups on the relevance to slavery of free trade and East Indian sugar.[39]

The Committee at once accepted Cropper's proposals. They formally requested Clarkson to tour the country at their expense; they took measures to provide him with names and thanked Cropper for his offer of financial aid, should it be needed; finally, they accepted gratefully his offer to undertake a tour on his own account.[40] Cropper had brought about an important shift in policy, and by turning attention to the need for itinerant agents to arouse public interest had helped prepare the way for the later Agency Committee.

If Cropper was pleased by the success of this plan, he must have been even more gratified on October 24 when the London Committee took official cognizance of the economic aspect of slavery, resolving that discussions of impolicy, as well as principle, fell naturally within their province.[41]

Having accumulated considerable evidence to support his theories, Cropper now took many occasions to explain and reiterate his views to the public. He argued that removal of the bounty on exporting refined sugar would reduce the price of domestic sugar, enable exporters to compete more favorably in foreign markets, and stimulate production in the East Indies. This measure, accompanied by an equalizing of import duties, would make slavery unprofitable and also save the British public an annual expense of some £1,200,000. The country could thus afford to relieve West Indians of any temporary hardships by granting a bounty directly to proprietors, scaled to the number of their slaves appearing in the registry. This bounty would be tied to regulations for meliorating the Negroes' condition and would be gradually reduced as sugar production increased. Far from being a strict free trade measure, the plan

39. *Ibid.*, 36.
40. *Ibid.* The Committee was encouraged by Clarkson's reports on his travels during the summer. In December they requested him to canvass the fourteen counties he had not yet visited.
41. *Ibid.*, 65.

was designed to cushion the shock of moving from a slave to a free economy.[42]

Cropper professed interest in helping the West Indian planters, but their spokesmen saw him as a malicious hypocrite bent on destroying their lives and property.[43] In the fall of 1823 he became entangled in a vicious controversy with John Gladstone, a fellow Liverpool merchant, proprietor of West Indian estates, and father of William E. Gladstone. On October 31 *The Liverpool Mercury* published an anonymous article by Cropper drawing attention to the vast markets and unlimited production denied to Britain by unwise support of West Indian produce.[44] Gladstone replied anonymously in *The Liverpool Courier,* and the debate raged on through November and December.

Although the "correspondence" smoldered with personal animosity and covered the widest range of subjects, from the origin of evil to Cropper's alleged instigation of the Demerara insurrection, the two men were fundamentally disputing over economic theory. Cropper was confident that abolition of slavery would bring incalculable benefits for everyone, since whatever contradicted the immutable principles of justice must also be at variance with sound policy and the true interests of man. This was his central belief, adhered to with religious intensity, around which he spun an elaborate web of theory, evidence, and anecdote. He assumed that the East Indies possessed a nearly unlimited capacity for sugar production, that the potential demand for sugar was similarly unlimited, and that supply would immediately respond to demand once prices were allowed to seek their natural level. Abolition of slavery would be a by-product of this great transformation. Gladstone, on the other hand, assumed a rigidly limited demand for sugar. If prices were lowered, Britain would find she had destroyed her only certain supply of sugar, causing untold suffering for both planters and slaves. East Indian cultivation would not increase unless stimulated by increased prices, which would, in fact, be the result of a scarcity of sugar after the West Indies had been ruined.

Cropper was perhaps most vulnerable when it came to the effect of competition and falling prices on West Indian slaves. He had much to

---

42. Cropper, *Relief for West-Indian Distress* . . . (London, 1823), pp. 30–32. In his *Letter Addressed to the Liverpool Society* (pp. 26–27), Cropper had recognized the need for some indemnity and also the moral obligation to aid the Negroes.

43. Joseph Marryat, *A Reply to the Arguments Contained in Various Publications, Recommending an Equalization of the Duties of East and West Indian Sugar* (London, 1823), p. 28; [Anon.], *A Statement of the Claims of the West India Colonies to a Protecting Duty Against East India Sugar* (London, 1823), pp. 2–3.

44. James Cropper and John Gladstone, *The Correspondence Between John Gladstone, Esq., M. P., and James Cropper, Esq.* . . . (Liverpool, 1824), pp. 4, 8–9.

say on the suffering of the Negroes, which he attributed solely to ill
treatment and an oppressive system. While he admitted that slaves might
endure temporary hardships as sugar prices fell, his supreme faith in the
goodness of economic laws led him to expect that either the masters
would be forced to adopt more efficient procedures, supposedly beneficial to their slaves, or the property would soon pass to wiser and more
humane men. He thought it inconceivable that free trade and competition would bring more neglect, longer working hours, less food, or more
severe treatment.

Gladstone dealt savagely with Cropper's past involvement with slave-
grown cotton. Cleverly exploiting every inconsistency, he ridiculed the
Quaker's piety and impugned his motives. Cropper soberly explained
how he had ceased importing American cotton, observing that if wealth
had been his object, he would not have given up the most lucrative part
of his business. Yet Gladstone, if often grossly unfair, doubtless had
the best of the argument. Compared with Cropper's pedestrian logic and
bare statistics, Gladstone's prose sparked with wit and mockery, and he
had a manifest advantage in taking the firm ground of a worldly man of
shrewd common sense. In the end, Cropper committed a fatal blunder
in disapproving the Liverpool West India Association's publishing the
entire controversy. This allowed his opponents to represent him as being
afraid to give the final decision to the public.

Cropper's defense of his sincerity was convincing, but his arguments,
often shot through with elaborate rationalizations, revealed a mind that
moved in rigid compartments. But if his theories were sometimes wrong,
if his preoccupation with free trade obscured his interest in slavery,
there can be no doubt that Cropper was moved by a religious sense of
responsibility. And for him, this was all that mattered in the end. Writing to his son Edward in 1823, he expressed humility at the thought that
however small an individual's contribution must be, God's purposes were
fulfilled only through the united efforts of many individuals. If only, he
exclaimed, he could bring this sense of awful responsibility to the minds
of benevolent people in Liverpool—for, "How do any of these know
but they may be designed as a link in this chain of circumstances, and
that on them hangs, not the life of an individual but the everlasting
welfare, for aught they know, of hundreds of thousands."[45]

45. Extracts, fol. 21.

II:1823–1833

By the fall of 1823 James Cropper could view the rising anti-slavery movement with a mixture of optimism and frustration. During the past year he had organized an anti-slavery society in Liverpool and had played an important part in establishing a national society in London. As a devout Quaker who had struggled to reconcile a Quietist ideal of selflessness with a successful mercantile career, he found in anti-slavery an ennobling cause that seemed to confirm his faith that moral and material progress were inseparable. If he suffered violent personal abuse from the pen of John Gladstone, this only strengthened his belief that affliction was the inevitable result of righteousness. He could draw moral support from his association with eminent philanthropists, while helping to infuse philanthropy with the practical values of the business world. Yet the London Committee seemed cautious in fully committing itself to Cropper's program, despite the Government's failure to adopt an acceptable plan for gradual emancipation. He felt certain that the Committee would support an exposure of the impolicy of slavery, "But, if it is to be done, who is to do it? . . . How is the Anti-Slavery Society to act, if I go into the front of the battle?"[1]

Cropper was already in the front of the battle and saw the wrath of the West Indians as proof that he had thrust to the enemy's most sensitive and vulnerable spot. But the London abolitionists, thrown on the defensive by the Demerara insurrection and a storm of shrill indignation from the colonies, discreetly awaited the results of the Government's program. When it became apparent, however, that the Government meant, in Buxton's words, *"to forfeit their pledge,* and to do next to nothing," the Anti-Slavery Society evinced new interest in economic arguments.[2] As Cropper traveled to London for the spring campaign of 1824, the

1. Letter to the Anti-Slavery Society, reprinted in James Cropper and John Gladstone, *The Correspondence Between John Gladstone, Esq., M.P., and James Cropper, Esq. . . .* (Liverpool, 1824), p. 55.

2. Charles Buxton, ed., *Memoirs of Sir Thomas Fowell Buxton* (London, 1848), p. 143.

Committee sent copies of one of his pamphlets, along with other works on the economic waste of slavery, to the House of Commons. And on May 12 he was appointed to a subcommittee, including Buxton, Macaulay, and William Smith to prepare a formal address on the impolicy of slavery and draft resolutions for the Society's public meeting.[3]

As the anti-slavery public became aroused by the Government's caution and West Indian intransigeance, by persecution of missionaries and the death of John Smith, there was a mounting interest in destroying slavery by forcing its products from the English market. In August, 1824 a special subcommittee on East Indian sugar, appointed by the Anti-Slavery Society, established a temporary depot for the sale of sugar grown by free labor. And when James Heywood informed the Society on September 23 that he was about to inaugurate another depot for supplying East Indian sugar, the Committee advanced him £171 to finance the experiment.[4] For some years anti-slavery leaders urged their friends to buy Heywood's sugar, assuring the public that it was the genuine product of free labor. Although West Indian planters were soon badly hurt by competition from slave-grown sugar from Mauritius, the Society stuck to principle and cautioned friends against buying any slave-grown sugar, regardless of origin.[5]

A boycott of West Indian sugar might stimulate public interest and give people a sense of participating in a righteous cause, but it could also arouse a militancy that would shock more conservative anti-slavery leaders. In 1824 a Quaker named Elizabeth Coltman Heyrick, who had previously written such inoffensive books as *Instructive Hints, in Early Lessons for Children,* published the most passionate and uncompromising work on slavery to that date, entitling it *Immediate, Not Gradual Abolition.*[6] Renouncing all schemes of melioration as illusory, she attacked the Government for conspiring with slave-holders and called on all true Christians to quit the "miserable hypocrisy" of pretending to commiserate with the slave when, "by purchasing the productions of

3. MSS Minutes of the Anti-Slavery Society (Bodleian Library), I, 104–105.

4. *Ibid.,* 133–135, 139, 141.

5. *Ibid.,* II, 81. Most East Indian sugar was cultivated by free peasants, but their condition was scarcely better than that of the hundreds of thousands of slaves that actually existed in British India. The blindness of anti-slavery leaders to East Indian slavery was largely the result of scanty and unreliable information, and the peculiar nature of Indian slavery itself. See William Adam, *The Law and Custom of Slavery in British India. . . .* (London, 1840), pp. 6, 11, 14–15, 82, 104–138.

6. The first edition (London, 1824) was anonymous. It was reprinted the same year in Philadelphia and ran serially in Benjamin Lundy's *Genius of Universal Emancipation.* On June 8, 1824 the London Society instructed its secretary to procure a dozen copies of the pamphlet and give them to any member who wanted them. At the same time the Committee considered a letter that George Harrison had written to Cropper, which was vaguely reported to deal with the views of some members of the Society on immediate emancipation. Minutes, I, 111–112.

his labour, they *bribe* his master to keep him in slavery."[7] She was confident that the British could annihilate slavery within a few months if friends of the Negro quit making speeches and presenting evidence, and bound themselves "by a solemn engagement,—an irrevocable vow, to participate no longer in the crime of keeping him in bondage."

Although Elizabeth Heyrick began as Cropper did, by deprecating measures for melioration and saying that Britain must compel the planter, by economic means, to see his own true interest, she went far beyond him in her contempt for expediency and compromise. Whereas Cropper looked to the Government for commercial regulations that would slowly induce planters to give their slaves more liberty, Elizabeth Heyrick preached a massive consumers' crusade, independent of all political authority, and demanded immediate and unconditional emancipation. Furthermore, Cropper was alert to the implications of boycotting *all* slave-grown produce, which would be the logical extension of Mrs. Heyrick's argument. He said he admired people who felt it their duty to avoid all contact with slavery; the problem deeply troubled him and at times his conscience nearly broke through his economic theorizing. But Cropper's sympathy for the slave was undeniably subordinate to his sweeping vision of material progress; and this vision rested ultimately on his faith that God's fingers pulled the levers and ran the wheels of the industrial revolution.

"It is a very difficult thing," he confided to Joseph Sturge, "to keep from touching in any shape slave produce." If he refused to take any slave-grown cargoes for his ships, he could not forget that their sails and cordage were made from hemp and flax produced by Russian slaves.[8] And if he gave up shipping, he admitted some years later, he was still "engaged pretty considerably" in the Liverpool and Manchester railway, whose cars rolled slave-grown sugar and cotton to the refineries and textile mills. Cropper well knew that if the British public suddenly abandoned all slave produce, hundreds of thousands of destitute textile workers would be thrown into the streets, fleets of ships would slowly decay at their moorings, machines would rest idly in silent factories, businesses would go bankrupt, and the slaves themselves would starve. This, of course, was precisely the point made by the West Indians. But Cropper replied that the country was not relieved from the duty of distinguishing right from wrong, when the distinctions could be clearly seen, merely because everyone was more or less implicated in the pro-

7. Heyrick, *Immediate, Not Gradual*, p. 11.
8. Extracts from letters of the late James Cropper, transcribed for his grandchildren (British Museum), fols. 63–64.

duce of slavery. The problem was that not everyone saw the same distinctions that Cropper did.

James Cropper had long before struggled with the timeless dilemma
of moral man in an immoral society, and rejecting an inclination to
retire from the world, had satisfied his Quaker conscience by adopting
an unquestioning faith in the unity of moral and material progress. The
evils of slavery he associated exclusively with an archaic system of privilege and restriction that broke the normal relation between self-interest
and economic behavior. Thus slavery reversed the natural course of economic laws, rewarding waste, sterility, oppression, and bad management. But if slave cultivation could once be brought into competition
with free labor, "it will stand much the same chance as the old modes
of spinning, or of manufacturing iron, or of drawing water from our
mines, to oppose the modern improvements of industry."[9]

He often compared the support of slavery to the support of outmoded
techniques of production; but ultimately he was forced to confront the
problem of American cotton, on which depended the future of British
industry. It was with cotton textiles that Cropper hoped to buy India's
free-grown sugar and thereby emancipate West Indian slaves.[10] Thus a
distinction had to be drawn between cotton and sugar; cotton stimulated
trade and industry, which in the end would prove to be the most powerful agents of freedom. Grasping desperately for arguments to justify
his stand, Cropper talked of the comparative mildness of American slavery. Since no bounties protected it from the competition of free labor,
since the slave population increased remarkably, and since the Cotton
Kingdom prospered, Cropper concluded that the system must be both
more efficient and more humane than that in the West Indies.[11] Presumably American slavery was only a temporary stage induced by an abundance of land, a scarcity of labor, and an intensely exploitive and speculative spirit. It would disappear as soon as population increased on the
frontier and prices and wages fell accordingly.[12] Cropper also reassured
himself that cotton would soon be raised by free labor in India, once
the last protective duties had been removed. But it is doubtful whether
he entirely convinced even himself. He was clearly troubled by the spread
of slavery in America, which seemed to undercut his theory that bon-

9. Cropper, *Letter Addressed to the Liverpool Society for Promoting the Abolition of Slavery.*
. . . (Liverpool, 1823), p. 6.
10. Extracts, fols. 63–64; Cropper and Gladstone, *Correspondence,* pp. 56–57.
11. Cropper, *Letter to Liverpool Society,* pp. 19–22; Cropper, *Relief for West Indian Distress.*
. . . (London, 1823), p. 19.
12. Cropper, *The Support of Slavery Investigated* (London, 1824), pp. 5–16.

dage was utterly incompatible with economic progress.[13] If slavery did not soon begin to recede, he told Sturge, many people would feel obligated to abandon all use of slave produce, regardless of consequences.

Cropper may at times have been naive and inconsistent, but most of his difficulties arose from a desire to be realistic without ignoring fundamental moral distinctions. In the fall of 1823, for instance, he tried to resolve in a single paragraph the problems of slave produce and Negro colonization. It doubtless would have been best if Europeans had from the beginning refused to buy slave produce and compelled the planters to restore Negroes to their African homes. But now, centuries later, slave produce was interwoven with the national economy; and the transportation of American or West Indian Negroes to Africa would be no less cruel or inhumane than the original slave trade. Any solution to the problem would therefore have to move in accordance with economic realities and be directed toward preparing Negro slaves for the duties and responsibilities of free citizens.[14]

In the fall of 1824 Cropper worked out a grandiose plan that took him on a long trip through Ireland. If anti-slavery and East Indian groups were to abolish protective duties, they would need powerful allies. In the squalid huts and starved faces of Ireland, Cropper thought he found the answer to all his problems. The land, like that in the West Indies, had been rendered sterile by oppression and constant cultivation of a single crop. But Cropper noted the rushing streams which could be harnessed to mills and the crowds of idle men who would work for low wages.[15] Ireland, he felt certain, could be transformed into another Lancashire. This immense textile production would find its natural market in the vast population of India. But if Indians were to buy Irish textiles, they must find outlets for large amounts of tea and sugar. Thus the prosperity of Ireland would depend on the East Indies, and above all, on the removal of preferential duties and bounties.

Cropper became convinced that Irish poverty and West Indian slavery, the two dark evils that thwarted England's progress, were intimately connected. If Irish leaders could only be made to see this connection, if the cause of Ireland could be tied to that of West Indian slavery, then monopoly and special privilege were doomed and the Irish

---

13. *Ibid.* Since Cropper had always argued that slavery reduced the value of land, he was preoccupied in this essay with explaining why many land speculators in Illinois favored admitting slaves to the state. He had to admit that slavery could be supported by a frontier, as well as commercial privileges, an admission that weakened seriously his theory of progress. He was now forced to rely on a "normal" condition when jobs and land were scarce and wages low.

14. Cropper and Gladstone, *Correspondence,* p. 56.

15. Extracts, fols. 24–27.

laborer and West Indian Negro would rise together to a life of freedom and well-being. In Cropper's mind the science of political economy was primarily a search for the ingenious means provided by God for the advancement of the human race.

He discussed his plan with merchants and landowners, helped establish antislavery committees, asked for the cooperation of Daniel O'Connell, and became involved in a textile mill in Limerick. The sheer magnitude of his vision made Cropper so buoyant that he saw every courtesy as agreement and every conversation as a triumph for free trade and anti-slavery. After recent setbacks, the Irish were in a grim mood and willing to listen to any scheme that might win support to their cause in Parliament; in a few months O'Connell would begin publicly cooperating with the London Anti-Slavery Society. But Cropper was so deeply shocked by the actual spectacle of suffering that he almost forgot the sharp distinction abolitionists always drew between slaves and a poor but free peasantry:

> . . . indeed if the question of slavery was not so closely connected as it is with the condition of the Irish people, I should despair of any thing being done for the cause of slavery here, for though I am sure none of these civil, kind-hearted, and generous minded poor people, would change their miserable condition for that of West Indian slavery; yet in food, clothing, and houses, many of them must be infinitely worse off than many of the slaves; and being so, if I were an Irishman, I would say, it is my first duty to raise these my poor neighbours to a greater state of comfort—but happy am I in believing, that the cause of one, is the cause of the other, and I am in great hopes that I can convince the people here that it is so.[16]

The London Anti-Slavery Society watched Cropper's travels with interest and at the same time gave increasing attention to the question of sugar.[17] Early in 1825, as the Government moved toward a general tariff reform, the Committee printed tracts on the advantages of free-grown sugar and decided to call a public meeting in London if the Government seemed indisposed to revise existing duties and bounties.[18] When they learned that Huskisson had no interest in altering regulations on sugar and that Canning talked as if he had not heard of the subject before, the abolitionists angrily assumed a more militant stance.[19]

Having returned from Ireland, Cropper participated in the Committee's meetings through March and April; at the public meeting of April

16. *Ibid.*, fol. 37.
17. Minutes, I, 145–149.
18. *Ibid.*, I, 153, 155; II, 1–2.
19. *Ibid.*, II, 3–6.

30 he saw an impressive triumph of his doctrines. Speakers dwelt in detail on the impossibility of abolishing slavery by mere Parliamentary resolutions or royal recommendations while the system received continuing economic support. Daniel Sykes publicly eulogized Cropper; the *Second Report* of the Society, which was a product of the meeting, was little more than a summary of Cropper's previous writings.[20] By the spring of 1825 James Cropper had become the unofficial philosopher of the anti-slavery movement.

In Ireland Cropper had acquired experience in publicizing the anti-slavery cause by talking with leading citizens, holding meetings, making speeches, and forming societies. In October, 1825, he launched a brave campaign to organize similar support in the industrial Midlands. He was aided in this arduous enterprise by Joseph Sturge, a robust, impetuous corn merchant from Birmingham, whose rural Quaker origins were somewhat similar to Cropper's. Sturge, however, was twenty years younger, and in 1834 would become Cropper's son-in-law. Cropper had been impressed by Sturge's speeches in the London Yearly Meetings of 1823 and 1824, and was delighted to learn that he could count on the younger man's help: "It does me good to feel there are persons, who feel so warmly in the great cause, as to be willing to accompany me to the neighbouring towns."[21]

Certain members of the London Committee strongly opposed any plan of arousing popular feeling by itinerant agents and public meetings, probably for fear that anti-slavery would become associated with the tactics of Henry Hunt and Major Cartwright. Cropper informed the Committee of the exact course he planned to pursue, but he did not travel with their official sanction. He himself had doubts about the wisdom of speaking at very large meetings, apparently because he felt unsure whether he could make them understand his motives and economic arguments. But though he hoped to concentrate on small groups of influential citizens, he also intended to speak in every town and village where people were disposed to listen. And by the end of November he wrote to Sturge that public meetings were the best means for spreading knowledge on the subject.

Much of the time Cropper appears to have traveled alone, keeping Sturge well informed on the state of public opinion and the success of anti-slavery gatherings. He was particularly gratified by enthusiastic

20. *Ibid.,* II, 18–21; *The Anti-Slavery Monthly Reporter,* I (June 30, 1825), 6; Society for the Mitigation and Gradual Abolition of Slavery, *Second Report. . . .* (London, 1825), pp. vii, 16–17, 20–25, 33–37, 44–45, 63 188ff. The *Report* recommended Cropper's writings and included a copy of his map of potential sugar-producing areas of the world.

21. Extracts, fol. 56.

meetings at Leicester, Derby, and even Lancaster, "an old West India place," though the crowd at Coventry had been disappointingly small. Elated by a sense of active participation and personal involvement in the cause, he went on indefatigably, speaking in York, Hull, Manchester, Sheffield, and Leeds. Early in 1826 he moved into the West, to Bath, Exeter, and Plymouth, growing more optimistic as he went, interpreting every vote or resolution as a powerful blow to slavery. Like many missionaries and evangelists, he saw acceptance of his creed as a test of personal virtue, but made little effort to evaluate his program or its probable consequences.[22]

In 1826 and 1827 the anti-slavery movement sank into a state of lethargy and hopelessness. The infrequent meetings of the London Committee were occupied with minor details of business; slavery itself almost dropped from sight. Cropper remained active, continuing his travels, speaking to public meetings, and encouraging the formation of women's anti-slavery associations;[23] but such exertions could have little effect until either the Government or the Anti-Slavery Society radically altered the course it had been following.

During 1828 and 1829 the Anti-Slavery Society passed through a period of transition, often assessing the state of the cause and debating questions of policy. Most abolitionists agreed that Parliament must be brought to intervene directly in West Indian affairs; but the method of influencing Parliament and the nature of the intervention were matters of bitter controversy. James Cropper took a leading part in these debates, presiding occasionally over meetings of the London Committee, and writing lengthy letters of advice from Liverpool.

He had already done much to promote the idea of sending agents through the provinces to form auxilliaries and address public meetings. On August 6, 1828, after reading a letter from Cropper reviewing the state of the cause, the Committee resolved "that much good might arise from the appearance at Public Meetings in the Country of individuals properly qualified to exhibit the real state of Slavery in our Colonies."[24] But the country was torn by the crisis of Catholic emancipation, and the Society cautiously postponed a program of direct public agitation.

The Committee also debated the question of how Parliament should intervene in colonial affairs. In 1823 Buxton's motion had urged the

---

22. *Ibid.*, fols. 56–61.

23. *Ibid.*, fols. 59–61; *Monthly Reporter*, I (May 31, 1826), 185–188; J. A. Picton, *Memorials of Liverpool, Historical and Topographical* (London, 1873), I, 461, 477; Minutes, II, 75–76, 86, 90, 94, 177, 139.

24. Minutes, II, 141. It is not clear whether Cropper's letter advocated this, but it seems probable.

emancipation of slave children after a fixed date, but this proposal had been dropped from Canning's Resolutions and the subsequent recommendations of the government. When Henry Pownall revived the plan in February, 1829, the Society held a special meeting to consider asking William Smith to introduce a bill emancipating all slave children born after January 1, 1830.[25] But more members of the Committee were hopeful that Wellington's Government would cooperate in enforcing milder measures and thus establish a precedent for direct intervention.

Cropper became discouraged by this delay and a lessening of interest in the economic aspects of slavery. In March, 1830, he wrote Sturge that it was time for all abolitionists to unite behind some definite plan, which, to be practicable, would have to include some form of compensation to slave owners. He reported that the London Society was considering three programs—the emancipation of children, the purchase of slave women, and his own proposal, which was doubtless a version of a program he had recommended in 1829 for a graduated scale of compensation and removal of protective duties and bounties. He thought the cost to the country would be about the same whichever plan were adopted, but was confident his own scheme would involve the least delay.

The Anti-Slavery Society had already been reanimated by a new spirit of desperation. In February its leaders were stunned when Sir George Murray, the Colonial Secretary, coolly informed a deputation of abolitionists that the Resolutions of 1823 had been a mere declaration of opinion and not a pledge, that the Government had no intention of interfering with slavery in the chartered colonies, and that spokesmen for the West Indies had told him public interest in the question had subsided.[26] The Society concluded that slavery, if left solely in the hands of the Government, might exist with little mitigation for ages to come. And in drafting resolutions for a general meeting, they moved well beyond a policy of gradual melioration. Parliament, they agreed, should be petitioned to consider the best means of "speedily abolishing" slavery throughout the British Dominions; and until such measures for total emancipation had been adopted, a bill should be introduced that would free all children born after January 1, 1831.[27]

25. *Ibid.* III, 4–5.
26. Minutes, III, 20–21.
27. *Ibid.*, 27. The Committee approved these resolutions on April 6, 1830. But when the resolutions were actually proposed at the general meeting of May 15 at Freemasons Hall, there was no mention of a specific date. Buxton's opening speech called strongly for emancipation of children, but the crucial third resolution was made purposefully vague. Henry Pownall then rose from the floor, delivered an impassioned speech against compromise, and, amid loud cheers, proposed an amendment calling for liberation of children born after January 1, 1831 (according to the *Monthly Reporter* the date was January 1, 1830; but the London *Times* of May 17 recorded it as 1831 and later speeches made clear it was 1831.).

The Government's extreme caution jarred the Society from its policy of deference and from its years of hopeful waiting. Invigorated by the addition of new members, many of whom were clergymen, the Society reorganized itself in the summer of 1830 for more efficient and concentrated action. The General Committee focused its energies on raising petitions and stirring up public interest; it greatly expanded its correspondence with auxiliary societies, coordinated its activities more closely with *The Anti-Slavery Monthly Reporter,* and resolved finally to employ at least one traveling agent to diffuse information and attend meetings of provincial societies.[28] By September the Committee had begun dividing London and its vicinity into districts for holding public meetings and gathering petitions.

Illness prevented Cropper from taking an active part in this renewed activity of 1830, but he returned to London in February, 1831, and became immediately involved in efforts to mobilize public sentiment against slavery. Apparently reconciled to postponement of economic questions, he actively supported political measures and advocated direct appeals to public opinion. The Committee had already secured hundreds of petitions and was considering names recommended for traveling agents. Instead of deferring to the day-by-day diplomacy of its spokesmen in Parliament, the Society framed drafts of various bills and resolutions, ranging from emancipation of children to a code of regulations to follow total emancipation, so that its leaders would be prepared for whatever contingency that might arise.[29]

Many historians have been misled by Sir George Stephen's account of the last years of the anti-slavery movement, which pictures a struggle in 1831 and 1832 between the conservative party and the democratic "young England Abolitionists."[30] According to Stephen, the radicals formed their own Agency Committee as an independent body after the conservative Anti-Slavery Society had vehemently rejected the plan of employing itinerants to arouse public support.[31] In actuality, the agency idea had long been proposed by Cropper and others; the Society had accepted it in principle in 1828 and had begun making specific plans in 1830. By the spring of 1831 the Committee had abandoned its earlier

28. Minutes, III, 49–62.
29. *Ibid.,* 79.
30. Stephen had planned to write a history of the movement in 1834 and had formally asked the Anti-Slavery Society for access to its records (Minutes, IV, 67). The Committee did not act on this request; some twenty years later when Stephen wrote *Antislavery Recollections* (London, 1854) as a series of letters to Harriet Beecher Stowe, his account was at variance with the Society's records, which he had probably never seen. It is surprising that so many historians have uncritically accepted Stephen's work as a primary source.
31. Stephen, *Antislavery Recollections,* pp. 128–135.

caution and conservatism. The general meeting of April 23, at the newly-opened Exeter Hall, displayed a sense of crisis and a desire to mobilize political power to force emancipation directly upon the colonies. Abolitionists no longer considered slavery a mere evil that might be slowly mitigated by indirect laws, but talked of the guilt and criminality of the institution, which could be extinguished only by swift and powerful intervention.[32] The Society called on its friends throughout the country to form committees, to meet regularly and to make strict inquiries of every candidate "not only whether he is decidedly favourable to the extinction of Slavery, but whether or not he will attend the Debates in Parliament when that question shall be discussed. . . ."

Cropper attended the crucial meetings of May 25 and June 1, 1831, when the Anti-Slavery Society appointed a special subcommittee to engage stipendiary agents to travel through the country and promote public discussions of slavery. This "Agency Committee," which was part of the general Society, at first included such outsiders as George Stephen, Stephen Price, Emmanuel Cooper, and Charles Stuart. But though the Society had unanimously approved the agency plan, some members feared that the subcommittee might become too independent, perhaps adopting policies deemed inexpedient by the General Committee. Membership in the subcommittee was thus confined to members of the Anti-Slavery Society; outsiders were given the role of special advisers.[33] Further attempts were soon made to ensure the right of the Society to supervise and approve policies of the subcommittee, although these restrictions were resisted or disregarded. Dissension did not arise over the wisdom of arousing public opinion, but rather over the control of such efforts and the coordination of policy by a central authority. Because the Anti-Slavery Society was still closely geared to Parliamentary strategy, its leaders naturally feared the potential power of a body whose operations would be solely concerned with the state of popular feeling.

Although Sir George Stephen's history of the Agency Committee is misleading, there is some truth to his account of Cropper's important part in its formation. Cropper reported having had an interview with Stephen at the time when the Agency Subcommittee was formed; and while he made no mention of the sumptuous dinner and dramatic decision described by Stephen, he did subscribe £500 to the new body, and his sons added another £100 apiece.[34] More significant, however, was

32. Minutes, III, 84–88.
33. *Ibid.*, 94–100.
34. Extracts, fol. 79; *Report of the Agency Committee of the Anti-Slavery Society, Established in June, 1831* . . . (London, 1832), p. 21.

the role he played as an intermediary between the General Committee
and its rebellious offspring.

The Agency group presented regular reports of its activities to the
General Committee, but was unwilling to submit all its documents for
approval prior to publication.[35] The first intimation of a division came
on March 7, 1832, when Cropper presented the Society a request from
the Agency body that its funds be kept in a separate account at the
bank.[36] He continued to work with both groups, transmitting messages
from one to the other. After the final separation, on July 4, 1832, he
helped create a mediating authority to ensure their cooperation. He told
the General Committee that the Society of Friends had decided to make
strenuous efforts to raise large funds to promote emancipation. Such
information would have been of considerable interest, since the Quakers
had all along supplied the principal support for both Agency and Anti-
Slavery Committees. This new fund, Cropper said, would be entrusted
to Josiah Forster, George Stacey, and Richard Barrett, who would transmit money to either of the two societies at their discretion.[37] Thus with
Cropper's aid an independent financial authority had been created to
mediate between the two anti-slavery societies and encourage their cooperation.

The division of July 4 had been preceded by increasing disagreement
over immediate objectives. When Buxton failed in 1831 to carry a motion for freeing children born after a fixed date, many reformers turned
to immediate emancipation as the only alternative. The idea of freeing
newborn children, which had been a radical proposal in 1830, now became the leading plan of the more cautious members. Influential leaders, such as the elder James Stephen, argued hotly against any proposal
short of immediate and general abolition. On several occasions in the
spring of 1832 the Committee showed its impatience with Buxton's
leadership and its desire for a policy devoid of compromise. The secession of the Agency Committee was only one symptom of a deeper spirit
of frustration; and even after this separation, the General Committee
was divided between those who would prudently defer to the judgement
of Buxton and Lushington, and those who favored immediate emancipation and close cooperation with the Agency Committee.[38]

Meanwhile, Cropper had been busily engaged in writing pamphlets
for the cause. He was violently opposed to any plan of apprenticeship,

35. Minutes, III, 97, 100, 111, 121. Many members of the General Committee favored greater
independence for the Agency group.
36. *Ibid.*, 124.
37. *Ibid.*, 174.
38. *Ibid.*, III, 131–134, 142–147, 152–153; IV, 2–3.

which, he felt, would only stifle the initiative of both masters and slaves. He was similarly against outright compensation, since for him it was unthinkable that legitimate losses could result from abandoning a wasteful and uneconomical system.[39] He saw, however, that the idea of compensation might be altered to fit his own theories. If Britain advanced a loan of £15,000,000, in return for equalization of sugar rates, planters could pay off their debts and redeem their mortgages, diversify crops, and adopt a profitable system of free labor. The relevance of his plan to Negro slavery was not always clear, but he at least emphasized the importance of economic reorganization and public responsibility for providing necessary supports for free labor.[40]

Although Cropper's writings were more concerned with the bounty on exporting refined sugar than with the moral evils of slavery, Cropper himself played a distinct part in the final months of anti-slavery action in 1833. He sat on various subcommittees of the London Society and occasionally acted as chairman of joint meetings with the Agency Committee. He led the move to summon deputies to London from the provincial societies, and helped revise the memorial which a parade of 339 delegates carried on April 18 to Downing Street.[41]

When Edward Stanley outlined the Government's plan on May 14, Buxton was generally satisfied, accepting compensation as a necessity and hoping to modify the apprenticeship plan once the Government had firmly committed itself.[42] While the Anti-Slavery Society refrained from openly criticizing Buxton's leadership, they attacked the Government plan and organized a United Committee, representing both provincial deputies and the metropolitan Committees, to meet with Members of Parliament and devise strategy for securing a better measure.[43] Cropper helped prepare pamphlets on the state of the cause and on objections to the Government's program; he doubtless had a part in creating the United Committee, since he had frequently pressed for unity between the Agency group and the Anti-Slavery Society.

On the morning of July 24, just before the crucial Parliamentary struggle, Cropper, Sturge, George Stephen, and others visited Buxton with the hope of committing him to a last-ditch fight against Stanley. He wisely insisted, however, on entering the House with full liberty to

39. Cropper, *A Vindication of a Loan of £15,000,000 to the West India Planters. . . .* (London, 1833), pp. 3–4.

40. *Ibid.;* Cropper, *The Interests of the Country and the Prosperity of the West India Planters Mutually Secured by the Immediate Abolition of Slavery. . . .* (London, 1833), pp. 24–25; Cropper, *Another Bonus to the Planters. . . .* (London, 1833), *passim*.

41. Minutes, IV, 30.

42. Buxton, *Memoirs*, pp. 324–326.

43. Minutes, IV, 40–43.

choose his tactics according to circumstances.[44] Oddly enough, once the bill had been passed, most abolitionists forgot their high principles and gloomy predictions. Cropper quit attending meetings of the Society after the 24th and wrote his son that he was actually joyful over the improved law.[45] The great object had been achieved, the battle was over, and the Society turned to the settling of its financial accounts.

But Cropper had already become involved in another slavery controversy that would not end so amicably. In October, 1832, he had warned the London Committee not to be deceived by the pretensions of the American Colonization Society.[46] The following month he wrote a biting letter to Thomas Clarkson deploring the latter's endorsement of a society founded on racial prejudice and dedicated to the perpetuation of slavery.[47] Some forty years earlier Clarkson and other abolitionists had assumed that slavery would be mitigated and gradually destroyed when abolition of the slave trade increased the value of West Indian Negroes. But Cropper had long held that slavery would disappear only when the natural increase of Negroes so reduced the price of labor that slavery could not be profitably maintained. For over a decade he had expected American slavery to show signs of expiring under pressure of increasing Negro population and the falling price of cotton. Yet something was clearly blocking the natural consequences of economic laws. As Cropper looked closer at the perplexing problem, he found racial prejudice and discriminatory laws which prevented free Negroes from competing with slaves. The "diabolical scheme" of the American Colonization Society was to remove free Negroes and thus prevent the emancipation which otherwise would accompany expanding production and population. The American Colonization Society helped Cropper solve a dilemma he had long faced. If slavery persisted in the free American economy, it was because this Society had spread the poison of racial prejudice.

As a Quaker, a merchant, and the moving spirit of the Liverpool Anti-Slavery Society, Cropper had long had important contacts with American abolitionists. He had written to Arnold Buffum, approving the formation of the New England Anti-Slavery Society; and when Gar-

---

44. Buxton, *Memoirs*, p. 333.
45. Extracts, fol. 92.
46. Minutes, III, 170. Elliott Cresson, the Colonization Society's agent, had explained the purposes of his organization to the London Committee on August 3, 1831; he was doubtless challenged, however, by Charles Stuart, who was also present (*Ibid.*, 105).

47. Cropper, *A Letter to Thomas Clarkson* (Liverpool, 1832), pp. 1–2. This published letter undoubtedly strained relations between the two men; yet in 1835 Clarkson wrote Cropper without mentioning the colonization matter, and Cropper replied in the same spirit (Extracts, fols. 104–105). In September, 1840, Clarkson wrote to Garrison, admitting his error and apologizing for having been taken in by Cresson (Bodleian C 107/108).

rison made preparations for his trip to England in 1833, he sought first of all a letter of introduction to Cropper.[48] When Garrison arrived in Liverpool he went immediately to Cropper's home, where he was hospitably entertained, though Cropper himself was in London, engaged in the last critical struggle. Some days later Cropper greeted Garrison in London and introduced him to the high command of the British anti-slavery forces.[49]

Just as Cropper had once served as an intermediary between the Agency Committee and Anti-Slavery Society, so now he sought to unite the efforts of British and American movements. On June 10 and July 13, 1833, he presided over public meetings at which Garrison violently denounced the Colonization Society. Many Americans would have later smiled at his description of Garrison as "a man very highly recommended and esteemed by the respectable part of the community in his own country. . . ."[50] The result of the debates, however, was clearly a defeat for Elliott Cresson and an arousal of British opinion against colonization. In this campaign of exposure Cropper had been Garrison's chief support.[51]

In the late summer of 1833 Cropper was tired of controversy and eager to proceed with his plans for an industrial and agricultural school. Though in poor health, he traveled through Germany and Switzerland, observing schools and discussing educational philosophy. On August 1, 1834, the day when West Indian slavery officially came to an end, he helped lay the foundation for his school at Fearnhead. For the six remaining years of his life Fearnhead school was the center of his existence. It offered him a chance for withdrawal from politics and militant reform and yet gave him a sense of fulfilling his obligations as a steward of great wealth.[52]

But Cropper by no means forgot the question of slavery.[53] He contributed to a fund in 1834 to enable Charles Stuart to tour America as an anti-slavery agent.[54] And he remained in close touch with Sturge,

48. W. P. Garrison and F. J. Garrison, *William Lloyd Garrison . . . the Story of his Life Told by his Children* (New York, 1885), I, 328, 342.

49. *Ibid.*, 350–351.

50. [William Lloyd Garrison, ed.], *Speeches Delivered at the Anti-Colonization Meeting, in Exeter Hall, London, July 13, 1833. . . .* (Boston, 1833), p. 3.

51. Cropper had long been opposed to the colonization plan and was far more influential than Charles Stuart. He supported Garrison further in his tract, *The Extinction of the American Colonization Society the First Step to the Abolition of American Slavery* (London, 1833).

52. Extracts, fols. 92–98.

53. It is interesting to note that Cropper's son Edward married Margaret Macaulay, daughter of Zachary and sister of Lord Macaulay, and that his son entertained Harriet Beecher Stowe during her visit in 1853.

54. Garrison, *William Lloyd Garrison,* I, 444.

who was leading a mounting attack on apprenticeship. Although East and West Indian sugar rates were equalized in 1836, Cropper became increasingly depressed by reports on the evils of apprenticeship. While many abolitionists looked back on the past movement as a holy crusade, Cropper came to see anti-slavery history as a series of disastrous blunders. By first attacking the slave trade and then working for meliorative measures, the reformers had only demonstrated their ignorance of economic laws. The course of history leading to the dismal system of apprenticeship gave somber vindication, Cropper thought, to his own warnings and exhortations.[55]

It is clear that Cropper's anti-slavery sentiment was of a different stamp from that of John Woolman, Thomas Clarkson, or William Lloyd Garrison. For him the movement was obviously not a vehicle for attacking worldliness, materialism, or economic change; nor did he find anti-slavery a means for achieving status or power, since he already had both and actually stood to lose reputation. His devotion to the cause was not an all-consuming passion that led him to throw off every association with slave-grown produce or castigate slavery as the essence of human sin. Though cognizant of its moral evils, he discussed slavery on a highly abstract level and thought of it as part of an old regime of unenlightened bounties, monopolies, and other economic restrictions that stifled man's enterprise and natural instinct to achieve abundance, freedom, and happiness. Thus whenever the facts of slavery seemed to contradict his economic theories, he stuck by his theories, even at the risk of seeming to favor American over West Indian slavery, or of advocating a reduction in prices and wages that might produce all the evils of slavery, if not, as in India, promote slavery itself.

It would be rash, however, to conclude that Cropper's vision was less noble than that of other anti-slavery leaders, or that his contribution was lessened by his doctrinaire approach. He brought the values and techniques of the business world to a movement largely dominated by moralists and politicians. From 1822 to 1833 he played a prominent part in nearly every important shift of policy; he was largely responsible for developing the plan of itinerant agents, which was to become so important in America; he served as an intermediary between the London and Liverpool groups, the Agency Committee and parent Society, the Quakers and non-Quakers, the abolitionists and East India merchants. And it was he who provided Garrison with access to the British anti-slavery leadership. His vision did not stop at the saving of souls or at the moral uplifting of individuals; his faith did not rest in mere legal measures.

55. Extracts, fols. 126–127.

He perceived, however dimly, the vital relation between economic and social progress, and foresaw a world of expanding population enjoying increased productivity and material abundance. In Cropper's mind the intensity of Quaker Quietism had fused with the economic optimism of Adam Smith. Anti-slavery confirmed this union, endowing laissez-faire with an immediate moral and spiritual purpose, and enriching his faith in the inevitability of human progress.

19

American Slavery and the American Revolution

The ideological connections between American slavery and the American Revolution have been carefully studied and fully documented by numerous historians.[1] There is no need to repeat the story they have told or to dwell further on the notable inconsistency between American ideals and American practice. Yet a broader understanding of the connections between the Revolution and the fate of black slavery can perhaps be furthered by engaging in some highly speculative reasoning. I hesitate to use the fashionable term *counterfactual*, which suggests that mathematical precision can be given to a fantasy. At the outset, however, I frankly acknowledge that this is an experiment in disciplined fantasy—disciplined because its plausibility and ultimate value depend on reasoned inferences and analogies based on empirical knowledge,

---

1. Benjamin Quarles, *The Negro in the American Revolution* (Chapel Hill, N.C., 1961); Arthur Zilversmit, *The First Emancipation: The Abolition of Slavery in the North* (Chicago, 1967); Winthrop D. Jordan, *White over Black: American Attitudes toward the Negro, 1550–1812* (Chapel Hill, N.C., 1968); Betty Fladeland, *Men and Brothers: Anglo-American Antislavery Cooperation* (Urbana, Ill., 1972); Duncan J. MacLeod, *Slavery, Race and the American Revolution* (Cambridge, England, 1974); Donald L. Robinson, *Slavery in the Structure of American Politics, 1765–1820* (New York, 1971); David Brion Davis, *The Problem of Slavery in the Age of Revolution, 1770–1823* (Ithaca, N.Y., 1975); Robert McColley, *Slavery and Jeffersonian Virginia*, 2d ed. (Urbana, Ill., 1973); A. Leon Higginbotham, Jr., *In the Matter of Color: Race and the American Legal Process* (New York, 1978); John Chester Miller, *The Wolf by the Ears: Thomas Jefferson and Slavery* (New York, 1977).

From *Slavery and Freedom in the Age of the American Revolution*, edited by Ira Berlin and Ronald Hoffman (Charlottesville, Va.: University Press of Virginia for the United States Capitol Historical Society, 1983). Reprinted by permission.

and a fantasy because it departs from reality and arbitrarily assumes that certain events could have been different without altering every other variable. It will be assumed, for example, that the North American colonies remained part of the British Empire but that this counterfactual change did not prevent the French Revolution or the wars against France by the various European coalitions. The intention is to question some of the tacit assumptions historians often make about the effects of the American Revolution on slavery and abolition—for example, that emancipation would have come earlier within a united British Empire.

Suppose, then, that the American Revolution failed and that the British succeeded early in the conflict in suppressing armed resistance and in vindicating Parliament's constitutional supremacy. In this scenario there is no compromise settlement leading to semiautonomy within a confederated empire, but henceforth Parliament would be more sensitive to the prerogatives of the chartered or legislative colonies, refraining from overt intervention in domestic affairs. This was in fact the case, at least through the 1820s, with respect to the chartered colonies in the British West Indies. Assume also that the skirmishes and ultimate showdown of the mid-1770s did not involve a total disruption of colonial society or the intervention of foreign powers; and that the broad social, economic, and intellectual trends of the pre-Revolutionary period were little affected by the abortive struggle for independence.

The most striking consequence of this fantasy for the future of slavery would have been an enormous strengthening of the British slave system, especially when compared to that of Britain's chief rival, France. In 1770 there were 379,000 slaves in the French Caribbean and 428,000 in the British Caribbean. By 1790, after years of wartime depression, the slave population in the British islands had increased only slightly, to 480,000; but in the French colonies, thanks to provisions from the United States and to the great sugar boom in Saint-Domingue, the number had soared to 675,000. If there had been no war for American independence, the French would still have gained the advantage of a larger labor force in the sugar colonies, but the British would have retained nearly 700,000 slaves in North America—not even allowing for the tens of thousands of blacks who died, escaped, were carried off, or were freed as a direct result of the war. In such a case the British New World colonies would have contained by 1790 roughly twice as many slaves as the French colonies.

Moreover, as Stanley L. Engerman has recently emphasized, the American Revolution led initially to "a significant impairment of the economic conditions in the southern states," signified by a dramatic decline in the southern share of the nation's wealth and exports.[2] One can argue that by maintaining beneficial commercial ties with Britain, the upper South in particular would have avoided much of the economic decline of the 1780s and 1790s, and the South as a whole would not have lost to the Middle Atlantic states its regional dominance over American wealth and exports.

Imperial unity would also have meant that Britain would retain possession of Florida and of the Gulf coast extending to Spanish Louisiana. Assuming that the North American colonies would have participated in the war against France and then Spain, following the precedent of earlier imperial conflicts, it seems likely that Britain could easily have added Louisiana to Trinidad and other New World conquests. Even if the British and French armies would have failed to subdue the rebellious blacks of Saint-Domingue—as was in fact the case—Britain would have entered the nineteenth century as the unrivaled master of the New World's slave colonies and of virgin lands, ideal for plantation agriculture, extending from Guiana to eastern Texas.

The scenario from this point is now clear-cut if one accepts the assumptions of Eric Williams and his followers. According to this school of thought, the American Revolution hastened the inevitable decline and fall of the British West Indies. It gave a temporary though self-destructive advantage to the French colonies, and enabled British capitalists to see the light and to begin disengaging themselves from the burned-out cornucopia that had originally financed the Industrial Revolution. Henceforth, they could afford the moral luxury of condemning the sin of slaveholding while investing in the expansion of slavery in Brazil, Cuba, and the United States, regions where the institution was still economically indispensable and which supplied British industry with essential raw materials, especially cotton. If American independence marked the political separation of an ascending and profitable slave system from one that was declining and already becoming an economic burden, then the retention of the North American colonies would logically have weakened the motives for antislavery. The first and telling reversal of actual British policy would have been the successful defense and continuation of the British slave trade, which Parliament outlawed in 1807.

But this line of reasoning is untenable. First of all, Britain did enter the nineteenth century as the leading "Slave Power" in the New World. By 1805, with the victory at Trafalgar, Britannia literally ruled the waves.

---

2. Notes on the Patterns of Economic Growth in the British North American Colonies in the Seventeenth, Eighteenth and Nineteenth Centuries,'' in Paul Bairoch and Maurice Lévy-Leboyer, eds., *Disparities in Economic Development since the Industrial Revolution* (London, 1981), pp. 51–52.

As a result of its strategic conquests and virtual monopoly of the African slave trade, Britain enjoyed unprecedented control over the labor supply of Caribbean and Latin American plantation societies that had not begun to achieve a self-reproducing labor force. While American independence infuriated British slave merchants, who complained bitterly about unpaid debts and the temporary ban on slave imports even by Georgia and South Carolina, British ships, merchants, and capital continued to dominate the post-Revolutionary slave trade to the latter two states. Between 1790 and 1807 the United States imported more African slaves than during any twenty-year period of the colonial era. Yet in 1806, a year before Congress moved to outlaw this trade, Parliament prohibited British subjects from transporting African slaves to any foreign markets, including those of the United States.

The argument that Britain sought by this prohibition to cripple foreign competitors hardly applies to the southern United States, which never posed an economic threat to the British West Indies. There is little reason to think that Parliament would have been less eager to suppress the African slave trade if the United States had remained part of the empire. On the contrary, it may reasonably be supposed that a variety of American interests, prejudices, and aspirations would have reinforced the growing public sentiment in Britain for outlawing the slave trade. For it was in America that this sentiment first crystallized. The motives, to be sure, were not altogether humanitarian. As Gary B. Nash has recently shown, social and economic conditions following the Seven Years' War brought a marked protest against all forms of bound labor in Boston, New York, and Philadelphia, as well as an extraordinary decline in slave imports and in the proportion of black slaves in the North. A largely artisan insistence on free white labor drew support from racial prejudice and from fear that an Africanized population would feed the conceits and power of a colonial aristocracy. In the Chesapeake colonies tidewater planters had long profited from the rapid natural increase of their slave population and from the sale of slaves to the south or west. A desire to retain a monopoly in supplying this interregional trade, coupled with fears of black demographic density and surplus labor, intensified opposition to further imports of African slaves. Moreover, Americans of every colony resented British vetoes on legislative acts to tax or restrict the importation of slave labor.[3]

To note such American opposition to further slave importation is by

3. *The Urban Crucible: Social Change, Political Consciousness, and the Origins of the American Revolution* (Cambridge, Mass., 1979), pp. 109–10, 320–21, and 343–45. It is also true that continuing prosperity in the Chesapeake colonies might have muted opposition to the slave trade in the decades before cotton became a major American export.

no means to endorse the hypocritical argument, repeated both during and after the Revolution, that the perfidious British had imposed an unwanted burden of black slavery upon the American colonists. The United States Constitution not only barred Congress from prohibiting the importation of slaves before 1808 and from imposing a tax of more than ten dollars upon "such persons," but specifically exempted this provision from the power of amendment. New Englanders and New Yorkers long continued to outfit slave ships; and in 1803, following the purchase of Louisiana and the promise of unlimited demand for labor in the Southwest, South Carolina legalized a short-lived but prodigious slave trade from Africa.

Yet there can be no doubt that even by the 1780s Americans overwhelmingly opposed the continuation of the African slave trade. In 1794 Congress forbade Americans from selling slaves in foreign markets. By 1798 even Georgia permanently outlawed further slave imports. South Carolina's defiant action at the end of 1803, based on the expectation of a national prohibition in 1808, shocked and outraged the rest of the nation. Despite the agitation of southern extremists in the 1850s, reopening the slave trade was never a realistic option even for the Confederate States of America. Given this unmistakable commitment, reinforced by interest, prejudice, and humanitarian values, it can reasonably be predicted that a unified empire would not have delayed the abolition of the slave trade beyond 1807. Even if South Carolina had allied with Jamaica and the other West Indian islands, British public opinion would have been incalculably strengthened by the division among slaveholding colonies. The North American colonies would have proved that a British-governed population of black slaves was capable of rapid natural growth, presumably as a result of humane treatment and planter foresight, although today we know that slave demography involved many complex variables. For some decades British abolitionists were in fact inclined to applaud the putative enlightenment of the southern states; as British colonies, they would have been far more forceful models of the advantages of the so-called breeding system. Since Parliament came close to abolishing the slave trade in the 1790s, the example and support of Virginia, Maryland, North Carolina, Pennsylvania, and other northern colonies might well have hastened the decision by a decade or more.

It is not really paradoxical to add that imperial unity would have removed a major barrier to subsequent British efforts to suppress the illegal slave trade to foreign markets, especially Cuba and Brazil. For in defiance of American law, American ships continued to play a crucial role in this traffic, and the American flag often protected foreign ships from British search and seizure. It was not that the American government covertly encouraged smugglers; the United States simply lacked the will and the naval power to enforce its own laws. Moreover, the Revolution and the War of 1812 bequeathed a hypersensitivity to any pretexts for British policing of the high seas. If, however, Britain had retained an increasingly effective control of imperial trade, most Americans probably would have approved the trial and punishment of fellow subjects who persisted in such a widely reprobated crime. Even had other nationals taken up some of the smuggling abandoned by the Americans, it is almost certain that in the nineteenth century fewer African slaves would have been transported to Cuba and Brazil.

But thus far only the African slave trade has been considered. How would the robust expansion of British North American slavery have affected the supposedly declining fortunes of the British West Indies? In the first place, Seymour Drescher has marshaled considerable evidence to show that the British slave system was actually expanding well into the nineteenth century, at least in terms of its capital value and its share in Britain's overseas trade.[4] It is also true that for decades the West Indians complained about the hardships entailed by American independence and by subsequent British restrictions on trade with the North American mainland. It can therefore be assumed that a flow of cheap foodstuffs and other essential commodities from a still British North America, as well as access to North American markets for muscovado sugar, molasses, and rum, would have further accelerated West Indian economic growth. There is no point in speculating here on the needed and perhaps unlikely adjustments in British mercantile policy. It is sufficient to emphasize that preservation of the Old Empire would have united within a single polity two prosperous, expanding, and complementary slave systems. If this would have diminished the relative importance of the Caribbean system—at the turn of the nineteenth century it constituted the most important market, outside Europe, for British imports and exports—the British West Indies could only have gained from a relatively noncompetitive alliance with North America.

By 1790, however, it was easy to caricature Britain's remaining New World colonies as a fringe of clearings in the Canadian woods and a cluster of sugar islands owned by absentee proprietors and populated essentially by African slaves. Jamaica and the new state of Virginia each contained over a quarter million slaves, but there were no more than 20,000 whites in Jamaica while in Virginia they numbered 442,000. The survival of the Old Empire would have retained over three million whites in the British colonial population, a fact that profoundly compli-

4. *Econocide: British Slavery in the Era of Abolition* (Pittsburgh, 1977).

cates every colonial issue as well as the very meaning of colonial labor. In British America, even taken as a whole, free white laborers would always outnumber black slaves.

From what is known of the growing shortage of productive land along the Atlantic seaboard, the central political issue would clearly have been the rich, uncleared lands of the West. In one sense, the independence of the United States freed Britain from the dilemmas of formulating and enforcing a western land policy, except in the ultimately self-defeating role of a foreign adversary lending support to Indians and other resisters. In 1763 the British government drew a "proclamation line" intended to close the transappalachian West to white settlers; this general policy of protecting the Indians and the Indian fur trade, confirmed by the Quebec Act of 1774, was one of the causes of the American Revolution. While the imposition of such a barrier was actually vague and relatively unenforceable, presumably Britain would have persisted, in our counterfactual scenario, in trying to thwart or at least restrict the advance of American squatters and speculators.

Faced with such restraints, westerns might have forged an alliance with Spain or France. Even disregarding this option, it is clear that in the Mississippi Valley Britain would have had less administrative control than in the newly conquered territories of Trinidad and Guiana, which will be considered shortly. On the other hand, a wise restrictionist policy, especially if it could have been separated from the claims of the Catholic population in Quebec, would have drawn increasing support from northeastern Protestant groups who feared that westward migration would increase their labor costs and weaken their communities, who expressed outrage over the despoliation and removal of the Cherokees and other so-called civilized tribes, and who protested bitterly the admission of Missouri as a new slave state. The discrediting of the Federalists as an essentially un-American party contributed to the image of cramped, mean-spirited Anglophiles who selfishly tried to preserve their labor supply while thwarting the manifest destiny of the West. But these same groups might have appeared more liberal and even humanitarian if allied on the winning side with Parliamentary leaders like William Wilberforce and with Colonial Office officials intent on protecting Indians, restricting the expansion of slavery, and ensuring a gradual and orderly settlement of designated regions of the West.

If this is an idealized view of British policy, it is nevertheless instructive to look at the forces that encouraged or opposed development of the Carolina backcountry in the era of the Revolution. From the 1760s onward, the South Carolina Regulators and patriots represented a rising planter class eager to consolidate landholdings, establish commercial ties with Charleston, and guarantee the security of slave property in a back-country still populated with Indians, white hunters, fugitive slaves, and outlaws of various kinds. Tories and British officers enlisted the support not only of Cherokees but of various antiplanter groups of woodsmen and bandits, some of whom included white women, free blacks, and escaped slaves. Such British allies posed a temporary obstacle to the kind of planter-class expansionism later symbolized by Andrew Jackson. Indeed, it is worth noting that Jackson's obsessive Anglophobia arose from his boyhood experiences with the guerrilla warfare on the South Carolina frontier; his famous invasion of East Florida in 1818, ostensibly to end British-instigated Indian raids and remove a fugitive slave refuge, was foreshadowed in the early 1780s when patriots invaded East Florida in pursuit of tories and interracial outlaw gangs.[5]

This is not to say either that the British and the tories were inclined toward abolitionism or that restrictions on westward expansion would have condemned slavery to an inevitable economic death. With regard to the first point, it is true that after capturing Charleston in 1780 Sir Henry Clinton issued a proclamation promising freedom to those slaves who deserted their rebel owners and took up arms for the king. But Clinton scrupulously returned fugitive slaves to tory owners; and even in the Caribbean, where the British later enlisted thousands of African troops with promise of freedom upon discharge, British commanders restored slavery in the conquered French islands where it had earlier been abolished. The question of restricting slavery's expansion is far more complicated. Historians have tended to accept the nineteenth-century dogma, championed by the Free Soil and Republican parties, that slavery could not survive economically without being rejuvenated by constant expansion into undepleted western lands. This assertion always evoked significant dissent in the South, and it has been challenged by modern economists who contend that the slave economy would have benefited from less rapid geographic expansion. It is therefore conceivable that British restrictions on western settlement actually would have promoted the economic growth of the Cotton Kingdom, especially if British policies had been increasingly guided by the central interests of the cotton textile industry.

But economic questions should not be divorced from political ones. Although John Randolph of Roanoke bitterly opposed continental expansion as a threat to the slaveholders' world, he also understood that a political power that could restrict the expansion of slavery could even-

5. This and the following paragraph are much indebted to Rachel Klein, "The Rise of the Planters in the South Carolina Backcountry, 1767–1808," Ph.D. diss., Yale University, 1979.

tually be used to emancipate slaves. British policies with respect to the
conquered and ceded colonies in the West Indies, especially Trinidad
and the Guianese colony of Demerara, in fact bore out Randolph's fears.
These policies should be taken into account when considering a hypothetical Anglo-American empire, in order to appreciate that economic
interests would have been complicated by administrative, strategic, political, and humanitarian objectives. While the fertile and undeveloped
lands of Trinidad promised almost unlimited supplies of cheap sugar,
the Demerara frontier was especially prized for cotton, which became
the latter colony's initial and most valuable export to Britain during the
early years of the nineteenth century, before the United States emerged
as a major producer. Beginning in the late 1790s, investors, speculators,
planters, and merchants exerted intense pressure for the rapid sale of
these frontier lands and for unlimited supplies of African slave labor.
Nevertheless, Britain denied these colonies the legislative form of self-
government enjoyed by the older West Indies, delayed the sale of crown
lands, prohibited in 1805 the further importation of slaves from Africa,
and in 1806 imposed effective restrictions on the flow of slave labor
from the older colonies. It would range too far afield to debate the motives of policies that unquestionably curbed production of British sugar,
cotton, coffee, and other tropical staples. It should be noted, however,
that various orders-in-council were designed to make Trinidad in particular a model for ameliorating the condition of black slaves.

Extending this model to North America suggests that such new states
as Alabama, Mississippi, Florida, and Louisiana might have been governed as crown colonies and subjected to free-labor experiments on crown
lands. According to this scenario, they would have been ruled by successive secretaries of state who relied on the expertise of a permanent
abolitionist bureaucrat, James Stephen the younger. In 1813 Stephen
became legal counsel to the Colonial Office; his influence over the details of administration increased until, first as assistant undersecretary
and then as permanent undersecretary in the 1830s, he helped to ration-
alize and reorganize the entire colonial system. In 1833 it was Stephen
who drafted the government's bill for slave emancipation.

Of course such policies could not have been pursued in North America without provoking revolution. In 1810, to choose a potentially explosive year, the power of a few thousand West Indian planters and
speculators was hardly comparable to that of two million southern whites.
But the examples of Trinidad and Guiana show that the British government was capable of restricting and regulating the expansion of black
slavery, even to the probable detriment of imperial economic interests.
From 1812 to the end of slave apprenticeship in 1838, the slave popu-

lation of British Guiana dropped from 100,000 to less than 83,000. By 1841, when most freedmen had deserted regimented plantations for the relatively free but subsistence agriculture of backwoods villages, officials estimated the effective labor force at a mere 25,000. Sugar production fell accordingly. In a disciplined fantasy of imperial unity, such policies would doubtless have been modified in response to southern and British industrial demands. Yet it still seems probable that the future Cotton Kingdom would have assumed a different form, less characterized by rampant speculation and "herrenvolk democracy." In the likely event of an Anglo-American war against Spain and France, the West Indian analogy also suggests a widespread dependence on black troops, large-scale manumission, and an imperial policy prescribing at least minimal civil rights for freedmen.

The point of this theorizing is not to idealize British authority, which could be as tyrannical in America as in suppressing British workers or Irish peasants. What needs to be emphasized is that the American Revolution freed southern slaveholders from various imperial restraints, opening the way for Indian removal and for a westward expansion of slavery that met no serious opposition until the rise of the Republican party in response to the Kansas-Nebraska Act of 1854. The United States Constitution gave slaveholders privileges and powers that exceeded the wildest dreams of the beleaguered West Indian whites, who had to deal with official "protectors of slaves" and with imperial reorganizations intended to assure that colonial governors would represent the crown. Guaranteed state autonomy within a federal system, southern slaveholders could count on disproportionate national power as a result of slave representation, federal assistance in the recovery of fugitive slaves or the suppression of insurrections, and noninterference in matters relating to race and labor. Perhaps even more important was the political neutralization of the natural opponents of an expanding slavocracy. Fearful of being stigmatized as tories and "Anglomen," as Jefferson called them, these potential opponents quickly discovered that concessions on slavery were indispensable for winning southern votes on such pressing questions as credit and the public debt. As Howard A. Ohline has recently shown, the Congressional debates over slavery in 1790, decisive in establishing a framework of basic consensus, were governed by the northern desire to win southern support for Hamilton's financial program.[6] From 1790 onward, at least to the late 1850s, it became increasingly clear that any effective national coalition depended on appeasing slave-

6. "Slavery, Economics and Congressional Politics, 1790," *Journal of Southern History* 46 (1980):335–60.

holder demands. Within the South, Federalists and Republicans, Whigs and Democrats, represented conflicting local interests and also competed to present the most convincing defense of black slavery.

Because the structure of American politics served so many vital needs and interests, even at the cost of reinforcing the local and national power of slaveholders, it is difficult to imagine the realignments that might have emerged within a single British empire. As late as the 1830s and 1840s, when abolitionism in both countries had enlisted wide popular support and had become intertwined with various radical causes, American politicians could still successfully stigmatize the movement as a popular front for antirepublican despotism. It is hardly cheering to think of America being ruled by men whose power would have depended on the patronage of Pitt, Liverpool, Castlereagh, Canning, and Wellington. Yet is is conceivable that under British rule, implemented mainly by the men who led the Federalist and Whig parties, southern slaveholders would have been unable to "make" the autonomous, paternalistic world which Eugene D. Genovese has empathetically described.

But a disciplined fantasy of this kind should lead to questions, not answers. It should not only generate contradictory scenarios but point to intermediary zones which blur and confuse accepted categories of historical understanding, just as actual historical events confound conventional labels and expectations. Therefore, before suggesting a tentative choice among various possibilities, a few extreme but not impossible options can be explored. First, one can imagine a revitalized British West Indies joining the South in a fused American Revolution and Civil War, precipitated by British and northern attempts to restrict the expansion of slavery. Second and less conventional, one can picture an irreconcilable conflict in which land-hungry northern farmers and artisans, galvanized by racial prejudice and by the republican ideology which Eric Foner has eloquently described, would have pitted themselves against a constraining, conservative alliance of southern planters, northern cotton-textile magnates, and British industrialists and landed gentry. In this scenario it would have been the northern and northwestern radical Republicans, led perhaps by Lincoln, who would have seceded from a multiracial British empire based on slave-grown cotton, factory production, centralized government, and control of world markets. It is worth emphasizing, in this respect, that Britain's global hegemony depended in large measure on the manufacture and export of cotton textiles, and that after the 1820s the entire British economy became dependent on low-cost, slave-grown American cotton, much as modern Western economies have become dependent on Mideastern oil. During the pre-Civil War decades of soaring demand, and despite frantic searches for alternative sources of supply, Britain relied on the South for over 70 percent of all its cotton imports. America's national independence meant that British statesmen never had to face the political implications of this economic dependence. Within a united empire, such a compelling national interest would surely have led to drastic political realignments. One can imagine, for example, southern and West Indian proprietors abandoning some of their states rights and agrarian doctrines and forging a Junker-like alliance with leading Anglo-American industrialists. Or there might have been a reactionary swing on the part of British capitalists, faced now with the political consequences of their American investments and dependence on American cotton, and with the need for suppressing antislavery along with other forms of radicalism. This script could have led finally to a revolutionary alliance of Anglo-American workers, slaves, and abolitionists, with minds inflamed on both sides of the Atlantic, as in the French Revolution, by the exploits of a John Brown or Toussaint Louverture.

Thus far, however, these speculations have omitted reference to the ideology of the American Revolution and to its continuing influence on history. It is clear that antislavery arguments, taken in the abstract, preceded the Revolution. One can even argue that the Revolution cut off and then fragmented the antislavery efforts of the Quakers, who led the way in translating abstract ideals into personal decision and organized pressure on central and local governments. Both British and American Quakers deplored the imperial conflict as a violation of their pacifist principles and as a rupture of their transatlantic fellowship; American Quakers, including prominent abolitionists, suffered a loss of political influence and even imprisonment, as suspected tories. Anthony Benezet, unsure of the war's outcome, sent copies of his antislavery pamphlets to General Howe as well as to the Continental Congress.

Nevertheless, the Declaration of Independence was the touchstone, the sacred scripture for later American abolitionists, for blacks like David Walker as well as for whites like Benjamin Lundy and William Lloyd Garrison. It was no less important for tories and British critics who scoffed at the arrogance of slaveholders who preached the inalienable rights of man. Less directly, the words of the Declaration inspired French and Latin American champions of emancipation. The 1791 manifesto of the French Amis des noirs was more explicit than Jefferson's Declaration: "We hold that all men are born free and with equal rights, regardless of their color, their nationality, or the condition of birth. We hold that no man can give up his freedom, and no man can seize the freedom of his fellow man, and that no society can legitimate such crime."[7]

7. *Adresse de la Société des Amis des Noirs, à l'assemblée nationale* . . . , 2d ed. (Paris, 1791), pp. 107–8.

As early as A.D. 869 thousands of black slaves had risen in revolt against their masters, in that case against the Arabs of Mesopotamia. But such earlier slave revolts had never challenged the justice of slavery as an institution. It was a wholly unprecedented ideology that led American blacks of the early 1770s to petition for their freedom on the grounds of natural rights. Never before in human history had slaves challenged the general principles justifying slavery. If the American Revolution is eliminated from these calculations, the pride of subsequent generations of free blacks whose ancestors had won freedom by fighting for the rebel cause, and who looked back upon the War of Independence as a struggle betrayed, is also lost.

The Revolution was also of crucial psychological importance in combining the secular philosophy of individual rights and political equality with a millenarian vision of national mission and retributive justice. The history of religion provides innumerable examples of millenarian and revitalization movements, many of which have attacked secular sins and impurities. There were no precedents, however, for the clerical condemnations of slaveholding that suddenly erupted during and after the American Revolution. These apocalyptic warnings and denunciations, which merged an affirmation of natural rights with threats of divine judgment, flowed from southern Baptists, Presbyterians, and Methodists, as well as from the New England followers of Jonathan Edwards. If the rhetoric of such jeremiads inevitably allowed for later declension and accommodation, the testimony could not be forgotten. Historians have too often slighted the clerical founding fathers who established a prophetic tradition that later American abolitionists, both black and white, revived and reformulated to suit their needs.[8]

Without such a tradition American antislavery might have been more moderate and institutionally oriented. Yet the Revolution was directly responsible for the most striking example of such conservative reform: the acts of gradual emancipation in Pennsylvania, Connecticut, Rhode Island, New York, and New Jersey. These laws were designed to free only the future-born children of slaves, at ages ranging from twenty-one to twenty-eight. Robert W. Fogel and Stanley L. Engerman, computing some eighteen variables, such as maintenance expenditure and "the ratio of the value of the childbearing capacity of a woman of a given age to her price at that age," conclude that these earliest emancipation laws imposed little if any capital losses on northern slaveholders. In effect, the labor of northern slaves subsidized the costs of emancipation. More-

---

8. This subject is ably explored by James David Essig, "Break Every Yoke: American Evangelicals against Slavery, 1770–1808," Ph.D. diss., Yale University, 1978.

over, many northern owners seem to have reaped substantial capital gains by selling their slaves in the South.[9] It is almost certain, however, that even this grudging and self-serving emancipation would have been infinitely delayed without the spur of Revolutionary ideology and the heightened consciousness of political self-determination.

The example of Canada raises a possible objection to this argument, because in 1793 the House of Assembly and Legislative Council of Upper Canada passed an emancipation act resembling Connecticut's law of 1784. While this measure conflicted with the Imperial Act of 1790, which permitted free importation of black slaves and other chattel property into British North America, it received the crown's assent. It appears, however, that Upper Canada was decisively influenced by the example of the northeastern United States and by the desire of loyalist refugees to prove their own liberality. If the states south of Maryland had remained within the empire, it seems highly probable that the British government would have vetoed all such emancipation acts in the interest of imperial unity and security. Restraints might even have been applied on the judges who actually succeeded in undermining slavery, without benefit of positive law, in Massachusetts, New Hampshire, and the eastern provinces of Canada. Certainly British courts gave no encouragement to the idea of extending to the colonies the common-law principles of the famous Somerset case of 1772, which denied legal support for slavery in England. As late as 1827 Lord Stowell ruled in the Court of Admiralty that the Somerset decision implied no more than a suspension of colonial slave codes during a slave's residence in England. Far from affecting the status of slaves in the colonies, Somerset could not even prevent the reestablishment of slave status for a black who had voluntarily returned to the colonies from England. The most revealing point, however, is that despite the example of some northern states which by the 1820s had totally outlawed slavery, black slavery remained legal in all parts of British America until August 1, 1834.

It is impossible to imagine Parliament passing the celebrated Emancipation Act of 1833 if the United States had remained part of the empire. Cotton was by then far more vital for British industry and trade than sugar had ever been. Moreover, both contemporary British observers and later historians agree that no emancipation plan was politically feasible unless it included monetary compensation from the British government to West Indian proprietors. Parliament finally assented to the staggering figure of £20 million because of the pressing need to win the

---

9. "Philanthropy at Bargain Prices: Notes on the Economics of Gradual Emancipation," *Journal of Legal Studies* 3 (1974):377–401.

cooperation of slaveholders, to affirm the sanctity of private property, and to guard against other and more threatening forms of expropriation. But this twenty million-pound grant, which the so-called black apprentices were to supplement for a period of six years with forty-five hours of unpaid labor for their masters out of a sixty-hour working week, was clearly an upper limit for British taxpayers. Slave prices tended to be higher in the United States than in the British colonies. But even at the same average compensation per slave, the more than two million slaves in the southern states would have increased the taxpayers' bill by another £51 million.[10] It is true that the addition of the United States would have increased the number of taxpayers, but if British leaders had managed to preserve the empire for fifty-seven additional years, they presumably would have been sensitive to American feelings about taxes. As Thomas Jefferson put it in 1824, after making somewhat similar calculations of the costs of African colonization, "it is . . . impossible to look at the enterprise a second time."[11]

Where, then, does this leave us? On the one hand, continuing imperial unity probably would have hastened the international suppression of the African slave trade, slowed down the westward expansion of slavery, strengthened pressures for amelioration in accordance with standards prescribed in London, and delayed slave emancipation especially in such colonies as New York and New Jersey, where there was significant resistance to even gradual emancipation.

On the other hand, it is also indisputable that the American Revolution opened the way for Britain's emancipation of 780,000 colonial slaves. This worthy achievement, celebrated as the dawning of a millennial era of universal emancipation, confirmed Britain's self-image as the world's altruistic champion of liberty and civilization. It cast shame upon the United States, inspiring both abolitionists and their opponents to vindicate in different ways the revolutionary mission of the founding fathers. If imperial unity would have precluded legislative emancipation in 1833, it also would have muted sectional rivalries and blurred sectional boundaries; there would have been no Northwest Ordinance and no truly "free soil," even if there were imperial experiments with contract or indentured labor in the West. Assuming that British administrators would have been flexible enough to avoid revolution—and we must remember

---

10. Ibid. The figure would be £42.6 million if one allows for the discounted late payments calculated by Fogel and Engerman. Even when the British subsidy is discounted to the value of £16.6 million, Fogel and Engerman estimate that it amounted to 49 percent of the actual value of the emancipated slaves, whose continuing labor covered most of the balance.

11. Andrew Lipscomb and Albert Bergh, eds., *The Writings of Thomas Jefferson*, 20 vols. (Washington, D.C., 1903–4), 16:8–13.

that the ideology of the American Revolution would now lack the radiance of success—the alliance between manufacturers and planters would have given politics a more conservative cast on both sides of the Atlantic. This is not to deny a probably inevitable conflict between capitalism and slavery. Emancipation would no doubt have come eventually—but perhaps as slowly and as ambiguously as it did in British Africa.